Creativity and Successful Aging

Carolyn E. Adams-Price, Ph.D., received her Bachelor's Degree in Psychology from the University of California at Santa Cruz. She received her M.A. in Social/Developmental Psychology from Brandeis University, and her Ph.D. in Life-span Developmental Psychology from West Virginia University. She was a Postdoctoral Fellow at the Institute of Gerontology at the University of Michigan. She is currently an Associate Professor of Psychology at Mississippi State University, where she also chairs the Gerontology Program. Dr. Adams-Price is the author of several journal articles on aging and cognition. She is also married and the mother of two children.

Creativity and Successful Aging

Theoretical and Empirical Approaches

Carolyn E. Adams-Price, PhD

Editor

 Springer Publishing Company

Springer Publishing Company, Inc.
536 Broadway
New York, NY 10012-3955

Cover design by Margaret Dunin
Acquisitions Editor: Bill Tucker
Production Editor: Kathleen Kelly

98 99 00 01 02 / 5 4 3 2 1

Library of Congress Cataloging-in-Publication-Data

Creativity and successful aging : theoretical and empirical approaches
   / Carolyn Adams-Price, editor.
        p.   cm.
     Includes index.
     ISBN 0-8261-9910-0
     1. Creative ability in old age.   2. Creation (Literary, artistic,
   etc.)   3. Aged—Psychology.   I. Adams-Price, Carolyn.
   BF724.85.C73C74   1997
   153.3'5'0846—dc21   97-23168
                                                                  CIP

Printed in the United States of America

Contents

Contributors

Carolyn Adams-Price, PhD
Department of Psychology
Mississippi State University
Mississippi State, MS 39762-6161

Cheryl Anagnopoulos
Department of Psychology
Black Hills State University
Spearfish, SD

Hélène Croteau, MA
Department of Psychology
University of Montreal
Case postale 6128, succursale A
Montreal, Quebec H3C 3J7

Stéphanie Z. Dudek, PhD
Department of Psychology
University of Montreal
Case postale 6128, succursale A
Montreal, Quebec H3C 3J7

Carol Emmons, MFA
Department of Communications
    and the Arts
University of Wisconsin
Green Bay, WI 54311

Ravenna Helson, PhD
Institute of Personality and
    Social Research
University of California
Oxford Court Building, Room 2C
2150 Kittredge Street
Berkeley, CA 94720

M. Catherine Kelley, PhD
Institute of Gerontology
300 North Ingalls
Ann Arbor, MI 48109-2007

Susan Kemper, PhD
Department of Psychology
University of Kansas
426 Fraser Hall
Lawrence, KS 66045-2160

Christie A. Kenyon, MFA
History of Art Dept., U-M, Ann Arbor
2792 Clear Lake
Grass Lake, MI 49240

Martin S. Lindauer, PhD
3864 25th Street
San Francisco, CA 94114

Todd I. Lubart, PhD
Université René Descartes
Labortoire de Psychologie
  Differentiale
28 Rue Serpente 75006 Paris
France

Wayne State U.

← **Mark R. Luborsky, PhD**
Clinical Research Center
Philadelphia Geriatric Center
5706 Old York Road
Philadelphia, PA 19141

Michael Marsiske, PhD
Assistant Professor of Psychology
  and Gerontology
Institute of Gerontology
Wayne State University
87 E. Ferry St.
Detroit, MI 48202

Lucinda Orwoll, PhD
1401 Culver Street
Ann Arbor, MI 48103

Karen Powers, BA
Department of Psychology
University of Wisconsin
2420 Nicolet Drive
Green Bay, WI 54311-7001

James G. Ravin, MD
The Eye Center of Toledo
3000 Regency Court, Suite 100
Toledo, OH 43623

Dean Rodeheaver, PhD
University of Wisconsin
2420 Nicolet Drive
Green Bay, WI 54311-7001

Dean K. Simonton, PhD
Department of Psychology
University of California, Davis
Davis, CA 95616

Jan D. Sinnott, PhD
Psychology Department
Towson State University
Baltimore, MD 21204

Robert J. Sternberg, PhD
Department of Psychology
Yale University
P.O. Box 11A Yale Station
New Haven, CT 06520-7447

Sherry L. Willis, PhD
Human Development and Family
  Studies
110 Henderson Building South
The Pennsylvania State University
University Park, PA 16802

Introduction

Books on creativity usually include elaborate discussions of different definitions of creativity. This volume is an exception in that regard; there will be no attempt to provide an elaborate definition of creativity. For the purpose of this volume, *creativity* will be defined as the range of cognitive and emotional processes involved in the "creation," of meaningful products, as reflected in those products. The entire range of processes involved in the creation of a complex product such as a painting or a literary work are unknowable.

This book is not simply a book on creativity, but also a book on successful aging. My purpose in bringing together these chapters is to demonstrate the creative abilities of older adults, and the extent to which these abilities reflect their special characteristics, including the circumstances of their lives and their wisdom. Connections between research on successful aging and new or classic approaches to creativity are also a major emphasis of this volume.

The first section of this volume describes major theoretical models of age changes in creativity. In the first chapter, Dean Simonton discusses his classic work on the relationship between age and creative productivity, including new findings about the productivity of persons who begin artistic careers relatively late. Simonton's chapter emphasizes the theme of late life potential that permeates this volume. The second chapter, by Todd Lubart and Robert Sternberg, describes the range of social, personality, cognitive, and environmental factors that determine the style and quantity of late life creative products. They suggest that the factors that influence late life creativity are complex and work differently in different individuals.

The second section includes two chapters linking creativity and cognitive processes in late life, especially in the domain of problem solving. Jan Sinnott's chapter discusses the extent to which postformal reasoning allows older people to be particularly creative problem solvers. The chapter by Michael Marsiske and Sherry Willis discusses the role of three components of creativity: fluency, flexibility, and originality in the practical problem solving of elderly persons. Both chapters suggest that the unique nature of the cognitive processes of older persons contributes to their everyday creativity.

The third section of the volume includes chapters on personality variables and creativity; three of the four chapters emphasize the variables that are predictive of creativity in older women. It should also be noted that the chapters by Ravenna Helson and by Stephanie Dudek and Helene Croteau are based on some of the most important longitudinal studies ever conducted in the field of creativity. Dudek and Croteau focus on personality change in MacKinnon's famous studies of exceptionally creative architects. Their findings suggest that the architects have aged with great dignity and continued interest in their profession. Lucinda Orwoll and Catherine Kelley suggest that older artistic women have achieved a balance of masculine and feminine qualities in their struggle for recognition in the art world. Helson reports a longitudinal follow-up study of the Mills College art students studied by the Institute of Personality Assessment and Research in the 1950s. Taking a life course perspective, she discusses the identity statuses and personality types that are predictive of continued artistic production in older women. Helson also ties continued productivity in women artists to the circumstances and life management skills of these women. The last chapter in this section, written by Dean Rodeheaver, Carol Emmons, and Karen Powers, includes the perspectives of both psychologists and artists. They criticize the relevance of traditional male- and youth-oriented perspectives to the subject of the creativity of the female artist, suggesting that late life changes in cognition and personality can create new opportunities for the older woman artist.

The fourth section of the book discusses aging and specific creative domains—in this case, art and writing. Martin Lindauer's chapter is an excellent introduction to aging in famous artists. It takes a historiometric approach similar to that of Simonton. Lindauer also discusses artistic style in late life. Ravin and Kenyon have used case histories to examine age changes in artistic style in two famous artists, Monet and Degas. They explore the positive and negative effects of serious eye diseases on the motivation and quality of work in these artists. Their chapter is important because it suggests that some of the losses that come with age can have a positive impact on creative production.

The third and fourth chapters in this section emphasize age changes in writing and literature. Susan Kemper and Cheryl Anagnopoulos have written an elegant chapter describing longitudinal age changes in the writing style of professional and nonprofessional writers. In my own chapter, I describe the variety of ways in which age changes in literature have been studied and might be studied in the future, and the extent to which such research would advance our understanding of both aging and creativity.

In the last chapter of the book, Mark Luborsky examines the ability of older persons to create meaning in their lives. Luborsky, an anthropologist, describes the forms of narrative used by depressed and nondepressed older people in recounting their life stories. He suggests that the telling of the life story is a creative act within reach of all people.

I would like to thank several people, without whom I could not have put together this volume. First of all, I would like to thank Martin Lindauer and Carolyn Phinney for encouraging me to get started on the book, for introducing me to some of the individuals who contributed chapters, and for reading and commenting on several chapters. I would also like to thank all of the authors for their excellent chapters, but give special recognition to several of them, who contributed their time to comment on the chapters of others, including Dean Simonton, Susan Kemper, Ravenna Helson, and Lucinda Orwoll. Finally, I would like to thank my husband, Marty Price, who not only gave me huge amounts of moral and emotional support, but who also helped with the proofing and editing of all chapters.

CAROLYN ADAMS-PRICE

Theoretical Approaches

Career Paths and Creative Lives: A Theoretical Perspective on Late Life Potential

Dean K. Simonton

Making a mark as a creative genius is not a one-shot affair. Rather, it requires the commitment of a lifetime. Indeed, this necessity is implicit in many conceptions of genius. For example, according to Albert's (1975) behavioral definition,

> The key ingredient to genius is productivity—large in volume, extraordinary in longevity, more or less unpredictable in content. . . . Long-term creative behavior, as evidenced in influential productivity, is the "carrier" of genius qua eminence. The earlier a person starts and the more he does, the more likely will his impact on others be significant and, eventually, the higher his eminence will be. (pp. 144–149)

A genius is thus a long-term generator of significant contributions. This fact implies the need to study creativity from a life span developmental perspective. Creative behavior has a career course that we must closely follow, or else we will fail to appreciate the phenomenon. Most obviously, this career course has a beginning and an end. Yet it also has a middle, and a characteristic way of going from beginning to middle to end.

Furthermore, this career trajectory varies from creator to creator. Some creative minds are "early bloomers" while others are "late bloomers." Hence, a complete analysis of creativity across the life span must accommodate individual differences in the equation. Variations in career paths may reveal different facets of what it takes to commit oneself to a creative life.

This chapter presents a theoretical model that handles both longitudinal changes and cross-sectional variation in creative output. The model was originally designed to explain the vast amount of research that has accumulated on the relation between age and achievement (e.g., Cole, 1979; Dennis, 1966; Lehman, 1953, 1962; for reviews, see Simonton, 1988a, 1990b, 1990c). However, because the model leads to rather specific predictions about career trajectories, it has also successfully guided a program of empirical research (e.g., Simonton, 1977a, 1984a, 1985, 1989a, 1991a, 1991b, 1992a).

Both the theory and the data, moreover, feature some crucial implications for the amount of creativity we can expect in the final years of life (Simonton, 1990a). These implications we shall draw out once the theoretical perspective has been presented (see also Simonton, 1990c).

THEORETICAL PERSPECTIVE

The description here is a mere sketch of a model that has evolved over the years. Portions of the model can only be accurately communicated using the language of mathematics, especially differential equations and covariance algebra (Simonton, 1984a, 1991a). Yet presentation of the formalistic elements is not essential to an appreciation of the model's implications. More important, the model can be subsumed under a comprehensive explanatory system that derives ultimately from Donald Campbell's (1960) blind variation and selective retention theory of creativity (Simonton, 1988b, 1988c). The factors of this more encompassing framework we must consider here are (a) the connection between age and creative output, (b) the relation between quantity and quality of output, and (c) the effects of individual variation in creative potential and career onset.

AGE AND OUTPUT

Empirical research on how creative productivity varies with age dates back to 1835 (Quetelet, 1835/1968), and hundreds of studies have been conducted since then (Simonton, 1988a). Taken together, this huge volume of literature suggests that creative output increases fairly rapidly to a career peak, after which a gradual decline sets in. Although a big debate has raged about the magnitude of the post-peak drop, the reality of the decrease cannot be doubted (see Cole, 1979; Dennis, 1954c, 1956, 1966). Exceptions exist to every generalization, but at least the downturn occurs when we average across a large sample of representative careers. Notwithstanding the cornucopia of empirical studies, theoretical inquiries are all too few (see Beard, 1874; Cole, 1979; Diamond, 1984). Even worse, most theories that have been put forward cannot handle the fine details of the phenomenon. That failure led me to propose my own model in 1984. The model begins with three assumptions:

1. An individual launches his or her career with what I call an initial creative potential (m). This is a hypothetical count of the total number of products the creator would be capable of producing in an unlimited life span.[1]

2. During the course of the career, this potential is actualized into overt products by the two-step procedure of ideation and elaboration. Ideation entails coming up with ideas for new projects, while elaboration involves the laborious process of transforming these works-in-progress to actual products. Corresponding to each of these two processes is a transformation rate. We must thus speak of an ideation rate (a) and an elaboration rate *(b)*.

3. This conversion of potential to actual productivity begins at the moment a career effectively begins. In other words, if we express productivity as a function of time, or *p(t)*, then $t = 0$ at the career onset. Hence, the age curve that results is defined according to career age, not chronological age. This definition sets the model apart from many rival theories (Simonton, 1988a).

Given these three assumptions, we can derive a function that predicts the annual output of finished products as a function of career age. The age curve and the corresponding equation are shown in Figure 1.1. This curve has been tested against a large number of data sets, including the data gathered by Lehman (1953), Dennis (1966), Cole (1979), and Zuckerman (1977). The results have been uniformly gratifying. The correlations between predicted and actual levels of productivity range in the middle to upper .90s (Simonton, 1984a, 1988a, 1989a). The theoretical curve accurately reflects details such as the career path's concave downward commencement, its single prominent peak, and its concave upward finish (Simonton, 1984a, 1989a).

This theoretically derived age curve provides a summary of the typical career path for a creative career. The model also can accommodate

---

[1] Technically speaking, m should be defined in terms of the number of original ideas a person can produce. Actual output is then a fraction of this value, according to the "least publishable unit" of a discipline (e.g., brief articles versus monographs). Because this nicety has no consequences for our conclusions, we will ignore the distinction here.

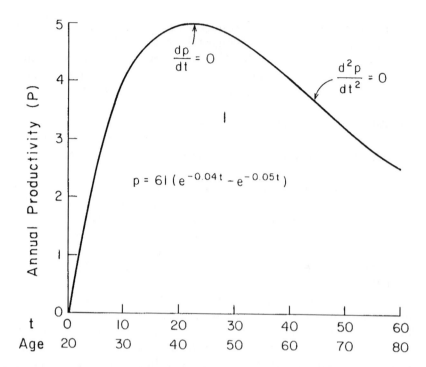

FIGURE 1.1   Predicted relation between productivity p(t) and career age t according to a two-step model of the creative process (from Simonton, 1984a).

the data from a single career, albeit with less precision. For instance, the correlation between Thomas Edison's output of patents and the productivity predicted by the model is an impressive 0.87 (Simonton, 1989a).

However, to maximize the fit between predicted and observed output, we must make adjustments in the equation. In particular, the two information-processing parameters a and b vary across creative disciplines (Simonton, 1984a, 1988a, 1989b). In some fields, such as poetry and pure mathematics, ideation and elaboration proceed rather quickly (e.g., $a = 0.04$ and $b = 0.05$). In other domains, such as history and geology, the two-step procedure moves more slowly (e.g., $a = 0.02$ and $b = 0.03$). These may appear like small differences, but they are not. Poets consume their creative potential at over twice the rate as do historians, for example. In addition, small contrasts in ideation and elaboration rates result in large differences in the expected career trajectories. For example, the predicted career peak for historians comes 18 years later than that for poets. Figure 1.2 shows the predicted curves for two

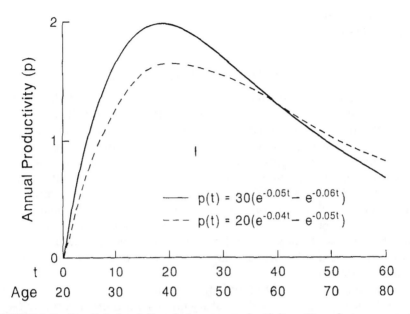

FIGURE 1.2   Predicted relation between productivity p(t) and career age t for two disciplines that differ slightly in the rates of ideation *(a)* and elaboration *(b)*, but with creative potential and career onset identical (from Simonton, 1991a).

hypothetical disciplines with only the slightest discrepancy in the two information-processing parameters (and holding initial creative potential constant).

These contrasts have to do with the nature of the cognitive material that must be manipulated in a given creative enterprise. The more simple, abstract, or finite the array of concepts that the creator deals with, the faster the information-processing rates. In contrast, the more complex, associatively rich, or unbounded this repertoire, the slower the same rates. Thus, poetry deals with a smaller range of topics and a more restricted vocabulary than does history. Likewise, pure mathematics handles more refined and restricted concepts than does geology. Moreover, the ideation and elaboration processes are somewhat independent of each other. What is required to elaborate a poem is different than what is necessary to perfect a mathematical proof. Accordingly, the two information-processing rates may be freely varied to capture the signature trajectory of various creative activities. For example, two fields may peak at the same career age, yet one may exhibit a rapid post-

peak decline while the other displays a more gradual loss in output
with age (Simonton, 1989a).[2]

QUANTITY AND QUALITY

So far we have been speaking of total output per age period. Needless
to say, not every idea that a creator offers the world has any wide
impact. Therefore, we must distinguish the hits from the misses. Only
the hits represent genuine creativity, whereas the hits and misses
combined together represent only mere productivity. For some time
researchers believed that the age curves for exclusive quality differed
from those for inclusive quantity (e.g., Dennis, 1966). Yet this conclusion
was based on flawed data analysis (Simonton, 1988a). Tabulations of
total output from one data set had been compared with tabulations of
selective output from another data set. Consequently, it was not possible to determine whether any differences were due to contrasts in the
samples studied.

However, more recent studies have compared quantity and quality
with the same creators, and the story comes out quite differently (e.g.,
Over, 1989, 1990; Simonton, 1977a, 1984b, 1985). The age curves for
quality and quantity are basically identical. The former is merely a
scaled-down version of the latter. This congruence holds not only for
the overall trajectory, but for the period-to-period fluctuations besides.
Those periods in which a creator produces the most masterpieces are
often the same periods in which that same creator generates the most
forgettable pieces.

The same point is made more dramatically by the quality ratio
(Simonton, 1977a, 1984b, 1985). This is the ratio of hits to total attempts
in consecutive age periods (e.g., 10-year or 5-year intervals). This ratio
neither increases nor decreases with age, nor does it exhibit some
curvilinear form. This means that the odds of hitting a bull's eye is a
probabilistic function of the total number of shots. The more attempts,
the more successes, but also the more failures. Hits and misses go
together so that the ratio does not vary systematically across the
creative career. This result leads to an important empirical generalization: The equal odds rule.[3] The principle holds that quality correlates

---

[2] If the ideation and elaboration rates happen to be identical for a particular discipline
(i.e., $a = b$), the solution to the differential equations becomes $p(t) = a2mte - at$. The
resulting curve looks the same as what we see in Figure 1.1, however.

[3] In earlier writings, I referred to this rule as the constant-probability-of-success model or
principle (e.g., Simonton, 1988a). This change in terminology was motivated only by a
desire for elegance. The concept is unaltered.

positively with quantity, so that creativity remains constant across as well as within careers. In any sample of contributors to a particular domain, the variation in total lifetime output will be tremendous (Dennis, 1954a, 1954c, 1955; Lotka, 1926; Price, 1963; Simonton, 1984b, 1988c).

Usually the most prolific 10% account for around half of everything produced. The most prolific have bibliographies or lists of works that are at least 100 times longer than their least productive colleagues. Nonetheless, those who are the most productive are producing both hits and misses. They have more successes only because they have more failures, too. W. H. Auden put his finger on this essential reality when he said, "The chances are that, in the course of his lifetime, the major poet will write more bad poems than the minor" (quoted in Bennet, 1980, p. 15). Hence, whether we are looking across lifetimes or within careers, the equal odds rule operates.

This principle is indispensable if we wish to comprehend the longitudinal placement of career landmarks. There are three such critical turning points in any creative career: the first, the best, and the last masterpiece, hit, or influential contribution. The age at the first hit then marks the onset of the creative career, when quantity finally produces something of quality. The age at the best hit defines the career peak, when a creator produces that work that most enhances his or her reputation. And the age at the last hit indicates when the creative portion of the career has terminated. The creator may evince further output, but this will count as the aftermath of a creative life now spent.

Where are these three landmarks placed during the course of a career? I will provide a complete answer in the next section, so for the moment let me concentrate on the middle landmark. If quality is a function of quantity, then creators will produce the most hits in those periods in which they are the most prolific. Yet the equal odds rule applies to the collection of hits as well as to all output regardless of quality. This implies that those periods in which the most hits appear will, on the average, contain that single hit that we can consider the best hit of all. It follows that the single most significant creative product will fall around the same age as the point of maximum output. In other words, we can reinterpret the curve in Figure 1.1 as expressing the likelihood that a creator's magnum opus will appear at a given age across the life span.

POTENTIAL AND TIMING

Two final variables are necessary to complete the model. Both factors concern individual differences or cross-sectional variation. The first variable is a direct consequence of our stipulation that the trajectory be defined according to career age. Although career age correlates very highly with chronological age, the correlation is not perfect (Bayer & Dutton, 1977; Levin & Stephan, 1991). This means that creators can vary in age at career onset (Simonton, 1991a, 1991b). Some individuals launch their creative enterprises at incredibly youthful ages, while others get a late start. Variation in the age at career onset does not alter the shape of the age curve, but only its location within a person's lifetime. For example, those who get a quick start will peak earlier than those who were late bloomers.

The second variable is more subtle but no less essential. According to the model, the career trajectory is founded on the realization of a beginning amount of creative potential, which we designated as m. Yet we must emphasize that this initial creative potential varies considerably across creators (Simonton, 1984a, 1991a, 1991b). Some are essentially "one-idea" intellects, and therefore run out of steam early on. Others are phenomenally prolific in the generation of ideas, and cannot be stopped except by death. In any case, individual differences in m have an interesting consequence for the career trajectory. This variation does not affect the shape of the curve (for two persons working in the same discipline), but it does determine the curve's height. The parameter that scales the magnitude of annual output is given by: $c = abm/(b - a)$. Holding a and b constant, c becomes a direct linear function of m (Simonton, 1984a). In concrete terms, this means that the higher an individual's initial creative potential, the faster the average output rate throughout the career. But the peak age for output will remain unchanged.

Now according to both theory and data, these two variables—average output rate and peak age for output—are uncorrelated with each other (Simonton, 1991a, 1991b). Someone high or low in initial creative potential may get either an early or a late start on his or her career. The orthogonal nature of these factors enables us to put forward a typology of career trajectories for creators working in the same discipline. Such a hypothetical typology is graphed in Figure 1.3. Here a and b are held constant, while the two individual difference variables vary across the extremes, yielding four idealized trajectories: early bloomers with either high or low creative potential and late bloomers with either high or low creative potential.

Given this typology, we can return to the question of where the three career landmarks are placed over a creator's life span. Because the creator's best work appears around the time of peak productivity, it is clear that this is affected solely by individual differences in the age of

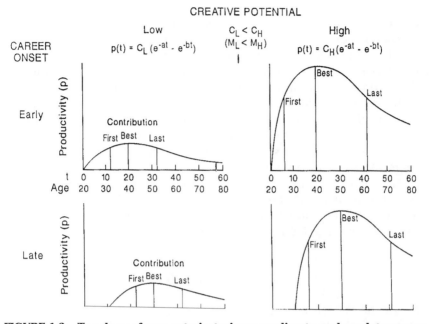

FIGURE 1.3 Typology of career trajectories according to early or late career onset and low or high initial creative potential (from Simonton, 1991a).

career onset. Those who commence their careers earlier will peak earlier. On the other hand, the age at which one's best work is done is not influenced by cross-sectional variation in creative potential. Highly creative persons will produce more masterpieces at their career acme, but that optimum will occur at the same place as it does for anyone else who began their career at the same age and within the same discipline (see Raskin, 1936; Simonton, 1991a, 1991b, 1992a; Zusne, 1976; see also Horner, Rushton, & Vernon, 1986). What about the first and last career landmarks? Here we must again apply the equal odds rule. Notice the difference between the career trajectories for people who differ widely in initial creative potential; right from the career's onset they are producing works at a far more hectic pace than their colleagues with lower initial potential. This faster accumulation of total attempts increases the likelihood that those with higher creative potential will get a hit at an earlier stage in their careers. In contrast, those who have less potential come out with ideas more slowly, and therefore the odds are stacked against their having an early career success.

The same argument applies for the last career landmark. Higher initial creative potential means more prolific output in the later years.

This raises the chance of a hit late in life. In comparison, those with lower potential will most likely produce their last important work not long after they produce their best work. Hence, holding other variables constant, the higher a creator's initial potential, the earlier appears the first landmark and the later appears the last landmark, while the middle landmark stays in the same place. On the other hand, a person with very low initial potential will have the first landmark happen so late and the last occur so early, that all three landmarks will appear within only a few years of each other. In the extreme case, we have the "one-book author" whose single contribution to human culture represents all three career landmarks at once!

Although other, more complicated predictions can also be derived from the model (Simonton, 1991a, 1991b), the discussion presented above provides enough theoretical background to justify moving to the more practical implications of the next section.

LATE LIFE POTENTIAL

Given the theoretical perspective just presented, what can we say about the prospects for creativity in the later part of life? A lot! The following six points deserve special emphasis:

1. Because the career trajectory is a function of career age rather than chronological age, the course of a creative life has an endogenous determination. This renders implausible any attempt to attribute any declines in creative output to exogenous factors. For example, much work has been done identifying age decrements in performance on tests of intelligence and creativity (e.g., McCrae, Arenberg, & Costa, 1987). Whatever the intrinsic merit of this research, it cannot help us understand the career course. By expressing longitudinal changes in terms of chronological age, these findings fail to explicate that the rise, acme, and decline are actually determined by (a) the field in which the individual is working and (b) the number of years the creator has been contributing to that field. Besides, the predictive validities of these psychometric measures are so small that we can not attribute much explanatory power to these variables (Simonton, 1988a).[4]

---

[4] This argument applies to attempts to explain the creativity age curves in terms of physical health as well (e.g., Lehman, 1953). Such an exogenous factor would be tied to chronological rather than career age, and therefore could not explicate contrasts due to different disciplines and career onsets (Simonton, 1988a).

2. Given the significance of career age, we cannot dismiss the possibility that late bloomers may attain career peaks at ages at which their colleagues might be well past their prime. A concrete illustration is the life of the classical composer, Anton Bruckner. Spending much of his life as a provincial Austrian organist, he discovered his true mission—that of a symphonist—at a relatively mature age. His first mature composition in this form, the First Symphony, did not appear until he was 42 years old. Beethoven had already completed his first eight symphonies by this age. Consequently, Bruckner was 50 when he produced his first unquestioned masterpiece, the Fourth *(Romantic)* Symphony. And what many devotees consider his greatest symphonies, the Seventh and the Ninth, emerged when he was 59 and 70 years old, respectively. This example assumes special importance now that we have so many mature adults becoming "reentry students" in order to launch themselves on new careers.

3. We must always remember that the career trajectory is contingent on the specific endeavor that occupies the creator's attention. Although some activities show early peaks and rapid declines, others are characterized by gradual ascent, relatively flat maxima, and rather slow declines with age. Data collected by Dennis (1966) suggests a wide range of possibilities in some scholarly activities, including history and philosophy. Accordingly, creators in these fields often will produce masterpieces at advanced ages. Immanuel Kant, for instance, did not produce his Critique of Pure Reason until he was 57, while his last two critiques, of practical reason and judgment, had to wait until he was in his 60s. Needless to say, if an individual happened to choose an activity represented by an early peak and a precipitous decline, he or she can always undergo a mid-life career change to a more forgiving field like philosophy or history. Wordsworth's own switch from poetry to criticism and philosophy offers an example. And as noted in the preceding point, such switches reset the career clock, so that the individual can expect a secondary peak.

4. Individual differences in creative potential are so substantial that they largely supersede the longitudinal shifts (see, e.g., Dennis, 1954b; Over, 1982a, 1982b; Simonton, 1977b, 1991a, 1991b, 1992a). A genius-grade creator who has become an octogenarian can easily out-produce a lesser creator who basks at the peak of his or her career. In fact, as can be inferred from Figure 1.3, those individuals who produce their first big contributions at unusually youthful ages tend to produce their last influential works at unusually advanced ages. Guiseppe Verdi composed his first operatic hit, *Nabucco,* when he was 29. His last hit, *Falstaff,* appeared when he was 80 years old. Because cross-sectional variation in creative potential is unrelated to variation in career onset, these two factors can combine to yield some exceptionally late-maturing

careers. Alexander von Humboldt was something of a late bloomer, but once his scientific career got off the ground, he became quite prolific. He was still working on the fifth volume of his masterpiece, *Kosmos,* when he died in his 90th year.

5. In one critical aspect, the theoretical model offers a worse-case scenario for latelife creativity. According to the theory that generates the age curves in Figures 1.2 through 1.3, the initial amount of creative potential is consumed as a career unfolds. Yet clearly, this is a simplifying assumption only. Although few mature creators can spend the time to completely retool themselves every several years, this is not utterly impossible. This rejuvenation process was implicit in our earlier remarks about the advantages of switching fields. Nevertheless, even should one remain in the same creative enterprise throughout the life span, creative potential may undergo at least partial resuscitation. For example, those creators who most prolong their careers will be those who, through extensive reading and study, keep up on the major developments in their own field as well as adjacent activities (see, e.g., Dennis & Girden, 1954). In addition, the intellectual stimulation of colleagues, collaborations, and rivalries can serve much the same function (see, e.g., Simonton, 1992b).

6. We must never forget that the equal odds rule holds throughout the creator's career. This means that the odds of getting a hit are a direct function of the number of total attempts, no matter what the creator's age. Thus, the quality ratio suffers no systematic change with age. One vital implication cannot be overlooked: This principle implies that on a contribution-for-contribution basis we cannot speak of age decrements at all! In other words, if we are handed two creative products, one from the hand of a 40-year-old and the other from that of a 80-year-old, we cannot use age as a predictor of their differential merits. A second implication is no less consequential: If, for any reason, a creator undergoes a resurgence of productive output in the last years of life, we should expect the emergence of new masterworks. Notable creators often display just such a personal renaissance in productivity (Haefele, 1962). Even if this secondary peak comes nowhere close to the magnitude seen at the career high point, the swan-song phenomenon (Simonton, 1989b) enables the greatest creators to end their career trajectories with a bang, not a whimper.

CONCLUSION

The picture just presented supports a very optimistic outlook on late life creative potential. Creativity of the highest caliber can continue until a person's final days. To be sure, I have based these conclusions on a specific theoretical model of how creative productivity varies across and within careers. Would these forecasts hold up were the model to be proven substantially incorrect? My answer is: Yes! The theoretical model was based on over a hundred years of empirical research (Simonton, 1988a). Since its presentation, it has been utilized in many more recent inquiries based on new data (Simonton, 1991a, 1991b, 1992a). Hence, even if some later psychologist offers an alternative model that explains the same facts, the facts themselves will remain. For example, the existence of distinct career paths for different creative activities cannot be denied. The contrasts have been too well documented, especially in the sciences (e.g., Adams, 1946; Dennis, 1966; Lehman, 1953; Simonton, 1991a). Moreover, the contrasts appear to be cross-culturally and transhistorically invariant (Lehman, 1962; Simonton, 1975).

Accordingly, whatever alternative accounts future investigators may offer, the six encouraging propositions about late life potential will probably survive unscathed, still supported by both data and theory. Under a wide range of conditions, the most senior members of a creative enterprise may out-perform a large proportion of their discipline's whippersnappers.

REFERENCES

Adams, C. W. (1946). The age at which scientists do their best work. *Isis, 36,* 166–169.

Albert, R. S. (1975). Toward a behavioral definition of genius. *American Psychologist, 30,* 140–151.

Bayer, A. E., & Dutton, J. E. (1977). Career age and research—professional activities of academic scientists: Tests of alternative non-linear models and some implications for higher education faculty policies. *Journal of Higher Education, 48,* 259–282.

Beard, G. M. (1874). *Legal responsibility in old age.* New York: Russell.

Bennet, W. (1980, Jan.-Feb.). Providing for posterity. *Harvard Magazine,* pp. 13–16.

Campbell, D. T. (1960). Blind variation and selective retention in creative thought as in other knowledge processes. *Psychological Review, 67,* 380–400.

Cole, S. (1979). Age and scientific performance. *American Journal of Sociology, 84,* 958–977.

Dennis, W. (1954a). Bibliographies of eminent scientists. *Scientific Monthly, 79,* 180–183.

Dennis, W. (1954b). Predicting scientific productivity in later maturity from records of earlier decades. *Journal of Gerontology, 9,* 465–467.

Dennis, W. (1954b). Productivity among American psychologists. *American Psychologist, 9,* 191–194.

Dennis, W. (1954). Review of *Age and Achievement. Psychological Bulletin, 51,* 306–308.

Dennis, W. (1955). Variations in productivity among creative workers. *Scientific Monthly, 80,* 277–278.

Dennis, W. (1956). *Age and Achievement:* A critique. *Journal of Gerontology, 9,* 465–467.

Dennis, W. (1966). Creative productivity between the ages of 20 and 80 years. *Journal of Gerontology, 21,* 1–8.

Dennis, W., & Girden, E. (1954). Current scientific activities of psychologists as a function of age. *Journal of Gerontology, 9,* 175–178.

Diamond, A. M., Jr. (1984). An economic model of the life-cycle research productivity of scientists. *Scientometrics, 6,* 189–196.

Haefele, J. W. (1962). Creativity and innovation. New York: Reinhold.

Horner, K. L., Rushton, J. P., & Vernon, P. A. (1986). Relation between aging and research productivity. *Psychology and Aging, 1,* 319–324.

Lehman, H. C. (1953). *Age and achievement.* Princeton, NJ: Princeton University Press.

Lehman, H. C. (1962). More about age and achievement. *Gerontologist, 2,* 141–148.

Levin, S. G., & Stephan, P. E. (1991). Research productivity over the life cycle: Evidence for academic scientists. *American Economic Review, 81,* 114–132.

Lotka, A. J. (1926). The frequency distribution of scientific productivity. *Journal of the Washington Academy of Sciences, 16,* 317–323.

McCrae, R. R., Arenberg, D., & Costa, P. T., Jr. (1987). Declines in divergent thinking with age: Cross-sectional, longitudinal, and cross-sequential analyses. *Psychology and Aging, 2,* 130–137.

Over, R. (1982a). Does research productivity decline with age? *Higher Education, 11,* 511–520.

Over, R. (1982b). Is age a good predictor of research productivity? *Australian Psychologist, 17,* 129–139.

Over, R. (1989). Age and scholarly impact. *Psychology and Aging, 4,* 222–225.

Over, R. (1990). The scholarly impact of articles published by men and women in psychology journals. *Scientometrics, 18,* 71–80.

Price, D. (1963). *Little science, big science.* New York: Columbia University Press.

Raskin, E. A. (1936). Comparison of scientific and literary ability: A biographical study of eminent scientists and men of letters of the nineteenth century. *Journal of Abnormal and Social Psychology, 31*, 20–35.

Quetelet, A. (1968). *A treatise on man and the development of his faculties.* New York: Franklin. (Reprint of 1842 Edinburgh translation of 1835 French original).

Simonton, D. K. (1975). Age and literary creativity: A cross-cultural and transhistorical survey. *Journal of Cross-Cultural Psychology, 6*, 259–277.

Simonton, D. K. (1977a). Creative productivity, age, and stress: A biographical time-series analysis of 10 classical composers. *Journal of Personality and Social Psychology, 35*, 791–804.

Simonton, D. K. (1977b). Eminence, creativity, and geographic marginality: A recursive structural equation model. *Journal of Personality and Social Psychology, 35*, 805–816.

Simonton, D. K. (1984a). Creative productivity and age: A mathematical model based on a two-step cognitive process. *Developmental Review, 4*, 77–111.

Simonton, D. K. (1984b). *Genius, creativity, and leadership: Historiometric inquiries.* Cambridge, MA: Harvard University Press.

Simonton, D. K. (1985). Quality, quantity, and age: The careers of 10 distinguished psychologists. *International Journal of Aging and Human Development, 21*, 241–254.

Simonton, D. K. (1988a). Age and outstanding achievement: What do we know after a century of research? *Psychological Bulletin, 104*, 251–267.

Simonton, D. K. (1988b). Creativity, leadership, and chance. In R. J. Sternberg (Ed.), *The nature of creativity: Contemporary psychological perspectives* (pp. 386–426). New York: Cambridge University Press.

Simonton, D. K. (1988c). *Scientific genius: A psychology of science.* Cambridge: Cambridge University Press.

Simonton, D. K. (1989a). Age and creative productivity: Nonlinear estimation of an information-processing model. *International Journal of Aging and Human Development, 29*, 23–37.

Simonton, D. K. (1989b). The swan-song phenomenon: Last-works effects for 172 classical composers. *Psychology and Aging, 4*, 42–47.

Simonton, D. K. (1990a). Creativity in the later years: Optimistic prospects for achievement. *The Gerontologist, 30*, 626–631.

Simonton, D. K. (1990b). Creativity and wisdom in aging. In J. E. Birren & K. W. Schaie (Eds.), *Handbook of the psychology of aging* (3rd ed., pp. 320–329). New York: Academic Press.

Simonton, D. K. (1990c). Does creativity decline in the later years? Definition, data, and theory. In M. Perlmutter (Ed.), *Late life potential* (pp. 83–112). Washington, DC: Gerontological Society of America.

Simonton, D. K. (1991a). Career landmarks in science: Individual differences and interdisciplinary contrasts. *Developmental Psychology, 27,* 119–130.

Simonton, D. K. (1991b). Emergence and realization of genius: The lives and works of 120 classical composers. *Journal of Personality and Social Psychology, 61,* 829–840.

Simonton, D. K. (1992a). Leaders of American psychology, 1879-1967: Career development, creative output, and professional achievement. *Journal of Personality and Social Psychology, 62,* 5–17.

Simonton, D. K. (1992b). Social context of career success and course for 2,026 scientists and inventors. *Personality and Social Psychology Bulletin, 18,* 452–463.

Zuckerman, H. (1977). *Scientific elite.* New York: Free Press.

Zusne, L. (1976). Age and achievement in psychology: The harmonic mean as a model. *American Psychologist, 31,* 805–807.

PART TWO

Creativity and Cognition

Life Span Creativity:
An Investment Theory Approach

Todd I. Lubart and Robert J. Sternberg

> It is too late! Ah, nothing is too late
> Till the tired heart shall cease to palpitate . . .
> Chaucer, at Woodstock with the nightingales,
> At sixty wrote the Canterbury Tales;
> Goethe at Weimar, toiling to the last,
> Completed Faust when eighty years were past.
> These are indeed exceptions; but they show
> How far the gulf-stream of our youth may flow
> Into the arctic regions of our lives,
> Where little else than life survives. . . .
> Whatever poet, orator, or sage
> May say of it, old age is still old age.
> It is the waning, not the crescent moon,
> The dusk of evening, not the blaze of noon. . . .
> What then? Shall we sit idly down and say
> The night hath come; it is no longer day? . . .
> Something remains for us to do or dare;
> Even the oldest tree some fruit may bear; . . .
> For age is opportunity no less
> Than youth itself, though in another dress,
> And as the evening twilight fades away
> The sky is filled with stars, invisible by day.
>
> Henry Wadsworth Longfellow, *Morituri Salutamus*

Longfellow (1876) touches on three aspects of life span creativity in his poem. First, he notes that some individuals produce creative work in late life. These "exceptions," however, are contrasted with a basic decline in creativity with age. The poem ends by noting that creative work may also take a different form in old age as compared to youthful productions. To a surprising degree, Longfellow captures basic research findings that have emerged during the last 100 years. We begin our analysis of creativity over the adult life span by reviewing evidence of age-related changes in the quantity, quality, and form of creative work. Then, we briefly present our investment approach to creativity (for details see Sternberg & Lubart, 1991). The *investment theory* identifies six resources—intellectual processes, knowledge, intellectual style, personality, motivation, and environmental context—that interactively yield creative performance. As each resource is described, we consider how changes in the resource over the life span may contribute to observed changes in creativity with age.

CREATIVE PERFORMANCE OVER THE LIFE SPAN

THE QUANTITY OF CREATIVE WORK

Lehman (1953) and Simonton (1988, 1990a, 1990b) have thoroughly documented age-related variations in the quantity (or productivity) of creative work. Productivity can be measured by counting the number of works that an individual produces during a certain span of time, such as a decade. In general, productivity increases rapidly with age to a peak, often around age 40. Productivity then decreases slowly through the rest of the life span, often declining until productivity is half of its peak rate. This general relationship of productivity and age has been found in both artistic and scientific fields, and across different cultures (Simonton, 1988, 1990a, 1990b).

The exact location of the peak and the rate of change in productivity depend on the field of endeavor. In some fields, such as pure mathematics, the productivity peak is early (e.g., age 30) and productivity rapidly declines with age to one quarter of the peak performance level. In contrast, domains such as history and philosophy show a later age peak for productivity (e.g., age 50) with small decreases beyond the peak.

It is important to note that productivity of creative work declines asymptotically and there are numerous cases of creative work by people in their eighties and older. Furthermore, there are large individual differences in the productivity changes with age. McLeish (1976) identified several "Ulysseans" who showed high productivity during old age. For example, Thomas Mann published three major novels after he was 70, including *Dr. Faustus*. Thus, there are well-documented changes in the quantity of creative productions with age, but there are also important variations due to the domain of work and individual differences.

THE QUALITY OF CREATIVE WORK

In contrast to productivity, which varies over the life span, the quality of creative work tends to follow a constant-probability-of-success model (Simonton, 1990b). The number of masterworks during a specified time period is a probabilistic function of the number of works produced in the period. In other words, during very productive periods of a person's life, there is a higher chance that a creative masterwork will be produced. The ratio of high-quality works to total number of works in any given period, however, does not show any developmental pattern. For example, in one study Simonton (1985) used citation counts to establish major and minor works for the careers of 10 eminent psychologists. The ratio of major (high-quality) works to total publications per unit of time showed no systematic changes with age. The same result was demonstrated with 10 classical composers (Simonton, 1977).

Changes in productivity, therefore, seem to drive the basic age function for creativity. In accord with this finding, when we describe the resources for creativity, posited by the investment theory, we will focus on age-related changes in the resources that affect creative productivity rather than purely the quality of creative work over the life span.

THE FORM OF CREATIVE WORK

Analysis of creative products suggests that the form and substance of creativity varies with age. Arieti (1976), for example, proposed that "young creativity," produced by those in their 20s or 30s, is spontaneous, intense, and "hot from the fire." Older creators, age 40 and above, "sculpt" their products with more intermediate processing. This view receives some support from Simonton's (1975) study of 420 literary creators. Creators were drawn from 25 centuries using histories, anthologies, and biographical dictionaries of Western, Near Eastern, and Far Eastern literatures. Poets produced their most frequently cited works at a significantly younger average age than imaginative prose writers and informative prose writers. Poetry is often seen as a literary form involving emotional content and play with language; in other words, poetry involves creativity "hot from the fire" (Cohen-Shalev, 1986).

Several researchers have suggested that as creativity evolves over the life span certain features emerge. Although the details depend on the domain of work, we suggest that an "old age style" with four main characteristics can be identified in the creative products of elderly adults. First, creative work by older adults tends to emphasize subjective rather than objective experience. In art, there seems to be a movement away from objective depiction and formal perfection. In writing, this feature may involve the use of an introspective approach and a focus on inner experiences (Cohen-Shalev, 1989). Second, there is an emphasis on unity and harmony. In art, this concept can be expressed through even tonality, muted colors, and decreased tension and dynamics. For musical composition, Simonton (1989) examined 1,919 works by 172 classical composers. The composers' last works, their "swan songs," showed increased melodic simplicity and shorter duration. Third, Lehman (1953) has observed that creative achievements during old age often involve a summing up or integration of ideas. Creative work in basic science, social science, and philosophy often consists of writing memoirs, histories of a field, and textbooks, or recording observations accrued over a life span. Fourth, there is a recurrent emphasis on aging in the content of older creators' work. Issues of living with old age and coping with death emerge in novels, scholarly works, and musical compositions, such as Verdi's opera, *Falstaff* (Beckerman, 1990; Lehman, 1953; Wyatt-Brown, 1988).

The presence of an old-age style is supported by evidence from a variety of fields. Thus, in addition to changes in creative productivity with age and related patterns in the quality of creative work, there are changes in the form and content of creative work over the life span.

THE INVESTMENT THEORY OF CREATIVITY

Creativity can be defined as the production of works judged to be novel, appropriate, and of high quality. To understand creativity we draw on concepts from the realm of investment. The most obvious and trivial advice that one can give an investor in the financial markets is to "buy low and sell high." Despite its obviousness, few people follow this advice (Dreman, 1982). Successful investors have to be (a) intelligent in spotting future investment trends, (b) knowledgeable about investment markets, (c) willing to act on their discernments and knowledge, (d) prepared to take risks, (e) motivated to follow their beliefs even as they go against the crowd, and (f) positioned in an environment where going against the existing trends is encouraged, or at least permitted. When these investors go against the existing trends in a contrarian fashion, they may be seen as foolish. If or when the investment comes to be widely recognized as a good one, however, its price rises rapidly, and it is no longer possible to buy it at a low and hence favorable price. The person formerly seen as foolish may now be seen as prescient.

An analogous situation is observed for creative performance. A person who follows the crowd and produces work that is already in vogue may be viewed as competent, but not as creative. In effect, the price for this kind of work is already high. In contrast, an individual who chooses projects and formulates ideas in domains or with paradigms that are at least slightly out of favor is taking some risk. But if others come to recognize the value of the work, the individual may be viewed as highly creative. The same kinds of attributes described above as relevant to successful investing are relevant to successful creative performance.

We suggest that cognitive aspects of the person (processes of intelligence, knowledge, intellectual style), conative aspects (personality, motivation), and the environment provide relevant psychological resources for creativity. An individual's "portfolio" of resources allows the initiation and completion of a range of projects. The observable products that result from a person's work can be evaluated for creativity by appropriate judges.

Our theory, of course, draws heavily upon the work of others (see Sternberg & Lubart, 1991). For example, Amabile (1983) has proposed a componential model describing creativity as the result of intrinsic motivation, domain-relevant skills, and creativity-relevant skills. Csikszentmihalyi (1988) notes the importance of the person, the field, and the domain structure for creative work. And, Gruber and Davis (1988) trace creative work over long periods with an evolving system approach. We also acknowledge Walberg's (1988) views of education, creativity, and human capital which relate to the investment metaphor plus many other sources that helped us designate the specific resources for creative performance. Nevertheless, we believe that our particular conceptualization of variables and integration of these variables through the investment theory adds something new to the theoretical literature on creativity. Consider each investment resource for creative performance and the way resource changes with age may contribute to changes in creative performance over the life span.

RESOURCES FOR CREATIVITY

INTELLECTUAL PROCESSES

Creative performance involves the intellectual processes of defining and redefining problems, choosing appropriate problem-solving strategies, and using insight processes to solve problems (Sternberg, 1985; Sternberg & Lubart, 1991). In regard to problem definition, John Dewey is credited with the maxim: "A problem well put is half solved." And, research on problem solving in both art and general domains supports the importance of problem formulation (Getzels & Csikszentmihalyi, 1976; Kotovsky, Hayes, & Simon, 1985). Strategy selection is another high-level process involved in creativity. Depending on the stage of a project, it may be useful to employ either a divergent or convergent mode of thinking (Brown, 1989). Divergent thinking refers to the generation of responses from given information with an emphasis on variety of output. Convergent thinking involves the use of information to arrive at a single "correct" solution. Divergent thinking at an early stage of work may be especially important because it helps a person move beyond easily obtained mundane ideas and provides alternative paths for task completion (Osborn, 1963; Torrance, 1974, 1988).

Finally, the importance of insight processes for creative work has often been noted (Davidson & Sternberg, 1984; Sternberg, 1988a; Sternberg & Lubart, 1991). Selective encoding involves sifting out information that is relevant for one's purposes and seeing as relevant information that others may pass over. Selective comparison involves seeing connections between present and past ideas that may elude others' notice. Selective comparisons are often made through analogies and metaphors. Selective combination involves the meaningful synthesis of disparate information fragments. Janusian thinking (i.e., the simultaneous integration of opposing or antithetical ideas) and bisociation (the unification of disparate thought matrices) can be viewed as specific forms of selective combination that have previously been linked to creativity (Koestler, 1964; Rothenberg, 1979).

The intellectual processes involved in creative performance are subject to both positive and negative age influences. On the positive side, problem definition, strategy selection, selective encoding, comparison, and combination can become more efficient with experience (Berg & Sternberg, 1985). Also, dialectical thinking is believed to develop with age (Berg & Sternberg, 1985). This form of thinking involves posing a thesis and its antithesis to find a coherent solution. Dialectical thinking may enhance problem definition and the selective combination process. Dialectical thinking also could contribute to the harmony and decreased tension that form part of old age style.

On the negative side, fluid abilities—the general ability to think flexibly and handle new kinds of situations, divergent thinking, and selective attention (relevant to selective encoding)—show declines with age (Belsky, 1990; McCrae, Arenberg, & Costa, 1987; McDowd & Birren,

1990; Simonton, 1990b). The declines in these specific abilities, however, may be relatively small and partially due to the use of time-limited tests of the abilities or domain-general tests for abilities that become increasingly domain specific with experience (Salthouse, 1990; Schaie, 1990; Simonton, 1988). The most insidious effect of age is probably a generalized slow-down of information processing (Cerella, 1990). Reduced cognitive speed could cause changes in productivity of creative work without specifically affecting quality of the work.

KNOWLEDGE

To make an informed creative contribution in any domain, knowledge is necessary. Hayes (1989), for example, examined over 500 notable musical compositions produced by 76 "great" composers. Only three pieces were composed before year 10 of the composers' careers. An analysis of 131 painters showed that 6 years of preparation were needed. The literature on expertise strongly supports the importance of knowledge in a given field (e.g., Chase & Simon, 1973; Chi, Glaser, & Rees, 1982).

We noted earlier that the age at which peak creativity occurs varies across domains. Fields also vary on the average age at which the earliest contributions occur. This variation is found across disparate fields (e.g., mathematics and history) and within subdisciplines of a large domain such as science (e.g., chemistry and physics) (Simonton, 1991). These age-related variations may be caused, in part, by differences in the amount of start-up knowledge that a field requires before creative work is possible (Amabile, 1983).

For creative performance, knowledge has many benefits. First, knowledge allows a person to be contrarian, as successful investors often are in financial markets; to go against the current trends, one needs to know what they are. Second, knowledge can prevent a person from reinventing ideas or products that society has already experienced. Third, knowledge helps a person to produce work of high quality, which is a component of most creativity judgments. Fourth, with an adequate knowledge base, a person may notice and use chance occurrences; as Pasteur said: "Chance favors the prepared mind" (quoted in Rosenman, 1988). Finally, knowledge, in the form of practice, allows a person to devote greater cognitive resources to the processing of new ideas.

In terms of the knowledge resource, aging usually involves increases in general knowledge, life experience, and career experience. For older adults a large knowledge base can help buffer decrements that may occur in the intellectual processes resource (Salthouse, 1990). Also, changes in the content of knowledge, such as a greater awareness of the aging process and disease, can move a creator's work in new directions (Gardner & Monge, 1977). This change in the content of creative work is one feature of old age style, described earlier.

While noting the benefits of knowledge, research indicates that more knowledge does not always lead to higher creativity. When formal education is taken as a measure of knowledge, an inverted-U function for creativity and knowledge is demonstrated, with an undergraduate level of knowledge at the peak (Simonton, 1983, 1984). Experts may lose flexibility and become entrenched in a standard or "correct" way of approaching a problem (Frensch & Sternberg, 1989; Langer, 1989). As a result of entrenchment, the rate of knowledge acquisition may decrease with age. With less novelty in the knowledge base, there may be less idea generation and less creative productivity. Also, if an individual fails to keep up with changes in the domain of work, his or her work may become dated. The tendency for knowledge to become outdated more quickly in some domains as compared with others can account for variation across fields in the average age of final creative contribution (Simonton, 1991).

INTELLECTUAL STYLES

Intellectual style refers to a preferred way of using one's abilities to approach a task or situation (see Kogan, 1973). People do not have one style exclusively and styles interact with situations. Nevertheless, people do seem to have stylistic preferences. The theory of intellectual styles used here is Sternberg's (1988b) theory of mental self-government, according to which people apply their intellectual processes to tasks in ways analogous to those that governments use to rule a nation. Three styles that are particularly relevant for creative performance are the legislative, liberal, and global ones.

A person with a legislative style is someone who likes to come up with his or her own rules, procedures, or ideas. The person likes to invent, discover, and work on problems that are not prefabricated. Such a person can be contrasted with both the executive and judicial stylist. The executive stylist likes to be given a set of guidelines within which to operate, implement plans, and solve problems. Schooling often promotes the executive style through assignments that involve following a preset route for task completion. A person favoring the judicial style likes tasks that involve analysis, comparisons, and criticisms of various approaches to a topic.

A second style dimension is the liberal-conservative leaning of one's mental self-government. (It should be noted we refer here to personal, not political style.) The person with a liberal style likes change in his or her way of seeing or doing things, whereas a person with a conservative style prefers traditional approaches and maintenance of the status quo. The novelty component of creative performance clearly favors liberal stylists.

Corresponding to the levels at which government can operate, people also vary on the extent to which they favor a global or local approach to tasks. The global person likes to deal with larger and often fairly abstract problems, in comparison with the local stylist, who prefers to deal with details and smaller, often fairly concrete problems. Clearly, both global and local levels are involved in every task and an ability to move between levels is beneficial. However, we suggest that high levels of creativity require a global proclivity.

At this point, we can only speculate on changes in mental self-government styles over the life span. In general, age-related changes in cognitive styles have been observed (Kogan, 1973). For example, there are age differences in conceptualization style, the way people categorize or group objects together. For the mental self-government styles described above, two shifts are hypothesized. First, liberal stylists may shift toward the conservative pole as aging adults grow to accept the world as they find it and their lives as they lived them. This change could reduce creative productivity in general. Second, there may be shifts from legislative to judicial styles with age. This shift could be reflected in the nature of creative work by older adults. Lehman (1953), as noted earlier, observed that late life creative achievements often involved the writing of histories or important textbooks. These types of integrative reviews are primarily judicial tasks.

PERSONALITY

Several personality attributes have been linked to creativity. We include five that we believe to be essential. The first, tolerance of ambiguity (Barron & Harrington, 1981; Golann, 1963), is necessary during those periods of creative endeavor in which things are not quite fitting together, but in which premature closure would negate the likelihood of creative contribution. Tolerance for ambiguity may affect the quality of work and the decision to pursue projects—the quantity of work. A study with 111 teachers (age 20–83) found scores on the Barron-Welsh Art Scale to decline with age, especially beyond age 50 (Alpaugh & Birren, 1977). The Barron-Welsh Art Scale consists of a set of figures that vary in complexity, symmetry, and ambiguity (Golann, 1962; Ridley, 1977). Subjects respond "like" or "dislike" to each figure. Changes in tolerance of ambiguity with age need to be further substantiated.

The second attribute, perseverance (Golann, 1963; Roe, 1952), is essential in any kind of contrarian efforts, where one's going against vested and entrenched interests is likely to threaten those who have a stake in the existing order. It has often been suggested that old age is accompanied by decreased stamina and decreased willingness to battle frustration (Abra, 1989; Lehman, 1953). However, there are numerous cases of creativity in old age despite physical ailments. For example, Renoir continued to work although rheumatism forced him to have a paint brush tied to his hand (Simonton, 1990b). Further research is needed on whether life span changes occur for perseverance.

The third attribute, willingness to grow and openness to new experiences (McCrae, 1987), becomes especially important as one attempts to go beyond one's past contributions to make new ones that are genuinely different and perhaps different in kind. Older workers may be content with their earlier accomplishments. They also must compete with their own record when they produce new work (Abra, 1989; Lehman, 1953). Due, in part, to the possibility of devaluing their own work, Planck (1949) and others have proposed that older achievers are less receptive than younger achievers to new ideas in their discipline. Hull, Tessner, and Diamond (1978) tested this hypothesis with historical records of British scientists who reacted to Darwin's theory of evolution in the decade after it was published. Scientists who accepted the theory were significantly younger (mean age = 41.7) than those who rejected the theory (mean age = 53.0).

The fourth attribute, willingness to take risks (Glover, 1977; McClelland, 1956), is emphasized in our investment approach. During creative work there is a potential for gain (internal and external rewards) or loss (time, energy, criticism) and the outcome is uncertain. Botwinick (1984) has documented the tendency for increased cautiousness with age. Several studies have measured risk taking through a set of hypothetical situations that involve choice dilemmas (Kogan & Wallach, 1964). Subjects were asked to indicate the odds of success they would require before advising the person in the scenario to choose the risky course of action. The possible odds for success were: 1 in 10, 3 in 10, 5 in 10, 7 in 10, or 9 in 10. A subject could also refuse the risky alternative "no matter what the probabilities." Elderly subjects showed a tendency to avoid risk in these scenarios by refusing to endorse the risky course of action "no matter what the probability" of success. On cognitive tests, elderly subjects also show a tendency to omit answers rather than guess incorrectly. However, in further studies, when subjects were forced to choose among options that involved some risk, then the elderly's risk preferences were similar to younger subjects' (Botwinick,

1984; Okun, 1976). This finding suggests that older adults often opt out of risk taking but are willing to take average levels of risk when required to choose the lesser evil.

Okun and DiVesta (1976) further examined risk taking in actual performance with a vocabulary task. Older subjects (age 60–76) showed less risk taking than young subjects (age 18–30) by choosing problems that offered them a high probability of success and refusing to increase their risk level when they did succeed at the less risky problems. Declines in risk taking may reflect a fear of failure in old age and will negatively affect creative performance. The tendency of elderly people to opt out of risky situations especially limits creative productivity.

The fifth attribute is individuality and a supporting courage of one's convictions (Barron & Harrington, 1981; Dellas & Gaier, 1970; Golann, 1963; MacKinnon, 1962, 1965). One needs to value oneself and one's difference from others, and to believe in one's ideas even as they go against the entrenched ones. Individuality may be expressed in the work of older creators by emphasizing subjective, introspective material, or rejecting formal styles for one's own style. Research suggests, however, that individuality tends to decline in older adults. Adults age 60 and older display more conformity than younger adults on projective tests such as the Thematic Apperception Test (TAT) and in experimental settings (Botwinick, 1984). Klein (1972), for example, tested young adults (16–21 years) and old adults (60–86 years) in a perceptual judgment task. When given false feedback about other subjects' judgments, the older subjects conformed significantly more often and this tendency was even stronger for more difficult versions of the task. Relating to courage of convictions, Jaquish and Ripple (1981) found decreased self-esteem in elderly subjects (ages 61–84) as compared with younger subjects (ages 18–60). In the elderly group, self-esteem was significantly correlated with response fluency for divergent thinking test performance, suggesting an effect of changes in self-esteem on creative productivity.

Taken together, the aspects of personality described above are viewed as necessary for maintaining high levels of creative performance over long periods of time. Research suggests that negative changes may occur in each component, which in turn affect creativity.

MOTIVATION

Intrinsic rewards—such as realizing one's potential and satisfying one's curiosity—and achievement motivation have often been viewed as important driving forces for creators (Amabile, 1983; Crutchfield,

1962; Golann, 1962). These motivators share the common feature of tending to focus attention on the task.

Goal-focusing motivators, in contrast, lead people to see a task as a means to an end. If the goal, which may be money, recognition, or an intangible reward, such as pride in one's accomplishment, remains salient during task completion then creative performance suffers because attention is drawn away from the task itself. It is important to note, however, that extrinsic motivators like money are not always antithetical to creativity; some people can maintain a focus on their task. Thus, we emphasize the way in which motivation focuses attention (task vs. goal) rather than the specific motivator (see Sternberg & Lubart, 1996).

Life span research, to date, has not directly addressed the possibility of changes in task- or goal-focused motivation with age. A few studies, however, have shown changes in the level of specific motivators, which may affect creative productivity (Kausler, 1990). For example, Veroff, Reuman, and Feld (1984) used projective measures of achievement motivation with representative samples of more than a thousand adults in 1957 and 1976. Achievement motivation was highest for the age 21–34 group, declined slightly for the 35–54 year old group, and declined somewhat more for the 55–80+ group. This pattern was more pronounced for women than men. In contrast, a longitudinal study with college students, who were retested when they were in their thirties or forties, showed increases in self-reported achievement motivation, as measured by the Edwards Personal Preference Test (Stevens & Truss, 1985). Taken together, these two studies offer somewhat conflicting accounts, but do suggest that some motivational changes occur. These changes might be due partially to the structure of career advancement, retirement policies, or other environmental influences (Mumford & Gustafson, 1988; Skinner, 1983).

ENVIRONMENTAL CONTEXT

The final resource for creativity is environmental context. Environments can provide physical and social stimulation, which help new ideas to form. Environments also vary on the extent to which creativity is fostered (Amabile, 1983; Lubart, 1990). When conformity is valued, new ideas may be squelched as soon as they are conceived.

Aging is associated with a host of environmental changes. First, older people often experience decreased income, decreased social networks for support, and declining health (Belsky, 1990). These elements create a context in which creative work is difficult. Second, as a person advances in a field, and attains some fame for creative work, there are requests for lectures, committees on which to serve, and other chores. Essentially, with age, people have increased responsibilities for the maintenance of their field. These "taxes" limit the time available for creative productivity (Bjorksten, 1946). Third, there may be cohort differences in the overall economic climate and the availability of benefactors to support creative work (Simonton, 1988); publication practices and the amount of competition in a field can also change over time (Botwinick, 1984; Simonton, 1977).

As an interesting aside, the tendency for precocity, longevity, and output rate to be positively correlated can be explained through the nurturing environment. Simonton (1990b) has noted that those who produce creative work at a young age also tend to be highly productive and have long creative careers. This co-occurrence may stem from accumulative advantage, or the "Matthew effect" (Allison & Stewart, 1974; Merton, 1968). Recognition for creative work at an early age reinforces achievement and provides the person with increased resources for further work. This cycle feeds on itself. The person produces more work, gains more recognition, and acquires more resources. In contrast, a person who begins with failure or is simply slow to start a creative career receives little recognition and support at first. This poor beginning, often, is discouraging enough to spiral the person away from creative work. The accumulative advantage hypothesis has received empirical support through an analysis of chemists, physicists, and mathematicians (Allison & Stewart, 1974).

Beyond the nurturance of creativity, the social environment serves to evaluate products and performances. The very same contribution viewed as creative by one group of judges may be viewed as mundane by another (Csikszentmihalyi, 1988). Changes in life span creativity can be traced, in part, to changes in implicit standards for creativity over time, and to rater bias against the elderly. Consider each of these possibilities.

Each age cohort may have a different standard for creativity (Romaniuk & Romaniuk, 1981). Cohorts may have their own preferred genres of work, as well as distinct preferences for artists or musicians that were novel during the cohort's youth. Products that an older cohort may consider novel could very well be deemed ordinary by a younger cohort because that novelty has been incorporated into the culture.

In a preliminary study of the investment theory of creativity, we obtained some evidence for a cohort effect (Lubart & Sternberg, 1992; see also Sternberg & Lubart, 1996). We asked 48 New Haven area adults (ages 18–65, X = 33.4, SD = 13.8) to complete two drawings, two short stories, two advertisements, and two scientific problem-solving tasks. In each domain, subjects were given a choice of topics as the starting point for their productions. For example, drawing topics included "hope," "rage," and "earth from an insect's point of view." Advertising topics included "bow ties," "brussel sprouts," and "the Internal Revenue Service." Subjects also completed a battery of psychometric measures. Fifteen additional subjects (X age = 41.07, SD = 13.02) rated the overall creativity and several other attributes of each product. The creativity ratings showed high interrater reliability (α = .88). Specific to the advertising domain, a forward stepwise regression for the advertising domain showed that there was a nonsignificant linear age trend, $F < 1$, and a significant quadratic age trend, $F(2,45) = 3.30$, $MSe = .48$, $p < .05$, $R^2 = .13$. This pattern could be caused by an age-related mismatch between raters' and producers' conceptions of novelty and creativity. For example, a 65-year-old subject might have produced an advertisement that she considered creative; a 30-year-old rater might have regarded this product as outdated. We suggest that the characteristics of creative work may change rapidly in some domains, such as advertising, but exhibit slow changes in other domains, such as writing. Bias against work produced by elderly persons also seems to occur. Cohen-Shalev (1989) points to several instances of critics in art and literature dismissing creative works because the producer was "mentally fatigued" or senile due to old age. This tendency is especially strong when the work produced is difficult to interpret or uses a new style. Elderly creators, in some critics' eyes, may also be constrained by their early products to follow a developmental course in their work. If a person produces work that does not fit into a progression in style or content (as imposed by the critics) then the work may be dismissed. Finally, critics may set unrealistic standards for elderly creators, believing that the products of old age must offer a profound message and surpass the creator's earlier works in order to be considered creative. Thus, the evaluative environment can have a profound effect on creative performance. The environment often contains obstacles for older adults that, at the very least, provide negative incentives for producing any work in old age.

THE CONFLUENCE OF RESOURCES

The investment theory is a confluence theory: It holds that the resources of creativity work in conjunction with each other. For example, all the knowledge in the world may be to no avail if an individual does not have the intelligence to use the knowledge effectively, or the legislative style to turn that knowledge toward creative ends. Similarly, great intelligence must be combined with a willingness to take risks with that intelligence. In addition to the need for multiple resources to be active together, some resource combinations can interactively boost creative performance. For example, when a high level of perseverance and a high level of task motivation co-occur in a person, creative performance is predicted to increase multiplicatively.

Our treatment of life span creativity reflects the investment theory's confluence approach. We have indicated that the cognitive, conative, and environmental resources are subject to age-related changes. These resources are not static over the adult life span. We suggest that the multiple changes with age work together to yield the general life span trends in productivity, quality, and form of creative work. In our view, theories that try to account for life span creativity using only a few cognitive or conative variables may appear attractively simple. However, these parsimonious theories, in our opinion, either require untenable assumptions or do not adequately capture the course of life span creativity (see Simonton, 1988).

CONCLUSION

Between 18 and 81 creativity changes. Productivity, quality, and the form and style of creative work vary over the life span. We can understand these changes through the confluence of six resources—intellectual processes, knowledge, intellectual style, personality, motivation, and environmental context—which themselves change with age. Changes in the resources over the life span may enhance creativity in some ways and detract from it in other ways. The combined set of resource changes is hypothesized to lead to observed creative performance during the adult years.

It is important to note three points before closing. First, the investment theory focuses on the psychological variables for creative performance. Physical energy and disease clearly are important (Simonton, 1977, 1984). We believe, however, that the influence of these variables are mediated through the psychological resources. For example, decreased energy may reduce motivation and physical impairments may decrease productivity because perseverance is lacking. Second, we have used chronological age throughout this chapter to index changes in creative performance and changes in the resources for creativity. Chronological age denotes biological age, cohort age, and career age. Although these aspects of age are highly correlated, it may be useful to separate the age effects in future work. Third, we acknowledge limitations in our current theory. For example, the investment theory is posed at a global, somewhat descriptive level and has been subject to only a preliminary empirical test (Lubart & Sternberg, 1992). In future work, we plan to specify the confluence of resources in greater detail and link the resources to a process model of creative work. In conclusion, we hope that some of the conjectures that we have offered will further an understanding of life span creativity and provide useful directions for research.

ACKNOWLEDGMENTS

This chapter was written, in part, while the first author was supported by a Jacob K. Javits Fellowship and a Yale University Graduate Fellowship. The work reported herein was further supported under the Javits Act program (Grant #R206R00001) as administered by the Office of Educational Research and Improvement, U.S. Department of Education. The findings and opinions expressed in this report do not reflect the positions or policies of the Office of Educational Research and Improvement or the U.S. Department of Education. Correspondence and requests for reprints should be addressed to Todd I. Lubart or Robert J. Sternberg, Yale University, Department of Psychology, Box 11A Yale Station, New Haven, CT 06520.

REFERENCES

Abra, J. (1989). Changes in creativity with age: Data, explanations, and further predictions. *International Journal of Aging and Human Development, 28*(2), 105–126.

Allison, P., & Stewart, J. (1974). Productivity differences among scientists: Evidence for accumulative advantage. *American Sociological Review, 39,* 596–606.

Alpaugh, P. K., & Birren, J. E. (1977). Variables affecting creative contributions across the adult life span. *Human Development, 20,* 240–248.

Amabile, T. M. (1983). *The social psychology of creativity.* New York: Springer-Verlag.

Arieti, S. (1976). *Creativity: The magic synthesis.* New York: Basic Books.

Barron, F., & Harrington, D. M. (1981). Creativity, intelligence, and personality. *Annual Review of Psychology, 32,* 439–476.

Beckerman, M. B. (1990). Leos Janá_ek and "the late style" in music. *The Gerontologist, 30,* 632–635.

Belsky, J. K. (1990). *The psychology of aging: Theory, research, and interventions* (2nd ed.). Pacific Grove, CA: Brooks/Cole.

Berg, C. A., & Sternberg, R. J. (1985). A triarchic theory of intellectual development during adulthood. *Developmental Review, 5,* 334–370.

Bjorksten, J. (1946). The limitation of creative years. *Scientific Monthly, 62,* 94.

Botwinick, J. (1984). *Aging and behavior* (3rd ed.). New York: Springer.

Brown, R. T. (1989). Creativity: What are we to measure? In J. A. Glover, R. R. Ronning, & C. R. Reynolds (eds.), *Handbook of creativity* (pp. 3–32). New York: Plenum.

Cerella, J. (1990). Aging and information-processing rate. In J. E. Birren & K. W. Schaie (eds.), *Handbook of the psychology of aging,* (3rd ed., pp. 201–221). San Diego: Academic Press.

Chase, W. G., & Simon, H. A. (1973). The mind's eye in chess. In W. G. Chase (ed.), *Visual information processing.* New York: Academic Press.

Chi, M., Glaser, R., & Rees, E. (1982). Expertise in problem solving. In R. J. Sternberg (ed.), *Advances in the psychology of human intelligence* (Vol. 1, pp. 7–76). Hillsdale, NJ: Erlbaum.

Cohen-Shalev, A. (1986). Artistic creativity across the adult life span: An alternative approach. *Interchange, 17*(4), 1–16.

Cohen-Shalev, A. (1989). Old age style: Developmental changes in creative production from a life-span perspective. *Journal of Aging Studies, 3*(1), 21–37.

Crutchfield, R. (1962). Conformity and creative thinking. In H. Gruber, G. Terrell, & M. Wertheimer (eds.), *Contemporary approaches to creative thinking* (pp. 120–140). New York: Atherton.

Csikszentmihalyi, M. (1988). Society, culture, and person: A systems view of creativity. In R. J. Sternberg (ed.), *The nature of creativity* (pp. 325–339). New York: Cambridge University Press.

Davidson, J. E., & Sternberg, R. J. (1984). The role of insight in intellectual giftedness. *Gifted Child Quarterly, 28*(4), 58–64.

Dellas, M., & Gaier, E. L. (1970). Identification of creativity: The individual. *Psychological Bulletin, 73,* 55–73.

Dreman, D. (1982). *The new contrarian investment strategy.* New York: Random House.

Frensch, P. A., & Sternberg, R. J. (1989). Expertise and intelligent thinking: When is it worse to know better? In R. J. Sternberg (ed.), *Advances in the psychology of human intelligence* (Vol. 5, pp. 157–188). Hillsdale, NJ: Erlbaum.

Gardner, E. F., & Monge, R. H. (1977). Adult age differences in cognitive abilities and educational background. *Experimental Aging Research, 3,* 337–383.

Getzels, J., & Csikszentmihalyi, M. (1976). *The creative vision: A longitudinal study of problem-finding in art.* New York: Wiley-Interscience.

Glover, J. A. (1977). Risky shift and creativity. *Social Behavior and Personality, 5,* 317–320.

Golann, S. E. (1962). The creativity motive. *Journal of Personality, 30,* 588–600.

Golann, S. E. (1963). Psychological study of creativity. *Psychological Bulletin, 60,* 548–565.

Gruber, H. E., & Davis, S. N. (1988). Inching our way up Mount Olympus: The evolving-systems approach to creative thinking. In R. J. Sternberg (ed.), *The nature of creativity* (pp. 243–270). New York: Cambridge University Press.

Hayes, J. R. (1989). Cognitive processes in creativity. In J. A. Glover, R. R. Ronning, & C. R. Reynolds (eds.), *Handbook of creativity* (pp. 135–146). New York: Plenum.

Hull, D. L., Tessner, P. D., & Diamond, A. M. (1978). Planck's principle: Do younger scientists accept new scientific ideas with greater alacrity than older scientists? *Science, 202,* 717–723.

Jaquish, G. A., & Ripple, R. E. (1981). Cognitive creative abilities and self-esteem across the adult life-span. *Human Development, 24,* 110–119.

Kausler, D. H. (1990). Motivation, human aging, and cognitive performance. In J. E. Birren & K. W. Schaie (eds.), *Handbook of the psychology of aging* (3rd ed., pp. 171–182). San Diego: Academic Press.

Klein, R. L. (1972). Age, sex, and task difficulty as predictors of social conformity. *Journal of Gerontology, 27*(2), 229–236.

Koestler, A. (1964). *The act of creation.* New York: Dell.

Kogan, N. (1973). Creativity and cognitive style: A life-span perspective. In P. B. Baltes, & K. W. Schaie (eds.), *Life-span developmental psychology: Personality and socialization* (pp. 145–178). New York: Academic Press.

Kogan, N., & Wallach, M. A. (1964). *Risk taking: A study in cognition and personality.* New York: Holt, Rinehart, and Winston.

Kotovsky, K., Hayes, J. R., & Simon, H. A. (1985). Why are some problems hard? Evidence from Tower of Hanoi. *Cognitive Psychology, 17,* 248–294.

Langer, E. J. (1989). *Mindfulness.* New York: Addison-Wesley.

Lehman, H. C. (1953). *Age and achievement.* Princeton, NJ: Princeton University Press.

Longfellow, H. W. (1876). *The masque of Pandora.* Boston: Osgood.

Lubart, T. I. (1990). Creativity and cross-cultural variation. *International Journal of Psychology, 25,* 39–59.

MacKinnon, D. W. (1962). The nature and nurture of creative talent. *American Psychologist, 17,* 484–495.

MacKinnon, D. W. (1965). Personality and the realization of creative potential. *American Psychologist, 20,* 273–281.

McClelland, D. C. (1956). The calculated risk: An aspect of scientific performance. In C. W. Taylor (ed.), *The 1955 University of Utah research conference on the identification of creative scientific talent* (pp. 96–110). Salt Lake City: University of Utah Press.

McCrae, R. R. (1987). Creativity, divergent thinking, and openness to experience. *Journal of Personality and Social Psychology, 52,* 1258–1265.

McCrae, R. R., Arenberg, D., & Costa, P. T. Jr. (1987). Declines in divergent thinking with age: Cross-sectional, longitudinal, and cross-sequential analyses. *Psychology and Aging, 2*(2), 130–137.

McDowd, J. M., & Birren, J. E. (1990). Aging and attentional processes. In J. E. Birren & K. W. Schaie (eds.), *Handbook of the psychology of aging* (3rd ed., pp. 222–233). San Diego: Academic Press.

McLeish, J. A. B. (1976). *The Ulyssean adult: Creativity in the middle and later years.* New York: McGraw-Hill Reyerson.

Merton, R. K. (1968). The Matthew effect in science. *Science, 159,* 56–63.

Mumford, M. D., & Gustafson, S. B. (1988). Creativity syndrome: Integration, application, and innovation. *Psychological Bulletin, 103,* 27–43.

Okun, M. A., & Di Vesta, F. J. (1976). Cautiousness in adulthood as a function of age and instructions. *Journal of Gerontology, 31*(5), 571–576.

Osborn, A. F. (1963). *Applied imagination* (3rd ed.). New York: Scribners.

Planck, M. (1949). *Scientific autobiography and other papers,* (F. Gaynor, Trans.). New York: Philosophical Library.

Ridley, D. R. (1977). Preference for stimulus complexity and architectural creativity. *Perceptual and Motor Skills, 45,* 815–818.

Roe, A. (1952). *The making of a scientist.* New York: Dodd, Mead.

Romaniuk, J. G., & Romaniuk, M. (1981). Creativity across the life span: A measurement perspective. *Human Development, 24,* 366–381.

Rosenman, M. F. (1988). Serendipity and scientific discovery. *Journal of Creative Behavior, 22,* 132–138.

Rothenberg, A. (1979). *The emerging goddess.* Chicago: University of Chicago Press.

Salthouse, T. A. (1990). Cognitive competence and expertise in aging.

In J. E. Birren & K. W. Schaie (eds.), *Handbook of the psychology of aging* (3rd ed., pp. 310–319). San Diego: Academic Press.

Schaie, K. W. (1990). Intellectual development in adulthood. In J. E. Birren & K. W. Schaie (eds.), *Handbook of the psychology of aging* (3rd ed., pp. 291–309). San Diego: Academic Press.

Simonton, D. K. (1975). Age and literary creativity: A cross-cultural and transhistorical survey. *Journal of Cross-Cultural Psychology, 6,* 259–277.

Simonton, D. K. (1977). Creative productivity, age, and stress: A biographical time-series analysis of 10 classical composers. *Journal of Personality and Social Psychology, 35,* 791–804.

Simonton, D. K. (1983). Formal education, eminence and dogmatism: The curvilinear relationship. *Journal of Creative Behavior, 17,* 149–162.

Simonton, D. K. (1984). *Genius, creativity, and leadership.* Cambridge, MA: Harvard University Press.

Simonton, D. K. (1985). Quality, quantity, and age: The careers of 10 distinguished psychologists. *International Journal of Aging and Human Development, 21,* 241–254.

Simonton, D. K. (1988). Age and outstanding achievement: What do we know after a century of research? *Psychological Bulletin, 104,* 251–267.

Simonton, D. K. (1989). The swan-song phenomenon: Last-works effects for 172 classical composers. *Psychology and Aging, 4*(1), 42–47.

Simonton, D. K. (1990a). Creativity in the later years: Optimistic prospects for achievement. *The Gerontologist, 30,* 626–631.

Simonton, D. K. (1990b). Creativity and wisdom in aging. In J. E. Birren & K. W. Schaie (eds.), *Handbook of the psychology of aging* (3rd ed., pp. 320–329). San Diego: Academic Press.

Simonton, D. K. (1991). Career landmarks in science: Individual differences and interdisciplinary contrasts. *Developmental Psychology, 27*(1), 119–130.

Skinner, B. F. (1983, September). Creativity in old age. *Psychology Today,* 28–29.

Sternberg, R. J. (1985). *Beyond IQ: A triarchic theory of human intelligence.* New York: Cambridge University Press.

Sternberg, R. J. (ed.) (1988a). *The nature of creativity.* New York: Cambridge University Press.

Sternberg, R. J. (1988b). Mental self-government: A theory of intellectual styles and their development. *Human Development, 31,* 197–224.

Sternberg, R. J., & Lubart, T. I. (1991). An investment theory of creativity and its development. *Human Development, 34*(1), 1–31.

Sternberg, R. J., & Lubart, T. I. (1996). Investing in Creativity. *American Psychologist, 51,* 677–688.

Stevens, D. P., & Truss, C. V. (1985). Stability and change in adult personality over 12 and 20 years. *Developmental Psychology, 21,* 568–584.

Torrance, E. P. (1974). *Torrance tests of creative thinking.* Lexington, MA: Personnel Press.

Torrance, E. P. (1988). The nature of creativity as manifest in its testing. In R. J. Sternberg (ed.), *The nature of creativity* (pp. 43–75). New York: Cambridge University Press.

Veroff, J., Reuman, D., & Feld, S. (1984). Motives in American men and women across the adult life span. *Developmental Psychology, 20,* 1142–1158.

Walberg, H. J. (1988). Creativity and talent as learning. In R. J. Sternberg (ed.), *The nature of creativity* (pp. 340–361). New York: Cambridge University Press.

Wyatt-Brown, A. M. (1988). Late style in the novels of Barbara Pym and Penelope Mortimer. *The Gerontologist, 28,* 835–839.

Creativity and Postformal Thought: Why the Last Stage Is the Creative Stage

Jan D. Sinnott

Data shows that postformal thought, which develops in the second half of life, is a major area for expression of adult creativity and a major way to describe the process of adult creativity. Creative postformal thinking is expressed in many domains, including interpersonal relating, everyday problem solving, and making sense of the world through which humans so briefly pass. In this chapter I will argue that creativity in midlife and old age takes on specific cognitive qualities (i.e., those of postformal thought) that are adaptive in everyday life because they regulate the integration of intellectual and emotional stimulation from events or people. This complex cognition is a bridge between affect and cognition and between a person and other persons, and is a way to make the demands and practical concerns of adult life bearable and meaningful. This complex cognition can be described using research data and can be manipulated experimentally. Its style changes during the adult life span, as is evident in cross-sectional studies. The products of this mature thought are better reflections of the union of emotion and cognition, of heart and mind, than are products which the younger person creates. The purposes of this chapter are to show the nature and use of this form of creativity, and to suggest applications and future studies.

In the next few pages I will discuss the following topics: the qualities of postformal thought, broader definitions of creativity, links between postformal thought and creativity, the utility of postformal thought for development, the regulation of life stage–specific stimulation, making life meaningful (e.g., reaching Eriksonian integrity, phenomenological epistemology, spirituality), and a summary of findings from my own and others' work on adult "postformal creativity." The topics addressed include adults' creative production of ways to attack everyday problems, young vs. mature styles of problem solving, and creative *social* construction of reality.

BROADER DEFINITIONS OF CREATIVITY

What kind of creativity will we be addressing in this chapter? The definitions of creativity are broad, although dictionary definitions usually are restricted to something like "intellectual inventiveness." In practice we see creativity in dichotomous ways, polarized around seven issues:

1. *process* focus vs. *product* focus
2. art (the emotional, the visual, the aural) vs. *ideation* (verbal, cognitive)
3. *uniqueness or originality* of products vs. *a high volume of high quality work*
4. representation of the product to others *(communication)* vs. *private experience* for one's own growth
5. quality *judged by others* vs. quality *judged by creator*
6. presence of *emotion and synthesis required* vs. *no need for these*
7. life's *pain* vs. life's *fullness* as a source of creativity

All these aspects are valid, but only some are consciously addressed by any given researcher or critic. Thus, it is hard to compare creativity across various studies.

Some combinations of these dimensions seem to yield higher quality than others. For example, many parents have received very creative breakfasts as special surprises for their birthdays, breakfasts made by young children using a creative process involving every pan in the house. These creations are full of emotion and color ("Look!! There are catsup and Jello faces on the toast!"), are very unique, and are clearly communicated ("I made this special breakfast just for you. See, the faces are smiling at you!"). These creations are creative to their creators, and might be called a synthesis of all meals the creators have ever liked. Yet is this as good a creation as the Mona Lisa? If one polar dimension of creativity is changed to "quality judged by others," the creativity of the breakfast seems to disappear, even though the breakfast, unfortunately, does not. It is not surprising then that creativity seems somewhat ephemeral.

The links of creativity to the happiness and psychological development of the creator are the subject of many stories, too. Is creativity "good" or "bad" for development? Mad artists and starving, rejected geniuses people our imaginations, although it also seems true that those who live creatively are the happiest adults. These happy people can't even commute to work without being moved by the wild and wonderfully strange behavior of others on the highway, seeing them all in creative ways. Even the mystics' truism that the enlightened soul sees *all* places as Nirvana and finds the Kingdom of Heaven within and all around seems to describe good psychological health and development. Is creativity a blessing or a curse?

For this chapter I have chosen to view creativity in only some of its possible dimensions. I am interested most in the creativity that is part of good psychological midlife development. In focusing on the creative process, and the concomitant presence of emotion, synthesis, and ideation, I ask how adults show the development of creative processes of thinking. Creative thinking can synthesize knowledge and emotion and experience, lets the thinker grow in real life social contexts, and can lead to a high volume of high quality, behaviorally productive work. I have approached the question of how persons develop the ability to make masterpieces of their lives during adulthood, with all its demands, by studying *postformal thought,* the cognitive side of what makes this all happen. Postformal thought allows one's life to be crafted consciously in creative ways.

Creativity takes place in a real interpersonal context, in a real period of history, and has a real impact on people and society. The kind of creativity a society values determines, in general systems theory terms (Miller, 1978; Sinnott, 1989c, 1989e, 1992b), how open the society is to solution of its problems. The creativity I will discuss takes place in such a context, which helps shape it. Each individual develops an ability to be postformal and to be creative in order to be more adaptive personally. He or she also, then, contributes to the adaptivity of the society or the family or the dyad in which he or she creates. For example, if I become capable of postformal thought and become more creative, my partner and I can more creatively shape our marriage (in the United States in the 20th century, where marriage has many forms). The quality of the marriage will reflect my partner's and my levels of creativity. In another example, how creatively my society attacks problems of the environment reflects the postformal cognitive creativity of the society's members, acting together.

Because creativity takes place in a life span context, too, the age and experience of the creator would seem to make a difference to the quality of creation. The younger or less experienced artist or author more often creates products communicating raw emotion and less refined ideas; the older or more experienced one more often produces the interpreted emotional expression and the integrated, synthesized idea. Again, in general systems theory terms, the younger society creates structures and processes that are less politicized, less subtle, and less integrated than the older society. For example, the United States has gone through its early, adolescent creative phase where simple, idealistic, emotion-laden solutions were imposed on social problems by strong-willed charismatic individuals. The young thinker creates new simple solutions ("shoot the developers, save the earth") or new specific products to help the environment, like the automotive catalytic converter. But our society may be transitioning to its midlife creative phase of refining creative solutions and interpreting and integrating them by consensus. The mature thinker wants to create better processes to help the environment (e.g., the Earth Summit), as well as be open to many new products.

The differences between values of young and mature creative societies can also be seen in the political realm or in science. The young society likes maverick, iconoclastic politicians and scientists who campaign for a simple or unspecified "change" and against the system or who seem to be lone geniuses. The mature society also values the creativity of the program to be put into place and the creativity of the brilliant scientific mentor and agenda setter.

Adolescent and mature societies frequently dismiss each others' creations as "uncreative." In the competitive adolescent creative society, one creative individual sometimes tears down what another creative individual creates; among mature creators individual geniuses are sometimes dismissed as troublemakers. Ideally, individual genius can be integrated into the creative mass for better cooperative problem solving or teamwork to occur. (Note that this does not mean the individual creator is a replaceable part!)

The role of creative social organizations also reflects the creative life cycle of the society. For example, the role of the university in a young culture is to produce the clever "lone wolf" creator; the university's role in a mature culture may be to produce good processes or questions or solutions which show integration across persons and problem parts. Mature creative societies integrate a historical prospective and social cooperativeness. (See Sinnott, in press-d, for a discussion of the future of the university.)

In this chapter, I will be focused on postformal thought as a component of the development of mature creative processes. I will also discuss the creative products of postformal thinkers.

NATURE OF POSTFORMAL THOUGHT, THE BASIS OF MATURE COGNITIVE CREATIVITY

What is postformal reasoning? In Piagetian terms, it is the way an adult structures thinking, over and above the operations of the formal operational adolescent, in order to optimally be in touch with reality, to make sense of the world and to live optimally. Two skills seem necessary to an intelligent creative adult. The first is cognizance of interpersonal and social reality in family, work, and other cultural situations. The second is knowledge of how to apply a variety of abstract formal operations selectively based on experience as needed in practical situations. But is there anything special or complex about the operations that would underlie those interpersonal, social, and practical skills? Are they different from Piaget's concrete or formal operations on physical relations?

There is at least one important difference to these creative postformal skills (Sinnott, 1984). It is the concept of necessary subjectivity which includes the knowledge of one's own reality creation. Knowledge of physical relations, such as number, volume, conservation, binary relations, and transitivity, are the result of abstractions from action on the physical world. Practically speaking, "local" physical relations are objectively present in reality (Sinnott, 1981) and are not so much the creation of the observer. The knower structures physical reality without seriously changing the local physical phenomena. Interpersonal relations, in contrast, are mainly a reflection of how people interact socially and how they know this interaction. Interpersonal relations seem to change constantly in their reality as a function of their being known or perceived in different ways by different individuals in the relationship. Relations may be very concrete or abstract or postformal or mixed, depending on the skills of those relating. Postformal structures develop through knowing interpersonal reality and, therefore, are inherently creative.

Postformal operations form a stage in a developmental hierarchy of cognitive operations that goes beyond Piagetian formal operations. As such, they construct a system of formal operational systems, or metatheories. Relativistic operations permit selection of one formal operational system among many, based on a necessarily subjective selection of *a priori* assumptions, or "givens." This selection occurs in a situation where several contradictory formal operational systems could apply. Formal operations presume logical consistency. In contrast, relativistic operations presume subjective selection among logically contradictory formal operational subsystems, each of which is internally consistent. They presume both creative idea production and creative appropriate application. Today our realities are often contradictory: Is reality new physics or Newtonian? Is our reality our neighborhood or the global village? Is what is really happening now what we see at this moment on TV, although it was taped last week, or what we don't see at all, but which actually is happening today? There is need for this cognitive skill to sort these realities out.

The postformal stage of relativistic operations presupposes Piaget's findings (summarized in Furth, 1969; Inhelder & Piaget, 1958) that the developing child passes through the following stages of cognitive growth at an individual rate in an invariant order: sensorimotor, preoperational, concrete operational, and formal operational. Piaget's analysis of formal operational thought provides sufficient structure to describe scientific thought up to and including the operations of Newtonian physics. It is insufficient, however, for the description of Einsteinian and later physics. The intellectual operations used by contemporary physicists can and may be used by other adults in other areas of life, including interpersonal relationships. Relativistic, self-referential postformal operational thought is a description of how this may be accomplished, because it permits sophisticated, necessary subjectivity to be ordered within complex adult thought. (See Sinnott, 1981, for an overview of relativistic thought in light of relativity and quantum physics theory).

Postformal thought has social implications. First, an individual reasons that if one choice of reality is necessarily partly subjective, perhaps other choices about reality are, too. The individual next reevaluates other formal systems already in use. Then, several persons together judge the "best fit" system in a case where no system completely fits a reality that involves them all and is seen somewhat differently by each. Finally, group explorations concerning system choice lead to a consensus on the formal reality system to utilize in a given case. Necessary subjectivity leads to a collective cognition and collectively agreed upon reality. So, shared invariants—agreed-upon metrics, logics, assumptions, parameters, and so on—persist beyond an individual or a group. (Such shared referents may become a dominant philosophy or culture of belief if the necessary subjectivity or arbitrariness of the system choice is forgotten.) If the fit is still not perfect, this imperfection eventually becomes apparent. Alternative, logically competing systems are again explored. Finally, the expenditure of energy involved probably precludes frequent collective postformal choices; so searches for best-fit systems go on at the individual level. Social change may result if a new best-fit system is found and is collectively agreed upon. Success, that is, construction of a formal reality system that fits with reality in a particular content area, would most likely lower the use of relativistic operations in the area but increase their use in other areas. But there is no limit to use of relativistic operations in understanding interpersonal relations in which one takes part, because the nature of the reality is constantly changing as a function of being known by the participants.

All theories of postformal thought (Arlin, 1975; Basseches, 1984; Commons & Richards, 1984; Labouvie-Vief, 1984; Perry, 1975; Sinnott, 1984) more-or-less share the belief that such thought goes beyond Piagetian formal operations and involves a kind of emotional commitment to one or the other of many generated views of truth in order for the thinker to take action. (Also see Commons et al., 1990; Commons, Richards, & Armon, 1984; Commons, Sinnott, Richards, & Armon, 1989; Sinnott, 1989a, 1989d, in press-a; and Sinnott & Cavanaugh, 1991.)

While some have compared postformal self-referential thought to simple relativism or to dialectical thought, it goes beyond those two forms. Simple relativism (e.g., Perry, 1975) leads to the conclusion that one's choice of truth is totally arbitrary because truth cannot be known; postformal thought concludes that truth can indeed be known and choices made because one can know the process by which any formal truth comes to be true. Dialectical thought (e.g., Basseches, 1984), leading to a synthesis of opposites, also differs from postformal self-referential thought. The former leads to understanding of higher order organization of opposites; the latter leads to awareness that the "rules of the game" of synthesizing a new truth are decided by the players as they play that truth game together. But despite the differences among relativism, dialecticism, and postformal self-referential thought on general theoretical levels, there are many similarities and in a given context all three might predict the same conclusions.

Responses of an individual in a given situation can be scored for presence or absence of the operations which together indicate postformal thought (see Sinnott, 1984, 1989a, 1989b). These operations include metatheory shift, problem definition, process/product shift, parameter setting, and multiple solutions and methods, among others. (See Table 3.1 and Sinnott, 1984, 1989b, 1991a, 1991b).

A summary of the genesis and results of postformal thought is in Figure 3.1.

divergent thinking (handwritten marginal note)

**TABLE 3.1 Criteria for Relativistic, Self-Referential
Postformal Operations**

1. *Metatheory shift.* There is the production of abstract and practical (real life) solutions as well as a shift between conflicting abstract *a priori* and real *a priori.* This shift is stated by the subject. The solution always includes problem definitions. For example, the subject might ask whether we want the hypothetical solution that is logical on paper or the solution that would really be viable. (The respondent may or may not then proceed to give both solutions.)

2. *Problem definition.* There is a statement of the meaning and demands of the problem for the subject. There is also the decision to define problems in a certain, chosen way. The subject indicates a change in the types of parameters from solution to solution. Defining the problem is the first concern, but the subject need not give alternative solutions, since these solutions might be precluded by the problem definition. The problem definition may include a metatheory shift. For example, the subject might wonder what the real problem is, whether it is the need to have peace in the family or to use all the space. The subject might then decide to treat it like an algebra problem.

3. *Process/product shift.* This is a description of a process as one answer and an outcome as another. Or there may be a description of two processes that achieve the same outcome. Often there is a statement by a subject that there is a solution and that finding the solution is actually a never-ending process.

4. *Parameter setting.* The subject names key variables to be combined or made proportional in the problem other than those given in the written demands of the problem. Often the subject explicitly writes out key variables. Alternatively, the subject may change the variables that limit the problem from solution 1 to solution 2. Parameter setting differs from problem definition in that it is less inclusive and more concrete.

5. *Pragmatism.* One can choose a best solution among several, or one can choose the best variant of a solution that has two processes. For example, the subject might say that if you want the most practical solution, it's number 2, but if you want the quickest, easiest solution, it's number 1. This is the only operation that cannot be given a passing score unless the subject actually gives more than one solution.

6. *Multiple solutions.* There is a direct statement that there are many correct solutions intrinsic to a problem with several causes, or that no problem has only one solution. Also, the subject may create several solutions. For example, the subject might respond that he or she sees four solutions that could be termed correct, or that there are limitless arrangements that would be correct if you change the constraints.

TABLE 3.1   *(Continued)*

7. *Multiple causality.* There is a statement that multiple causes exist for any event or that some solutions are more probable that others. For example, some subjects state that the solution depends on all past relations of the persons in the problem; that is, when the three persons in the problem get together anything could happen, depending on personalities and on how each reacts.

8. *Paradox.* The subject gives a direct statement or question about perceived, inherently conflicting demands that are integral to the problem, not simply two solutions with different parameters. For example, the Bedroom Problem can be read in two conflicting ways. The subject notices that two different things are being said at once, both of which could change the way the problem should be solved.

9. *Self-referential thought.* Awareness that the subject must be the ultimate judge of which belief system dominated his or her thinking; that is, of what is "true." For example, the subject might say that she, a therapist, can never be free of a bias but can only be aware of which bias is coloring her view of a client. But she knows all the views are true, and she must choose one and go on with the treatment sessions.

LINKS BETWEEN POSTFORMAL THOUGHT AND CREATIVITY

Postformal thought is linked to creativity because it describes the process by which mature adults think creatively. Postformal thought also is linked to creative production by virtue of its production of multiple views of reality and its multiple solutions, definitions, parameters and methods obtained empirically during problem solving. It is also linked to creativity because it changes the creative product from solely intellectual or solely emotional to a combination of subjective and objective understanding. The postformal creative production occurs within an experiential context with a historical perspective, and with awareness of social consequences. Notice that postformal thought develops after young adulthood and adolescence, during midlife and old age. This increased creativity thus presents a possibly positive expectation for cognitive growth and development of thinking in maturity and old age.

Postformal thought is a means by which mature adults can express creativity in a number of content domains. These include for example:

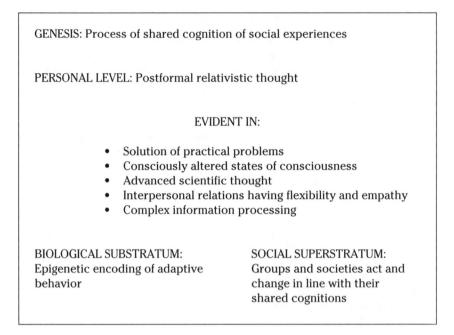

GENESIS: Process of shared cognition of social experiences

PERSONAL LEVEL: Postformal relativistic thought

EVIDENT IN:

- Solution of practical problems
- Consciously altered states of consciousness
- Advanced scientific thought
- Interpersonal relations having flexibility and empathy
- Complex information processing

BIOLOGICAL SUBSTRATUM: SOCIAL SUPERSTRATUM:
Epigenetic encoding of adaptive   Groups and societies act and
behavior   change in line with their
                                shared cognitions

FIGURE 3.1   Relativist thought: Genesis, effects, and behavioral evidence.
Note. "Postformal Reasoning: The Relativistic Stage" by J. D. Sinnott. Adapted
by permission.

interpersonal relations, everyday problem solving, family problems, logical thought about career choices, works of art, intragroup conflicts in the workplace, transpersonal issues and spirituality, psychotherapy, expertise, and cross-cultural understanding (e.g., Armstrong, 1991; Basseches, Kramer, & Sinnott, 1991; Johnson, 1991; Lee, 1991; Luszcz & Orr, 1991; Rogers, Sinnott, & Van Dusen, 1991; Sinnott, 1987b, 1989a, 1989b, 1991c, 1992a, 1992b, 1992c, in press-a, in press-b, in press-c, in press-d; Sinnott & Cavanaugh, 1991; Tanon, 1991; Weibust & Thomas, 1993). Some of these domains will be explored in a later section of this chapter.

Since it is the process (rather than the product) that is inherently creative in postformal thought, and the process that is productive, if a thinker has access to a postformal process in any domain at all, she or he has the cognitive processes that equate with creativity. Whether the product of these processes is considered valuable, and to whom, is not an issue here. The essence of postformal thinking is to realize that "reality" and "quality" are socially constructed (and sometimes socially agreed upon), that they demand choice of one of many solutions produced in response to a problem. Yet productivity alone is not equivalent to postformal creativity, since simply making a lot of something, even ideas, would not necessarily include the two essential acts of postformal thought, namely, (a) ordering logically disparate formal reality systems and (b) being self-referential. One would also need to make many systems, and then be able to select one as "true," knowing that this choice is somewhat arbitrary and done in reference to one's chosen view of the world. Postformal creativity, then, is like creating many romantic possibilities or relational systems by dating many persons and even falling in love with more than one, followed by consciously choosing to make a commitment to one person and forsaking all others. Ideally the head and the heart are both operating in complex ways.

The developmental demand for adaptivity makes the creative process here more complex. Being able to create multiple formal systems or views of reality seems adaptive because, with more systems, the odds of finding the best, most useful ones for a given context increase. But this only seems adaptive if the thinker can finally choose among inadequate solutions. Simon (1982) called this sort of choice "satisficing." It is not adaptive to be forever indecisive and caught in relativism. And thought is only adaptive if the emotional components of the situation are also satisfied. Thus both production and choice are part of the adaptive creative act. Furthermore, this kind of creativity seems adaptive only when the formal solutions created, and among which one chooses, involve more than intellectualizations. This coordination and production is certainly no less creative than painting a masterwork of art; in this case, the work of art is one's life. The systems, to be adaptive, should coordinate thought with emotion, meaning, intention, and action, within the behavioral context of the person and the times, including the person's developmental stage and world history. In the next section, we'll see how we found in research that intellectualization was not enough.

CREATIVE PROCESS AND CREATIVE PRODUCTION OF SOLUTIONS ARE HALLMARKS OF POSTFORMAL THOUGHT

When we first examined the nature of thinking done by normal 18- to 97-year-old respondents faced with everyday or abstract problems to solve, we noticed that some respondents saw each problem as many problems. One reason that some respondents seemed to do so poorly on ordinary logical problem-solving tests was just this tendency to see each problem in many different ways. Respondents sometimes really were solving not one problem but many. The more focused test creator saw one problem; the more experienced test taker saw multiple problems, solutions, methods, and was carefully sorting out which to explore. Sometimes—to the irritation of the test creator—some respondents would then "solve" the problem, not by giving a content-specific answer, but by giving a generally useful process to use in problems of this type. Even more irritating, some respondents—especially "slower" and older ones—would turn to the experimenter who had labored to set up a high-demand "absolutely clear and objective" problem, and complain, "This problem makes me mad! I have to decide how to interpret it (and it is somewhat arbitrary how I interpret it) before I ever solve it." At that point, at first, the test creator would worry that the stimulus materials were flawed, and would try to write a clearer problem that would induce less emotion.

Further questioning of these troublesome test takers led to a better understanding of why some weren't producing the logic desired at first by the test giver. Some of the respondents didn't produce logical answers because they didn't seem to have mastered logic. In other words, they really just failed. Other test takers, usually older but not cognitively struggling, could produce the logical response desired at first by the test giver once they knew that such a response was the "right" one, the one the test giver wanted. "Oh, you want abstract logic," they might say, "you don't want me to be realistic." All they needed was a good clue as to which logic the test giver wanted. They worked intellectually in a larger cognitive problem space (Newell & Simon, 1972), so to speak, than the test giver!

Still further questions to this large problem space set of respondents revealed that they made use of many logics, and that the parameters, operations, methods, and solutions they adopted differed based on the logic they chose to articulate. At that point we test givers began to explore the nature of these self-referential postformal logical operations with which respondents co-constructed their test experience reality along with us. What is the link to creativity here? It is that these test takers were generating multiple logics, methods, processes all the time, in real, everyday life!

How ironic that what was really creative had been labeled *stupid* by the experimenter! Just as we are now aware of gender bias and ethnic bias in correctness of answers, age bias in cognitive style needs to be reexamined. The richness and diversity of everyday human thought are being overlooked (see Sinnott, in press-e).

POSTFORMAL THOUGHT AND LIFE STAGE DEVELOPMENT

MOTIVATION FOR POSTFORMAL CREATIVITY

Midlife issues may be the key issues which motivate creative thinking about the shifting nature of socially constructed reality in everyday cognitive events. The psychologist's awareness that the person has such postformal thought processes can help him or her explain the behavior of the person at that developmental point in life.

In thinking about this further, let's examine one or two typical tasks of midlife and old age that are present in various cultures and theories. At the entry point of midlife, perhaps around the age of 30, one must choose a path through life in industrial cultures of multiple possibilities (Perry, 1975; Levinson, 1978). Even as the younger adult sees the relativity of many truths, he or she must make a passionate commitment (Frankl, 1963; Perry, 1975; Polanyi, 1971) to live out one choice or truth. That choice also involves relinquishing several illusions, including (Gould, 1978) the one that there is only one correct way to proceed in life, and that one's parents have the knowledge of that single way.

Erikson (1950) describes the tasks of the midlife and old individual as developing generativity and integrity, that is, a mentoring and caring for others, a creation of children and contributions which will outlast the self, and a sense of the satisfying completeness of one's life story and one's place in the overall story of life. Again the sense of meaning is in relations with others and the creation of a personal truth. Many authors speak of midlife as a time to deepen commitment and to choose deliberately what one's life will mean (e.g., Havighurst, 1953). One must choose when (and why!) to deploy one's resources, newly aware of their limits. This choice of meaning, if it is truly adaptive, also incorporates one's emotional side, allowing for conscious orchestration of emotional and cognitive life, leading to emotional self-regulation (Labouvie-Vief, 1987), maturity, and wisdom (Chinen, 1992).

The midlife adult begins to see a bigger picture that involves time and persons existing before and after him or her. As Riegel (1975) suggests, discord or disharmony, whether from other people, a rapidly shortening lifetime, or the pressure of multiple social roles, demands a new adaptive stance. Jung (1930/1971) speaks of the incorporation of the unknown sides of the personality into the conscious self at midlife.

These midlife tasks involve bridging realities, entering the reality of another person, and developing complex concepts of the self, of success, of personal continuity. By this time in life the person has gathered the skills and the experience to make this potential midlife leap in thinking structures. Spurred by everyday social encounters, fresh from the everyday problem-solving tasks of creating a marriage, a long-term friendship, a parent-child relationship, an organization, a social role, a self, the adaptive midlife adult is primed to make new realities. Like the developing child in Piagetian theory, the midlife adult seems to use assimilation and accommodation to reach new ways of filtering life with a new postformal subjective/objective logic.

We can see a tendency for adult development in these theories to include wisdom—more sophisticated interpersonal skills, concern for the group (over and above the self), deepening spirituality, and the ability to deal with paradoxes whether they are within the self, among persons, or in life itself. Troll (1985) has reviewed major theories of adult development. These theories all hypothesize that developed mature adults have a tendency to tie things together, to give overall meaning to emotions and events, to find overall purpose in one's feelings, life and death. Adult development, including postformal development, seems to mean increasing maturity, by all the definitions of maturity set out by Whitbourne and Weinstock (1979). The goal of later development seems to be to tie the individual's life to the group and to anchor both in a meaningful story that makes the struggle of existence worthwhile.

POSTFORMAL THOUGHT ALLOWS CREATIVE REGULATION OF MIDLIFE STIMULATION

At each stage of life the organism is confronted with multiple demands related to sustaining life. It is also confronted with demands specific to growth during that particular stage of life. For example, a two-year-old or any human adult must meet the demands of his or her body for food, drink, rest, and an emotional bond with another person. The two-year-old also feels specific developmental stage-related psychological and social demands for greater personal control and autonomy, demands that have already been met by the older adult. Creativity at age two may lead to production of numerous clever ways to get one's way and to bond by subtly pleasing others, so that needs will be met. The more ways one gets autonomy, caretaking, and emotional support, the better.

On the other hand, the stage-related needs which confront the teen are different in some ways. They still include needs for food, water, and social connection, but they also compel the teen to construct a logic encompassing physical demands, work life, and love life in order to make sense of strong impulses and feelings. This logic must be consistent internally for the life to "work" and the teen to enter adulthood. It must be consistent with the current epoch of history in which the teen lives as well. The creative production of a consistent logic (i.e., formal operations) is needed.

The midlife and older adult is faced with some similar demands for food, drink, bonds with others, and so forth, but there are some new demands, too. The new ones are generated by the broader social identity usually found in midlife due to family and generativity connections. The demands are overwhelming and often contradictory. The individual may need to support his or her partner, and parents, and children, while meeting demands of a job and colleagues. The individual may need to refocus a career, as he or she sees the finite timetable of life, but also may need to mentor new workers in the current career. The formal systems employed to control impulses and to find a transcendent meaning in life may not be compatible with the formal systems used to meet the other needs. Generating more systems may help, since productivity could create more adequate answers to life's dilemmas. But the ante has been raised by life; there are too many contradictory demands. Enter the logic of self-referential choice of truth, the realization that life is an ill-structured problem (Churchman, 1971) where one must creatively choose one's reality and go on, or none of the needs will be met. The demands, in a best case scenario, lead to the development of cognitive processes that creatively transcend and enlarge the self and retap emotional strengths. When demands lead people to suppress emotions and the self, the worst-case possibility exists.

OVERLOAD

With the onset of deteriorative aging the organism must control the amount of stimulation it receives and handle cognitions more efficiently (Sinnott, 1989f, 1991a, 1991e). Resources are diminishing prior to death, so overload of information from people or events must be regulated or the system will no longer function effectively. Postformal thought at this point allows the creative consolidation of experience which in turn lets the organism handle more events for a longer time.

Overload can be handled by postformal operations and can sometimes be caused by them, too, since they generate multiple possibilities. The overload dilemma may be resolved nonadaptively and noncreatively: Adults may limit their experience to those situations where only one formal system need be considered, and may not develop postformal thought at all. The overload dilemma might also be resolved adaptively and creatively. Relativistic operations might provide an advantage over formal operations by permitting consensus understandings and maximal use of large amounts of conflicting information.

Maturity probably brings acceptance of the necessary subjectivity inherent in relativistic operations carried out on interpersonal reality. This acceptance would be apparent in creative tolerance of others' beliefs and ways of life. If the evaluator has postformal thought, the painful struggles of the young adolescent and young adult to reason concretely or formally about relationships could be interpreted more empathically as a youthful attempt to force relativistic postformal reality into one "correct" formal system. Relativistic postformal operations can thus maximize use of conflicting information and minimize social conflict, too.

Individual Coping with Overstimulation

If overload is distressing, the individual might respond with various creative coping strategies to minimize personal distress, sometimes at the cost of adaptivity. Since the adaptive choices, those related to relativistic thought, are often found in interpersonal cognitions, coping strategies might be seen there, too. For example, consider a middle-aged adult with a family, a career, civic responsibilities, and a social life. This person is faced with endless demands to conform to the data of this social world by choosing a viable formal operational system for interacting with each individual at an appropriate level. If this adult makes these choices and solves these interpersonal problems, it will not happen by means of formal operations alone. Nor will the use of relativistic operations often be perfectly consistent with reality. But relativistic postformal operations will provide the best possible match. Postformal creativity processes will provide the largest number of inclusive, real-life problem-solving possibilities.

These are possible uncreative, nonpostformal solutions to overload in interpersonal midlife contexts:

1. The adult might reduce stimulation by retreating cognitively and perceiving all interpersonal relations at a lower level of cognitive or emotional complexity. Instead of "receiving" the behaviors of others as they are encoded, or trying to receive them at a higher, more integrated level of complexity, the adult might *interpret* all of them *in a simplistic way*. For example, instead of trying to understand the relations that are possible with a certain individual, the adult may resort to dealing with him or her only as a member of a feared racial group.

2. The adult might reduce stimulus overload by developing a *rigid social identity* that permits only certain messages to be received. If, in such a case, the adult has a self-definition capable of only certain relations, other relational stimuli are ignored. All problems are simplified.

3. The adult can reduce overload by *focusing on* only *selected goals* or interests. The effect of this tactic is similar to the effect of the second tactic. All levels of complexity are available to be used in analyzing an event, but the individual limits the types of content considered.

These are some possible creative, adaptive, postformal solutions to overload in interpersonal midlife contexts:

1. The adult might reduce overload by understanding the possible structures that can underlie a perceived interaction. This is an adaptive strategy that can only come from experience and familiarity with many types of systems and possession of postformal cognitive ability. If the receiver can *match reception to the encoded level,* conflict can be reduced. This receiver is flexible in the use of the structures. The key to this operation would be access to a good system of transformations to relate the sets of coordinates using relativistic operations.

2. The adult might reduce stimulus overload by making a *more efficient total integration.* Developing the integrative skill is an adaptive solution to overload. It makes use of metatheorizing that is based on experience. No content or complexity is lost when this technique is used. The mapping surface is so large and the topography so varied that most messages fit in somewhere through use of relativistic operations.

MAKING LIFE PERSONALLY MEANINGFUL: INTEGRITY, PHENOMENOLOGY, SPIRITUALITY AND CREATIVE POSTFORMAL THOUGHT

Humans want their lives to make sense to them, personally. In the face of death we struggle to make our life story meaningful. Abstract logics and others' judgments matter less and less as we approach the end of life; we want our own experiences to make sense to us, above all. We look for transcendent meanings that can link us to the flow of humanity, to God, to the spirit of life itself. Yet we are aware that lives and fortunes are various and appear somewhat arbitrary. We realize, too, that our choices of how to frame our lives have often determined our fate.

For example, Carlos Castaneda said in his (1981) book, *A Separate Reality,* that the sorcerer don Juan reminds Carlos that, after all, anything is one of a million paths . . . a path is only a path, and there is no affront to oneself or others in dropping it . . . All paths are the same; they lead nowhere . . . Look at every path closely and deliberately . . . Then ask yourself and yourself alone one question. This question is one that only a very old man [sic] asks: Does this path have a heart? If it does, it will make for a joyful journey . . . [but] the other will make you curse your life.

To tolerate the arbitrariness of life, he seems to say, we must jump up to a bigger picture that ties together the logics of many paths and lives, many emotions, many meanings. Having "jumped out of our system," we can choose the reality to impose on our own smaller lives, then jump back in to set up a logic of our own life.

Postformal creative thought can give us multiple logics from which we can choose the best one in a given context (though all are inadequate) to commit to and then live as our personal truth. Without both the productivity and the choice, though, we are left, in mature years, adrift without meaning in a large and confusing multigenerational and transpersonal reality (Weibust & Thomas, 1993). (For further discussion of postformal thought and spirituality, see Sinnott, 1992a.)

SOME DATA: ADULT POSTFORMAL CREATIVITY

Over 20 years of my and others' studies have related adults' practical creativity to their complex postformal thought and have described creative processes developed along with postformal thought itself. Other studies have examined age differences in creative postformal styles. Some studies of other investigators were referenced earlier. The major results of some of my work as it relates to creativity are summarized in Table 3.2. The table then offers one example for each entry of how postformal creativity may regulate organism overload and basic and applied ideas for future studies. The reader is urged to examine data in the original sources used for summary in the table, since it is difficult to do justice to 20 years' of data in a few pages.

As seen in Table 3.2, whether one looks at creativity as process or as product, postformal thinkers are creative. Postformal thought is mainly a symbolic, ideational form of creativity that incorporates emotional elements and synthesizes and integrates across domains. There are both unique products and high productivity of solutions, methods, goals, and metatheories organizing logical systems. This creative representation is sometimes for communication and sometimes for private, uncommunicated analysis. The quality of products is sometimes judged by the thinker and sometimes judged by others, too. Postformal creative thought seems to be a form of positive life span development, a form of thought which is useful and adaptive to individuals. The processes suggest that a large research program with many applications is possible in this area.

TABLE 3.2 Summary of Theory and Data on Postformal Creativity from Sinnott's Main Studies: Proposed Mechanisms of Stimulation Regulation with Suggested Studies

Source	One Main Point/Finding	One Possible Mechanism for Organism's Regulation of Midlife/Aging Stimulation	One Future Study Needed
1. Sinnott, 1984	1.a. Experimental study. Mature subjects (Ss) give > 1 paradigm for solving problems.	1.a. Adaptive shifts in logic process more stimuli at low cost in energy.	1.a. How is this developed?
	1.b. Content analysis. 2-person dialogues demonstrate that speakers influence each other's cognitive development and make it more creative.	1.b. Coconstruction of reality leads to more adaptive consensual reality.	1.b. Do speakers always stimulate each other toward cognitive *growth*?
	1.c. Experimental study. Experience of Ss and social content in problems lead to more creative solutions.	1.c. Interpersonal experiences lead to creative ways of processing reality which reduce overstimulation.	1.c. Is it experience or some other factor that releases creative cognition?
	1.d. Experimental study. Postformal operations showing creative production of multiple solutions and a priori's were shown by about ⅓ of Ss, sometimes as high as 75% for interpersonal problems.	1.d. Creativity is *commonly* expressed in a problem-solving context postformally in mature adults.	1.d. Does creative problem solving depend on other thinkers' being present?

(continued)

TABLE 3.2 *(Continued)*

Source	One Main Point/Finding	One Possible Mechanism for Organism's Regulation of Midlife/Aging Stimulation	One Future Study Needed
2. Cavanaugh, Kramer, Sinnott, Camp, & Markley, 1985	2. Synthetic model can be made to describe adults creatively coconstructing reality.	2. Postformal thought seems to describe this way to handle complex interpersonal experience.	2. Does postformal thought provide a model for studying the connection of complex, creative cognitive and interpersonal/emotional factors?
3. Sinnott, 1987a, 1988, 1989a, 1991a	3.a. Experimental study. Mature adult creative postformal thought is reliably present.	3.a. It's adaptive in some way for mature adults to think in a creative postformal way.	3.a. Are there conditions under which adults will not reliably produce thought? Which ones?
	3.b. Correlational study. Health variables, such as blood pressure (bp), do not seem to influence presence of creative postformal thought.	3.b. The use of creative postformal thought is a "durable" ability, a core skill, not a cognitive process used only when energy is overabundant.	3.b. Does acute illness influence use of creative thought?
	3.c. Correlational study. Memory and verbal ability are related to postformal creative problem solving.	3.c. Creative postformal thought is part of an integrated package of adaptive cognitive skills.	3.c. If memory changes over time, will postformal creative thought change?
	3.d. Model. Goal clarity and heuristic availability would seem to be related to postformal thought.	3.d. Complex situations would be prime occasions for use of creative postformal thought.	3.d. Does manipulation of goal clarity in real life setting influence use of creative postformal thought? How?

3.e. If older Ss are pressured to give *specific* answers, do they still prefer process answers?	3.e. Process answers reduce overstimulation due to losses with advancing age.	3.e. Correlational study. Older Ss produce general-creative-process answers to problems, though younger adults produce larger number of solutions.
3.f. Can induction of negative emotion ("depression") lead to lessened creative postformal thought?	3.f. Creative postformal thought is a synthesis of emotion and cognition in service to organism goals.	3.f. Experimentally manipulating emotion, mind-wandering, demand for production caused interpersonal logical problem-solving differences. Positive emotion led to greater productivity. Instruction to mind-wander led to more postformal thought.
3.g. What criteria do variously aged Ss use to censor their responses?	3.g. Ss limit overstimulation by deciding how much creativity to show.	3.g. Experimental study. Probes exploring set responses led to greater productivity and more creative postformal thought.
3.h. Chart a descriptive taxonomy of noncognitive processes useful to cognition, especially postformal creative cognition.	3.h. Postformal creative thought is a synthesis of emotion and cognition in service of the organism's goals.	3.h. Descriptive study. As high as 75% of Ss incorporated emotion or mind-wandering into their creative problem solving.

(continued)

TABLE 3.2 *(Continued)*

Source	One Main Point/Finding	One Possible Mechanism for Organism's Regulation of Midlife/Aging Stimulation	One Future Study Needed
	3.i. Models. Individual models of creative, logical problem solving can be created, and demonstrate points in the problem-solving process in which creative postformal thought has impact on creative process and/or productivity.	3.i. Individuals use their adaptive mechanisms at individually specific points in their thinking process.	3.i. Can individuals' models form the basis of an artificial intelligence (AI) model of creative postformal thought?
	3.j. Experimental study. Given solvers' creative or noncreative postformal or nonpostformal processing style, predictions can be made about solvers' errors and processes on later problems. There are age-related styles.	3.j. Individuals show individually specific patterns of weaknesses and strengths in this area.	3.j. Can AI models be created for average performance of different age cohorts?
4. Sinnott, 1991c	4. Single case experiment. Postformal creativity seen in mature adult's adaptive solution to family mental health problem.	4. Creative postformal thought can bring order to crisis situations.	4. How do the cognitive levels of family members play into the genesis of the individual's problem?

Reference	Finding/Model	Research Question
5. Rogers, Sinnott, & Van Dusen, 1991	5. Experimental study. Married couples demonstrated more creative postformal thought when working together on problems if well-adjusted as couple.	5. Creative postformal thought is adaptive in couples' interactions.	5. What *nonverbal* data correlates with creative postformal problem solving, or the lack of it? Does couple's process influence their family's process?
6. Sinnott, 1992b	6. Model. Creative postformal thought can be useful in the classroom.	6. Creative postformal thought can assist communication to prevent student overload.	6. Does teacher personality correlate with these skills?
7. Sinnott, 1992a, 1992c	7. Model. Creative postformal thought can be used in the workplace for personal and group development during intragroup conflicts.	7. These skills can be useful for group and personal development by ordering conflict situations.	7. Does the initial social level of functioning influence the growth potential of the group member trying to be creative during the conflict?
8. Sinnott, 1993	8. A computerized version of the creative, postformal problem-solving test can be created and used in place of other means, such as interviews.	8. Average performance and norms can be created for these adaptive skills.	8. Test the computerized version against paper-and-pencil and interview forms.

AN EXAMPLE FROM A CASE STUDY

In order to see several of these characteristics of creativity as they are manifest in real life postformal thought, Sinnott (1984, 1996) presents a case history of the process of a family member deciding what to do about an acutely psychotic sibling's care. The same case was analyzed in a later work (Sinnott, 1991c). Figure 3.2 shows the steps in the decision-making process, based on the informant's thinking aloud description and journal notes. Was creativity evident in this postformal (and less than postformal) thought process? Did it matter to the outcome in real life?

Most of the criteria for postformal thought (see Table 3.1) were present in this process, and they involved creativity. The informant created several goals, solutions, and methods to attack the problem. She shifted realities to "try on" the logical, formal world views of the doctor, mother, and father. She expanded possible definitions about the nature of the problem and the relevant variables. The social factors in the problem (Sinnott, 1991c) describe creative use of a multiperson, consensus postformal reality about the mentally ill family member, "John." And postformal thinking was demonstrated in the following ways:

- Ability to "speak" in "others' languages" or belief systems: better communication (for more discussion of communication and postformal thought, see Johnson, in press)
- Ability to argue within others' logics; better communication
- Flexible view of what is possible for a family
- More effective interventions, based on others' psychological realities
- Awareness of one's own biases and filtered world views
- Ability to limit overstimulation without limiting information flow
- More flexible interpersonal relations
- Ability to get perspective on family problems
- Ability to be more effective in emotion-laden interpersonal situations
- A flexible view of who the other "is"
- Ability to reach the best solution in view of all realities
- Lessened need for control and defenses—lower anxiety level
- Ability to interact with all the other group members at their level

Creative processes used in the postformal solution of the problem of John's psychosis fit within the broader description of creativity found earlier in this chapter. They were used to deal with people and events, and to generate creative products (goals, solutions). The creativity

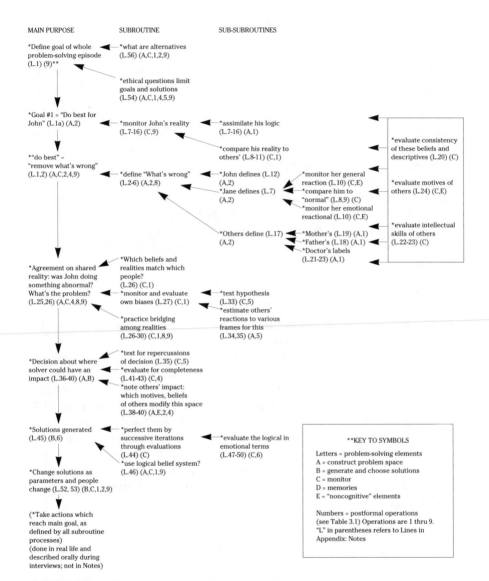

MAIN PURPOSE   SUBROUTINE   SUB-SUBROUTINES

*Define goal of whole   ◄── *what are alternatives
problem-solving episode   (L.56) (A,C,1,2,9)
(L.1) (9)**

                             *ethical questions limit
                             goals and solutions
                             (L.54) (A,C,1,4,5,9)

*Goal #1 = "Do best for ◄── *monitor John's reality ◄── *assimilate his logic
John" (L.1a) (A,2)   (L.7-16) (C,9)   (L.7-16) (A,1)   ◄──
                                                                                        *evaluate consistency
                                                         *compare his reality to   ◄── of these beliefs and
                                                         others' (L.8-11) (C,1)   descriptives (L.20) (C)

*"do best" =   ◄── *define "What's wrong" ◄── *John defines (L.12)   *monitor her general
"remove what's wrong"   (L.2-6) (A,2,8)   (A,2)   reaction (L.10) (C,E)   *evaluate motives of
(L.1,2) (A,C,2,4,9)   *Jane defines (L.7)   *compare him to   others (L.24) (C,E)
                                                         (A,2)   "normal" (L.8,9) (C)
                                                                                 *monitor her emotional
                                                                                 reactional (L.10) (C,E)
                                                                                                         *evaluate intellectual
                                                         *Others define (L.17) ◄── *Mother's (L.19) (A,1)   skills of others
                                                         (A,2)   *Father's (L.18) (A,1) ◄── (L.22-23) (C)
                                                                                  *Doctor's labels
                                                                                  (L.21-23) (A,1)   ◄──

                             *Which beliefs and
*Agreement on shared   realities match which
reality: was John doing   people?
something abnormal?   (L.26) (C,1)
What's the problem?   ◄── *monitor and evaluate ◄── *test hypothesis
(L.25,26) (A,C,4,8,9)   own biases (L.27) (C,1)   (L.33) (C,5)
                                                         *estimate others'
                             *practice bridging   reactions to various
                             among realities   frames for this
                             (L.26-30) (C,1,8,9)   (L.34,35) (A,5)

                             *test for repercussions
*Decision about where   ◄── of decision (L.35) (C,5)
solver could have an   ◄── *evaluate for completeness
impact (L.36-40) (A,B)   (L.41-43) (C,4)
                             *note others' impact:
                             which motives, beliefs
                             of others modify this space
                             (L.38-40) (A,E,2,4)

*Solutions generated   ◄── *perfect them by   ◄── *evaluate the logical in
(L.45) (B,6)   successive iterations   emotional terms
                             through evaluations   (L.47-50) (C,6)
                             (L.44) (C)
*Change solutions as   *use logical belief system?
parameters and people   (L.46) (A,C,1,9)
change (L.52, 53) (B,C,1,2,9)

(*Take actions which
reach main goal, as
defined by all subroutine
processes)
(done in real life and
described orally during
interviews; not in Notes)

┌─────────────────────────────────────┐
│   **KEY TO SYMBOLS   │
│   │
│ Letters = problem-solving elements │
│ A = construct problem space   │
│ B = generate and choose solutions   │
│ C = monitor   │
│ D = memories   │
│ E = "noncognitive" elements   │
│   │
│ Numbers = postformal operations   │
│ (see Table 3.1) Operations are 1 thru 9. │
│ "L" in parentheses refers to Lines │
│ in Appendix: Notes   │
└─────────────────────────────────────┘

FIGURE 3.2   Summary of processes used by key informant based on her notes and thinking aloud description.

67

was ideational and focused on issues of identity, roles, and the nature of reality (midlife issues). Creative, unique views of the problem were sometimes for public consumption, something for private resolution of issues. Synthesis of emotion and ideation, as well as synthesis across ideations was required. This creative problem solving was fueled initially by pain, but later was seen as growth. The creativity of the informant had an impact on the family's overall creativity and logic about the problem, as theirs did on her logic. The informant, being a mature adult, was solving for some overall better (i.e., more flexible) future family reality process as well as for a "quick fix" product for John that day. And the creative postformal process ultimately addressed (for her) the nature of good and evil, love, truth, and the existence of God.

The last developed stage of logic—postformal thought—seems to have potential for being the creative stage at which life is tied together. It also seems to be the stage when the richness of life's possibilities is given logic, a name, a spirit and meaning. With creative postformal thought, logical thought finally moves outside the limits of one's head to a larger creative reality.

ACKNOWLEDGMENTS

This research was supported in part by grants from the Public Health Service, from the National Institute on Aging, and from Towson State University. Thanks to David Arenberg, PhD., Donna Baumgartner, Kevin Bochenek, Janis Carlos, Dina Cortese, Carolyn Dunmyer, Jean Foley, Al Giovetti, Kathleen Henderson, Debbie Johnson, Michelle Kim, Lisa Klein, Lena Phillips, Judith Plotz, Donna Rogers, June Sacktor, Cliff Santiago, Lisa Shannahan, Helene Shiffman, Barbara Skinner, Fran Spencer, Diana Sutton, and the participants and staff of the Baltimore Longitudinal Study of Aging for their help, and to reviewers for their comments and suggestions. This chapter is based in part on a presentation at the 1985 Harvard University Symposium on Postformal Thought, Cambridge, MA.

REFERENCES

Arlin, P. (1975). Cognitive development in adulthood: A fifth stage? *Developmental Psychology, 11,* 602–606.

Armstrong, J. (1991). Keeping one's balance in a moving system: The effects of the multiple personality disordered patient on the cognitive development of the therapist. In J. Sinnott & J. Cavanaugh

(Eds.), *Bridging paradigms: Positive development in adulthood and cognitive aging* (pp. 11–18). New York: Praeger.

Basseches, M. (1984). *Dialectical thinking and adult development.* Norwood, NJ: Ablex.

Basseches, M., Kramer, D., & Sinnott, J. D. (1991, June). *Dialectical perspectives on psychotherapy and human growth.* Symposium presented at 6th Adult Development Symposium, Suffolk University, Boston.

Castaneda, C. (1981). *A separate reality.* New York: Washington Square.

Cavanaugh, J., Kramer, D., Sinnott, J. D., Camp, C., & Markley, R. P. (1985). On missing links and such: Interfaces between cognitive research and everyday problem solving. *Human Development, 21,* 327–333.

Chinen, A. (1992). *Once upon a midlife.* Los Angeles: Tarcer.

Churchman, C. (1971). *The design of inquiring systems: Basic concepts of systems and organizations.* New York: Basic Books.

Commons, M., & Richards F. (1984). A general model of stage theory. In M. Commons, F. Richards, & C. Armon (Eds.), *Beyond formal operations: Late adolescent and adult development* (pp. 120–140). New York: Praeger.

Commons, M., Armon, C., Kohlberg, L., Richards, F., Grotzer, T., & Sinnott, J. D. (Eds.). (1989). *Beyond formal operations: Models and methods in the study of adult and adolescent thought* (Vol. 3). New York: Praeger.

Commons, M., Richards, F., & Armon, C. (Eds.). (1984). *Beyond formal operations: Late adolescent and adult cognitive development.* New York: Praeger.

Commons, M., Sinnott, J. D., Richards, R., & Armon, C. (Eds.). (1989). *Adult development: Comparisons and applications of adolescent and adult development models* (Vol 2). New York: Praeger.

Erikson, E. (1950). *Childhood and society.* New York: Norton.

Frankl, V. (1963). *Man's search for meaning.* New York: Washington Square.

Furth, H. (1969). *Piaget and knowledge.* Englewood Cliffs, NJ: Prentice-Hall.

Gould, R. (1978). *Transformation.* New York: Simon & Schuster.

Havighurst, R. (1953). *Human development and education.* New York: Longmans.

Inhelder, B., & Piaget, J. (1958). *The growth of logical thinking from childhood to adolescence.* New York: Basic Books.

Johnson, L. (1991). Postformal reasoning facilitates behavioral change: A case study of an international development project. In J. D. Sinnott & J. Cavanaugh (Eds.), *Bridging paradigms: Positive development in adulthood and cognitive aging* (pp. 59–72). New York: Praeger.

Jung, C. (1971). The stages of life. In J. Campbell (Ed.), *The portable Jung.* New York: Viking. (Originally published 1930).

Labouvie-Vief, G. (1984). Logic and self-regulation from youth to maturity: A model. In M. Commons, F. Richards, & C. Armon (Eds.), *Beyond formal operations: Late adolescent and adult cognitive development* (pp. 158–179). New York: Praeger.

Labouvie-Vief, G. (1987). *Speaking about feelings: Symbolization and self-regulation through the life span.* Paper presented at the 3rd Beyond Formal Operations Conference at Harvard University.

Lee, D. M. (1991). Relativistic operations: A framework for conceptualizing teachers' everyday problem solving. In J. Sinnott & J. Cavanaugh (Eds.), *Bridging paradigms: Positive development in adulthood and cognitive aging* (pp. 73–86). New York: Praeger.

Levinson, D. (1978). *The seasons of a man's life.* New York: Knopf.

Luszcz, M. A., & Orr, R. L. (1991, April). *Constructed knowing and everyday problem solving in adults.* Paper presented at the 12th Biennial Life Span Conference, April, West Virginia University, Morgantown, WV.

Miller, J. (1978). *Living systems.* New York: Basic Books.

Newell, A., & Simon H. (1972). *Human problem solving.* Englewood Cliffs, NJ: Prentice-Hall.

Perry, W. B. (1975). *Forms of intellectual and ethical development in the college years: A scheme.* New York: Holt, Rinehart & Winston.

Polanyi, M. (1971). *Personal knowledge.* Chicago: University of Chicago Press.

Riegel, K. (1975). Toward a dialectic theory of development. *Human Development, 19,* 50-64.

Rogers, D., Sinnott, J. D., & Van Dusen, L. (1991, June). *Marital adjustment and social cognitive performance in everyday logical problem solving.* Paper presented at the 6th Adult Development Symposium, Suffolk University, Boston.

Simon, H. (1982). *Models of bounded rationality.* Cambridge, MA: MIT Press.

Sinnott, J. D. (1981). The theory of relativity: A metatheory for development? *Human Development, 24,* 293–311.

Sinnott, J. D. (1984). Postformal reasoning: The relativistic stage. In M. Commons, F. Richards, & C. Armon (Eds.), *Beyond formal operations: Late adolescent and adult cognitive development.* (pp. 288–315). New York: Praeger.

Sinnott, J. D. (1987a, June). *Experimental studies of relativistic self-referential postformal thought: The roles of emotion, intention, attention, memory and health in adaptive adult cognition.* Invited paper presented at the 3rd Harvard University Conference on Positive Adult Intellectual Development, Cambridge, MA.

Sinnott, J. D. (Ed.) (1987b). Sex roles in adulthoods and old age. In D. Bruce Carter (Ed.), *Current conceptions of sex roles and sex typing* (pp. 155–180). New York: Praeger.

Sinnott, J. D. (1988, April). *"Noncognitive" processes in problem solving: Are there age differences in use of emotion, personal history, self-evaluation and social factors during combinatorial problem solving?* Paper presented at the Cognitive Aging Conference, Atlanta, GA.

Sinnott, J. D. (Ed.). (1989a). A model for the solution of illstructured problems: Implication for everyday and abstract problem solving. In J. D. Sinnott (Ed.), *Everyday problem solving: Theory and applications* (pp. 72–99). New York: Praeger.

Sinnott, J. D. (1989b). Adult differences in use of postformal operations. In M. Commons, J. D. Sinnott, F. Richards, & C. Armon (Eds.), *Beyond formal operations* (Vol 2, pp. 239–278). New York: Praeger.

Sinnott, J. D. (1989c). Changing the known, knowing the changing. In D. Kramer & M. Bopp (Eds.), *Transformation in clinical and developmental psychology* (pp. 51–69). New York: Springer.

Sinnott, J. D. (Ed.). (1989d). *Everyday problem solving: Theory and application.* New York: Praeger.

Sinnott, J. D. (1989e). General systems theory: A rationale for the study of everyday memory. In L. Poon, D. Rubin, & B. Wilson (Eds.), *Everyday cognition in adulthood and old age* (pp. 59–70). New Rochelle, NY: Cambridge University Press.

Sinnott, J. D. (1989f). Life span relativistic postformal thought: Methods and data from everyday problem solving studies. In M. Commons, J. Sinnott, F. Richards, & C. Armon (Eds.), *Adult development: Comparisons and applications of developmental models* (pp. 239–278). New York: Praeger.

Sinnott, J. D. (1991a). "Noncognitive" processes in problem solving: Are there age differences in use of emotion, personal history, self-evaluation or social factors? In J. D. Sinnott & J. Cavanaugh (Eds.), *Bridging paradigms: Positive development in adulthood and cognitive aging* (pp. 169–202). New York: Praeger.

Sinnott, J. D. (1991b, June). *Scoring protocols for self-referential postformal thought.* Workshop presented at the 6th Adult Development Symposium, Suffolk University, Boston.

Sinnott, J. D. (1991c). What do we do to help John? A case study of postformal problem solving in a family making decisions about an acutely psychotic member. In J. Sinnott & J. Cavanaugh (Eds.), *Bridging paradigms: Positive development in adulthood and cognitive aging* (pp. 203–220). New York: Praeger.

Sinnott, J. D. (1992a, August). *Development and yearning: Cognitive aspects of spiritual development.* Paper presented at the American Psychological Association Convention, Washington, DC.

Sinnott, J. D. (1992b). Teaching in a chaotic new physics world: Teaching as a dialogue with reality. In P. Kahaney, J. Jananglo, & L. A. M. Perry (Eds.), *Teachers and change: Theoretical and practical perspectives.* Norwood, NJ: Ablex.

Sinnott, J. D. (1992c). The use of complex thought and solving intragroup conflicts: Means to conscious adult development in the workplace. In J. Demick (Ed.), *Development in the workplace* (pp. 155–175). Hillsdale, NJ: Erlbaum.

Sinnott, J. D. (1993). *Test of Postformal Thought: Computer Version.* Available from author, Psychology Department, Towson State University, Baltimore, MD 21204.

Sinnott, J. D. (Ed.). (in press-a). *Interdisciplinary handbook of adult life span learning.* Westport, CT: Greenwood.

Sinnott, J. D. (in press-b). New science models for teaching adults: Teaching as a dialogue with reality. In J. Sinnott (Ed.), *Interdisciplinary handbook of adult life span learning.* Westport, CT: Greenwood.

Sinnott, J. D. (in press-c). Postformal thought, adult learning, and life span development: How are they related? In J. Sinnott (Ed.), *Interdisciplinary handbook of adult life span learning.* Westport, CT: Greenwood.

Sinnott, J. D. (in press-d). The longterm future of adult life span learning: Making the most of adults in times of change. In J. Sinnott (Ed.), *Interdisciplinary handbook of adult life span learning.* Westport, CT: Greenwood.

Sinnott, J. D. (in press-e). Yes, it's worth the trouble! Unique contributions from *everyday* cognition studies. In H. Reese & J. Puckett (Eds.), *Life span developmental psychology: Mechanisms of everyday cognition.* Hillsdale, NJ: Erlbaum.

Sinnott, J. D., & Cavanaugh, J. (Eds.). (1991). *Bridging paradigms: Positive development in adulthood and cognitive aging.* New York: Praeger.

Tanon, F. (1991). The influence of formal vs. informal education on planning skills: A cultural perspective. In J. Sinnott & J. Cavanaugh (Eds.), *Bridging paradigms: Positive development in adulthood and cognitive aging* (pp. 221–236). New York: Praeger.

Troll, L. (1985). *Early and middle adulthood* (2nd ed.). Monterey, CA.: Brooks/Cole.

Weibust, P., & Thomas, L. E. (1993). Learning and spirituality: A hound, a bay horse, and a turtledove. In J. Sinnott (Ed.), *Interdisciplinary handbook of adult life span learning.* Westport, CT: Greenwood.

Whitbourne, S., & Weinstock, C. (1979). *Adult development.* New York: Holt, Rinehart, Winston.

CHAPTER FOUR

Practical Creativity in Older Adults' Everyday Problem Solving: Life Span Perspectives

Michael Marsiske and Sherry L. Willis

There has been an increasing emphasis in the research literature on contextually relevant assessments of older adults' problem-solving capabilities (e.g., Denney, Tozier, & Schlotthauer, 1992; Poon, Rubin, & Wilson, 1989; Sinnott, 1989; Sternberg & Wagner, 1986; Willis, 1991). Researchers of everyday problem-solving try to understand the cognitive competence of individuals in their real world environments; these everyday competencies have been labeled *practical intelligence* by Sternberg and Wagner (1986).

Practical creativity has remained understudied. For the present purposes, practical creativity is defined as the fluent, flexible, and original generation of solutions to real world problems. Practical creativity is hypothesized to operate in situations where linear reasoning and prior knowledge are insufficient for the solution of particular everyday problems. Prototypical situations could include any or all of the following: (a) problems that are highly novel or are in unfamiliar domains, (b) problems for which previously successful solutions (e.g., well-rehearsed strategies) are no longer effective or useful, (c) problems for which available sources of information (e.g., reference books, close others) are not relevant or useful. Although the concepts of creativity, problem solving, and intelligence have been linked in the theoretical literature, essentially no empirical investigations of creativity or problem solving in late life have actually examined these relationships. In this chapter, creative problem solving in the everyday lives of older adults is considered from an individual differences perspective. Drawing on psychometric and life span psychological data, we will consider the potential adaptive value of creative mental ability as individuals confront the challenges of old age.

Inattention to practical creativity is somewhat surprising, because some theorists (e.g., Wagner, 1986) have argued that the problems of everyday life tend to be ambiguous, without clear goals or means of solution, and they may be effectively solved with a multitude of potential solutions (i.e., they are ill-structured problems) (Neisser, 1976). It is precisely these kinds of problems that have been identified as requiring creativity for their effective solution (e.g., Voss & Means, 1989). Despite conceptual linkages between intelligence, creativity, and problem-solving, most studies of older adults' problem-solving capabilities to date have focused on what might be called *convergent production* (Guilford, 1970), or individuals' abilities to produce "correct" responses to relatively well-structured problems. In contrast, it is *divergent production* (Guilford, 1970), or individuals' ability to devise original and flexible solutions, that has been linked with creativity. Thus, while well-structured problems undoubtedly constitute a substantial proportion of the problems confronted by older adults, the lack of attention to how individuals differ in their responses to everyday problems characterized by greater ambiguity and novelty appears to limit the generalizability of everyday cognition research to highly structured situations. This leads to the question of what role(s) creativity-related mental abilities might play in the everyday competence of older adults.

In contrast to other points in the life span, where creativity in academic, workplace or leisure contexts may be more important, practical creativity in later adulthood may be increasingly focused on dealing with the challenges of daily life (see Willis, 1991). Flexibility in identifying novel ways of achieving important objectives in the face of age-associated physical losses may constitute a very important adaptive characteristic of individuals in late life (Baltes & Baltes, 1990). Arranging for the completion of tasks like self-care and home care activities under conditions of physical disability, for instance, might be one example of the need for a kind of pragmatic creativity in late life. Furthermore, as one moves out of the formal institutional contexts of school and work (which surround much of young and middle adulthood), there may be an increasing probability of confronting new, idiosyncratic life challenges for which prior experience may only be of limited usefulness. In addition, some of the everyday challenges with which individuals are confronted in late adulthood and throughout the life span may not have a correct answer; for example, how should an older adult deal with a spouse who becomes cognitively impaired?

In this chapter, we will consider the concept we have labeled practical creativity, with a particular emphasis on how mental abilities related to creativity might be important for understanding the everyday competence of older adults. The main position of this chapter is that divergent production abilities of fluency, flexibility, and originality are to practical creativity what other, convergent, production abilities (like inductive reasoning and crystallized knowledge) are to linear, logical everyday problem solving. This chapter is organized into five major sections. First, definitions and theoretical perspectives on everyday problem solving in late life are considered, with a particular emphasis on how cognition in everyday contexts might relate to cognition as it has been traditionally assessed in the laboratory. Second, the concept of practical creativity is discussed from the viewpoint of psychometric intelligence conceptions, and in terms of its application to problem solving. Third, evidence concerning the development of intelligence, creativity, and everyday problem solving across adulthood is reviewed, with the goal of providing an understanding of how basic mental abilities thought to undergird creative everyday problem solving might vary with age. Implications for the developmental trajectory of practical creativity are considered. Fourth, the literature on the adult developmental trajectory of everyday problem solving is considered, with a particular emphasis on problem solving involving fluency, flexibility, and originality. Fifth, a view of one possible role of creativity-related mental abilities in the everyday lives of older adults is presented. This perspective argues that the mental abilities associated with practical creativity may have substantial adaptive value in the later years.

EVERYDAY PROBLEM SOLVING: DEFINING THE DOMAIN

Willis and Schaie (1993) have argued that across several definitions of everyday cognition (Charlesworth, 1976; Neisser, 1976; Wagner, 1986) there are some areas of agreement. In general, everyday cognition seems to involve the application of basic abilities to naturalistic or everyday contexts. Furthermore, everyday problems seem to be complex and multidimensional, requiring the use of multiple abilities and skills (e.g., knowledge, reasoning, memory), and not just single abilities.

As well as consensus, however, there is also disagreement on some of the prototypical features of everyday tasks. Wagner (1986), for example, has argued that traditional measures of intellectual functioning, labeled *academic intelligence,* are

(1) well-defined; (2) linear, in the sense of having but one correct solution and one method of obtaining it; (3) disembedded from an individual's ordinary experience and of little intrinsic interest; and (4) complete in that all needed information is available from the start (Wagner, 1986, p. 362, adapted from Neisser, 1976; Wagner & Sternberg, 1985).

Practical intelligence tasks, or "one's cognitive responses to almost everything that happens outside the school" (Wagner, 1986, p. 362) are defined by exclusion. In other words, everyday tasks in adulthood are thought to be comprised of ill-structured problems with multiple potential solutions. These tasks are relevant to daily experience, and their means of solution are incomplete or uncertain. Similar views have been expressed by Resnick (1987).

Wagner (1986) also recognized the existence of other possible definitions. In another view, the kind of ill-structured tasks mentioned by Wagner constitute only a subset of the broader body of daily challenges with which individuals might be confronted. As Willis and Schaie (1993) have noted, some everyday problems (e.g., banking or the use of airlines and other transportation services) are highly structured and would be more likely to have one correct answer (e.g., one must fill out a deposit form correctly; one must get to the correct airport gate on time).

Consequently, this chapter argues that everyday problem solving cannot be defined by exclusion, but rather by inclusion. The everyday experiences in which individuals engage, across the life span, are characterized by substantial breadth and diversity, with a blend of novel and familiar challenges, characterized by variation in intrinsic ambiguity and information provided.

Differences in theoretical definitions of what constitutes everyday tasks have come to be reflected in differing predictions about the relationship between basic intellectual functioning and performance in everyday environments across adulthood. One broad class of theoretical perspectives, *contextual/expertise*-based views, notes the familiarity and repeated occurrence of many everyday challenges, particularly in late life. As a result, these theories emphasize the particular importance of accumulated domain-specific knowledge in understanding the everyday cognitive competence of individuals. A second class of theories, so-called *hierarchical models,* emphasizes the role of a full breadth of intellectual abilities, including knowledge, in everyday task performance. The primary conceptual emphasis of these two approaches, however, has been on convergent problem solving and linear reasoning. There has been a lack of explicit consideration of divergent production abilities.

CONTEXTUAL/EXPERTISE VIEWS

The three dominant contextual/expertise views of the relationship between intellectual ability and everyday activities, and their developmental trajectories, are associated with P. Baltes (P. Baltes, 1987; P. Baltes, Dittmann-Kohli, & Dixon, 1984; Staudinger, Cornelius, & P. Baltes, 1989), Berg and Sternberg (1985, see also Wagner & Sternberg, 1986), and Denney (1984, 1989). While their conceptual models seem to primarily emphasize convergent production, all three research groups listed here have actually studied everyday problems that one might consider ill-structured problems of daily living.

With regard to everyday functioning, P. Baltes and colleagues have emphasized what they call the *pragmatics* of intelligence, which individuals acquire in the course of social participation. Drawing on a broad body of cross-sectional and longitudinal literature, cognitive pragmatics appear to evince selective maintenance and growth until very late in the life span (Lindenberger & Baltes, in press; Salthouse, 1991).

P. Baltes and colleagues further assume that the cognitive pragmatics represent the accumulated, experienced-based knowledge which underlies the performance of many routine everyday tasks. Thus, the kinds of tasks embedded within cognitive pragmatics are reading and writing, language, educational achievements, professional competence, and even self-related knowledge and coping skills (P. Baltes, 1993), tasks in which individuals may be said to have a kind of expertise (Ericsson & Smith, 1991). Given high levels of accumulated procedural and declarative knowledge in these familiar task domains, the expectation is that, in selected everyday activities, high levels of pragmatic knowledge may ensure continued preservation of functional competence, despite potential age-related losses in the underlying cognitive mechanics (see also P. Baltes, 1987, 1993).

A related, but somewhat different perspective has been advanced by Denney (1984, 1989). Denney makes a distinction between unexercised potential and optimally exercised potential. Unexercised potential is seen in tasks which are unpracticed and untrained; optimally exercised potential reflects the maximum performance an individual might demonstrate under conditions of practice and training. By implication, the most frequently performed tasks of daily living would be those which most approximate optimally exercised performance levels, although they may not actually reach the highest potential levels. Regarding developmental predictions, the general expectation is that both exercised and unexercised abilities may follow an inverse U function, with exercised abilities showing a slower rate of decline until advanced old age. Regarding the relationship of everyday tasks to basic intellectual abilities, Denney writes that "traditional problems tend to measure general problem solving *ability,* everyday problems tend to measure *ability plus experience*" (Denney, 1989, p. 46). Thus, basic intellectual abilities should be better predictors of novel everyday tasks, but in familiar everyday problems, acquired experience (possibly reflected in domain-specific knowledge) should be an additional and substantial predictor of performance.

The position advanced by Sternberg and colleagues (Berg & Sternberg, 1985; Sternberg, 1985), the *triarchic theory of intelligence,* also expects a difference between novel tasks and familiar tasks. Although the triarchic theory also considers components of intelligence and contexts in which it operates, its "experiential subtheory of intelligence" describes the cognitive effort required to adapt to novel challenges:

> The first time one encounters a task the ability to deal with novelty is involved. One of the important elements in dealing with novel tasks and situations is the eventual ability to automatize aspects of task performance . . . tasks are apt measures of intelligence when component operations are in the process of becoming automated (Berg & Sternberg, 1985, p. 357).

Thus, the common threads that run through the various contextual-experiential theories reviewed is

1. Emphasis on individual differences and age-group differences in contextually relevant tasks of everyday functioning
2. A view of everyday activities as consisting largely of highly familiar, practiced tasks
3. The assumption that such highly familiar, practiced tasks may show attenuated age-related disadvantages (relative to basic ability functioning) because they are decoupled somewhat from the basic cognitive architecture (since reserves of experience-based procedural and declarative knowledge may ensure at least preserved functioning in these familiar domains)
4. The expectation that older individuals may be at a disadvantage, relative to younger adults, on novel or unfamiliar tasks that pose high levels of challenge. Successful adaptation in such cases relies more heavily on the operation of basic cognitive

components, which are expected to have shown some age-related degradation in efficiency.

In the next section, a hierarchical view of everyday cognition is considered. While compatible with experiential models, the hierarchical view differs in emphasis.

HIERARCHICAL VIEWS

The hierarchical model of the relationship between basic intellectual ability and everyday task performance has been most explicitly advanced by Willis, Schaie, and colleagues (Marsiske & Willis, 1995; Meyer, Marsiske, & Willis, 1993; Willis, 1991; Willis, Jay, Diehl, & Marsiske, 1992; Willis & Marsiske, 1991; Willis & Schaie, 1986a, 1993); it is also prominent in the writing of Berry and Irvine (1986).[1] The differences between the hierarchical and contextual-experiential models center on three major points:

1. The hierarchical model views everyday tasks as falling along a continuum of familiarity to novelty.
2. Therefore, in trying to understand the range of individual differences across a broad array of everyday tasks, the emphasis is on the predictive salience of all intellectual abilities (including knowledge-based crystallized abilities).
3. With its origins in a psychometric, individual differences perspective, the hierarchical model has not focused on the measurement of domain-specific knowledge, since good measures of such knowledge (and a meaningful selection of domains to assess) remain to be developed (Willis & Schaie, 1993).

Thus, while not disputing that knowledge-based functioning and expertise may predict high-level performance within particular, individually varying domains, the hierarchical position places a greater emphasis on understanding the predictors of individual differences in a broad

---

[1] It is important to note here that hierarchical model is not used in the sense of traditional ability structural modeling (e.g., Cattell, 1971), where lower order factors are regressed upon higher order factors, such that higher order factors (e.g., second-order abilities) subsume the lower order factors (e.g., primary abilities), and are not measured independent of the primary abilities. Rather, *hierarchical* in this context is used to reflect the idea that multiple basic cognitive abilities may, together, explain substantial variance in a (independently measured) more complex everyday task.

array of tasks.[2] Furthermore, the hierarchical position has a particular concern with the adaptive feature of everyday problem solving, which (as argued by Berg and Sternberg, 1985) would be best assessed in novel, less familiar (but still ecologically relevant) tasks. Consequently, within a hierarchical view, there has been a greater emphasis on how individuals perform on multiple, critical tasks of daily living, tasks which must be performed well if individuals are to continue to live independently in the community (e.g., Lawton & Brody, 1969).

The hierarchical model is schematically illustrated in Figure 4.1. As the figure attempts to show, this model argues that basic abilities reflect the operation of relatively universal cognitive processes. Particular tasks of daily life will reflect the operation of subsets of basic abilities, and different tasks may draw not only on different abilities, but on different admixtures of those abilities. Regarding the adult development of everyday cognitive capabilities, "age-related change in performance on a practical intelligence dimension should also be reflected in a pattern of change in underlying abilities and processes" (Willis & Marsiske, 1991, p. 185). Note that the hierarchical model assumes that both basic abilities and accumulated domain-specific knowledge are important predictors of individual differences in everyday task performance.

PRACTICAL CREATIVITY AND PROBLEM SOLVING

In the cognitive psychological literature on traditional problem solving, links between creativity and problem solving have been considered explicitly. The information processing approach to problem solving can be credited to Newell and Simon (1972). In their description, they present problem solving as a move from an initial knowledge state to a goal state. To reduce the large number of potential pathways from initial state to goal, individuals are hypothesized to draw on their prior knowledge and a set of heuristics (e.g., rules of thumb, metastrategies for problem solving) to search through these alternative paths. The efficiency and limits on the problem-solving process are determined by basic information-processing capabilities. As a summary of the key features of this problem-solving process, Mayer (1990) listed four major aspects in the definition of problem-solving:

> First, problem solving is cognitive, . . . so that its existence can only be inferred directly from the behavior of the problem solving. Second, prob-

---

[2] Similar issues have been discussed with regard to job performance.

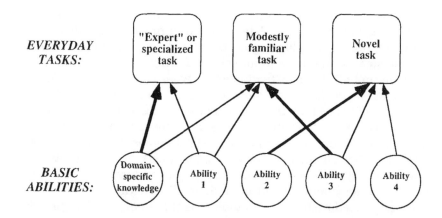

FIGURE 4.1 **Schematic of a hierarchical model of the relationship of intellectual abilities and everyday tasks.** Bold arrows represent strong predictive relationships, other arrows represent weaker relationships. Different everyday tasks draw on different abilities, and the strength of their relationship may vary by task. When domain-specific knowledge has not been acquired, task performance will rely more heavily on general intellectual competence. This is an elaboration of a figure which appeared in Willis & Marsiske, 1991. From "Life-Span Perspective on Practical Intelligence," by S. L. Willis and M. Marsiske. In *The Neuropsychology of Everyday Life: Issues in Development and Rehabilitation,* by D. E. Tupper and K. D. Cicerone (Eds.), 1991. Boston: Kluwer. Copyright 1991. Adapted by permission.

lem solving is a process—that is, it involves manipulating knowledge in the problem solver's mind. . . . Third, problem solving is directed—that is, it is intended to produce a solution to a problem. Fourth, problem solving is personal . . . the difficulty of transforming a given state of a problem into a goal state depends on the existing knowledge of the problem solver (Mayer, 1990, p. 284).

As already suggested, there is also a conceptual distinction between well-defined problems and ill-defined problems (e.g., Reitman, 1965; Simon, 1973). In fact, criticisms of problem-solving research have sometimes centered on the fact that laboratory simulations of problem solving often use puzzles characterized by being too well-defined and unfamiliar (i.e., problems requiring little pre-experimental knowledge; Eysenck & Keane, 1990). Ill-defined problems (thought to be more "ecologically valid") are those in which one or more of the given state, goal state, and allowable operators for the problem are not known (Mayer, 1990). With regard to creative problem solving in late life, the emphasis on novelty and problem structure also seems to neglect one major element of the age-related context of practical creativity: When prior solutions to familiar problems are no longer useful (e.g., because the physical competence to implement particular solutions may have been disrupted), then a situation exists where new means to old problems must be devised. Frustration of old solution strategies will require the availability of alternative solution possibilities, and their flexible use.

Research on the cognitive aspects of problem solving can be traced back, in a fashion, to learning theorists (Kendler, Kendler, & Carrick, 1966) and Gestalt theorists (Wertheimer, 1959). In current years, the dominant perspective has been that advanced by Newell and Simon (1972). Under conditions of unfamiliar, ill-structured problems, the solution procedure becomes complex, as the problem solver proceeds through steps of generating potential actions, testing them, and planning next steps based on the success or failure of the previous step. In this ability to generate potential solutions, presumably via an active search of prior knowledge (Sternberg & Lubart, 1991), creativity is thought to come into play.

Models of creative problem solving have emphasized *analogical mapping* (e.g., Gentner, 1983; Holyoak, 1985; Keane, 1988) in the problem-solving process. Describing a process implicit in the use of metaphor, a base domain of concepts is mapped onto a new target domain. Creative problem solving is evidenced in the transformation of base knowledge that is indirectly applicable to the new goal state. Thus, new problems are solved by transforming old knowledge in novel and flexible ways.

Guilford, arguably the originator of current psychometric conceptions of creativity, proposed that creativity had a special role to play in the solution of novel problems (Guilford, 1977). Divergent production was important in the flexible combination of and reinterpretation of past information to generate new (emergent) ideas (cf. Michael, 1977). Flexible transformation of knowledge, components of which were actually classified as "convergent production," was described as an obvious basis for creative progress (Guilford, 1970, p. 162). As Sternberg and Lubart (1991) and Voss and Means (1989) have noted, creativity seems to be involved in recasting an ill-defined problem.

Implicit in these formulations of the creative problem-solving process is an association between the concepts of creativity and ability; creativity is a part of the intellect, according to Guilford (1977). Indeed, creativity is reflected in the novel use and combination of stored knowledge and old strategies for the solution of problems. Sternberg (1982) and Sternberg and Lubart (1991) have argued that there is a certain conceptual link between creativity and fluid intelligence, both of which are hypothesized to be important abilities in the solution of novel, unfamiliar problems (e.g., Cattell, 1971). According to this perspective, creativity, therefore, should not be considered a set of mental skills apart from intelligence, but rather a unique use and application of prior knowledge, memories, and reasoning abilities.

For the present purposes, we take three major ideas from this literature: First, cognitive psychologists have explicitly considered the links between creativity and problem solving, but they have too often emphasized creativity in novel problems. Second, a major contribution of this literature has been the elucidation of the processes of analogical mapping and selective search. These processes emphasize the use of prior knowledge from base domains, and their application to new problem domains. This emphasis is congruent with the flexibility and originality notions of Guilford's notion of creativity, reviewed below. Third, the emphasis on processing has largely neglected application. The role of creative problem solving in everyday life, particularly in older adulthood, needs further consideration. We do not mean to imply that creativity is solely cognitive. While the present treatment emphasizes the cognitive abilities underlying and the cognitive results of creativity, there is a substantial body of work which has emphasized the personality (e.g., Barron, 1963; McCrae, 1987) and motivational/environmental features of creative contributions (e.g., Amabile, 1983).

FLUENCY, FLEXIBILITY, AND ORIGINALITY

Before explicitly considering the divergent production abilities of fluency, flexibility, and originality, it is important to mention that, as Brown (1989) has noted, creative divergent thinking has not been as rigorously subjected to tests of its criterion or predictive validity as other intellectual ability factors. The link between divergent production and creativity was more theoretically than empirically established (Wallach, 1986). This helps to explain why subsequent measurement research has tended to question the utility of the divergent production approach (see Brown, 1989; Hocevar & Bachelor, 1989; Kogan & Pankove, 1974; Weisberg, 1986). Similarly, in specifying domain-general divergent production abilities, the Guilford model of the structure of intellect did not address the question of whether creativity is, in fact, a domain-general ability (Simonton, 1990). Is creativity in the visual arts the same as scientific creativity? Differing developmental trajectories for eminent members of different professions have tended to suggest that there are at least some domain-specific variations in creative achievement (Simonton, 1991). Furthermore, beyond the threshold of average intelligence, intellectual ability appears to have little utility for predicting outstanding creative achievements in particular domains (Simonton, 1985), undoubtedly due to the greater relevance of domain-specific knowledge (Ericcson & Smith, 1991).

For the present purposes, however, one must note that while the link between fluency, flexibility, and originality and creative achievement in various fields of endeavor may be tenuous, the specific linkages between these three abilities and creative problem solving seem clearer. Fluency of thinking and response flexibility seem directly relevant to the kinds of flexible uses of base knowledge for analogical mapping that define creative problem solving.

Models of Creative Mental Ability

A dominant view on this question was proposed by Guilford (1970), for whom the most important abilities in understanding creativity were those relied on in the operation of divergent production. This concept was broadly defined as an operation involved in the generation of many and varied responses. Guilford's ability model, the structure-of-intellect model, was highly complex, and it is not possible to substantially consider it here; however, it is important to note that Guilford himself did not make the simple distinction between convergent and divergent production that much subsequent investigation has come to rely upon (including the present chapter). But Guilford highlighted the notion that a subset of intellectual operations might not be concerned so much with finding correct answers, but with devising and evaluating new, different, unusual, or varied ideas.

In his earlier writings on the topic (Guilford, 1950), Guilford mentioned a number of abilities: sensitivity to problems, fluency, novel ideas, flexibility, synthesizing abilities, analyzing abilities, complexity, and evaluation (see Brown, 1989, for more detailed critical discussion). Although he later tried to reemphasize the full range of abilities (Guilford, 1970), Guilford and others (especially Torrance, e.g., Torrance, 1988) primarily emphasized fluency, flexibility, and originality as the major components of creative mental ability. *Fluency* was assessed in measures that required individuals to generate as many ideas as possible (number of words beginning with a particular letter, number of words in a particular category). *Flexibility* was assessed in terms of how many different kinds of solutions people were willing to try. *Originality* was assessed as the number of novel, or unusual, ideas people generated; number of rare and loosely related words in word-association tests might be used as an indicator.

Beyond these operational definitions, in this chapter we have attempted to develop the broader conceptual meanings of these abilities, as major constituents of practical creativity. Fluency, then, is a summary of the availability and accessibility of potential solution strategies. An illustration from common usage may clarify this: To be fluent in a language implies both the availability of a substantial and sufficient vocabulary, but also implies a certain smooth, natural polish in its use. It connotes efficient and appropriate selection from a larger body of knowledge. Flexibility refers to the tendency to adopt multiple or alternative means to particular ends. Borrowing from its use with regard to physical objects, flexibility suggests a certain pliability or malleability. Flexibility presupposes fluency in problem solving (i.e., alternative solution means must be available); if a particular strategy for solving a problem does not meet with success, flexibility is an index of the ability and proclivity to try other strategies. This use of flexibility highlights its location at the intersection of personality (Costa & McCrae, 1985; McCrae, 1987), intellectual style (Sternberg, 1988) and mental ability (Schaie, Dutta, & Willis, 1991). Finally, originality here refers to both the origin of a solution, and its prior natural history. My idea is original if I produced it; an effective solution proposed by another person is not a reflection of my originality. An original work of fiction is one written by the author, and not directly adapted from another source. In a different sense, originality also describes the newness and unusualness of ideas. A solution that has never been tried before, by anyone, might be classified as original. In addition, however, a solution that applies familiar ideas or strategies from another domain might also be an unusual solution in a new domain (e.g., use of a stapler as a hammer in an office; use of a rolling TV-tray as a walker), and might also be classified as original in particular contexts. A related concept is resourcefulness (connoting the effective use of the means at hand), which is considered in greater detail below.

Fluency can only be thought of as an indirect measure of creative potential. As Simonton (1990) has noted, the "linkage between quantity and quality can be subsumed under the more extensive constant-probability-of-success model of creative productivity" (p. 93). Fluency is presumed to measure the wealth of ideas, with the assumption that the more thoughts a person has, the more good thoughts such a person will have. Flexibility is conceived of as the ability to try many approaches to a problem. Flexibility seems to be a more direct indicator of creative processing. If one means of solving the problem proves to be ineffective, or is thwarted by certain constraints, the flexible individual will be able to proceed beyond the restrictions and devise other means of solving the problem, to transform old ideas in order to apply them in new situations (Guilford, 1970). Finally, originality seems to capture an important contextual feature of creative ability: the newness of the idea. Highly fluent and flexible individuals who nonetheless reproduce responses that have been produced by others would not be considered creative; rather, they might be considered effective implementors of others' good ideas. The creative response is not only to devise many, varied solutions, but also to produce solutions which are fresh or unique. It is important to note that an individual and his or her ideas are not intrinsically original; original is a evaluative term based, in part, on whether that individual or others have had similar ideas before.

It is also important to reemphasize that creative performance in problem solving is not conceived to be a sole function of divergent production abilities. Rather, divergent production seems to refer to a set of knowledge utilization and knowledge transformation abilities which presuppose the effective functioning of intelligence in general. Bodies of relevant knowledge, and basic reasoning and memory processes are required (as in all intellectually challenging tasks) for the divergent production abilities to be useful in the generation of good results.

The links between creativity and intelligence have been explicitly recognized by Sternberg and his colleagues. In their measurement of creativity-relevant mental abilities, for example, Sternberg and Lubart (1991) included measures of fluid reasoning, attentional capacity, knowledge, and intellectual style in their study of the predictors of creative production in writing, drawing, advertising, and scientific problem solution. Over all domains, fluid reasoning was the best predictor, accounting for almost 40% of the variance in some tasks.

Taken together, then, our central assumption, derived from a hierarchical model, is that the abilities of fluency, flexibility, and originality may be related to practical creativity in the same sense as more convergent intellectual abilities (e.g., reasoning and crystallized knowledge) are related to practical intelligence. Practical creativity is hypothesized to operate in everyday, challenging situations that are ill-defined, unfamiliar, and in which known or previously successful solution strategies are no longer useful. Practical intelligence is hypothesized to operate in situations that have greater structure (the problem, its goals, and potential means of solution are fairly easily identified), and in which prior knowledge and linear reasoning may be sufficient for solving presented problems. In the next section, the adult developmental trajectories of intelligence, the specific abilities of fluency, flexibility, and originality, and everyday problem solving are considered.

THE DEVELOPMENT OF CREATIVE MENTAL ABILITY IN ADULTHOOD

The investigation of the adult development and aging of psychometric intelligence (primarily nondivergent abilities) has been a topic of considerable research interest for most of the 20th century, and there have been a number of good reviews of the major findings (P. Baltes, 1993; Hoyer & Rybash, 1993; Lindenberger & P. Baltes, in press; Salthouse, 1991; Schaie, 1983, in press; Woodruff-Pak, 1989). Substantially less extensive research has been done on the aging of creativity-related mental abilities.

With regard to studies of adult intelligence, a few major summary findings are well accepted:

1. Cross-sectional research on adult age differences has shown that primarily reasoning-based *fluid* intelligence abilities show negative age trends beginning in early adulthood, while the relatively knowledge-based *crystallized* intelligence abilities show cross-sectional stability or increase until at least the seventh decade of life (Cattell, 1971; Horn & Hofer, 1992). There is evidence that speed-mediated ability-general declines in very late life (Lindenberger, Mayr, & Kliegl, 1993). Although suggestive of later mean ages of decline, and somewhat different change trajectories, longitudinal findings generally concur[3] (Schaie, 1994).

---

[3] Cross-sectional studies confound age differences with systematic differences in life history that differentiate age cohort groups. Longitudinal studies have other methodological problems, including selective subject dropout, uncontrollable nonmaturational influences on development between testings (period effects), and the effects of repeatedly retesting subjects (see P. Baltes & Schaie, 1976; P. Baltes, Schaie, & Nardi, 1971; Schaie, 1965; Salthouse, 1991). In an attempt to deal with the problems of both cross-sectional and longitudinal designs, Schaie has used a most efficient design (1977), which follows multiple cohorts of men and women over the adult life course, sampling from each cohort with replacement at each successive testing period. Although some methodological and substantive issues remain to be resolved (McArdle, Hamagami, Elias, & Robbins, 1991; Salthouse, 1991; Schaie, 1986), this method has provided the most systematic strategy of disentangling age, cohort, and period effects to date. One of the interesting outcomes of this research has been the documentation of substantial generational differences in intellectual performance. Recent cohorts, when compared to other cohorts at the same age, demonstrate positive shifts in some abilities (Inductive Reasoning, Verbal Memory, Spatial Orientation) but negative shifts in others (Perceptual Speed, Numeric Ability, and Verbal Ability) (Schaie, 1994).

2. There are wide inter- and intraindividual differences in the magnitude, timing, locus, and occurrence of age-related declines (see P. Baltes, 1987). Using hazard modeling, Schaie (1989) also documented that, for most subjects, two of five intellectual abilities studied remained stable up to age 74.

3. When a reliable negative change in intellectual functioning is present, there is increasing support for the reversibility of these changes. A substantial body of cognitive training research has demonstrated that older adults can produce significant (P. Baltes & Lindenberger, 1988; P. Baltes & Willis, 1982; Willis, 1987; Willis & Schaie, 1986b) and long-lasting (Willis & Nesselroade, 1990; Willis & Schaie, 1994) performance gains after just a few hours of training or practice (P. Baltes, Sowarka, & Kliegl, 1989; Hofland, Willis, & Baltes, 1981).[4]

Research on the adult development of creativity-related mental abilities has not been nearly as extensive as research on other (i.e., convergent) intellectual abilities. The dominant approach has been the cross-sectional research design, and there have been varied operational definitions of fluency, flexibility, and originality. From these studies, the picture has been one of negative age trends. Alpaugh and Birren (1977) studied a cross-section of adults from 20 to 83 years of age, administering two subtests of the Wechsler Adult Intelligence Scales, and seven Guilford (1967) tests of divergent production. Over all the Guilford tests, age was significantly and negatively related to performance. In terms of variable means, after age 30 older age/cohort groups tended to have successively lower divergent production scores. There was, however, an increase in these scores from age 20 to 30 years, yielding a quadratic curve with a peak in the mid-life, a finding that was subsequently replicated by Ruth and Birren (1985).

Jacquish and Ripple (1981) administered adaptations of Cunnington and Torrance's (1965) measures of fluency, flexibility, and originality to subjects who ranged in age from 18 to 84 years of age. For all three

---

[4] There is some evidence from cross-sectional studies of memory training, however, that there may be some effect of age on the maximum performance potential (i.e., developmental reserve capacity—Kliegl & P. Baltes, 1987). In studies in which younger and older subjects received up to 25 sessions of memory training and practice, older subjects rapidly reached a performance asymptote that was lower than the maximum performance achieved by younger subjects. At the conclusion of such studies, there was virtually no overlap in the performance distributions of younger and older subjects (P. Baltes & Kliegl, 1992). While there may be age differences in the maximum memory performance attainable, older subjects still evinced substantial cognitive plasticity: their mean performance increased from a recall of 5–7 words to 15 words, in correct order.

divergent production abilities studied, subjects aged 40 to 60 years of
age showed the best performance levels, while subjects aged 61 to 84
years of age performed at levels substantially lower than all other age
cohort groups, again yielding a quadratic function.

There have been relatively few longitudinal investigations of fluency,
flexibility, and originality, and these findings have been generally comparable to the cross-sectional results. Andersson, Berg, Lawenius, and
Ruth (1989) studied age changes in divergent production in Swedish
adults who were first tested at age 70, and who were retested 13 years
later. The authors found no significant effect of age over the period
studied, even though subjects had moved from young-old to old-old
age. Given the high dropout rate in this study (71% of subjects did not
return for follow-up), selective mortality probably attenuated some of
the age effects. More typically, in another investigation, which was
sequential in nature, McCrae, Arenberg, and Costa (1987) studied men
initially aged 17 to 101 over a period of approximately 6 years. Cross-sectional results found curvilinear associations between several measures
of fluency and age, while the relationship between age and originality
was linear. The magnitude of age effects was not large. Cross-sectional
age accounted for only 10% of the variance in a divergent thinking
composite score. Longitudinal findings on a highly selected returning
sample (less than 34% of subjects returned for follow-up) also documented a curvilinear pattern: In general, peak performances were observed
in the thirties and forties.

Fluency and flexibility have also been measured in the context of
the Seattle Longitudinal Study (SLS; Schaie, 1983), Schaie's operationalization of the "most efficient design," but were measured somewhat
differently from the traditional Guilford approach. Specifically, fluency
was measured as Verbal Fluency, and was assessed in terms of the
number of words beginning with a particular letter that subjects could
generate in a fixed time period. Cross-sectional findings suggested a
pattern of modestly negative and relatively monotonic age/cohort
trends from the period of 25 to 81 years of age. Longitudinally, a quadratic function was reported; there was relative stability or slight increase
in verbal fluency until about age 60, followed by a period of relatively
monotonic decline (about .2 of a standard deviation every 7 years)
(Schaie, 1994). With regard to flexibility, the SLS measured three
dimensions: Attitudinal Flexibility (comprised of items from various
personality scales), Motor-Cognitive Flexibility (the ability to change
response set), and Psychomotor Speed (requiring quick responses
under varying performance instructions). The three flexibility measures were significantly related to all factors of intellectual ability

assessed (Schaie, Dutta, & Willis, 1991). Developmentally, cross-sectional findings have supported linear, negative trends for all flexibility measures, with peak performances observed in the late twenties and early thirties. Longitudinal findings concurred, suggesting negatively accelerated quadratic functions for all rigidity-flexibility dimensions, but with relative stability characterizing the period from the twenties to the late sixties for Psychomotor Speed and Attitudinal Flexibility. Motor-Cognitive Flexibility did not show a significant shift in the direction of rigidity until age 81 (Schaie, 1983).

Other studies of adult intellectual development have also included measures of fluency and/or flexibility (e.g., Horn, 1982; Hultsch, Hertzog, Small, McDonald-Miszczak, & Dixon, 1992) and have reported generally negative effects of age on fluency and flexibility in the later adult years. Based on these findings, a general inverse-U function seems to constitute the developmental trajectory of fluency, flexibility, and originality. In both cross-sectional and longitudinal investigations, the evidence suggests that it is in midlife that peak levels of performance can be observed. Stability of interindividual differences may also be high; longitudinal stability coefficients for the rigidity-flexibility coefficients in the SLS exceed .85 (Schaie et al., 1991). The quadratic inverse-U or inverse-J function for creativity has also been supported, generally, by historiometric investigations of adult creativity development (Simonton, 1990).

Plasticity of creative mental ability in late life has also been studied. One investigation, the Quality of Life study at the University of Georgia (Goff, 1992, 1993; Torrance, Clements, & Goff, 1989) has documented some modifiability of older adults' fluency and flexibility. In a sample of 108 older adults ranging from 51 to 89 years, pretest-posttest changes in these abilities as a function of training were examined. Drawing on Torrance's "incubation model of teaching" (Torrance & Safter, 1990), experimental subjects received 4 months of training, 3 times a week. Compared to untrained controls, trained subjects showed significantly greater improvement on measures of fluency and flexibility.

From the hierarchical perspective, psychometric data on the adult development of fluency, flexibility, and originality (and other abilities) suggest that advanced age may be a time of lower levels of divergent production capabilities, but this can only be a tentative conclusion in the absence of more intraindividual change data. Nevertheless, one implication is that everyday problems that rely heavily on creative mental ability for their solution might also be expected to evince similar quadratic age trends across adulthood. At the same time, preliminary results from a creativity training study suggest that, as with intellectual functioning, there may be plasticity and modifiability in older adults' fluency and flexibility. In the next section, research which has attempted to assess the developmental trajectory of everyday problem solving directly is considered.

PRACTICAL INTELLIGENCE FINDINGS: A LITERATURE REVIEW

The relative recency of research on the adult development of everyday cognition (Woodruff-Pak, 1989) means that, to date, there is still little research on this topic. Furthermore, substantial heterogeneity in obtained functions for everyday problem solving (Marsiske & Willis, 1995) is undoubtedly due, in part, to the diversity in investigators' approaches to the measurement of this construct. Most of the research to date has also been cross-sectional in nature, inevitably confounded by age group differences in maturational status and life history. There has been virtually no explicit consideration of creative everyday problem solving.

In the research literature on older adults' everyday problem solving, there have been two broad areas of interest. One area has focused on the relationship between everyday cognition and traditional (nondivergent) measures of intellectual functioning. The second has concentrated on trying to estimate the developmental course of everyday cognition in adulthood. Most of the everyday cognition measures used have also emphasized convergent production (especially, coming up with correct answers).

With regard to the relationship between everyday cognition and psychometric intelligence, many studies have reported significant correlations of varying magnitudes. Indeed, significant relationships between measures of fluid and crystallized intelligence, memory, and everyday tasks have been reported for several multidomain measures of real life problem solving, in both cross-sectional (Camp, Doherty, Moody-Thomas, & Denney, 1989; Cornelius & Caspi, 1987; Denney, 1991; Hartley, 1989; Lindenberger, Mayr, & Kliegl, 1993; Poon et al., 1992; Willis, Marsiske, & Diehl, 1991; Willis & Schaie, 1986a) and longitudinal (Willis et al., 1992; Willis & Marsiske, 1991) studies. The variance accounted for by ability measures varied from under 10% (e.g., Camp et al., 1989; Cornelius & Caspi, 1987) to 70% or more (e.g., Willis & Schaie, 1986a; Lindenberger et al., 1993).[5] Fluid and crystallized factors

---

[5] A measure of practical knowledge and practical reasoning shared so much variance with other indicators of fluid and crystallized intelligence in the Lindenberger et al. (1993) study of adults between 70 and 105 years of age that the investigators chose to treat the practical measures as indicators of the psychometric ability factors.

of intelligence also accounted for 20% to 45% of the variance in every-day problem-solving competence as assessed through behavioral observation (Diehl, Willis, & Schaie, 1995), and fluid intelligence was substantially related (.60<r<.90) both to perceived functional (ADL/IADL) competence among adults aged 70 and above, and to the amount of time they spent in discretionary and leisure activities (M. Baltes, Mayr, Borchelt, Maas, & Wilms, 1993).

Findings regarding the developmental course of everyday problem solving have demonstrated even fewer regularities across studies than in the correlational results. While fluid and crystallized intelligence at least emerged as significant predictors of real life task performance in most studies in which they were assessed together, the obtained cross-sectional findings have shown less convergence across studies. This may not necessarily be a problem, if the empirical findings are taken to support a multidirectionality perspective (e.g., P. Baltes, 1987): different developmental functions might be expected to apply to different kinds of tasks (see also Denney, 1989).

In those cross-sectional studies which have emphasized (a) individual differences in problem solving, rather than just a comparison of novices and experts in particular domains, (b) problem solving in multiple everyday domains or situations, and (c) the performance of older adults, there has been substantial task specificity of findings. Early attempts to measure adult-relevant cognition supported a preserved competence view (Demming & Pressey, 1957; Gardner & Monge, 1977). In the more recent research literature, Cornelius and Caspi (1987) found incremental age trends in a sample ranging from 20 to 78 years of age, using a measure which assessed subjects' degree of endorsement of an idealized solution pattern for selected everyday problems.

A rather different pattern of findings was reported by Willis, Schaie, and their colleagues in several studies investigating document literacy and reasoning with everyday printed materials in such domains as food preparation, housekeeping, financial management, and transportation (e.g., Willis & Schaie, 1986a; Willis et al., 1992; Willis & Marsiske, 1991). In old and very old adults, a significant negative association with age was obtained (e.g., Marsiske & Willis, 1995), even when tasks were designed to be highly relevant to the everyday lives of older adults (Diehl, Willis, & Schaie, 1990). In one of the few longitudinal investigations of everyday problem solving in older adults, 7-year change was assessed. Despite significant mean decline over the longitudinal interval, 57% of subjects were actually classified as having remained stable over time (Willis et al., 1992).

Hartley (1989) has provided a nice illustration of the task specificity of obtained developmental trajectories; over three different everyday tasks, he obtained three very different cross-sectional age gradients. Taken together, all of these findings point to substantial measure specificity of obtained cross-sectional and developmental findings. This is supportive of Willis and colleagues' hierarchical contention that everyday problem solving is multidimensional, and developmental trajectories might be expected to vary with the trajectory of the constitutive abilities (Willis & Marsiske, 1991; Willis & Schaie, 1986a).

Data collected within other traditions, including studies of problem solving in particular, circumscribed domains (e.g., Klemp & McClelland, 1986; Lave, Murtaugh, & de la Rocha, 1984; Scribner, 1984), or studies of expertise in particular everyday practical and leisure domains (e.g., P. Baltes, Smith, & Staudinger, 1992; Charness, 1985; Ericsson & Smith, 1991; Krampe, 1992; Salthouse, 1991) have tended to support the view that domain-relevant expertise can buffer against age-associated losses. While a number of these studies have actually included ill-structured problems of daily living, they have not emphasized the creativity dimension in their scoring or analysis.

One major contributor of research on older adults' everyday problem solving, whose studies have appeared throughout the last decade, is Nancy Denney. In the next section, the focus is on Denney's problem-solving research, because it is Denney's work that Marsiske & Willis (1993) and others (e.g., Poon, et al., 1992) have seen as a potential empirical exemplar for the role of creativity and resourcefulness in everyday problem solving.

FLUENCY, FLEXIBILITY, AND ORIGINALITY IN EVERYDAY PROBLEM SOLVING

Earlier in this chapter, the Denney (1984, 1989) model of adult cognitive development was considered in the broader context of contextual/expertise models. Denney's research on the topic of everyday, or practical, problem solving has been cast within her theoretical notions of exercised and unexercised tasks. Traditional problem-solving measures (i.e., those used in cognitive psychological research, like Twenty Questions) are viewed as relatively unexercised tasks, while practical problems of daily life are considered to be exercised tasks whose developmental trajectories would be expected to fall somewhere between the hypothesized trajectories for unexercised and optimally exercised abilities.

Emerging from this theoretical orientation, Denney's earliest work on the topic of practical problem solving in late life took the form of performance comparisons on traditional and practical problems in adults of different ages. Practical problems were administered in the format of brief problem vignettes (e.g., the subject is instructed to imagine awakening in the middle of the night to find that the refrigerator is not working), and subjects were asked to generate the best solutions they could. Over several studies, a cross-section of adults ranging from 20 to 80 years of age was included. In the earliest research, (Denney & Palmer, 1981; Denney, Pearce, & Palmer, 1982), Denney and her colleagues selected the best solution generated for each problem, and rated the solution for efficacy or quality (with the highest scores going to solutions which emphasized effective, independent action). In more recent research, using problems designed to be particularly relevant for older adults (Denney & Pearce, 1989; Denney, Tozier, & Schlotthauer, 1992), subjects were prompted to generate as many solutions as they could for each problem. Subject scores were based on the number of safe and effective solutions generated for each problem, so that more solutions produced higher scores. Over problem and scoring variations, there has been a remarkably consistent pattern of findings: The relationship between practical problem-solving performance and age has been curvilinear, with peak performances observed in subjects between 40 and 50 years of age. Results, thus, were comparable to quadratic functions reported in divergent production research, although performance peaks tended to be younger in divergent tasks, and there were variations with the hypothesized age relevance of everyday tasks in Denney, Pearce, and Palmer, 1982.

The problem vignettes administered by Denney and her colleagues are not substantially different in content or format than those administered by Cornelius and Caspi (1987). However, in the Cornelius and Caspi study, subjects were provided with possible solutions, and asked to rate the likelihood of their using each solution. In Denney et al.'s studies, the emphasis was on solution generation rather than solution selection, so that solution finding was relatively less constrained. These features of open-endedness and relative lack of problem structure in Denney's measures intuitively make them seem useful as assessments of creative problem solving. Because their content focuses on situations from the daily lives of older adults, Denney's measures might be viewed as the application of creative mental ability to real world problems. Thus, Denney's measures might be considered an operationalization of older adults' practical creativity. At least two task features support this view. First, the problems are either ill-structured or semistructured: Problems in the Denney and Pearce (1989) measure included (a) asking how a newly widowed older woman should adjust to her new situation, or (b) asking how an elderly man with a heart condition and limited financial resources should arrange for his lawn to be mowed. Such problems permit a multitude of potential solutions, rather than only one correct response. Second, the recent shift to a fluency-based scoring of the measure (e.g., Denney & Pearce, 1989; Denney, Tozier, & Schlotthauer, 1992), with scores based on the number of effective solutions generated, highlights the similarity between task characteristics of this measure and those of traditional fluency (e.g., Torrance, 1988). Thus, the Denney and Pearce (1989) measure seems to represent the application of a divergent production task to everyday situations.

The apparent fluency-based scoring of the Denney and Pearce (1989) measure led Marsiske and Willis (1993) to consider whether other dimensions of divergent production might also be found in subjects' solutions to these problems. In a sample of 111 older adults ranging in age from 68 to 94 years, they examined subjects' responses to Denney and Pearce's practical problems. In addition to fluency, subjects' responses were also coded for flexibility and originality. Flexibility was coded as the number of different solution styles subjects used; of four possible styles, most subjects used an average of only two. Originality was coded as the number of "rare" (low frequency) responses given by subjects; by definition, there were relatively few such original responses. One third of subjects, however, generated at least one original response. There was also some evidence for convergent validity among the dimensions coded: each of the three dimensions correlated significantly (r = .19–.47). Thus, Marsiske and Willis (1993) argued, it may be useful to think in terms of fluency, flexibility, and originality when using the Denney and Pearce (1989) everyday tasks, and suggested that these tasks may constitute an operationalization of the application of creative mental ability in everyday contexts.

Poon et al. (1992) have offered a seemingly similar interpretation of older adults' performance on Denney-type practical problems. In the context of their Georgia Centenarian Study, they investigated the performance of individuals 60 and older on an adapted version of the Denney and Palmer (1981) measure. In contrast to subjects' performance on all other measures of intellectual and cognitive functioning in the study, there was no significant effect of cross-sectional age on practical problem solving. This finding led the researchers to speculate:

Which cognitive resources are important for survival? The data show that practical problem-solving ability is important. The data substantiate our observations that centenarians are a resourceful group. Resourcefulness may be the one ingredient that keeps these centenarians functioning independently or semi-independently in the community (Poon et al., 1992, p. 36).

Explicit in the Poon et al. (1992) view is the idea that the abilities assessed by the practical problem-solving measure may have functional value in very old age. The next section revisits the question of the potential adaptive significance of practical creativity in late life.

CREATIVITY IN EVERYDAY PROBLEM SOLVING: AN EMERGING VIEW

The increasing emphasis on older adults' everyday problem solving seems to have emerged, in part, out of an interest in the question of preserved competence in personally salient life domains (P. Baltes & M. Baltes, 1990). The remainder of this chapter considers more precisely how fluency, flexibility, and originality might play a role in maintaining functional competence in late life.

To date, the research on everyday problem solving in late life has often connected itself, following Sternberg and Wagner's (1986) edited volume, with the concept of practical intelligence. There is undoubtedly more to cognition in everyday contexts than this. Indeed, it has been suggested here that practical creativity, or what Poon et al. (1992) have called "resourcefulness," may be other important concepts related to everyday problem solving. Intuitively, these concepts, when tied to the divergent production view of creative mental ability, point to individuals' fluency, originality, and flexibility in the course of managing the challenges of daily living, and their ability to activate base knowledge for use in new target domains. When the old ways of doing things are frustrated in some way (e.g., an elderly person has had a hip fracture, and can no longer climb the stairs in his or her home to an upper level bedroom), practical creativity would seem to be involved in devising new means for achieving the same objectives. There may be many potentially effective solutions (e.g., sell the home and move to a bungalow or congregate housing facility; install a stair-climbing machine; employ a caregiver; engage in physiotherapy), and adaptive success (e.g., for some, this might be defined as maintaining one's independence in one's home) is contingent on the selective search for and effective implementation of alternative strategies. The term *resource-*

fulness here captures the idea of drawing on, evaluating, and applying one's knowledge of existing resources (financial, social, intellectual, motivational, biological)—it captures the ideas of active search and analogical mapping inherent in many models of creative problem solving (e.g., Voss & Means, 1989). It is a creativity that is highly practical because its focus is on managing real-world objectives.

Readers of the literature on adult development and aging may recognize some relationship between this view of practical creativity and ideas associated with successful aging (e.g., P. Baltes, 1993; P. Baltes & M. Baltes, 1990; Brandtstädter, Wentura, & Grove, 1993; Carstensen, 1993; Featherman, Smith, & Peterson, 1990; Heckhausen & Schulz, 1995; Marsiske, Lang, P. Baltes, & M. Baltes, 1995). In the section below, a major model of successful aging, and the role that practical creativity might have in such a model, are both considered.

CREATIVITY AND SUCCESSFUL AGING

One widely cited model of successful aging has been proposed by P. Baltes and M. Baltes (1990), who have suggested that *selective optimization with compensation (SOC)* constitutes general adaptive strategies which characterize successful development throughout adulthood. Success, here, is defined as the reaching of goals; the particular goals and the domains within which they fall may vary across individuals. Generally speaking, individuals' adaptive processes are viewed as being aimed at achieving progressively higher levels of functioning, and at the avoidance of negative outcomes. Individuals are thought to engage in these processes throughout life, and selective optimization and compensation are thought to operate either consciously or unconsciously, depending on the individual and the domain.

The SOC model is hypothesized to take on new meaning in late life, when normative losses in biological, social, and intellectual resources might occur. Progressive specialization (selective optimization) into individually defined life niches is thought to be a process occurring throughout adulthood. (An implication is embedded in this theory that optimization of functioning in individually relevant life domains comes at the cost of losses in nonoptimized domains [Lerner, 1984]). If performance cannot be optimized in important domains, then it must be compensated for. Old age is seen as a time of loss in reserve capacity (Kliegl & P. Baltes, 1987); under conditions of extreme challenge, older adults might lack the surplus biological, psychological, and socioeconomic resources for managing situations. Age is thus associated with an amplification of the general life SOC process, and the SOC processes are presumed to describe a set of strategies which may lead to resilient functioning in the face of age-associated losses (Staudinger, Marsiske, & P. Baltes, 1995). As summarized by P. Baltes,

> because of a loss in reserve capacity, we must select critical life domains to preserve at the expense of others. Furthermore, when age-related losses compromise maintenance of adequate performance in target behavior domains, we are challenged to find compensatory ways. (1993, p. 590)

In other words, optimization must become more selective, and compensation may become more important with age (see also Marsiske, Lang, et al., 1995).

As described by P. Baltes and M. Baltes (1990) with regard to aging, selection "refers to an increasing restriction of one's life world to fewer domains of functioning because of an aging loss in the range of adaptive potential" (p. 21). Optimization generally refers to the idea that people "enrich and augment their general reserves" and "maximize their chosen life courses" (p. 22), and also captures the idea that functioning in important domains will tend to be maintained at high performance levels. Compensation is defined as operating when "specific behavioral capacities are lost or are reduced below a standard required for adequate functioning" (p. 22). Compensation (see Bäckman & Dixon, 1992, and Dixon & Bäckman, 1995, for detailed treatments) involves satisfaction or partial satisfaction of goals via alternative means. Increased reliance on social supporters, use of a cane to support walking, or use of a pill reminder to ensure correct medication use in the face of memory loss would all constitute potential compensatory strategies.

While selective optimization and compensation strategies may be applied in selected domains, it is important to underscore that the processes are assumed to be domain general, and to represent a set of strategies which can lead to maintained adaptive competence regardless of phenotypic expression varying across individuals (P. Baltes & M. Baltes, 1990). P. Baltes (1993) has also argued that the life knowledge used to support selective optimization with compensation is a component of the "pragmatics of the aging mind," a kind of stored procedural and declarative knowledge that comes with experience in managing individually relevant life domains.

In our view, selective optimization with compensation provides a good frame within which to view the abilities associated with practical creativity. Compensation, in particular, which emphasizes the ability to come up with new ways of doing things when old ways no longer work and the activation of life knowledge in flexible and novel ways, seems closely allied to the kind of fluency, flexibility, originality, and everyday problem solving that have been emphasized throughout this chapter. The skilled selection of relevant life domains also seems to be conceptually associated with such ideas as "problem finding" and the imposition of constraints on problem solving, ideas associated in the information-processing literature with creative problem solving (e.g., Newell & Simon, 1972).

In order to provide a more concrete illustration of how elements of fluency, flexibility and originality might be important in everyday problem solving, Table 4.1 shows some older adults' responses to a prototypical problem. The problem, drawn from Denney and Pearce's (1989) work, posits an older man who has a restricted ability to mow his lawn (because of a heart condition), but who cannot afford to employ help. The subjects' responses in Table 4.1 are transcriptions of solutions actually generated by participants in the study reported in Marsiske & Willis, 1993, 1995). The problem presented here is an instantiation of an age-related restriction in means; the protagonist used to be able to mow his own lawn, but a physical condition has rendered this old solution no longer useful. Examining the responses of the four subjects, one notes substantial differences in solution fluency. Although there were no limits on how long subjects could take to consider and respond to the problem, the number of solutions generated varied from three to ten. Drawing on the constant-probability-of-success idea (Simonton, 1990), one implication is that the more fluent respondents might have more good ideas available. Flexibility, however, is also important. Subject A, for example, uses only two kinds of solutions. One is avoidant (refusal to mow the lawn), while the other two involve dependence on the help of others. In contrast, Subject B (who has produced only one more solution) shows a much broader range of solution strategies. Two of this subject's solutions involve problem-focused action (selling the house, bartering with a neighbor); another involves a combination of information acquisition (call a human services department) and dependency (get volunteers' help). The final solution is dependent, and very similar to Subject A's solutions. Note, however, that because of greater flexibility, Subject B is better buffered against possible constraints. For example, if no family members live nearby, or social service/help agency assistance is not available, Subject A will not be any closer to solving his/her problem. Subject B, on the other hand, still has at least two other options available. Of course, fluency and flexibility alone do not guarantee a successful solution. Many of the solutions proposed by Subject D (who has produced the largest

TABLE 4.1   Older Adults' Responses to a Semistructured Everyday Problem: Exemplars of Practical Creativity

Problem: **Let's say that a 67-year-old man's doctor has told him to take it easy because of a heart condition. It's summertime and the man's yard needs to be mowed, but the man cannot afford to pay someone to mow the lawn. What should he do?**

Example solutions:

Subject A:
> Do not mow the yard.
> Pray that someone will do it for me . . . Let my church know I have a need . . . Tell any help agency.
> If I have children . . . let them know of my need.

Subject B:
> If the man has a yard, he must be living in a house. The best thing he could do would be to sell the house and move into an apartment with no yard or upkeep.
> He could trade services with a younger neighbor. The neighbor would mow his lawn in return for the man walking the neighbor's dog, watching his children, etc.
> He could call his city or county human services department . . . and ask if there are volunteers.
> He could ask a grandson to mow it without pay.

Subject C:
> Immediately start planning to live in a situation that is suitable to his condition. Plan ahead.
> In the meanwhile, he should see if a relative or friend could help him until he changes abode.
> Possibly he could exchange the mowing for some service he can do, like babysitting or tutoring.
> Be sure to get a second medical opinion.
> Talk to his church or organization people. Trade services.
> Check civic organizations.
> Possibly [borrowing] a riding mower might be suitable—until he changes abode.
> Get a part-time job, and earn enough to pay for help.

Subject D:
> Move to quarters not having a yard to maintain.
> Cover lawn with black plastic sheeting . . . remove plastic in fall and sow rye grass.
> Rent a room to a man who will care for yard as part payment of room.
> Marry a young physical training teacher who loves yard work.
> Tether sheep in yard.

TABLE 4.1 *(Continued)*

> Buy a reconditioned remote controlled power mower, shrubbery and flowers.
> Plant shade trees.
> Cover yard with river rock and/or concrete and apply weed killer when necessary.
> Plant a vegetable garden in yard. . . .
> Plant grain seed and sell harvest.

Note: These solutions are transcriptions of responses generated by 111 older subjects (aged 68–94) from Marsiske & Willis (1993, 1995). The problem comes from Denney and Pearce (1989).

number) would involve an expenditure of economic resources (purchase of plastic sheeting, purchase of a sheep, purchase of landscaping requirements) and physical resources (e.g., the planting of trees and gardens entails some hard physical labor) that ignore the constraints of the problem. Originality is also evident, particularly in Subject C's responses. Two solutions (that were infrequently mentioned by other participants) include getting a second medical opinion, or getting a job. These solutions are not only original in terms of their rarity, but because they go beyond the constraints of the problem. Drawing on prior knowledge (it is good to get second opinions; older adults can still work), Subject C brings additional, fresh, and potentially effective strategies into the problem space, and these may confer an additional adaptive advantage.

Subjects' strategies can be fit into the SOC framework as well. Subjects B, C, and D all mention selection: by selling the house and moving to other quarters, they are suggesting that a reduction in domains of functioning may be an effective solution strategy. Numerous compensatory strategies are also mentioned. Solutions emphasizing the help of others draw on external (social and economic) resources. Subject C's suggestion to borrow a riding mower also involves compensation via substitute skills (Bäckman & Dixon, 1992), as the physically demanding properties of the task are changed. The bartering solutions mentioned by Subjects B and C capture the full range of selective optimization with compensation: by selectively optimizing functioning in effective domains (the marketable skills of walking a dog, babysitting, etc.), they are able to use those skills to acquire the compensatory lawn mowing skills of others.

In summary, then, it has been suggested that, for the subclass of problems in late life with which individuals have little direct experience, or for those which a lack of problem structure (e.g., such "messy" real-life problems as coping with widowhood, or adjusting to health restrictions), or for problems of aging associated with a loss of performance means and for which new means are consequently required, the ability to think creatively may be a meaningful predictor of the ability to solve (adapt to) such problems.

SUMMARY AND FUTURE DIRECTIONS

In this chapter, we have chosen to take a broad view of the role of creative mental ability in late life, arguing primarily from within the psychometric tradition of research into adult intellectual functioning. The goal was to highlight the potential value of considering practical creativity within the context of trying to understand older adults' intellectual competencies in the everyday world. While there has been relatively little systematic research into the adult development of creativity-related mental abilities, we have tried to advance a view which can be summarized as follows:

1. Creativity and intelligence are fundamentally intertwined constructs.

2. An adequate accounting of older adults' mental abilities must include the specification of domain-specific knowledge bases, general (convergent) intellectual abilities, and at least some divergent production abilities.

3. Domain-specific knowledge may be particularly important in understanding individual differences within selected domains. Across domains of functioning, however, other intellectual abilities (e.g., domain-general crystallized knowledge, domain-general fluid reasoning, functioning of learning and memory "mechanics") may be most important. For a particular individual, novel tasks will most likely require fluid reasoning skills; as tasks decrease in structure (and increase in complexity and ambiguity) fluency, flexibility, and originality may become increasingly important.

4. Developmental evidence suggests that late life is a period of normative loss in intellectual functioning, including fluency, flexibility, and originality. Despite this, many individuals may demonstrate substantial developmental stability on at least some intellectual abilities.

5. Practical creativity is seen as the application of creative problem solving and divergent abilities like fluency, flexibility, and originality to the ill-structured problems of daily life. Such problems might be described as messy or ambiguous. They are the problems which are

often regarded as definitional of practical intelligence (Wagner, 1986; Resnick, 1987), but we see them as a subset of a broader class of everyday tasks. We believe that the *practical intelligence* label applies more correctly to abilities required in relatively well-structured problems of daily living, and that *practical creativity* might be a better label for the additional abilities needed for the solution of such ill-structured problems.

6. Ideas associated with practical intelligence can be seen in some common views of successful aging. Particularly the P. Baltes and M. Baltes (1990) and Bäckman and Dixon (1992) conceptions of selective optimization and compensation include proposals that the successful management of the challenges of late life may involve the flexible reassignment of solution strategies and solution goals.

Clearly, the empirical evidence for the adaptive importance of practical creativity is not yet in hand. Existing research on adults' everyday cognition, in general, has not yet shown that "ecologically valid" measures of cognition are good predictors of real-world outcomes (e.g., maintained independence, mortality and morbidity, physical and emotional well-being), or that they are better predictors than traditional measures of intelligence (Willis, 1991). In our view, however, in order to determine whether mental abilities associated with practical creativity might be useful antecedents of successful aging, future research must: (a) include measures of basic cognitive and intellectual abilities, and measures of divergent production and creative problem solving, (b) establish the salience of measures of basic convergent and divergent production relative to measures of practical intelligence or practical creativity for the prediction of late life adaptive criteria (e.g., maintenance of functional independence) using longitudinal and prospective designs, and (c) more clearly specify the aspects of everyday cognition they wish to measure. Global conceptions of everyday problem solving or practical intelligence seem unlikely to be very useful.

In addition, this chapter has attempted to highlight the relative paucity of research on both creativity and everyday problem solving in late life. It is interesting to speculate why creativity has received so much more attention in the educational, industrial, and organizational literature than it has in the adult developmental literature. Has creativity been seen as relatively unimportant in the post-retirement years? While some researchers have suggested that creativity may be related to late life psychosocial outcomes (e.g., Goff, 1993), the practical or adaptive outcomes of creativity, creative problem solving, and divergent production have not been considered. On the other hand, while research on late life everyday problem solving appears to be an emerging field (Woodruff-Pak, 1989), this area has been plagued by a lack of consistent measurement and theoretical approaches (see Marsiske & Willis, 1995). In our view, however, research on the intersection of creative abilities and everyday cognition may be one promising avenue for understanding maintained adaptive competence and successful aging in late life.

ACKNOWLEDGMENTS

The writing of this chapter was supported, in part, by Grant AG-08082 from the National Institute on Aging to Dr. S. L. Willis. Dr. Marsiske was initially supported by the National Institute on Aging Training Grant, T32-AG-00048, awarded to the Pennsylvania State University. This chapter was completed while Dr. Marsiske was a postdoctoral fellow at the Max Planck Institute for Human Development and Education, Berlin, Germany. Dr. Marsiske is currently an Assistant Professor of Gerontology and Psychology at Wayne State University.

The authors gratefully acknowledge discussions regarding the issues considered in this chapter with our colleagues at the Max Planck Institute for Human Development and Education and the Pennsylvania State University. Special thanks is extended to Drs. N. W. Denney, late of University of Wisconsin-Madison; B. J. F. Meyer, the Pennsylvania State University; and Dr. J. Smith, Max Planck Institute of Human Development and Education for helpful suggestions regarding this paper, and to Drs. A. L. Horgas, Wayne State University, and D. F. Lopez, University of South Florida-Fort Myers, for helpful comments on earlier versions of this paper.

Correspondence concerning this chapter should be addressed to either Michael Marsiske, Institute of Gerontology, Wayne State University, 87 E. Ferry St., Detroit, MI, 48202 or Sherry L. Willis, Professor of Human Development, S-110 Henderson Building, The Pennsylvania State University, University Park, PA, 16802. Electronic mail can be sent to Marsiske@geroserver.iog.wayne.edu, or to SLW@psuvm.psu.edu.

REFERENCES

Alpaugh, P. K., & Birren, J. E. (1977). Variables affecting creative contributions across the adult lifespan. *Human Development, 20,* 240–248.

Amabile, T. M. (1983). *The social psychology of creativity.* New York: Springer.

Andersson, E., Berg, S., Lawenius, M., & Ruth, J. E. (1989). Creativity and age: A longitudinal study. *Aging, 1,* 159–164.

Bäckman, L., & Dixon, R. A. (1992). Psychological compensation: A theoretical framework. *Psychological Bulletin, 112,* 259–283.

Baltes, M. M., Mayr, U., Borchelt, M., Maas, I., & Wilms, H.-U. (1993). Everyday competence in old and very old age: An interdisciplinary perspective. *Ageing and Society, 13,* 657–680.

Baltes, P. B. (1987). Theoretical propositions of life-span developmental psychology: On the dynamics between growth and decline. *Developmental Psychology, 23,* 611–626.

Baltes, P. B. (1993). The aging mind: Potentials and limits. *The Gerontologist, 33,* 580–594.

Baltes, P. B., & Baltes, M. M. (1990). Psychological perspectives on successful aging: The model of selective optimization with compensation. In P. B. Baltes & M. M. Baltes (Eds.), *Successful aging: Perspectives from the behavioral sciences* (pp. 1–34). New York: Cambridge University Press.

Baltes, P. B., Dittmann-Kohli, F., & Dixon, R. A. (1984). New perspectives on the development of intelligence in adulthood: Toward a dual-process conception and a model of selective optimization with compensation. In P. B. Baltes & O. G. Brim, Jr. (Eds.), *Life-span development and behavior* (Vol. 6, pp. 33–76). New York: Academic Press.

Baltes, P. B., & Kliegl, R. (1992). Further testing of limits in cognitive plasticity in old age: Negative age differences in a mnemonic skill are robust. *Developmental Psychology, 28,* 121–125.

Baltes, P. B., & Lindenberger, U. (1988). On the range of cognitive plasticity in old age as a function of experience: Fifteen years of intervention research. *Behavior Therapy, 19,* 283–300.

Baltes, P. B., & Schaie, K. W. (1976). On the plasticity of intelligence in adulthood and old age: Where Horn and Donaldson fail. *American Psychologist, 31,* 720–725.

Baltes, P. B., Schaie, K. W., & Nardi, A. H. (1971). Age and experimental mortality in a seven-year longitudinal study of cognitive behavior. *Developmental Psychology, 5,* 18–26.

Baltes, P. B., Smith, J., & Staudinger, U. M. (1992). Wisdom and successful aging. In T. Sonderegger (Ed.), *Nebraska symposium on motivation* (Vol. 39, pp. 123–167). Lincoln: University of Nebraska Press.

Baltes, P. B., Sowarka, D., & Kliegl, R. (1989). Cognitive training research on fluid intelligence in old age: What can older adults achieve by themselves? *Psychology and Aging, 4,* 217–221.

Baltes, P. B., & Willis, S. L. (1982). Plasticity and enhancement of intellectual functioning in old age: Penn State's Adult Development and

Enrichment Project (ADEPT). In F. I. M. Craik & S. E. Trehub (Eds.), *Aging and cognitive processes* (pp. 353–389). New York: Plenum.

Barron, F. (1963). *Creativity and psychological health: Origins of personal vitality and creative freedom.* New York: Van Nostrand.

Berg, C. A., & Sternberg, R. J. (1985). A triarchic theory of intellectual development during adulthood. *Developmental Review, 5,* 334–370.

Berry, J., & Irvine, S. (1986). Bricolage: Savages do it daily. In R. J. Sternberg & R. K. Wagner (Eds.), *Practical intelligence: Nature and origins of competence in the everyday world* (pp. 236–270). New York: Cambridge University Press.

Brandtstädter, J., Wentura, D., & Greve, W. (1993). Adaptive resources of the aging self: Outlines of an emergent perspective. *International Journal of Behavioral Development, 16,* 323–349.

Brown, R. T. (1989). Creativity: What are we to measure? In J. A. Glover, R. R. Ronning, & C. R. Reynolds (Eds.), *Handbook of creativity* (pp. 3–32). New York: Plenum.

Camp, C. J., Doherty, K., Moody-Thomas, S., & Denney, N. W. (1989). Practical problem solving in adults: A comparison of problem types and scoring methods. In Sinnott, J. D. (Ed.), *Everyday problem solving: Theory and application* (pp. 211–228). New York: Praeger.

Carstensen, L. L. (1993). Motivation for social contact across the life span: A theory of socioemotional selectivity. *Nebraska Symposium on Motivation* (Vol 40, pp. 209–254). Lincoln: University of Nebraska Press.

Cattell, R. B. (1971). *Abilities: Their structure, growth, and action.* Boston: Houghton Mifflin.

Charlesworth, W. (1976). Intelligence as adaptation: An ethological approach. In L. Resnick (Ed.), *The nature of intelligence* (pp. 147–168). Hillsdale, NJ: Ablex.

Charness, N. (1985). *Aging and human performance.* New York: Wiley.

Cornelius, S. W., & Caspi, A. (1987). Everyday problem solving in adulthood and old age. *Psychology and Aging, 2,* 144–153.

Costa, P. T., & McCrae, R. R. (1985). *The NEO Personality Inventory manual.* Odessa, FL: Psychological Assessment Resources.

Cunnington, B. F., & Torrance, E. P. (1965). *Sounds and images.* Lexington, KY: Ginn.

Demming, J. A., & Pressey, S. L. (1957). Tests "indigenous" to the adult and older years. *Journal of Counseling Psychology, 4,* 144–148.

Denney, N. W. (1984). A model of cognitive development across the life span. *Developmental Review, 4,* 171–191.

Denney, N. W. (1989). Everyday problem solving: Methodological issues, research findings, and a model. In L. W. Poon, D. C. Rubin,

& B. A. Wilson (Eds.), *Everyday cognition in adulthood and late life* (pp. 330–351). New York: Cambridge University Press.

Denney, N. W. (1991, November). *Intellectual correlates of practical and social problem solving.* Unpublished manuscript presented to the Gerontological Society of America, San Francisco.

Denney, N. W., & Palmer, A. M. (1981). Adult age differences on traditional and practical problem solving measures. *Journal of Gerontology, 36,* 323–328.

Denney, N. W., & Pearce, K. A. (1989). A developmental study of practical problem solving in adults. *Psychology and Aging, 4,* 438–442.

Denney, N. W., Pearce, K. A., & Palmer, A. M. (1982). A developmental study of adults' performance on traditional and practical problem-solving tasks. *Experimental Aging Research, 8,* 115–118.

Denney, N. W., Tozier, T. L., & Schlotthauer, C. A. (1992). The effect of instructions on age differences in practical problem solving. *Journal of Gerontology: Psychological Sciences, 47,* P142–P145.

Dixon, R. A., & Bäckman, L. (1995). *Compensating for psychological deficits and declines.* Hillsdale, NJ: Erlbaum.

Ericsson, K. A., & Smith, J. (1991). *Toward a general theory of expertise: Prospects and limits.* New York: Cambridge University Press.

Eysenck, M. W., & Keane, M. T. (1990). *Cognitive psychology.* Hillsdale, NJ: Erlbaum.

Featherman, D. L., Smith, J., & Peterson, J. G. (1990). Successful aging in a "post-retired" society. In P. B. Baltes & M. M. Baltes (Eds.), *Successful aging: Perspectives from the behavioral sciences* (pp. 50–93). New York: Cambridge University Press.

Gardner, E. F., & Monge, R. H. (1977). Adult age differences in cognitive abilities and educational background. *Experimental Aging Research, 3,* 337–383.

Gentner, D. (1983). Structure-mapping: A theoretical framework for analogy. *Cognitive Science, 7,* 155–170.

Goff, K. (1992). Enhancing creativity in older adults. *Journal of Creative Behavior, 26,* 40–49.

Goff, K. (1993). Creativity and life satisfaction of older adults. *Educational Gerontology, 19,* 241–250.

Guilford, J. P. (1950). Creativity. *American Psychologist, 5,* 444–454.

Guilford, J. P. (1967). *The nature of human intelligence.* New York: McGraw-Hill.

Guilford, J. P. (1970). Creativity: Retrospect and prospect. *Journal of Creative Behavior, 4,* 149–168.

Guilford, J. P. (1977). *Way beyond the IQ: Guide to improving intelligence and creativity.* Buffalo, NY: Creative Education Foundation.

Hartley, A. A. (1989). The cognitive ecology of problem solving. In L. W. Poon, D. C. Rubin, & B. A. Wilson (Eds.), *Everyday cognition in adulthood and late life* (pp. 300–329). New York: Cambridge University Press.

Heckhausen, J., & Schulz, R. (1995). A life-span theory of control. *Psychological Review, 102,* 284–304.

Hocevar, D., & Bachelor, P. (1989). A taxonomy and critique of measurements used in the study of creativity. In J. A. Glover, R. R. Ronning, & C. R. Reynolds (Eds.), *Handbook of creativity* (pp. 53–75). New York: Plenum.

Hofland, B. F., Willis, S. L., & Baltes, P. B. (1981). Fluid intelligence performance in the elderly: Intra-individual variability and conditions of assessment. *Journal of Educational Psychology, 73,* 573–586.

Holyoak, K. J. (1985). The pragmatics of analogical transfer. *The Psychology of Learning and Motivation, 19,* 59–87.

Horn, J. L. (1982). The theory of fluid and crystallized intelligence in relation to concepts of cognitive psychology and aging in adulthood. In F. I. M. Craik & S. E. Trehub (Eds.), *Aging and cognitive processes* (pp. 847–870). New York: Plenum.

Horn, J. L., & Hofer, S. M. (1992). Major abilities and development in the adult period. In R. J. Sternberg & C. A. Berg (Eds.), *Intellectual development* (pp. 44–49). New York: Cambridge University Press.

Hoyer, W. J., & Rybash, J. M. (1993). Characterizing adult cognitive development. *Journal of Adult Development, 1,* 7–12.

Hultsch, D. F., Hertzog, C., Small, B. J., McDonald-Miszczak, L., & Dixon, R. A. (1992). Short-term longitudinal change in cognitive performance in later life. *Psychology and Aging, 7,* 571–584.

Jacquish, G. A., & Ripple, R. E. (1981). Cognitive creative abilities and self-esteem across the adult lifespan. *Human Development, 24,* 110–119.

Keane, M. T. (1988). *Analogical problem solving.* New York: Wiley.

Kendler, T. S., Kendler, H. H., & Carrick, M. A. (1966). Verbal labels and inferential problem solving of children. *Child Development, 37,* 749–763.

Klemp, G. O., & McClelland, D. C. (1986). What characterizes intelligent functioning among senior managers? In R. J. Sternberg & R. K. Wagner (Eds.), *Practical intelligence: Nature and origins of competence in the everyday world* (pp. 31–50). New York: Cambridge University Press.

Kliegl, R., & Baltes, P. B. (1987). Theory-guided analysis of development and aging mechanisms through testing-the-limits and research on expertise. In C. Schooler & K. W. Schaie (Eds.), *Cognitive functioning and social structure over the life course* (pp. 95–119). Norwood, NJ: Ablex.

Kogan, N., & Pankove, E. (1974). Long-term predictive validity of divergent-thinking tests: Some negative evidence. *Journal of Educational Psychology, 66,* 802–810.

Krampe, R. (1992). *Maintaining excellence: Cognitive-motor performance in pianists differing in age and skill level.* Unpublished doctoral dissertation, Free University, Berlin, Germany.

Lave, J., Murtaugh, M., & de la Rocha, O. (1984). The dialectic of arithmetic in grocery shopping. In B. Rogoff & J. Lave (Eds.), *Everyday cognition: Its development in social context* (pp. 67–94). Cambridge, MA: Harvard University Press.

Lawton, M. P., & Brody, E. M. (1969). Assessment of older people: Self-maintaining and instrumental activities of daily living. *The Gerontologist, 9,* 179–185.

Lerner, R. M. (1984). *On the nature of human plasticity.* New York: Cambridge University Press.

Lindenberger, U., & Baltes, P. B. (in press). Intellectual aging. In R. J. Sternberg et al. (Eds.), *Encyclopedia of intelligence.* New York: Macmillan.

Lindenberger, U., Mayr, U., & Kliegl, R. (1993). Speed and intelligence in old age. *Psychology and Aging, 8,* 207–220.

Marsiske, M., Lang, F. R., Baltes, P. B., & Baltes, M. M. (1995). Selective optimization with compensation: Life-span perspectives on successful human development. In R. A. Dixon & L. Bäckman (Eds.), *Compensating for psychological deficits and declines* (pp. 35–81). Hillsdale, NJ: Erlbaum.

Marsiske, M., & Willis, S. L. (1993, August). *Aspects of creativity in the everyday problem solving of older adults.* Paper presented to the American Psychological Society, Toronto, Canada.

Marsiske, M., & Willis, S. L. (1995). Dimensionality of everyday problem solving in older adults. *Psychology and Aging, 10,* 269–283.

Mayer, R. E. (1990). Problem solving. In M. W. Eysenck, et al. (Eds.), *The Blackwell dictionary of cognitive psychology.* London: Blackwell.

McArdle, J. J., Hamagami, F., Elias, M. F., & Robbins, M. A. (1991). Structural modeling of mixed longitudinal and cross-sectional data. *Experimental Aging Research, 17,* 29–51.

McCrae, R. R. (1987). Creativity, divergent thinking, and openness to experience. *Journal of Personality and Social Psychology, 52,* 1258–1265.

McCrae, R.R., Arenberg, D., & Costa, P. T. (1987). Declines in divergent thinking with age: Cross-sectional, longitudinal, and cross-sequential analyses, *Psychology and Aging, 2,* 130–137.

Meyer, B. J. F., Marsiske, M., & Willis, S. L. (1993). Text processing variables predict the readability of everyday documents read by older adults. *Reading Research Quarterly, 28,* 234–249.

Michael, W. B. (1977). Cognitive and affective components of creativity in mathematics and the physical sciences. In J. C. Stanley, W. C. George, & C. H. Solano (Eds.), *The gifted and the creative: A fifty-year perspective.* Baltimore: Johns Hopkins University Press.

Neisser, U. (1976). General, academic, and artificial intelligence. In L. Resnick (Ed.), *Human intelligence: Perspectives on its measurement* (pp. 179–189). Norwood, NJ: Ablex.

Newell, A., & Simon, H. A. (1972). *Human problem solving.* Englewood Cliffs, NJ: Prentice-Hall.

Poon, L. W., Rubin, D. C., & Wilson, B. A. (1989). *Everyday cognition in adulthood and late life.* Cambridge, MA: Cambridge University Press.

Poon, L. W., Martin, P., Clayton, G. M., Messner, S., Noble, C. A., & Johnson, M. A. (1992). The influences of cognitive resources on adaptation and old age. *International Journal of Aging and Human Development, 34,* 31–46.

Reitman, W. (1965). *Cognition and thought.* New York: Wiley.

Resnick, L. B. (1987). Learning in school and out. *Educational Researcher, 16,* 13–20.

Ruth, J. E., & Birren, J. E. (1985). Creativity in adulthood and old age: Relations to intelligence, sex, and mode of testing. *International Journal of Behavioral Development, 8,* 99–109.

Salthouse, T. A. (1991). *Theoretical perspectives on cognitive aging.* Hillsdale, NJ: Erlbaum.

Schaie, K. W. (1965). A general model for the study of developmental problems. *Psychological Bulletin, 64,* 92–107.

Schaie, K. W. (1977). Quasi-experimental designs in the psychology of aging. In J. E. Birren & K. W. Schaie (Eds.), *Handbook of the psychology of aging* (pp. 39–58). New York: Van Nostrand.

Schaie, K. W. (1983). The Seattle Longitudinal Study: A twenty-one year exploration of psychometric intelligence in adulthood. In K. W. Schaie (Ed.), *Longitudinal studies of adult psychological development* (pp. 64–135). New York: Guilford.

Schaie, K. W. (1986). Beyond calendar definitions of age, time and cohort: The general developmental model revisited. *Developmental Review, 6,* 252–277.

Schaie, K. W. (1989). The hazards of cognitive aging. *The Gerontologist, 29,* 484–493.

Schaie, K. W. (1994). The course of adult intellectual development. *American Psychologist, 49,* 304–313.

Schaie, K. W., Dutta, R., & Willis, S. L. (1991). Relationship between rigidity-flexibility and cognitive abilities in adulthood. *Psychology and Aging, 6,* 371–383.

Scribner, S. (1984). Studying working intelligence. In B. Rogoff & J. Lave (Eds.), *Everyday cognition: Its development and social context* (pp. 9–40). Cambridge, MA: Harvard University Press.

Simon, H. A. (1973). The structure of ill-structured problems. *Artificial Intelligence, 4,* 181–201.

Simonton, D. K. (1985). Quality, quantity, and age: The careers of 10 distinguished psychologists. *International Journal of Aging and Human Development, 21,* 241–254.

Simonton, D. K. (1990). Does creativity decline in the later years? Definition, data, and theory. In Perlmutter, M. (Ed.), *Late life potential.* Washington, DC: Gerontological Society.

Simonton, D. K. (1991). Career landmarks in science: Individual differences and interdisciplinary contrasts. *Developmental Psychology, 27,* 119–130.

Sinnott, J. D. (1989). *Everyday problem solving: Theory and applications.* New York: Praeger.

Staudinger, U. M., Cornelius, S. W., & Baltes, P. B. (1989). The aging of intelligence: Potential and limits. *Annals of the Academy of Political and Social Sciences, 503,* 43–59.

Staudinger, U. M., Marsiske, M., & Baltes, P. B. (1995). Resilience and reserve capacity in later adulthood: Potentials and limits of development across the life span. In D. Cicchetti & D. J. Cohen (Eds.), *Developmental psychopathology: Vol. 2, Risk, disorder, and adaptation* (pp. 801–847). New York: Wiley.

Sternberg, R. J. (1982). Natural, unnatural, and supernatural concepts. *Cognitive psychology, 14,* 451–488.

Sternberg, R. J. (1985). *Beyond I.Q.: A triarchic theory of human intelligence.* New York: Cambridge University Press.

Sternberg, R. J. (1988). Mental self-government: A theory of intellectual styles and their development. *Human Development, 31,* 197–221.

Sternberg, R. J., & Lubart, T. I. (1991). An investment theory of creativity and its development. *Human Development, 34,* 1–31.

Sternberg, R. J., & Wagner, R. K. (1986). *Practical intelligence: Nature and origins of competence in the everyday world.* New York: Cambridge University Press.

Torrance, E. P. (1988). The nature of creativity as manifest in its testing. In R. J. Sternberg (Ed.), *The nature of creativity* (pp. 43–75). Cambridge, MA: Cambridge University Press.

Torrance, E. P., Clements, C. B., & Goff, K. (1989). Mind-body learning among the elderly: Arts, fitness, incubation. *Educational Forum, 54,* 123–133.

Torrance, E. P., & Safter, H. T. (1990). *The incubation model of teaching: Getting beyond aha!* Buffalo, NY: Bearly Limited.

Voss, J. F., & Means, M. L. (1989). Toward a model of creativity based upon problem solving in the social sciences. In J. A. Glover, R. R. Ronning, & C. R. Reynolds (Eds.), *Handbook of creativity* (pp. 399–410). New York: Plenum.

Wagner, R. K. (1986). The search for intraterrestrial intelligence. In R. J. Sternberg & R. K. Wagner (Eds.), *Practical intelligence: Nature and origins of competence in the everyday world* (pp. 361–378). New York: Cambridge University Press.

Wagner, R. K., & Sternberg, R. J. (1985). Practical intelligence in real-world pursuits: The role of tacit knowledge. *Journal of Personality and Social Psychology, 48,* 436–458.

Wagner, R. K., & Sternberg, R. J. (1986). Tacit knowledge and intelligence in the everyday world. In R. J. Sternberg & R. K. Wagner (Eds.), *Practical intelligence: Nature and origins of competence in the everyday world* (pp. 51–83). New York: Cambridge University Press.

Wallach, M. A. (1986). Creativity testing and giftedness. In F. D. Horowitz & M. O'Brien (Eds.), *The gifted and the talented: Developmental perspectives* (pp. 99–123). Washington, DC: American Psychological Association.

Weisberg, R. W. (1986). *Memory, thought, and behavior.* Oxford, UK: Oxford University Press.

Wertheimer, M. (1959). *Productive thinking* (rev. ed.). New York: Harper & Row.

Willis, S. L. (1987). Cognitive training and everyday competence. *Annual Review of Gerontology and Geriatrics, 7,* 159–188.

Willis, S. L. (1991). Cognition and everyday competence. *Annual Review of Gerontology and Geriatrics, 11,* 80–109.

Willis, S. L., Jay, G. M., Diehl, M., & Marsiske, M. (1992). Longitudinal change and prediction of everyday task competence in the elderly. *Research on Aging, 14,* 68–91.

Willis, S. L., & Marsiske, M. (1991). Life-span perspective on practical intelligence. In D. E. Tupper & K. D. Cicerone (Eds.), *The neuropsychology of everyday life: Issues in development and rehabilitation* (pp. 183–200). Boston: Kluwer.

Willis, S. L., Marsiske, M., & Diehl, M. (1991, November). *Older adults' performance on Instrumental Activities of Daily Living and mental abilities.* Paper presented to the Gerontological Society of America, San Francisco, CA.

Willis, S. L., & Nesselroade, N. (1990). Long-term effects of fluid ability training in old-old age. *Developmental Psychology, 26,* 905–910.

Willis, S. L., & Schaie, K. W. (1986a). Practical intelligence in later adulthood. In R. J. Sternberg & R. K. Wagner (Eds.), *Practical intelligence: Nature and origins of competence in the everyday world* (pp. 236–268). New York: Cambridge University Press.

Willis, S. L., & Schaie, K. W. (1986b). Training the elderly on the ability factors of spatial orientation and inductive reasoning. *Psychology and Aging, 1,* 239–247.

Willis, S. L., & Schaie, K. W. (1993). Everyday cognition: Taxonomic and methodological considerations. In J. M. Puckett & H. W. Reese (Eds.), *Mechanisms of practical cognition* (pp. 33–53). Hillsdale, NJ: Erlbaum.

Willis, S. L., & Schaie, K. W. (1994). Cognitive training in the normal elderly. In F. Forett, Y. Christen, & F. Boller (Ed.), *Plasticité cérébral et stimulation cognitive.* Paris: Fondation Nationale de Gérontologie.

Woodruff-Pak, D. S. (1989). Aging and intelligence: Changing perspectives in the twentieth century. *Journal of Aging Studies, 3,* 91–118.

PART THREE

Creativity, Personality, and Gender

Aging and Creativity in Eminent Architects

Stéphanie Z. Dudek and Hélène Croteau

INTRODUCTION

The goal of the present study was to evaluate the evidence for continuing creativity in a group of aging eminent male architects 25 years after they were seen by MacKinnon (1962, 1963, 1965) and his colleagues at the Institute of Personality Assessment and Research (IPAR), University of California, Berkeley, in 1958–1960. The present report is limited to analysis of the Rorschach and Adjective Check List (ACL) test evaluations of Group I, the eminently creative group of architects.

MacKinnon's research focus was on personality: that is, on the forces that make for effective use of creative potential in committed persons. He was interested in creativity that resulted in acknowledged outstanding achievement. Thus success was an unwitting part of MacKinnon's definition of effectiveness. Creativity that was not put to effective use did not concern him. However, his use of three levels of creativity did tell us something about the personality traits that keep creative potential relatively dormant.

The 124 architects who accepted MacKinnon's invitation to participate in his research consisted of three groups. Group I represented the top of the heap, acknowledged as the most eminent, creative, and effective architects in America in the 1950s by an impressive jury of experts (MacKinnon, 1962). Groups II and III, chosen for comparison with Group I, were meant to better identify the personality characteristics that define effectiveness. They also served to provide a picture of the normal range of talent within this profession. Groups II and III were rated significantly lower on creativity by a number of highly qualified architectural professionals. The creativity range for the group was 1.9 to 6.5 with a mean of 5.46 for Group I, 4.25 for Group II, and 3.54 for Group III, (a statistically significant difference). However, the talent was not discontinuous. There was no difference in measured intelligence. The mean age of the group was 49 (range, 33–63 years). The mean age for the follow-up group was 71 (range, 62–86 years).

A concerted effort had uncovered addresses for 95 of the original 124 architects. Of these, only 83 could be traced. Seventy accepted, 8 refused the interview for a variety of reasons and the rest could not be located, leaving us with a total of 70 completed interviews. Of these, 23 belonged to Group I, 25 to Group II, and 22 to Group III. The 1983–1984 follow-up consisted of a visit to the domicile or office of each of the 70 architects who had agreed to participate in this research.

The interview lasted between 3 and 5 hours and included the administration of the four tests chosen as highly representative of MacKinnon's original extensive battery. The present report concerns only the most creative group of architects because this is the only group to whom Rorschachs were administered in 1958–1960. The present test battery consisted of the Rorschach (ROR), the Adjective Check List (ACL), the California Psychological Inventory (CPI) and the Barron Welsh Art Scale (BWAS). The 450-item CPI was to be returned by mail. Only 64% mailed it back and it will not be part of the present report. The BWAS will be treated in a separate report. The present chapter is limited to the Rorschach and the ACL.

Twenty (90%) of the 23 subjects constituting Group I reported they were still working, but only 14 (61%) claimed full-time status. Two of those claiming to work full-time were in allied occupations (architectural research). Of the four surviving Group I architects who did not participate in the present study, one was hospitalized for Alzheimer's disease, one was chronically ill and refused to be seen, one could not be reached and one of the most eminent of the group was literally too busy to find time for testing.

In reassessing creativity after a 25-year interval, at a late stage in the creative architects' lives, the questions that were pertinent in their prime were reexamined. At follow-up the main concern was not whether and what creative traits characterize the architect, but what remained of the original capital and how effectively it was being put to use. We needed to assess:

1. How much talent remained
2. How rich the psychic apparatus was

3. How adequate the transformative skills (clear thinking, accurate planning, good judgment) were when compared to the 1959 results
4. How great was the desire to deploy them now
5. Evidence of well-developed social skills for engaging in person-environment interactions, and attracting and negotiating job contracts.

For an architect to remain at the top, all of these facets must still be operating at reasonable levels. One of the goals of the follow-up was to assess to what extent age and experience had affected the five aspects of the creative architect's sense of self and his continuing creative performance.

STUDIES OF AGING POPULATIONS

The methodological defects of the studies carried out between 1940 and 1960 on the effects of aging on a variety of intellectual, perceptual-motor, and learning functions were so great as to totally invalidate the findings. There had been no attempt to control for the effects of socio-economic status (SES), education, intelligence, cultural differences across generations, the complexity or simplicity of subject's milieu, nature of vocational or professional work, or physical condition—all of which were found to be relevant moderating factors by later researchers. The 1970s and 1980s studies used cross and time sequential designs as well as cross-sectional and longitudinal designs. These improved methodologies established with reasonable certainty that serious aging deficits in intellectual functioning, in memory, in learning and organization need not begin until the seventh decade; more precisely at about age 74 (see Schooler & Schaie, 1987; Birren & Schaie, 1990). This was approximately the age of the architects in Dudek and Hall's study (1991).

Although the research since 1970 has drawn a more positive picture of aging decline it has also made clear that "increasing age is associated with a fairly substantial reduction in effectiveness across a broad range of cognitive abilities . . . [although] there are notable exceptions" (Salthouse, 1988, p.4). Among the processes in which age deficits are clearly evident is the speed of information processing and the ability to process complex information (Charness, 1988; Falduto & Baron, 1986; McDowd & Craik, 1988). Speed of reaction time has been shown to be from 1.6 to 2.0 times slower than in young adults for central decision processes (Cerella, 1985; Salthouse, 1985). Cerella maintains that new aging theories view age deficits as defects distributed along a neural network, reporting, "Information processing latencies taken from elderly subjects model qualitatively and quantitatively those that would be expected from a brain whose interconnections were systematically disrupted or attenuated" (p. 218). Cerella also postulates "axonal degeneration and attenuation" (p. 217), which lead to breaks in links in the neural network resulting in "exponential decline of functionality with age" (p. 203), also known as generalized slowing with age. On the other hand, McDowd and Birren (1990, p. 222) stressed "attentional deficits in information processing" as the crucial factor, as did Craik and Byrd (1982) and Stankov (1988). Other explanations for age-related deficits include strategy differences, cautiousness, and so on. However, Cerella (1990) contended that the clinical generalized slowing hypothesis is sufficient to account for age deficits in all task conditions.

Cerella pointed out that skill acquisition, speed-accuracy trade-offs, attentional capacity, strategy differences, and other phenomena offered as hypotheses by other researchers are also pertinent or do make a contribution, but they would obviously operate in the same way in young persons. It is evident that experience alters the thresholds for the speed of processing throughout the life course. Cerella's work has been heavily criticized, and he admits that his analyses have dealt with latencies computed with the use of group means. He has not carried out any individual trial by trial analyses. In response he has indicated that "modal parameters such as connectivity constants or the signal loss rate may emerge as powerful predictors of individual differences" (Cerella, 1990, p. 219).

Electroencephalograms (EEG) and event related potentials (ERP) have documented the evidence for generalized slowing of nervous system functioning (accelerating after age 45–50) "at peripheral, brain stem, sensory receiving and cognitive integrative levels" (Prinz, Dustman, & Emmerson, 1990, p. 145). There are also considerable data to indicate that inhibitive controls are weakened, and this would lead to impaired attention and concentration as well as to impulsiveness and mental inflexibility. Healthier central nervous system functioning has been related to lifestyles, favoring those that include strenuous physical activity (Prinz et al., 1990).

In short, the latest research on aging has been stressing the importance of central nervous system characteristics to explain age-related slowing at all functional levels of the brain. Attenuating factors, such as the demonstrated relevance of health, lifestyles, expertise, residual plasticity, the modifiability of impairment, and software disuse are much in evidence as means of explaining notable individual differences. The main concern now is "how to distinguish between processes that appear to decline in effectiveness across adulthood and the products of prior processing that may continually accumulate" (Salthouse, 1988, p. 4).

To respond to that issue, Salthouse and a team of researchers (Salthouse et al., 1990) conducted three studies using young and older college-educated men and young and older architects (age range, 20–71). They compared them on several spatial visualization tasks, on which the older architects had a lifetime of experience. They found that increased age was associated with lower levels of performance for both unselected adults and for the architects. The younger architects were significantly more proficient than their more experienced colleagues on several tests of spatial visualization. The inference is that "age-related effects in some aspects of cognitive functioning may be independent of experiential influences" (p. 128). This does not answer the problems posed by Charness (1988), namely that any model of cognitive aging must come to grips with continuing efficiency of information processing within a degenerating neuronal network.

The research focusing on continuity of personality over time is nearly as impressive as the research focusing on intellectual abilities (Caspi & Bem, 1988; Costa & McCrae, 1980; Moss & Suddman, 1980; Schaie & Parham, 1976; Schuerger, Tait, & Tavernelli, 1982). In this area the parameters are broader and include psychological, sociological and anthropological influences, making the job of interpretation more difficult. However, the evidence for consistency is so great that the concept of change occurs frequently only to denote the absence of consistency. Caspi and Bem (1988) concluded their review of the methodological issues involved in dealing with concepts of change by noting that even the "classic stage theories of childhood cognitive development are currently under challenge, with the challengers claiming that children already possess the same cognitive competencies as adults but merely lack domain-specific knowledge" (Caspi & Bem, 1987, p. 569). This suggests that future research should perhaps focus on central nervous system mechanisms that inhibit change by virtue of a built-in consistency.

IPAR ARCHITECTS, 1984:
A FOLLOW-UP STUDY

Our follow-up of the IPAR architects is not encumbered by the same complex problems that beleaguered the assessment of decline with age in the studies prior to the 1970s. The group is homogeneous. The subjects came from a superior socioeconomic class, falling into a narrow range of intellectual ability at the high end on Terman's (1956) Concept Mastery Test and of the Wechsler Adult Intelligence Scale. They had completed a similar superior education at the same architectural schools. The members of this group had worked constantly within a complex environment that had demanded of them intellectual alertness, social acumen, creative thinking and flexibility in dealing with new situations. On the whole the group boasted of superior physical health and vigor, most having succumbed to the normal illnesses of old age only in the last 5 years of their life (on average, approximately 68 years of age). Except for one person who was dying of cancer, all were in stable good health at time of testing.

CURRENT FOCUS

The present researchers' interest was primarily to evaluate the extent to which the surviving architects, particularly those engaged in full-time practice, still felt and were effective and creative and the extent to which the personality traits associated with creativity, as identified by MacKinnon (1963), still characterized them. Personality was MacKinnon's central focus; he defined personality as the stable structure that enables the individual to cope with reality, to plan a future, to adapt, restructure or compensate when appropriate or necessary. Neugarten (1977) pointed out that "personality is the pivotal factor in adaptation to aging" (p. 644). More recently, Costa and McCrae (1980) underscored this by stating that "personality may be seen as the stable basis within the individual for adaptation to a changing life" (p. 70–71).

MacKinnon's extensive analysis of the architect's personality by means of Q sorts, CPI, ACL, questionnaires, and a number of other tests left a clear picture not only of the self-image, value system, and personality traits associated with the effective use of creative talent at high levels of excellence in architecture, but also what traits are present or absent at the lower levels. It is against the 1958 assessment of these traits that the current Rorschach and ACL data will be compared.

Personality would appear to be central to the full development of talents and skills in early adulthood and midlife, as well as to success in adjustment to the vicissitudes of life. It is certainly a key factor in coping with the effects of aging. To assess carefully the current effectiveness of the architect's functioning in the five categories we consider essential to professional success, we chose the Rorschach test and the ACL.

THE EVALUATION TOOLS

PART I: ASSESSING CREATIVITY

Both the ACL and the Rorschach have been extensively used in creativity research and were used by MacKinnon in 1958–1960. MacKinnon (1964, 1965) analyzed the ACL profiles of the architects and Dudek (1989) used the Rorschach to identify traits specific to creativity in the architect group. The most important goal of the follow-up was to assess the architects' functioning level as creative persons, and was approached through an assessment of cognitive effectiveness and creative strength. Of all the tests that MacKinnon included in his extensive assessment battery, the Rorschach appeared to us as the most useful to reflect the ravages of age and experience in the targeted areas. The Rorschach has demonstrated its value over the years as a clinical diagnostic tool and as an instrument sensitive to both stability and change (Dudek & Kolivakis, 1983; Exner, 1978; Klopfer, Ainsworth, Klopfer, & Holt, 1956; Piotrowski, 1965). It has particularly proved its usefulness in providing valid estimates of intact versus impaired cognitive functioning. It can very well reflect the adequacy of reality contact, judgment, lucidity of thinking, and information processing. It is effective in stimulating the emergence of primary process ideation, in which affect is the principal component. Primary process—thinking that is closely linked to the unconscious (Martindale & Daily, 1996)—is deferred as drive-dominated thinking and its presence, within the context of good ego control, identifies creative talent and augurs well for its effective use (Dudek & Verreault, 1989; Holt, 1967).

The Rorschach fulfills our methodological needs for several reasons. The process of responding to unstructured blot stimuli for which the only specific directive is "feel free to use your imagination," depends on the cooperation of intellect and affect, and some degree of imaginative strength. To see images or scenes in blots which are rich in nothing but black or bright colors and shadings calls upon the dual cognitive process of encoding and retrieving. What the subject sees and reports is a construction of retrieved memory images or of parts of subliminal images that were stimulated by looking at (encoding) poorly differentiated blots. These new images must be organized into information in such a way that a response can be rationalized and later scored for its formal adequacy; and thus it lends itself to an evaluation in terms of superior (F+), ordinary (Fo) or defective (F–) form. Form-level accuracy has been shown to be correlated with intellectual level, with good judgment, and good reality contact (Exner, 1978).

The formal organization of the response can be richly elaborated or limited to the base essentials. Craik and Byrd (1982) maintain that aging is associated with "an attenuation or shrinkage in the richness, extensiveness, and depth of processing operations at encoding and retrieval" (p. 208). In the case of the more creative individual, both encoding and retrieval, but particularly retrieval and the resulting products, have been shown to be richer and more nuanced, more uniquely marked by personal and varied associative and inferential information, than in less creative or uncreative individuals (Dudek, 1968b, 1971; Gall, 1970). Gall (1970) was able to demonstrate that practicing creative artists were significantly more sensitive to the dynamic, affective, and aesthetic qualities of objects—and particularly of human percepts—that they projected into the Rorschach than normal nonartists and schizophrenic patients. Our own measure of richness of processing (sensitivity, extensiveness, and depth) used what Piotrowski (1965) labeled the *multiple determinant response*. This term refers to the presence of more than one determinant within one complex response. (See Appendix for key to Rorschach indices.) The following are examples: In card two the response "Two people dancing, wearing fluffy woolen coats and bright red hats" is scored W, M, FC, Fc whereas the response if given as follows: "Two people dancing" is scored W, M; thus a single determinant. Decreases in the richness of the elaboration may be attributed to reduced sensitivity, attentional narrowing, decreased motivation, or to a combination of the above; they may reflect some attenuation of the processing operations of encoding and retrieval as Craik and Byrd (1982) suggest. Whatever the true explanation may be, the reduction of multiple determinants would be interpreted as a sign of impoverished imaginative expression.[1]

Methodology for Rorschach Analysis

Twenty-three architects were administered the Rorschach, at their domiciles or offices. Seventy percent were seen by the principal inves-

---

[1] it can always be inferred that different examiners elicit different amounts of content. This is true for the inquiry, but it must be remembered that the initial performance is given without any interference from the examiner. However, even in the inquiry the reasons for the addition of nuances to enrich the original content are evident because one of the rules of Rorschach recording is to indicate when and what question was asked. It is to be further noted that in 1984 the senior author carried out 70% of the testing while 30% was carried out by a research assistant who was her student. Interindividual differences in eliciting content are therefore reasonably controlled in 1984. Moreover, if analysis is restricted to the performance part only, there is no methodological problem. This is what we did.

tigator and 30% were seen by a research assistant who was her student. An attempt was made to write down all the verbal content. The Rorschachs were all typed and later scored by two independent scorers, one of whom was the second author. The system of scoring was that of Klopfer et al., (1956). Form level was scored using Mayman's (1962) system. The inter-agreement rates for the Klopfer system based on all the Rorschachs were 85%, ranging from 69% to 100%, with the second author serving as one of the scorers. Disagreements in scoring were settled by discussion. The scoring of the creativity, drive, and social skills scales was carried out by the principal investigator and rescored by an experienced independent Rorschach scorer. Agreements were generally between 98% and 100%.

Estimating Cognitive Effectiveness

As already stated, the focus of the present research is on assessing continuing effectiveness in the use of available talent. Cognitive integrity is one of the most important vehicles by which this is guaranteed. The evaluation of the adequacy of the forms projected into unstructured inkblots (good form, F+, and poor form, F−) allows us to infer whether the subject is thinking clearly, accurately, and rationally. To evaluate this aspect, all the scorable responses in the 1959 and 1984 Rorschachs were scored for form adequacy. The scale, provided by Mayman (1962), is a weighted 7-point scale by which fine discriminations in the level of form accuracy can be scored. The reliability of the Mayman system has been demonstrated by Leibowitz (1977). Mayman's scoring system offers the following scores: F+ identifies excellent forms; Fo is for ordinary and popular forms; Fw+ is for weak acceptable forms; Fw− is for weak unacceptable forms; Fv, vague, identifies forms that are by definition vague and acceptable as such (e.g., clouds); Fs is for good forms that are spoiled in elaboration. Fa identifies amorphous forms and F− identifies bad forms. The mean form level accuracy score is derived from the sum of all the weighted scores. It is intended to reflect the overall adequacy of the subject's thinking. A mean level of 5 on a 7-point scale is more than adequate and reflects effective use of the intellect.

Adequate norms for high IQ, high SES aging populations do not exist for the Rorschach or the Mayman scale. The early Rorschach studies of aged populations suffered from severe methodological defects and are useless as points of reference. Ames, Metruax, Rodel, and Walker (1973) provided norms for normal, senile, and presenile populations, but these are only a rough guide, considering the elite nature of the present populations. However, since the subjects here are used as their own controls, the absence of norms is not a problem.

Estimating Creative Potential with the Rorschach

A number of researchers (Anderson & Munroe, 1948; Dudek, 1968b, 1984; Hersch, 1962; Piotrowski, 1965; Prados, 1944; Rorschach, 1951) have established the usefulness of the Rorschach in providing an estimate of creative potential. It is the idiographic technique par excellence for the study of the many subtle changes in creativity that may occur as a function of age, differing as they may in unique ways from one subject to another. As we have already indicated, in stimulating projection, the Rorschach calls out responses that reflect the integration of affect and intellect within perceptual forms that are then evaluated for perceptual accuracy as well as for richness of imaginative resources. In this way, an insight is gained into how a person transforms what may be seen as a banal, stimulus-bound response, for example, "this is a bat" (scored WFA) in Card 1 into a rich elaboration such as "I see a bat flying against a white sky at dawn. Its fangs are dripping blood, and its wings are tattered. The white spaces on the inside suggest that some animal has taken a few bites out of him during their struggle. It reminds one of a TV show I saw recently about vampire bats" (scored WS, FM, Fm, C'F, A). The latter response reveals a greater contribution of intellect, imagination, sensitivity, and desire as well as the defenses that make expression socially acceptable. The free, spontaneous, and creative person takes greater liberties, has more access to drive sources (is less inhibited or repressed) and expresses them symbolically in more complex ways, with ingenuity, awareness, humor, or ambivalence making them socially acceptable as contents. By contrast, a response to a structured test (e.g., IQ) requires the subject to be as free of affect as possible in order to allow pure intellect to do its job lucidly and succinctly, undistorted by personal fantasy.

In summary, the job of the present researchers was not to identify Group I as creative—the selection committee had already done that in 1958. It was to recognize to what extent the eminent architects had been able to maintain over the years the talent that had won them top honors. Whatever the quality and range of the original talent and of the propitious circumstances that moderated success, the job now was to compare the creative individual against his earlier self in order to evaluate whether he had retained his effectiveness over the years.

Components of the Rorschach
Creativity Index

In order to evaluate the presence of creative talent at two points in time, we needed to construct a creativity index. Our decision was to use a broad range approach. Humphreys (1962) pointed out that maximal heterogeneity, within limits set by the test, will lead to higher predictive validity for the test. It was his contention that "the largest genetic contribution will be found in the very broadest, most heterogeneous tests" (p. 482). And it is our contention that creativity, in contrast to talent (which tends to be specific), is a broad range characteristic (Dudek, 1971; Dudek & Hall, 1991; Taylor, 1975).

Greenacre (1957) worked intensively with artists and identified artistic creativity as very great innate sensitivity, thus a nonspecific attribute. Persons who show signs of creativity are expected to be able to achieve superior performance in one (or several) of their talents (sensitivities), if they choose to become committed to its development. There is reason to believe that personality plays a determining role in whether such a choice is made or not (Barron, 1972; Dudek, Berneche, Bérubé, & Royer, 1991). It was also MacKinnon's belief that personality is a catalyzer of creativity. He was able to identify different personality structures in the creative and noncreative architects in his sample. These differences have persisted over the years (Dudek & Hall, 1991). The standard Rorschach indices of creativity have been well established (Dudek, 1968b; Hersch, 1962; Klopfer et al., 1956; Mayman, 1962; Myden, 1959; Piotrowski, 1965) with human movement as the single most important index.

Primary process thinking is part and parcel of psychodynamic theory. Evidence of primary process in the Rorschach (Dudek, 1968a, 1968b; Dudek & Bouhadana, 1982; Holt, 1970; Myden, 1959) has been shown to be a good index of creative talent in artists and in architects (Dudek, 1984) as well as in children (Dudek & Verreault, 1989). For example, Dudek (1984) compared 15 of the most creative versus 15 of the least creative architects within MacKinnon's group of 40 of the most creative architects in America in 1958. She found that the sole differentiating Rorschach criterion between them was the significantly greater presence of libidinal sexual content (Holt's Level 1 primary process) in the more creative group. The 15 less creative architects of the 40 most creative in America must have found their creative energy in other sources. It is at least clear that their outstanding creativity was minimally fueled by Level 1 libidinal drive as assessed by the Rorschach.

Needless to say, the Rorschachs of all 30 architects reflected adequate levels of ego integrity (each in its own unique way). Moreover, human movement, shading, multiple determinants and color were evident in numbers sufficient to identify them as creative persons. However, these Rorschach components constituted their commonly shared character-istics as a creative group. They did not serve as differentiating indices of excellence. In constructing our creativity index, presence of sexual content remains one of the important indices. We readily contend that creativity as a broad range characteristic will have sources in other sensibilities, some of which show no obvious links to libidinal drive; but since our previous research identified libido as a useful index in the present population (Dudek, 1984) its continuing presence needed to be assessed.[2]

Hypotheses

Our hypotheses are based on the recent literature on research on aging (Birren & Schaie, 1990; Cerella, 1990; Charness, 1985; Stankov, 1988; Salt-house, 1985, 1990; Schooler & Schaie, 1987) which has convincingly documented the fact that central nervous system processing slows down with age. As a result, we can expect the normal aging person to show a reduction in productivity, a decrease in motivation and a ten-dency to avoid taking on complex tasks. However, this need not result in serious thinking deficits. The ability to reason, judge, make plans, arrive at decisions, and so on, may remain intact although memory slippage and momentary confusion may occur occasionally. Efficient functioning has been reported until age 74 (Hertzog & Schaie, 1986) and it would certainly be expected to continue where skills have been perfected and maintained over a lifetime and where selective optimiza-tion has been achieved to increase competence. On the other hand, autonomic nervous system processing (Prinz et al., 1990; Woodruff, 1985), unlike learned skills, is likely to be more vulnerable to stimulus overload or to social pressure. Thus, lability and impulsiveness are expected to increase with age. This may result in decreased emotional adaptiveness, but it need not result in impaired social skills, particularly where professional concerns are implicated. These are products of a lifetime of experience and are normally highly monitored by cognitive

---

[2] We feel that the Rorschach qualifies as a broad range test to the extent that each of the variables represented by a scoring determinant is identified with different sensibilities. This was Rorschach's (1951) contention.

processes. However, encroaching central and autonomic nervous system weaknesses may lead to an avoidance of competition and to diminished drive for achievement in the average person. In the present follow-up study, 90% of Group I architects were still engaged in various aspects of their complex profession and 60% were still competing actively with younger peers. There was no sign that their drive for achievement had decreased or that their desire to put their talents to creative use had diminished significantly.

The maintenance of creative talent at peak levels is a more complex matter. It presupposes the availability of reasonable degrees of imagination, flexibility, libidinal resources, and the presence of an attitude of active search for novelty, as well as evidence of persisting psychic complexity. Sound cognitive functioning alone does not guarantee these other blessings, although it is a prerequisite to obtaining and executing work contracts.

The above considerations guided the formulation of the following hypotheses in analyzing the data for this eminent group of high-level professionally engaged architects:

H1.   There will be few significant changes in the 1983 group Rorschach psychogram as compared to that of 1958. The eminent architects will have lost little of their original talents. Changes expected to occur as an inevitable consequence of aging are specified in subsidiary hypotheses.

H2.   The architects as a group are expected to show evidence of lowered Rorschach productivity (R) and decreased control over affect (increase in CF and C relative to FC).

H3.   Cognitive functioning is expected to be intact as reflected in ability to give responses of adequate form level (F+%, W+ and Mayman F).

H4.   Drive or desire to deploy energies into creative channels will be high as reflected in high W%, dilated M:Sum C, R (8–10)% of approximately 40%, evidence of undiminished libidinal responses.

H5.   Despite greater emotional lability, social skills will remain adequate as manifested in adequate FC+, Fc+, a ratio of Sum c to sum C of approximately 1:1, R(8–10) of approximately 40%, constructive M and a minimum of 5 popular responses (P).

The results will be presented following the description of part II of the research.

Part II: Personality Attributes

The second facet of our study dealt with the architect's sense of personality integrity. This issue was originally addressed by MacKinnon (1963) with the adjective check list (ACL). It was one of the instruments to which MacKinnon gave considerable weight and it offered, in 1984, the best basis for comparison. The ACL is a self-report instrument much used in the study of lives (notably by researchers at the Institute of Personality Assessment and Research, Berkeley, CA).[3] It consists of 37 scales derived from the checking of 300 adjectives (with the directive to "check only those that apply to you"). It offers a more empirically grounded image of the self than the Rorschach, which tends to tap deeper, less conscious levels of the personality.

As already indicated, MacKinnon considered personality to be a catalyst of creativity and he found significant personality differences between the three levels of creativity in his sample of 124 architects. The members of Group I were distinguished by traits that described them as dominant, aggressive, independent, autonomous, self-confident, flexible, outspoken, self-centered, and were much more free from conventional constraints and inhibitions than the other two groups. Our job at follow-up was to see to what extent these traits, once seen to be important moderators of their success, were still characteristic of them.

Background Literature on Personality

A review of the relevant research literature on personality in aging populations showed great stability, as we have already indicated. Change was, in fact, the exception rather than the rule (Caspi & Bem, 1987; Costa & McCrae, 1980; Moss & Suddman, 1980; Siegler, George, & Okun, 1979; Schuerger, Tait, & Tavernelli, 1982). However, this need not contradict the finding that aging brings with it increased heterogeneity (Haan, 1981). By heterogeneity, Haan was referring to more individuated ways of meeting new, age-specific situational challenges. Caspi, Bem, and Elder (1989), in fact, emphasized coherence rather than consistency. Coherence, or homotypic continuity, broadens the understanding of the range of behaviors that belong in the same category. This concept accommodates both the notions of consistency and change. It is to be noted that the greatest stabilities were to be found in measures of intellectual performance followed by personality traits such as extraversion,

---

[3] Renamed as Institute of Personality and Social Research.

emotionality (impulse control) and cognitive styles (Caspi & Bem, 1987; Costa & McCrae, 1980). It would seem that it was not the invariance of behavior patterns that needed to be stressed, but the predictable ways in which persons relate to the environment in different settings over a lifetime, as the Freudians have always maintained. In other words, what is remarkable is the way individuals characteristically modify their changing contexts to suit their points of view.

In spite of the more sophisticated methodologies developed since 1970, research on the effects of aging is still fraught with numerous problems, one of which is the failure to consider sufficiently carefully cohort differences in a period of rapid cultural change. Under the circumstances, inconsistent research results may not adequately represent intraindividual consistency or change and valid information can only come from longitudinal research.

If we look at the longitudinal findings on consistency of personality and consider also the view of it as coherent, we have to conclude that the parameters of personality change have narrowed. On the other hand, if we look at conceptual approaches and, particularly, at the studies implicating information processing, we have reason to believe that changes are inevitable. They will be particularly evident in activities where central and autonomic nervous systems exert more control in the maintenance of stability, that is, in behavior, in which social reinforcement cannot be the sole moderating force. For example, it has been demonstrated that inhibitory controls are weakened with age. "Difficulties in suppressing ongoing motoric and mental activity may contribute to impulsiveness, behavioral rigidity or mental inflexibility" (Prinz et al., 1990, p. 135; also see Woodruff, 1985). Weakened inhibitory controls are expected to result in lability, if not irritability, and possibly in a decrease of sensitivity. This suggests the likelihood of changes in processing. Changes that involve impulsivity, lability, irritability, sensitivity, confusion can be picked up by the Rorschach (by examining the color, shading, and form level of responses).

In summary, the extensive reviews of the literature on personality give us reason to believe that both consistency and change are valid hypotheses. Much will depend on the population to be surveyed. In looking at MacKinnon's eminent group of creative architects (mean age 73), 90% of whom were still professionally active and all but one of whom were in good health in 1984, we were led to expect consistency, rather than change, to predominate. Moreover, the fact that 61% were still actively competing against younger architects would indicate that the personality traits that characterized them at their peak (in 1959) and which differentiated them from their less successful peers, moderating their professional success, would still be characteristic of them in 1984. Thus, we formed our sixth hypothesis:

H6.   There will be no significant changes on the scales that were most characteristic of Group I architects in 1958: Autonomy (Au), Aggression (Agg), Change (Cha), Exhibition (Exh), Creative Personality (Cps), High intellegence (A_2), Order (Ord), Deference (Def), Self-control (Scn) and Endurance (End).

On the other hand, research with young and aging creative artists (Dudek et al., 1991) led us to expect changes in the direction of greater maturity and greater acceptance of self and others. Thus we would expect moderate but significant changes on the following scores: increases on the adult scale (A), Affiliation (Aff), Nurturance (Nur) and a decrease in unfavorable adjectives (Unf). Hence, there would be an increase on favorable adjectives (Fav). A more positive, less defensive attitude toward others would reveal itself in lower critical parent (CP) scores. We would also expect less disparity between real and ideal self-image, hence higher Iss scores.

H7.   There will be moderate but significant increases on the ACL scales of A, Aff, Nur, Fav and Iss; and decreases on Unfav and CP and Agg.

RESULTS

RORSCHACH

Table 5.1 gives a comparison of the 1959 Rorschach protocols with those of 1984. It reveals few changes in the group psychogram. (Two subjects were not used in the analysis of data. One subject produced 152 responses in 1959 and the other's record was not available at the time of the analysis of data). Although the 1984 Rorschachs were shorter (with means of 27.5 vs. 34.7 responses), a *t*-test analysis revealed that these differences were not significant. This aspect will be discussed in greater detail later. The only significant differences were in diminished number (but not percent) of W ($p < .05$), diminished color (FC) responses ($p < .05$), and diminished shading responses ($p < .01$). These changes do not invalidate Hypothesis 1.

Continuing evidence of talent and richness of psychic apparatus was supported by the presence of M, of multiple determinants (MD), and by the presence of responses of creative strength (Cr 4 and 5). Adequate evidence of social skills was supported by presence of constructive M,

TABLE 5.1   T-Test Comparisons of 1958 versus 1984: Rorschach
Psychograms of Group I Architects (*N* = 21)

Variable	1958		1984		
	Mean	*SD*	Mean	*SD*	*t*
R	34.71	14.91	27.57	18.19	–1.53
W	15.52	6.90	11.81	7.52	–2.26
M	4.86	3.69	3.41	3.28	–1.65
FM	4.60	3.36	5.19	4.50	0.63
Fm	3.05	2.17	2.60	2.05	–1.26
kF	0.33	0.97	0.14	0.36	–0.81
Fk	0.38	0.52	0.14	0.48	–2.35*
KF	0.55	0.79	0.17	0.29	–2.41*
FK	1.33	1.65	1.19	–0.25	–0.02
F	13.05	10.05	10.29	9.40	–1.01
Fc	2.17	1.21	1.45	1.50	–1.73
cF	0.31	0.72	0.45	1.18	–0.45
FC¹+C1F	0.95	0.86	1.07	1.09	0.41
FC	2.24	2.07	1.41	1.64	–2.13*
CF	3.74	2.30	2.48	2.12	–2.03
C	0.26	0.45	0.83	0.84	
Sum C	5.08	2.55	3.94	2.61	–1.63
Sum Texture	5.20	2.98	2.90	2.16	–2.99
F%	33.43	18.22	36.38	17.99	0.69
R(8–10)%	37.00	12.39	35.05	8.37	–0.67
P	7.60	2.86	7.83	2.90	0.27
A%	36.57	8.37	40.76	14.26	1.26
Klopfer F+	73.95	12.90	69.85	16.60	–1.14
Multiple Determinants	5.70	4.65	5.10	4.19	–0.67

*$p < .05$.   **$p < .01$.   *df* = 20

shading in a 1:1 ratio to color, undiminished R (8–10)%, and high P. Overall form level (Klopfer F+, Mayman F, W+) was adequate. The significant losses were in FC, W, and differentiated shading. Decreased W suggested a slight diminution in drive for complicated achievement, especially in view of the fact that R had not significantly decreased. The intactness of the rest of the psychogram suggested that Hypothesis 1 was supported. It is further supported by the fact that conversion of all the psychogram data into percentages, using an arcsin transformation to control for differences in number of responses, revealed significant changes only on P (< .01), FC¹ (< .01), and cF (< .01), all of them showing significant increases. (The other shading responses [Fc, Fk,

FK] showed no significant differences when converted to percentages). We will return to this point in the discussion section.

Hypothesis 2 predicted that there would be evidence of generalized slowing and of decreased control over affect, but was not supported. The data are complex and equivocal. The *t*-test analysis (Table 5.1) showed that R decreased from 34.7 to 27.5 (n.s.). The significant decrease in FC is theoretically consistent with a decrease in emotional control, but the decrease in CF attenuates this conclusion and suggests alternative explanations. This will be further examined in the discussion section. There was a positive correlation between Age and A% (.46, $p < .05$), and a negative correlation with Fm (–.51, $p < .05$).

Table 5.2 summarizes the data with respect to overall cognitive efficiency as evaluated by the Mayman 7-point scale and by Klopfer F+%. There was a nonsignificant decrease from 73.95 to 69.85 on Klopfer F+%, but the Mayman scale revealed virtually no change (5.14 in 1959 vs. 5.05 in 1984). However, the percentage of Mayman F– and Fs scores increased significantly. This increase was only 2.76%, going from 4.62% in 1959 to 7.38% in 1984. Mayman's (Fo + Fw+ + F+), which reflects only the good forms, remained unchanged, 65.8% versus 64.4%. Amorphous forms increased from 3.9% to 6.5%, but this change was not significant. Good form W, the essential index of ability to plan, organize and set goals, showed a nonsignificant gain of 5 points, going from 59.3% in 1959 to 64.8% in 1984. However, (Wa + Ws + W–)% increased significantly from 8.05 to 16.1 ($p < .05$). In short, Table 5.2 shows that in 1959, 70.6% of the W responses were scored as good forms, 19.1% were weak and vague forms (Ww– + Wv–), and 8.0% were definitely poor. Correlational analysis revealed that none of these changes were correlated with age either in 1959 or in 1984. They were products of individual differences rather than reflections of a generalized aging trend.

Table 5.3 summarizes the data with respect to the architects' level of drive and desire to deploy energies into creative performance. As evident from Table 5.1, W% remained unchanged (44.7 vs. 42.8), although W decreased significantly. Both M and Sum C responses were present in adequate quantities and R(8–10%) did not decrease.

The availability of libidinal drive had not decreased. The sum of sexual content, clothes and exhibitionistic responses was 5.9 (14%) in 1959 and 5.4 (19%) in 1984. On the basis of this index, we conclude that libidinal drive is still available to the aged architects' fantasies. On the other hand, the quality of creative imagination appears to have suffered. When the entire group of 23 subjects was evaluated for presence of high-level creativity responses (Mayman's Cr 4 or 5), only 13 (57%) of 23 subjects in 1984 compared to 17 (74%) of 23 in 1959 were able to produce

TABLE 5.2   Rorschach Form Level using Klopfer and Mayman Systems,
1958 versus 1983 (N=21)

| Variable | 1958 | | 1983 | | |
	Mean	SD	Mean	SD	t
F+% (Klopfer)	78.75	11.89	66.93	0.58	–2.64*
F de Mayman	5.14	0.42	5.05	0.64	0.04
(F+ + Fo + Fw+)%	65.85	12.88	64.43	15.81	0.13
Fa%	3.90	7.82	6.52	9.21	1.05
(Fs + F–)%	4.62	5.58	7.38	7.74	2.27

* p < .05.   df= 20

responses at this level of creative strength. Subjects who produced 2 or less M were least able to give responses at a Cr 4 or 5 level. There were 3 subjects with no M responses in 1984 compared to none in 1959.

The presence of good social skills was supported by evidence of adequate numbers of constructive M+, adequate R(8–10%) (see Table 5.1) and by a significant ($p < .01$) increase in percent of popular responses (arcsin transformation). The significant decrease in FC responses would be interpreted as a negative sign but there was also a decrease on CF ($p < .10$). Despite significant loss in shading responses there was still a Sum c to Sum C ratio of 1:1. Taken all together we would conclude that social skills have remained adequate. Thus Hypothesis 5 was supported.

ADJECTIVE CHECK LIST

Table 5.4 summarizes the *t*-test analysis for repeated measures of the 37 ACL scales. The results indicate that hypothesis 6 was supported. Nine of the 10 ACL scales shown to be most characteristic of subjects in 1959 (MacKinnon, 1963; Dudek & Hall, 1991) were still characteristic of them in 1984. There was a significant change only on A^2, which decreased from a mean of 58 to one of 54. It is still above the average population mean of 50. The previously low scores on Def and Scn, on which creative groups normally score low, were slightly, but not significantly, higher. The Cps scale was virtually unchanged (54.3 vs. 55.2). In short, the constellation of personality traits that described the group as creative, and on which they differed significantly from the less creative groups in 1959, showed remarkable consistency.

Hypothesis 7 was directed at evaluating maturity and a sense of social ease as a function of age in the context of a professionally successful life. Significant positive changes in the predicted direction occurred on all 7 scales.

TABLE 5.3   Organizational Effectiveness Based on Quality of W Responses,
1958 versus 1983 (N=21)

Variable	1958		1983		t
	Mean	SD	Mean	SD	
W	15.52	6.93	11.81	7.52	–2.268*
W%	44.71	22.69	42.84	21.53	–0.444
(W+ + Wo + Ww+)%	59.33	15.33	64.85	19.63	1.318
Wv+%	11.33	7.68	5.76	6.40	–3.161**
(Ww– + Wv–)%	19.10	11.73	11.14	12.56	–2.198*
Wa% (1)	2.20	5.19	7.60	11.83	2.003
(Ws + W–)%	6.43	8.83	9.29	9.69	1.322
(Wa + Ws + W–)%***	8.05	10.34	16.10	14.48	2.201*

* $p < .05$.   ** $p < .01$. $df = 20$
*** Leaving out one subject who gave 55% Wa in 1958.

DISCUSSION

PERSONALITY

When we compared the overall ratings of the ACL scales in 1984 with those of 1959, it was evident that they reflected a sense of greater inner equilibrium. The image that emerged was one of greater self-confidence, self-assurance, and social integration. The architects had matured successfully. The scores on Aff and Nur increased significantly as predicted. This is in keeping with Neugarten's (1977) conceptualizations. The increased Iss scale indicated that the discrepancy between real and ideal self-image diminished, from which we might infer that the architects were more appreciative of their real assets and achievements. There was, perhaps, an attempt to perceive the self in a manner that was consistent with ideals set early in life and used to give direction to projects at which they worked hard and in which they believed. The unpredicted increase on Scfd and decrease on Crs indicated more self-assurance and less vulnerability, less need for inner change. Mls, a scale pertaining to respect for duties, obligations and discipline, and one on which creative groups tend to score low, increased, attesting to a greater sense of responsibility. There were 4 unpredicted changes on Berne's transactional ego scales. Scores on CP and AC decreased and those on NP and FC increased. The increase on A was predicted. These are all positive changes reflecting greater adaptability, tolerance, spontaneity, and responsibility, changes expected in successful aging. We would conclude that the architects experienced greater contentment

TABLE 5.4 Evaluation of Personality Using the Adjective Check List,
1958 versus 1983 (*N* = 21)

	1958		1983		
Scale	Mean	*SD*	Mean	*SD*	*t*
1. No. Chd	56.00	8.06	53.48	11.11	−1.096
2. Fav	47.62	11.04	51.71	9.85	2.407*
3. Unfav	51.67	12.26	46.57	7.04	−2.713*
4. Com	50.24	10.04	51.24	7.06	0.444
5. Ach	54.10	7.53	54.05	7.99	−0.036
6. Dom	51.00	10.19	52.29	9.85	0.961
7. End	50.76	10.29	52.95	9.42	1.419
8. Ord	50.19	10.94	51.48	8.96	0.713
9. Int	47.29	11.39	51.29	9.22	2.002
10. Nur	45.33	10.73	49.86	10.20	2.807*
11. Aff	44.29	10.05	50.05	10.50	3.238**
12. Het	49.10	10.79	52.57	13.14	2.004
13. Exh	49.52	11.64	52.67	11.18	1.789
14. Aut	56.05	10.51	53.10	9.83	−1.685
15. Agg	54.62	9.62	52.00	8.96	−1.698
16. Cha	53.95	9.53	53.43	7.42	−0.322
17. Suc	51.71	10.44	50.10	9.23	−1.058
18. Aba	48.62	9.61	48.29	10.68	−0.246
19. Def	43.24	10.48	44.91	10.22	1.229
20. Crs	50.05	12.01	46.33	12.61	−2.114*
21. S-Cn	48.29	11.11	47.81	7.70	−0.285
22. S-Cfd	48.67	11.62	52.71	11.17	2.131*
23. P-Adj	48.19	10.03	52.00	10.17	2.012
24. Iss	48.43	10.93	54.43	11.99	2.748*
25. Cps	55.38	7.68	55.29	8.14	0.594
26. Mls	50.48	9.93	54.67	7.67	2.107*
27. Mas	45.29	8.37	46.00	9.74	0.337
28. Fem	49.95	8.79	49.43	7.75	−0.286
29. CP	56.87	7.41	51.67	9.66	−2.953**
30. NP	44.62	9.79	49.71	11.32	2.872**
31. A	48.67	9.90	53.00	9.64	2.636*
32. FC	52.33	13.48	56.71	13.82	2.905**
33. AC	53.57	11.21	49.48	11.88	−2.288*
34. A^1	44.62	9.08	47.67	7.71	1.354
35. A^2	58.81	11.02	54.05	7.56	−2.137
36. A^3	45.00	8.63	46.62	8.87	1.054
37. A^4	50.10	10.39	50.52	8.33	0.244

T-test analysis
* $p < .05$.   ** $p < .01$. $df = 20$

and a more responsible social adaptability without loss of spontaneity, autonomy, dominance, and aggressive drive. They still felt a need for, and pleasure in, novelty and change. Achievement needs, for which no prediction was made, remained unchanged. It must be remembered that 90% of the group were still maintaining some degree of engagement in their profession. Although the picture is one of greater conformity, it does not appear to be at the price of abandoning individuality. The Dom, Aut, Agg and Cha scales have retained their importance.

THE RORSCHACH PSYCHOGRAM

The Rorschach results are more complex. This test taps deeper levels of personality. Research has indicated (Goldstein, 1963; Piotrowski, 1965; Rorschach, 1951) that central and autonomic nervous system integrity can be inferred from the quality of the form and of the color responses.

The relatively intact 1984 group Rorschach psychogram derived from the Rorschachs of the IPAR architects, (mean age 73) compared to that of 1959, suggests that they have lost little in the way of creativity and personality integrity. In fact, if we look at both the ACL and the Rorschach, the personality ratings emerge as more sound than ever. The group ACL revealed a heightened sense of inner equilibrium and projected an image of greater maturity, self-confidence and self-acceptance. The interviews with the architects (Dudek & Hall, 1991) reflected a sense of personal satisfaction and of continued engagement. Table 5.1 indicated that the significant Rorschach losses were limited to W, FC, and differentiated shading responses. This leads us to infer, first, that there has been a decrease of interest in complicated achievement, since there was a significant decrease of W relative to a nonsignificant decrease of R. The greater emergence of W amorphous responses pointed in the same direction. Second, a significant decrease in FC would lead one to infer that controls over affect weakened. However, the decrease in CF attenuated this interpretation and led us to conclude that curtailment of emotional response, rather than increased impulsivity, was at issue. The significant decrease in shading points in the same direction. It should be considered more serious in view of the fact that sensitivity is the creative person's stock in trade. In fact, where affect is in low supply, sensitivity becomes the main creative energy. Creative persons generally give significantly more shading responses than the norm. Exner (1978) shows that for normal persons the expected Sum c:Sum C is 2.6 to 3.7 (1:1.4 ratio based on an N of 325). Dudek's analysis of the 1959 Rorschachs of MacKinnon's group of 40 architects revealed a Sum c to Sum C ratio of 5.6:5.2 (Dudek, 1984). The present significant decrease in shading responses with a ratio of Sum c:Sum C of 2.9:3.94 (ratio 1:1.36) is a shift in the direction evident in Exner's normal group. The decrease in sensitivity for a creative person is more than a question of diminished capacity to nuance emotional expression, or of fine tuning aimed at better adaptation. Because the creative person's emotional investment is primarily in his work rather than in human relationships, the decrease in shading suggests a dampening of the antennae that pick up subliminal stimuli both of an internal and external nature. It also implies a decrease of awareness over what "message" is being received. In more operational terms it would imply an attenuation of the intuitive approach that MacKinnon (1963) found to be a characteristic of 100% of the architects. In short, a decrease in shading responses reflects a dulling of one of the essential processing tools at the creative person's disposition.

The transformation of the data into percentages using an arcsin transformation to control for the number of responses produced only 3 significant differences. Fc^1, cF, and P increased significantly in 1984, and underscore the regressive direction already noted.

On the intellectual side of the psychic apparatus, the evidence shows no significant decline in Klopfer F+%, or in (W+, Wo, and Ww+)%. We can thus infer that cognitive efficiency is intact and reality testing, judgment, organizational skills, and elaboration are comparable to what they were in 1959. The significant increase in F– and Fs responses was only a 2.76% increase from 4.6% in 1959 to 7.3% in 1984. This small impairment is countered by the adequate overall form level (Mayman F, 5.1 in 1959; 5.0 in 1984). The psychogram offered sufficient evidence of imaginative resources (M), of a broad and rich range of determinants (MD), and of libidinal content. The ability to achieve high-level creative responses (Cr 4 and 5), however, decreased significantly and in 17.5% of the group it virtually disappeared.

Thus, looking at the underside of the evidence (the empty half of the glass), the effects of aging were visible and were exacting their toll. In some architects, there was a decrease in psychic energy (R) and drive (W) as well as a slight impairment in ability to think clearly and to organize with care and precision (a significant 2.76% rise in F– and Fs). The control over affect had weakened (lower FC), and spontaneity (CF) was reduced. And, most important, on the affective side, sensitivity had decreased significantly ($p < .01$), coupled with a decrease in willingness and in some cases, in capacity, to engage in complicated creative achievement.

On the other hand, the percentages reflecting distribution of energy had not changed significantly (Table 5.1), suggesting that psychic energies were being distributed and invested by the ego in the same fashion and given the same relative importance as they were in 1959. That is, the same value system and the same priorities were in operation. However, the significant increase in percent of popular responses (using an arcsin transformation) may suggest conformist values had assumed greater importance and may be attenuating originality.

These conclusions were arrived at on the basis of a group psychogram. With an eminently idiographic tool such as the Rorschach, to what extent can a quantitative, nomothetically biased analysis do justice to the data? The tendency of group psychograms is to wipe out individual differences. Some of the architects' personality styles may be better reflected than others, but the less typical and certainly the more marginal cases would disappear from sight, thus giving too much credence to the concept of a typical Rorschach profile of creativity. An idiographic analysis appeared to be warranted.

Decreases in Psychic Energy

A case by case inspection of individual protocols immediately brought into full relief the dramatic decreases in psychic energy that the nonsignificant R, emerging from a *t*-test analysis, had obscured. As Table 5.5 shows, relative to their 1959 production, 14 (61%) of the 23 architects (the losers) had diminished the number of responses by an average 42.5% (losing between 15.5% and 68%). Ten of these subjects decreased their production by more than 44%. Nine (39%) of the subjects (the gainers) increased their R productivity by an average of 21.8% (gaining from 10% to 56%, excluding one subject who tripled the number of responses given in 1959). A *t*-test comparison of the 1959 data revealed significant differences again only in number of R (20 vs. 38.6) with the two groups changing places in terms of original production (42 vs. 27, $p < .01$).

There were no significant differences between them on W, W%, and W+ responses. The Mayman F was 4.95 in both groups. The poor form responses (Mayman's Fa + Fs + F–%) were 16.0% for the losers and 11.7% for the gainers (not significant).

In short, the decrease in Rorschach productivity was radical in a group of 14 (61%) subjects, while gains for the remaining 9 (39%) ranged from modest to extreme. The loss of R naturally entailed decreases in number of other determinants and these varied from individual to individual in idiosyncratic ways.

A further idiographic analysis indicated that the 1984 psychogram had eliminated other important individual differences. Looking back at the 1959 data it was clear that some of the profiles were already atypical

TABLE 5.5   **1983 Rorschachs of Architects Who Gained or Lost Rorschach Responses (*N* = 23)**

Variable	Decrease of R *n = 14*		Stable or Gain of R *n = 9*		
	Mean	*SD*	Mean	*SD*	*t*
R	20.00	6.09	38.66	20.40	3.017**
W	11.08	4.62	15.67	9.41	1.478
W%	53.42	18.84	41.67	17.45	−1.459
(W++Wo+Ww+)%	61.33	19.16	69.56	20.62	0.343
M	2.88	2.16	4.78	4.11	1.374
F (Mayman)	4.95	0.70	4.95	0.90	0.000
(Fa+Fs+F−)%	16.08	12.53	11.77	12.89	0.771
R in 1958	42.08	12.80	27.11	7.80	−3.094**
(F Mayman)	5.11	0.42	5.24	0.43	0.692

* $p < .05.$ ** $p < .01.$ $df = 22$
T-test analysis

at that time, but all of the subjects had achieved a reasonable equilibrium (some with the help of therapy). There were no depleted Rorschachs in 1959 although some were highly idiosyncratic. Of the four cases who showed depletion in 1984, only one gave an atypical Rorschach in 1959, and he was now the most intact of the four. His current Rorschach was a marked exaggeration of the original structure.

The conclusions and results that emerged from the idiographic analysis of the Rorschach were:

1. Psychic energy (R) had decreased radically in 61% of the group and increased in 39%.
2. There were at least two types of expressive styles (low and high F) unrelated to creative excellence.
3. Responses of creative strength (Cr 4 and 5) had decreased and were virtually absent in Rorschachs where M was seriously reduced (between 0 and 2).
4. The four subjects who showed depleted Rorschach profiles were no longer engaged in "building."
5. Three subjects gave zero M responses in 1984 whereas no one gave zero M in 1959.
6. Most (*n* = 17; 83%) of the 23 subjects were demonstrating effective use of their emotional, intellectual and creative energies within the limits available to them.

7. Four (17.4%) of the group had virtually collapsed psychologically. At best they showed a depletion of energy, at worst there was a disintegrative process at work. In one case, the loss could be explained by a terminal case of cancer.

The relative normality of the group psychogram misrepresented some individual cases, but was accurate to the extent that 19 of 23 (83%) of the architects were functioning adequately and effectively. That each was doing so in his own idiosyncratic way could not be inferred from the group psychogram either in 1959 or in 1984.

It is tempting to interpret the decrease in R in 61% of the group as a function of aging. However, 39% of the architects increased their production. Moreover, only one of the Rorschach determinants (Fm) was correlated (negatively) with age. The changes were, therefore, a function of individual differences. It is possible to infer that some individuals responded to aging with a reduction of vital energy while others compensated more effectively or aged more slowly. The four architects who produced depleted Rorschachs were all engaged in tangential enterprises (ages 70 to 76). The architect dying of cancer was still doing consulting work in his office. In fact all four maintained offices and were hopeful of future projects. Only one of the four gave an atypical Rorschach in 1959, and it was virtually unchanged in 1984.

Idiosyncratic Patterns the Creative Norm

Typical personality profiles have been found for most professions (Holland, 1985; Roe, 1956), and the current Rorschach psychogram does, in effect, present a typical group creativity profile. Even at the mean age of 73, the architects achieved a higher than average R, M, M: Sum C, W, F+, Sum c to Sum C, adequate R(8–10%), and high evidence of primary process. But it is evident that not all the architects either in 1959 or in 1984 produced typical records. Dudek and Hall (1984) showed that MacKinnon's sample of 40 Group I architects could be divided into four distinct psychogram groups, only two of which gave the typically dilated group creativity profile.

The theoretical typical creativity profile (whether Rorschach or any other test) may be seen as an academic exercise when the real-world, eminent creative person is the object of study (at whatever age). Each creative person will necessarily project an idiosyncratic structure by which a unique created product is expected to be forged. Thus, there can be no ideal or typical creativity profile. This is to say that signs of creativity alone predict little about the nature of real-life creativity. It is obvious that not all creative persons demonstrate richness of psychic apparatus, prodigious fluency, or flexible creative flow. Yet they achieve eminence by creating "monuments of splendor" with whatever talents are available.

MacKinnon's creative architects earned their eminent status by virtue of work that was highly valued by their peers. Within a creator's lifetime, this is the only criterion of creative excellence. The real challenge to an understanding of creativity comes when the psychic structure of the genuine creator, as revealed by the Rorschach, or any other instrument, does not reflect the expected test indices of creativity. How the individual's unique idiosyncratic perception transcends the expected profile may tell us more about the riddle of creativity than the presence of expected creativity indices. The analysis of individual cases revealed that some psychograms reflected intricate, internal psychic systems through which what was different, what was unique, and what was distorted could be exploited and put to creative use. Supports from the outside were sometimes brought in to compensate for psychic narrowness or deviation. Some individuals chose to cash in on difference, to propose their uniqueness as the new way of perceiving, creating, and sometimes achieving a result that the world was ready to label as outstanding. None of this could be predicted before looking at test results, and it can only be rationalized later.

Loss in Rorschach Productivity

A radical decrease in R cannot be taken lightly. R decreases significantly when persons are physically very ill, when they become psychotic, are given ECT, become seriously depressed, are placed on massive doses of drug therapy, or suffer from cerebral organic disease. One of the first changes with psychological improvement or physical recovery is a significant increase in R.

Since all but one of the architects in the present group were in good health, and except for the subject dying of cancer, none saw themselves as depressed, the decreased R in 61% of the group may be seen as a function of the physiological changes that accompany aging. It is not at all clear whether such reduction in productivity or responsiveness is an attempt by the organism to decrease stress in a failing biological system or simply a decrease in motivation and particularly in energy (much as one sees in aging animals who spend their days sleeping although they become frisky during their daily jaunts outside, as if they had been storing up energy to make the things that really count more vital).

Certainly aging persons report a significant slowing down process, and certainly they are capable of great effort and concentration on those occasions where the motivation to produce is at peak level. One architect in the group who gained responses increased his R from 32 to 40 in 1983 at age 79. At the age of 84, when he was semiretired, he was able to give an amazing 101 responses when he was retested in his office by the author. He is one of the most eminent and successful architects in America today. He was the most intellectually gifted of McKinnon's Group I architects, but not the most original. However, at age 84, he was still breaking ground and creating controversy on the architectural scene.

The unusual sprint of energy is not an unusual phenomenon either in humans or in animals. What is unusual is the ability to maintain the level in a day-to-day self-monitored fashion at any age, but particularly at an advanced age. Deeply depressed patients regain their original level of productivity when they get well. Perceptual motor control, short-term memory, unusual stamina, speed, do not return to aged persons even under the most highly motivating conditions, although imaginative and productive flights of fantasy are always possible. However, the capacity to perform efficiently and to achieve outstanding creative products in art, or in architecture, never seems to disappear, because it does not depend on peak physical, emotional, or intellectual levels. (Naturally, in some areas, e.g. sports, this may have to be qualified). In fact, Perlmutter (1988) proposes that "in later life there may be advanced and presumably valuable forms of thinking" (also in Birren & Bengston, 1988, p. 270). Our architects reported they could function effectively despite physical or emotional setbacks. The architect dying of cancer was still working, albeit slowly. It requires only sufficiently adequate levels of available drive, imagination, and lucid thinking. And it requires intense concentration. The availability of all of these was evident in most of the IPAR Group I architects, and is evident in many other aged populations until a very late age (certainly until age 74).

In professional persons it seems evident that *selective optimization* (Baltes & Baltes, 1980) would characterize their work strategies as they age. Where innovative skills falter, a lifetime of experience, acquired "tricks of the trade," and "wisdom" pitch in to bridge the gap that diminishing energy and failing memory has created. To quote one famous septuagenarian, age 77: "With experience, an intuitive wisdom sets in and I know at a glance what the correct solution should be. Sometimes it takes weeks to work the details out." Another, age 73, stated, "I get there a lot faster than my young colleagues because I've been there before. I see the mistakes a lot faster. That's a skill that's always available to me."

In short, the unpredictable connection between old information and new input does not depend on availability of maximum energy or on peak physical condition. Creativity depends on an innovative mind, learned skills, a reflexive repugnance to the banal, an automatic search for the novel, and on the occasional good moment when things long worked on fall into place to allow the unusual creative breakthrough. The most active architects of the present group, most over 70 years old, were still successfully competing in capacities as chief designers and as sought-after consultants. At age 81, one world-famous architect was sitting down to revise a few details in a design for a megastructure for which he was negotiating a binding contract. It would take his firm approximately 10 years to construct it. To quote Baltes and Willis (1982), *"In our view, the level of maximum potential is inherently an unknown or dialectic quantity"* [italics added] (p. 382). As Simonton's (1984, 1988) historiometric research has indicated, products of exceptional excellence have the same chance of emerging in the creator's old age as at any age. More essential than a clear mind, a rich imagination, a broad psychic apparatus, is the "will to form," the passion to "make it new," the lifelong search for the perfect form of forms—Platonic, Dionysian, or whatever the individual temperament considers to be its truest expression of the white fire that takes form rather than flame.

REFERENCES

Ames, L. B., Metruax, R. W., Rodel, J. L., & Walker, R. M. (1973). *Rorschach responses in old age.* New York: Brunner/Mazel.

Anderson, I., & Munroe, R. (1948). Personality factors involved in student concentration on creative painting and commercial art. *Rorschach Research Exchange, 12,* 141–154.

Baltes, P. B., & Baltes, M. M. (1980). Plasticity and variability in psychological aging: Methodological and theoretical issues. In G. Gurski (Ed.), *Determining the effects of aging in the central nervous system* (pp. 41–66). Berlin: Schering.

Baltes, P. B., & Willis, S. L. (1982). Plasticity and enhancement of intellectual functioning in old age: Penn State's Adult Development and Enrichment Project (ADEPT). In F. I. M. Craik & S. E. Trehub (Eds.), *Aging and cognitive processes* (pp. 353–389). New York: Plenum.

Barron, F. (1972). *Artists in the making.* New York: Seminar.

Birren, J. E., & Bengston, V. (Eds). (1988). *Emergent theories of aging.* New York: Springer.

Birren, J. E., & Schaie, K. W. (Eds.) (1985). *Handbook of the psychology of aging* (2nd ed.). New York: Van Nostrand.

Birren, J. E., & Schaie, K. W. (Eds.) (1990). *Handbook of the psychology of aging* (3rd ed.). San Diego: Academic Press.

Caspi, A., & Bem, D. (1988). Moving away from the world: Life-course patterns of shy children. *Developmental Psychology, 23,* 824–831.

Cerella, J. (1985). Information processing rates in the elderly. *Psychological Bulletin, 98,* 67–83.

Cerella, J. (1990). Aging and information processing rate. In J. E. Birren & K. W. Schaie (Eds.), *Handbook of the psychology of aging* (3rd ed., pp. 201–221). New York: Academic.

Charness, N. (1988). The role of theories of cognitive aging: Comment on Salthouse. *Psychology and Aging, 3,* 17–21.

Costa, P. T., & McCrae, R. R. (1980). Still stable after all these years: Personality as a key to some issues in adulthood and old age. In P. B. Baltes & O. G. Brim (Eds.), *Life span development and behavior* (Vol. 3, pp. 65–102). New York: Academic.

Craik, F. I. M., & Byrd, M. (1982). Aging and cognitive deficits: The role of attentional resources. In F. I. M. Craik & S. E. Trehub (Eds.), *Aging and cognitive processes* (pp. 191–211). New York: Plenum.

Dannefer, D. (1988). What is in a name? An account of the neglect of variability in the study of aging. In J. E. Birren & V. L. Bengston (Eds.), *Emergent theories of aging* (pp. 356–384). New York: Springer.

Dudek, S. Z. (1968a). Regression and creativity. *Journal of Nervous and Mental Disease, 147,* 535–546.

Dudek, S. Z. (1968b). M: An active energy system—correlating Rorschach M with ease of creative expressing. *Journal of Projective Techniques and Personality Assessment, 32,* 453–461.

Dudek, S. Z. (1971). Portrait of the artist as Rorschach reader. *Psychology Today, 4,* 78-94.

Dudek, S. Z. (1984). The architect as a person: A Rorschach image. *Journal of Personality Assessment, 48,* 6, 597–605.

Dudek, S. Z., Berneche, R., Bérubé, H., & Royer, S. (1991). Personality determinants of commitment to the profession of art. *Creativity Research Journal, 4,* 367–389.

Dudek, S. Z., & Bouhadana, G. (1982). Primary process in creative persons. *Journal of Personality Assessment, 46,* 239–247.

Dudek, S. Z., & Hall, W. B. (1984). Some test correlates of high level of creativity in architects. *Journal of Personality Assessment, 46,* 4, 351–359.

Dudek, S. Z., & Hall, W. B. (1991). Personality consistency: Eminent architects twenty-five years later. *Creativity Research Journal, 4,* 213–231.

Dudek, S. Z., & Kolivakis, T. (1983). Stability of intellect and personality in chronic schizophrenia. *Canadian Journal of Psychiatry, 28,* 2–7.

Dudek, S. Z., & Verreault, R. (1989). The creative thinking and ego functioning of children. *Creativity Research Journal, 2,* 64–86.

Exner, J. (1978). *The Rorschach: A comprehensive system.* (Vol. 1). New York: Wiley.

Falduto, L. L., & Baron, A. (1986). Age-related effects of practice and task complexity on card sorting. *Journal of Gerontology, 41,* 659–661.

Gall, M. D. (1970). An investigation of verbal style in creative and noncreative groups. Dissertation submitted in partial requirement for the PhD, University of California, Berkeley.

Getzels, T. W., & Csikszentmihalyi, M. (1976). *The creative vision: A longitudinal study of problem finding in art.* New York: Wiley.

Goldstein, K. (1963). *The organism.* New York: American.

Gough, H., & Heilbrun, G. (1983). *Manual for the Adjective Check List.* Palo Alto, CA: Consulting Psychologists.

Greenacre, P. (1971). The childhood of the artist. In P. Greenacre (Ed.), *Emotional growth* (Vol. 2). New York: International University Press.

Gutmann, D. L. (1964). An exploration of ego configurations in middle and later life. In B. L. Neugarten & Associates (Eds.), *Personality in middle and late life.* New York: Atherton.

Haan, N. (1981). Adolescents and young adults as producers of their own development. In R. M. Lerner (Ed.), *Individuals as producers of their own development.* New York: Academic.

Hersch, C. (1962). The cognitive functioning of the creative person: A developmental analysis. *Journal of Projective Techniques, 26,* 193–200.

Hertzog, C., & Schaie, K. W. (1986). Stability of adult intelligence: I. Analysis of longitudinal covariance structures. *Psychology and Aging, 1,* 159–171.

Holland, J. L. (1985). *Making vocational choices: A theory of vocational personalities and work environments,* (2nd ed.). Englewood Cliffs, NJ: Prentice Hall.

Humphreys, L. (1962). The organization of human abilities. *American Psychologist, 17,* 475–483.

Klopfer, B., Meyer, B., Brawer, F. B., & Klopfer, W. G. (1970). *Developments in the Rorschach technique* (Vol. 3). New York: Harcourt, Brace, Jovanovich.

Klopfer, B., Ainsworth, M. D., Klopfer, W. G., & Holt, R. R. (1956). *Developments in the Rorschach technique* (Vol. 2). Tarrytown, NY: World.

MacKinnon, D. W. (1962). The nature and nurture of creative talent. *American Psychologist, 17,* 484–495.

MacKinnon, D. W. (1963). Creativity and images of the self. In R. W. White (Ed.), *The study of lives* (pp. 250–278). New York: Prentice Hall.

MacKinnon, D. W. (1964). The creativity of architects. In C. W. Taylor (Ed.), *Widening horizons in creativity* (pp. 359–378). New York: Wiley.

MacKinnon, D. W. (1965). Personality and the realization of creative potential. *American Psychologist, 20,* 273-281.

Martindale, C., & Daily, A. (1996). Creativity, primary process cognition, and personality. *Personality and Individual Differences, 20,* 409–414.

Mayman, M. (1962). *Rorschach form level manual.* Topeka, KS: Menninger Foundation.

McDowd, J. M., & Craik, F. I. M. (1988). Effects of aging and task difficulty in divided attention performance. *Journal of Experimental Psychology: Human Perception and Performance, 14,* 267–280.

McDowd, J. M., & Birren, J. E. (1990). Aging and attentional processes. In J. E. Birren & K. W. Schaie (Eds.), *Handbook of the psychology of aging* (3rd ed.). San Diego: Academic.

Moss, H. A., & Suddman, E. J. (1980). Continuity and change in personality development. In O. G. Brim & J. Kagan (Eds.), *Continuity and change in personality development.* Cambridge, MA: Harvard University Press.

Myden, W. (1959). Interpretation and evaluation of certain personality characteristics involved in creative production. *Perceptual and Motor Skills, 9,* 139–158.

Neugarten, B. L. (1964). *Personality in middle and later life.* New York: Atherton.

Neugarten, B. L. (1977). Personality and aging. In J. E. Birren & K. W. Schaie (Eds.), *Handbook of the psychology of aging.* San Diego: Academic.

Perlmutter, M. (1988). Cognitive potential throughout life. In J. E. Birren & V. L. Bengston (Eds.), *Emergent theories of aging.* New York: Springer.

Piotrowski, Z. A. (1965). *Perceptanalysis.* Philadelphia: Ex Libris.

Prados, M. (1944). Rorschach studies of artists—painters. *Rorschach Research Exchange, 8,* 178–183.

Prinz, P. N., Dustman, R. E., & Emmerson, R. (1990). Electrophysiology and aging. In J. E. Birren & K. W. Schaie (Eds.), *Handbook of the psychology of aging* (3rd ed., pp. 135–149). New York: Academic.

Roe, A. (1956). *The psychology of occupations.* New York: Wiley.

Rorschach, H. (1951). *Psychodiagnostics* (4th ed). New York: Grune & Stratton.

Salthouse, T. A. (1985). *Theory of cognitive aging.* Amsterdam: North Holland.

Salthouse, T. A. (1988). Initiating the formalization of theories of cognitive aging. *Psychology and Aging, 3,* 3–16.

Salthouse, T. A. (1990). Cognitive competence and expertise in aging. In J. E. Birren & K. W. Schaie (Eds.), *Handbook of the psychology of aging* (3rd ed., pp. 311–319). San Diego: Academic.

Schaie, K. W., & Parham, I. A. (1976). Stability of adult personality traits: Fact or fable? *Journal of Personality and Social Psychology, 34,* 146–158.

Schaie, K. W., & Willis, S. L. (1986). *Adult development and aging* (2nd ed.). Boston: Little Brown.

Schooler, C. (1987). Cognitive effects of complex environments. In C. Schooler & K. W. Schaie (Eds.), *Cognitive functioning and social structure over the life course.* Norwood, NJ: Ablex.

Schooler, C., & Schaie, K. W. (Eds.). (1987). *Cognitive functioning and social structure over the life course.* Norwood, NJ: Ablex.

Schuerger, J. M., Tait, E., & Tavernelli, M. (1982). Temporal stability of personality by questionnaire. *Journal of Personality and Social Psychology, 43,* 176–182.

Siegler, I. C., George, L. K., & Okun, M. A. (1979). Cross-sequential analysis of adult personality. *Developmental Psychology, 15,* 350–351.

Simonton, D. K. (1984). *Genius, creativity and leadership.* Cambridge, MA: Harvard University Press.

Simonton, D. K. (1988). *Scientific genius.* New York: Cambridge University Press.

Stankov, L. (1988). Aging, attention and intelligence. *Psychology of Aging, 3,* 59–74.

Taylor, I. A. (1975). *Perspectives on creativity.* New York: Aldine.

Terman, L. M. (1956). *Concept Mastery Test, Form T: Manual.* New York: Psychological Corp.

Woodruff, D. S. (1985). Arousal, sleep and aging. In J. E. Birren & K. W. Schaie (Eds.), *Handbook of the psychology of aging* (2nd ed.). New York: Van Nostrand.

Appendix

The appendix contains the four scales that were developed to evaluate the extent to which the architects were still functioning effectively on the five categories considered essential for continuing professional success. Both conceptual and empirical considerations entered into their construction.

INDICES OF COGNITIVE EFFICIENCY

1) The single most crucial index is evidence of clear, lucid thinking which is reflected in adequate form level on all Rorschach responses. Mayman's (1962) form level rating scale was the main instrument. 2) The second important index was the Klopfer F+%. Evidence of F–, Fa, and Fs were negative signs. 3) Adequate presence of W+, the ability for organization and synthesis, is essential.

CREATIVITY INDICES

The typical creative profile is expected to show: 1) a large number of responses *(R)* to reflect evidence of psychic energy and associational fluency; 2) a large number of human movement responses *(M)*; 3) a capacity to give nuanced, complex responses, identified by the multiple determinant score (MD); 4) presence of color with *CF* exceeding *FC* as evidence of spontaneous, free, or impulsive affect; 5) preferably a dilated experience balance, although this is not essential *(high M high Sum C)*; 6) highly developed sensitivity reflected in by differentiated shading *(Fc, Fk, FK)*; 7) good synthetic ability *(W+* or combinatory D+); 8) absence of constrictive control, i.e. *low F%*; 9) evidence of responses showing creative strength (Mayman's Cr4 or 5); 10) availability of libidinal and aggressive drive with libidinal predominating (Holt's primary process, level 1); 11) some *Fm* responses reflecting unresolved tension; 12) broad content range; 13) a creative Rorschach should not give evidence of stereotypy (A% < 50); and 14) there should be no simple perseveration. We would like to stress this is what the *ideal* profile would be expected to show.

INDICES FOR ASSESSING DRIVE

1) The single most important index was sufficient evidence of good form W. The presence of weak, cheap or amorphous W are considered to be contraindicative of a desire for complicated achievement. The Mayman 7 point weighted scale was applied to the evaluation of the form quality of W. A minimum of 8W is expected in a short record, while 40% is expected in a longer one. Drive, however, cannot be solely restricted to an intellectual desire for complicated achievement. 2) This must be supported by availability of emotional resources (primary process content both libidinal and aggressive); 3) Some essential tension (Fm) is desirable; 4) Some need to interact with others and to enjoy the challenge. Hence color responses with CF greater than FC should be evident as well as an R(8–10%) of 40% or more.

INDICES OF SOCIAL SKILLS

1) The primary index is presence of *constructive* M in numbers larger than *neutral* or *aggressive* M. 2) Presence of positive affect, and particularly of constructive FC to indicate appropriate affect. 3) Shading to indicate sensitivity and ability to nuance emotional responses. The ratio of shading to color should be a minimum of one to one although artists normally give more shading. 4) Presence of C is contraindicative unless shading and M occur in large numbers. 5) Sufficient P (To see the obvious, 5P or more is expected).

Some of the signs in the different scales overlap as might be expected. No talents or skills exist in isolation. Interdependence is expected. Not all the signs need to be present to indicate that a skill or ability is in evidence but one would expect the important signs to be present. For example, it is unlikely that anyone will show all of the 14 signs comprising the creativity scale. The most important signs are *M, MD,* CF & FC, high shading, some Cr4 or 5, W+, and primary process. However, heterogeneity of signs gives a better chance for the idiosyncratic display of talent.

CHAPTER SIX

Ego Identity and Trajectories of Productivity in Women with Creative Potential

Ravenna Helson

" **C** reativity, identity formation, and career choice come together in the late teens or early twenties for most people," writes Albert (1990, p. 13), but he is thinking particularly of young men and careers in math and science. Open to their complexity and disinclined to follow conventional paths, many young people with creative potential have difficulty in consolidating an identity. A young woman has a particular problem. She attempts to build or sustain an image of herself as a professional (Arnold, 1993) or artist (Barron, 1972). Her problems in identity may have no good solution, and identity work may extend well beyond the college years (Helson, 1990).

This chapter examines how ego identity in potentially creative college women is related to the area and timing of their productivity in later life. The main subjects are 30 women, who as seniors at a West Coast women's college in the late 1950s, were nominated by faculty as outstanding in creative potential and have continued as participants in a longitudinal study (Helson, 1967, 1985, 1987). Some 30 years since the study began, the nominees have been classified according to their trajectory of productivity: that is, as never productive in terms of creative achievement, productive in both early and middle adulthood, productive primarily in young adulthood, or productive beginning in middle adulthood. They have also been classified as to whether they worked in the arts or other fields.

Identity will be examined in terms of ego identity status, as conceptualized by Marcia (1966) on the basis of formulations of Erikson (1950). Marcia developed an interview to assess four adolescent identity statuses: achieved, in moratorium, foreclosed, and diffuse. Classification was based on the patterning of active searching and commitment shown by late adolescents, especially in the areas of occupation and values. The youth with an *achieved* identity had searched actively and then made commitments, whereas the youth in *moratorium* were actively searching without having made a commitment, the *foreclosed* youth had accepted an identity from parents without an active search, and the *diffuse* adolescent was neither searching nor committed.

Marcia later (1980) described ego identity as a relatively enduring aspect of a self-system. His interview was somewhat awkward for use with adults, but Mallory (1984, 1989) developed a set of ego identity prototypes based on the California Adult Q Deck (Block, 1978). This Q deck consists of 100 items that raters sort on a 9-point scale according to a fixed normal distribution. Mallory asked Marcia and other researchers who had worked with his concepts of ego identity to use the Q sort to describe their idea of the prototypical person whose identity was achieved, in moratorium, foreclosed, or diffuse. Table 6.1 shows the items that Mallory's judges placed highest and lowest to describe prototypical women who had achieved an identity or were in moratorium. Only these two dimensions of ego identity are used in the present study, because of the high negative correlations between diffuse and achieved identity and between foreclosed identity and identity status in moratorium.

It is somewhat unusual to translate the ego identity statuses, usually conceptualized in terms of adolescent behavioral processes, into personality characteristics. However, there are a number of advantages. The same measures can be used for people at different stages of life, and whereas Marcia thought in terms of categories that tended to be mutually exclusive, we can now use in our hypotheses the ideas of dimensions and patterns of scores on the dimensions.

As a basis for formulating hypotheses about the relation of identity to career trajectory, I turned to Simonton's (1984) presentation and elaboration of Beard's (1874) theory about aspects of creativity and how they affect productivity over the life span. Simonton exposited Beard's theory as follows: Creativity is a function of enthusiasm and experience. Enthusiasm tends to peak early in life, but experience gradually increases, and the best equilibrium is attained at about ages 38–40. Simonton suggested that fields vary in the optimum relation between enthusiasm and experience.

TABLE 6.1   Q-items Rated Most and Least Salient
in Two Identity Status Prototypes

Most Salient	Least Salient
Identity Achievement	
Values own independence	Self-defeating
Clear, consistent personality	Brittle ego-defense system
Ethically consistent behavior	Reluctant to act
Warm, compassionate	Withdraws from frustration
Productive	Lacks personal meaning
Insight into own behavior	Avoids close relationships
Identity Moratorium	
Values own independence	Emotionally blind
Philosophically concerned	Represses conflict
Basically anxious	Satisfied with self
Rebellious, nonconforming	Calm, relaxed in manner
Introspective	Submissive
Verbally fluent	Does not vary roles
	Avoids close relationships

Note. From "Longitudinal analysis of ego-identity status," by M. E. Mallory. In *Dissertation Abstracts International, 44,* 3955-B, p. 94. Adapted by permission.

Experience and enthusiasm are not quite the right words for what the achieved and moratorium dimensions represent, and we are more concerned with individual differences in patterns of creative productivity than with the general temporal relations stated above. Nevertheless, I have found it useful to think of affective and ordering principles, both important to creative achievement, that are differentially expressed over time and in different areas of work.

Let us think of the achieved dimension in terms of self-chosen integration and the moratorium dimension in terms of emotionally involved search. Self-chosen integration (achieved dimension) would seem to be necessary for the forcefulness and perseverance of the creative achiever; openness to new possibilities, rebelliousness, and emotionality (moratorium dimension) are often attributed to the creative personality. My first hypothesis is that creative nominees who were productive at age 52 (whether always or late) will have had identities in late adolescence that incorporated *both* self-chosen integration and emotionally involved search. This kind of identity would not be readily envisaged with the use of Marcia's categories of ego identity, as the hypothesis seems to assert that productive creative people are both committed to and not committed to—but rather searching for—an identity. From the point of view of creativity research, the creative personality is sometimes described in terms of an integration of opposite tendencies (e.g., MacKinnon, 1962). The Q-sort prototype measures of identity make it easy to test this conception.

One might extract from the Beard-Simonton formulation the suggestion that patterns of emotionally involved search and integration would differ in individuals with different career trajectories. In addition, work on women's career development in the Mills Study (Helson, 1987; Helson, Elliott, & Leigh, 1989; Helson, Mitchell, & Moane, 1984; Wink, 1992) supports the idea that the relative strength of integration and motivated search at age 21 may predict the trajectory of productivity. I expect the nominees who were productive only in young adulthood to consist preponderantly of women who postponed, avoided, or mitigated the conventional women's role through undertaking careers, but found it difficult to make and sustain commitments in either work or relationships. They would tend to be high on moratorium identity but low on achieved identity. Nominees who became productive only in middle adulthood I expect to consist preponderantly of women with creative interests who began their adult lives as full-time mothers and homemakers, as was customary in their cohort. They would be high scorers on achieved identity, moderate on moratorium identity. The women who were nominated for creative potential but never productive in careers may have included a number who were shy or conflicted introverts. Their caution, superficial conventionality, and stress avoidance would lead them to score particularly low on the moratorium dimension.

The characteristics of self-chosen integration and emotionally involved search can be used to predict not only the trajectory but also the area of creative productivity. Artists have been described as more unconventional and as expressing more negative affect than others (Barron, 1965; Drevdahl & Cattell, 1958; Raskin, 1936; Sheldon, 1994) and can use their conflicts to more advantage in their work (Bush, 1969; Suler, 1980). Thus, a reasonable hypothesis is that among nominees who will be productive in careers, those in whom emotional search is pronounced will be more likely to go into art fields, whereas nominees in whom integration is pronounced will be more likely to go into other fields.

The hypotheses that have been advanced assume some consistency of creative personality, for which there is considerable evidence (Albert, 1975; Cox, 1926; Dudek & Hall, 1991; Helson, Roberts, & Agronick, 1995). To test the assumption of consistency, the relationships obtained in observer Q-sort data at age 21 will be sought again in data from file-rater Q sorts, based on the abundant questionnaire material available at age 43.

However, if the Q-sort measures at age 43 are sensitive to processes of identity revision, there should be change along with consistency. Women whose creative productivity has ended should decline over time in measures of emotionally involved search, as they find niches that do not require creative effort. Those whose productivity is just beginning may show an increased salience of emotionally involved search, as they change from being primarily homemakers to engaging in creative careers. Such findings would be consistent with literature that creative patterns often change in midlife (Jaques, 1965) and that for women in particular identity is an issue in midlife as well as in late adolescence (Helson & McCabe, 1994; Hornstein, 1986).

This chapter seeks to improve our understanding of the implications of identity patterns for women's lifestyles and for their problems in actualizing creative potential. The patterns of productivity described were related to demographic descriptors of life path and to the women's own accounts of their most difficult and formative experiences since college.

METHODS

SAMPLES AND DESIGN

The original sample consisted of 141 seniors at a women's college on the West Coast, 32 of whom were nominated by faculty members for their creative potential. A subsample of creative nominees and comparison women, matched with the nominees on the basis of verbal aptitude and major field, came in groups of 12 to a 1-day assessment at the Institute of Personality Assessment and Research (IPAR). Ten women, including two creative nominees who had been missed before and three new comparison subjects, were assessed several years after leaving college. The total N was 56. Subsequent waves of investigation of all previous participants were conducted by mail when the women were average age 43 and age 52. Of the 32 creative nominees, personality data are available from 30 at ages 43 and 52. Of the 26 comparison women, personality data are available from 22 at ages 43 and 52.

Criteria of Creative Potential

Faculty members nominated members of the senior class whom they regarded as high in potential for creative contributions in the arts, sciences, or humanities, whether or not it seemed likely that they would actualize that potential. The school had an arts faculty that was particularly distinguished. Women were nominated for their work in the fields of visual art, music, dance, drama, writing, biology, history/government, mathematics, and psychology.

Names of all creative nominees and comparison women who had participated in the assessment study were later sent to the faculty to be rated on originality and commitment to sustained endeavor. Two of the comparison women who received high ratings on originality are now included among the creative nominees.

Productivity Trajectories

In subsequent work, the entire sample of women were classified as to whether they had launched an upwardly mobile career by age 28 (Helson, Mitchell, & Moane, 1984). At age 43 they were rated on status level of work (Helson, Elliott, & Leigh, 1989), that is, on the extent to which their work reflected characteristics such as advanced training, autonomy, opportunity for creative expression, recognition, and responsibility. Status level of work was rated again at age 52. For the purposes of this chapter, the career and status level measures were used to classify the women into one of four categories: women considered "never productive" ($n = 10$) had not launched a career by age 28 nor was their work ever rated above average on status level; women "productive early" ($n = 7$) had launched a career by age 28 but were on the decline by age 43. Women "productive late" ($n = 5$) had not launched a career by age 28 but were rated above average in status level usually by age 43 and always by age 52; and women "productive always" ($n = 10$) had launched careers by age 28 and were rated above average in status level at both ages 43 and 52.

THE CALIFORNIA Q SET AND PROTOTYPES OF EGO IDENTITY STATUS

The California Q set (Block, 1978) consists of 100 items that the rater places on a 9-point scale according to a forced normal distribution to describe an individual or the prototypical exemplar of a construct. As explained in the introduction, prototypes of the four ego identity statuses (achieved, foreclosed, in moratorium, and diffuse) were constructed by asking a group of experts to describe the prototypical exemplar of each construct in terms of the Q sort (Mallory, 1984).

At age 21, the women were Q sorted by psychologists who observed them in group discussions or charades and interacted with them at meals or in a social hour. At age 43, the women were Q sorted by file raters on the basis of abundant questionnaire data, including responses to many open-ended questions about various aspects of their life. The two Q sorts were provided by different research teams, without knowledge of which women had been nominated for creative potential. Both sets of Q sorts show adequate reliability (Helson, 1967; Wink, 1991).

At each age, each woman's Q sort was correlated with the four ego identity prototypes, and correlations were used as scores on each ego identity dimension. Although the Q sorts were based on different kinds of data at the two ages, stability coefficients for the assessed women ranged from .43 (achieved) to .57 (moratorium) over this 22-year period (Hart, 1990). Scores on achieved and diffuse identity were highly intercorrelated at both ages 21 and 43 (−.96 and −.95, respectively), and so were scores on the foreclosed and moratorium dimensions (−.89 and −.91, respectively). Therefore, we will make use of scores only on the achieved and moratorium dimensions. Low scores on the achieved dimension may be regarded as diffuse, and low scores on the moratorium dimension as foreclosed. These two dimensions showed an intercorrelation of .32, $p < .05$, in the age 21 data and an insignificant correlation of .15 in the age 43 data. A low positive correlation would be expected because a person with a diffuse self-system is unlikely to engage in sustained search.

No Q-sort data, and thus no measures of ego identity, are available for the age 52 time of testing.

MEASURES OF LIFE DATA

Demographic Data

The women provided demographic information at each time of testing. At age 43 they filled out work histories from which various measures have been derived. Besides status level of work, previously described, this study uses a rating of duration of participation in the labor force, stated as time after entry (Helson et al., 1989).

Life Plans and Accounts of Difficult Times

At age 21 the women were asked to describe their future lives, assuming that they could have just what they wanted in terms of marriage and other interests. Some of their responses will be quoted to illustrate identity processes among the creative nominees as college seniors in 1958 or 1960.

At age 52 the women were asked to describe their most difficult time since college, the one that had influenced their subsequent lives most. The themes of these accounts were reliably classified as involving Unhappy self, Bad partner, Search for independent identity or its sequelae (Abandonment and Putdowns at work), Unhappy self in bad relationships, or Overload (Helson, 1992).

OVERVIEW OF STUDY

Sketches about their future life written by several of the women when they were college seniors will introduce the members of the sample and illustrate how the identity constructs were reflected in their thought processes. Then scores on the achieved and moratorium dimensions of ego identity (based on observer Q sorts) for the creative nominees and comparison women at age 21 will be used to test hypotheses about the relation of ego identity to the women's subsequent trajectory of productivity (early, late, always, and never) and field of work. The next section will describe the life paths taken by women on each of the four productivity trajectories between ages 21 and 43. Then scores on the achieved and moratorium dimensions of ego identity at age 43 (based on file rater Q sorts) will be examined to test the hypothesis that the findings will be largely the same as at age 21 but with changes in the relative position of early and late groups on the moratorium dimension. Finally, the trajectories of productivity will be related to an examination of the women's difficult times in adulthood.

The small size of the sample of creative nominees requires some combining of groups and tolerance of slightly shifting numbers between ages 21 and 43. Nevertheless, the findings about these young women with creative potential over 30 years of adulthood are consistent and instructive.

IDENTITY AT AGE 21

EXAMPLES OF THOUGHTS ABOUT IDENTITY

To introduce both the women of the sample and the identity constructs, I will quote from sketches that the women wrote about their plans for the future when they were college seniors. Remember that they were writing in the late 1950s, a period when gender roles were quite differentiated. Young women weren't really expected to have serious plans of their own. They would marry, have children, and live within the life structure provided by the husband. Among the creative nominees and comparison subjects in the Mills sample, however, many women had concern for their individual interests. I will give sketches from three women who were all creatively productive over at least part of the period of the study.

Here, first, are the plans of a young woman who scored high on both the achieved and moratorium dimensions, especially the latter, so that we would expect her to have an idea about what she wanted to do along with characteristics such as openness to new lifestyles, intellectuality, anxiety, and concern for integration. Actually, she begins by saying that she wants a career as a musician (a clear expression of achieved identity), but she also wants a family life and is considering how to have both. This tension among possibilities is pronounced in moratorium identity. Her scores would lead to the prediction that she will be productive throughout the period of the study.

> I really see no way to reconcile the career I want as a violinist with a career in the home. I want music, I want a home and husband. The only possible way would be to limit my musical activities to the bounds of the community, and this isn't too happy a prospect. My home, if I ever have one, will be very different from that in which I've been raised. I hope there will be a deep bond of affection between my husband and me, and a feeling of security and stability for our children.

Below is the sketch of a young woman who was low on both the achieved and moratorium dimensions. She is so unsure and vacillating (diffuse) in what she expects or wants that she cannot make a plan. I would expect her to be productive early, if at all, but not to be able to sustain a career.

> If I marry, I must be allowed to continue my creative life. I honestly do not know at this time how far I would be willing to give in, should my husband's interests directly oppose this creative existence. His interests would probably come first, however, as creativity can be a flexible thing. Until very recently, I never wanted to have children. I like small children, but I didn't think I would like my own. . . . Recently I gained confidence, and I almost think I might like children.

Finally, following is the sketch of a young woman who scored high on both dimensions but higher on achieved identity. She has many creative interests and takes the task of describing her future life as an opportunity to fantasize a bit, but within the identity that she comfortably anticipates as wife and mother. In later life, however, one supposes that she might make a shift in identity and become productive in creative work.

Ideally, I would want to enter into the life of my husband, to go with him if he were an archeologist or diplomat, to help him if he were a writer or English professor. I would like to be active politically in my community because I think I owe this to my community, but I would want plenty of time to be with my family and freedom to attend university classes, go back to the piano, paint, and sculpt, and do some serious writing.

PREDICTING CAREER TRAJECTORIES AND FIELD FROM IDENTITY PATTERNS AT AGE 21

Figure 6.1 shows a plot of the scores of the 51 women assessed at age 21, supplemented with the 5 assessed at age 27, on the two Q-sort prototype dimensions of ego identity, achieved (vs. diffuse) and moratorium (vs. foreclosed). The women are identified as nominees who were productive always, early, late, or never, or as comparison subjects.

The first hypothesis about the relation of identity pattern to trajectory of productivity was that creative nominees productive at age 52 would be characterized at age 21 by both self-chosen integration (high on the achieved identity dimension) and openness to personal turmoil and new possibilities (high on the moratorium dimension). To test this hypothesis, let us consider the area of the graph above the approximate sample means of .30 on the achieved dimension and .20 on the moratorium dimension. Consistent with hypothesis, the scores in this area (high on both dimensions) include 13 of 14 nominees who by age 52 had shown late productivity or no productivity, 6 of the 10 women who were productive early or never, and 8 of 26 comparison women, chi square (2) = 15.08, $p < .001$ ($N = 56$).

To examine other hypotheses about trajectory of productivity among the subgroups of creative nominees, scores on the achieved and moratorium dimensions were classified as high, medium, or low ($n = 30$, because the 26 comparison women are now omitted). On the achieved dimension, the early group (unable to sustain their careers) was expected to score low and the late group high (their first career presumed to be the conventional one of homemaker). As one can derive from the information in Figure 6.1, this was the finding: the early group scored low, the late group high, and the other groups (always and never) were about equally divided, chi square (4) = 19.00, $p < .001$ ($n = 30$).

On the moratorium dimension the women never productive were expected to score lowest (because of their conventionality or stress-avoidance), the late group was expected to score above average (as specified in the first hypothesis), but moderately so (their first career

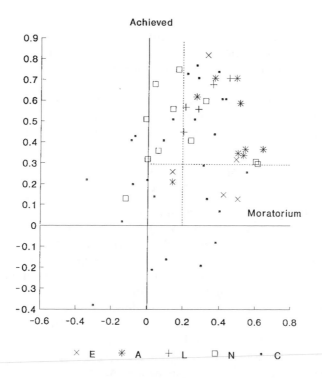

FIGURE 6.1 Scores of women assessed at age 21 on the achieved and moratorium dimensions. Dotted lines demarcate the high-high quadrant when the origin is at the sample means. Symbols identify creative nominees who were productive early (E), always (A), late (L), or never (N), and comparison women (C).

being assumed to be the conventional one of homemaker), and the early and always groups were expected to score high. As one can derive from the information in Figure 6.1, our predictions were borne out: chi square (4) = 15.70, $p < .01$ ($n = 30$).

It was hypothesized also that ego identity patterns at age 21 would predict an *area* of future creative productivity. In the interests of clarity this hypothesis was tested in 15 ever-productive women who had scores above the mean on both achieved and moratorium dimensions. Figure 6.1 shows a gap in the high-high quadrant (as defined above) between scores near the vertical and those towards the right horizontal. When the quadrant was divided diagonally into zones where achieved scores were higher than moratorium scores and vice versa, women whose future field of productivity would lie outside the arts were concentrated in the former zone (achieved scores higher) and women whose future field of productivity would be in artistic fields were concentrated in the latter (moratorium scores higher), chi square (1) = 7.82, $p < .01$ ($n = 15$).

In sum, creative nominees who would have different trajectories and areas of productivity over young and middle adulthood could be distinguished on the basis of their ego identity patterns as college seniors.

LIFE PATH BETWEEN COLLEGE AND AGE 43

The four groups of creative nominees differ strikingly in their life stories between graduation from college and the follow-up at age 43. The women who would never be productive (by the criteria of this study) all married and had children, and 7 of the 10 were in an intact marriage at age 43. Most of them did not do paid work in any sustained way until their children were in high school, and thus the group received the lowest score on duration of participation in the labor force of any of the four groups. At age 43 the women were generally dissatisfied with their career development, and we shall see that they sometimes held their spouses responsible.

In contrast, four of the seven women who were productive early never married and a fifth married but remained childless. Of the two who did have children, one was by standards of the cohort a "late" mother and the other divorced while her children were preschoolers. Of the six of these women for whom detailed work histories were available, all six received the maximum scores for length of participation in the labor force.

The five women who were productive late all married, had children, and were dedicated homemakers in the early years of the family. Three of them divorced by the follow-up at age 43. In length of participation in the labor force, the late group fell between the always and never groups, closer to the latter.

The 10 members of the group who were always productive show considerable diversity except for their commitment to work. They include two single women, one woman who married but did not have children, and seven mothers, four of whom were in intact marriages at age 43. The always group had worked almost as long as the early group.

These distinctive life paths reflect the expression and consequence of the differences in ego identity among the groups at age 21, made visible by the young adult pressures and subsequent opportunities available to this cohort.

IDENTITY PATTERNS AT AGE 43

The hypotheses now are, first, that the always and late groups will show the same ego identity pattern that characterized them at age 21, high on both the achieved and moratorium dimensions. We will also expect the early group to continue to score low on achieved identity and the late group to score high. Along with these expectations of consistency, we expect some of the groups to have changed in relation to each other. The late group who are now beginning careers, usually after a divorce or other difficult time, may have gained on the moratorium dimension relative to the early group, who have settled into niches.

Scores on the achieved and moratorium dimensions were plotted from the age-43 Q-sort data as previously from the age-21 data. Table 6.2 shows the three main findings that were consistent at ages 21 and 43. At age 43, as at age 21, creative nominees whose trajectory of productivity was classified as always or late had ego identity patterns high on both achieved and moratorium dimensions (high-high), whereas the comparison group and women who were productive early or never showed patterns other than high-high.

Second, among ever-productive nominees, women who were productive late all scored high on the achieved dimension, those productive always were medium or high, and those productive early scored low.

Third, at age 43, as at age 21, of ever-productive women with scores high on both the achieved and moratorium dimensions, all but one of those in non-art fields scored higher on the achieved dimension and all but one of those in art fields scored higher on the moratorium dimension.

Along with this evidence of continuity of creative personality there appears to have been some change. As predicted, the early and late groups reversed positions on the moratorium dimension. At age 21 the women in the always and early groups had higher scores on this dimension than women in the late or never groups, as reported previously, but at age 43 the women in the always and late groups had higher scores than members of early and never groups, chi square (1) = 6.71, $p < .01$ ($n = 30$).

This evidence for change needs to be interpreted cautiously, because the Q sorts were not based on the same kinds of data at ages 21 and 43, and because the participants were preponderantly but not entirely the same individuals.

TABLE 6.2 Scores on Achieved and Moratorium Dimensions: Consistent Findings at Ages 21 and 43

	Age 21		Age 43	
Productivity trajectory	High-high area	Other areas	High high area	Other areas
Always or late	13	1	13	1
Early or never	6	10	2	14
Comparison women	8	18	6	16
	$\chi^2(2) = 15.08, p < .001$		$\chi^2(2) = 22.75, p < .001$	

	Age 21			Age 43		
	Achieved identity			Achieved identity		
Productivity trajectory	High	Medium	Low	High	Medium	Low
Always	4	4	1	3	5	1
Late	5	0	0	5	0	0
Early	1	1	3	1	0	5
	$\chi^2(4) = 10.85, p < .05$			$\chi^2(4) = 19.07, p < .001$		

	Age 21		Age 43	
Field of productivity	Achieved>Moratorium	Moratorium>Achieved	Achieved>Moratorium	Moratorium>Achieved
Arts	1	5	1	7
Non-arts	8	1	8	1
	$\chi^2(1) = 7.82, p < .01$		$\chi^2(1) = 9.92, p < .01$	

Note. First row of tables includes all creative nominees and comparison women who were Q-sorted at each age. Second row includes all ever-productive nominees at each age, and third row includes all ever-productive nominees who scored high on both achieved and moratorium dimensions (high-high).

DIFFICULT EXPERIENCES IN ADULTHOOD

Each of the productivity groups shows considerable diversity, and certainly no life is like another. As a basis for identifying common problems in these women's actualization of their creative potential, I will draw upon their own descriptions of their most difficult times in adulthood.

This task was assigned them at age 52. The whole sample was asked to describe their most difficult time since college, the one that had most influenced their subsequent lives. They also gave their age when it occurred. The stories were reliably classified as accounts of Unhappy self, Bad partner, Search for independent identity, Consequences of independent identity (Abandonment or Putdown at work), Unhappy self in bad relationship, and Overload (Helson, 1992).

The women of the always and late groups showed a tendency to describe difficult times around age 30 or 40 (ages 27–46), whereas women of the never or early groups tended to report them in the first few years after college or after age 46, chi square (1) = 3.87, $p < .05$ ($n = 26$).

The difficult times described also differed in theme according to productivity group: the early and never groups tended to tell stories about an unhappy self, bad partner, or overload, whereas the late and always groups tended to tell stories about the search for independent identity or the consequences of independent identity, chi square (1) = 9.76, $p < .01$ ($n = 26$).

Among members of the early and never groups, several women described a time soon after college when they felt acute loneliness. This experience seems to have presented them with a "bad self" that they wanted to bury as deeply as possible. They were willing to drop career plans or make compromises in them to avoid the sense of isolation. One woman came to see her excellent creative work as the defensive expression of this isolated self, cutting her off from others. She first lowered the priority of her creative work out of economic necessity, then abandoned it entirely.

Several women classified as never productive described life with a partner who in one way or another had thwarted their development, beginning in early adulthood and sometimes continuing for a long time. For example, one husband developed a mental illness (due to a condition that was eventually corrected). He neglected his appearance and hygiene and was uncommunicative for many years. The wife could not do her creative work with him around and did not feel she could afford to spend the money to rent or build a "room of her own." These women classified as never productive were often dissatisfied with their career development at age 43, but in their 50s the departure of children had given them increased leisure and they engaged in modest forms of creative expression.

Members of the always or late groups sometimes described episodes leading to the establishment of an independent identity or discovery of what they wanted to do with their lives. Those who were productive late were very competent, intelligent women whose urge for creative expression was constrained by a strong need to love and be loved, a sense of responsibility, and an admiration, sometimes ambivalent, for their homemaker mothers. These women seemed to need to live out the homemaker role before they felt free to become careerists. Even so, it was not done without pain. Only frustration in relationships with partner or children brought them to the point of downplaying the role of strong supporter of others and investing seriously in a career of their own. The search for independent identity that they reported in their difficult times often involved the realization of aspects of their personality or marriage that had been unacknowledged in their young adult lives. "When I got my own sight straightened out, I put down my own order for grounding the rest of my life. No more need for compromise or schizoid deals with myself."

The women who were always productive had a desire for independence and strong career motivation as college seniors. Though they increased in independence, confidence, and clarity over time, it is not surprising that when they reported a difficult time in middle age, they did not describe a struggle to establish an independent identity but a struggle to deal with the consequences of having one. The experience coded most frequently as a consequence of independent identity was abandonment. Without exception, the women found the abandonment by partner to be extremely difficult. It led them to painful self-search. It required them to reorganize the remaining pieces of what had been a life structure conducive to their career productivity. Sometimes they had to change the nature of their work to support their children.

Most creative nominees who were never productive did not make a serious effort to change their lives, despite their dissatisfaction. One woman did leave an overbearing partner for a few weeks and tried to start an enterprise of her own, but she lacked the resources to sustain it. In contrast, several of the women who were always productive got started in the wrong direction, but they made decisions, sometime requiring considerable risk, to change their life circumstances in the interests of their creative work. For example, one ill and weak young woman had an abortion over the objections of her husband, and, taking three preschool children with her, moved to an area of the country propitious for her work. (A few months later her husband joined her.) The women who maintained their creative productivity had the confidence and courage—sometimes ruthlessness—to act on their urges and insights, or to hold to their creative goals, and they also had the judgment to minimize risks and the capacity to follow through with hard work.

Skill, dedication, and the ability to take informed risks are recognized as characteristics of creative people in relation to their work. What these life histories show is that the same characteristics go into the life management necessary for a woman's productive career.

Through their sustained efforts, the always-productive women developed valuable skills, emotional equilibrium, and confidence. But of course, successful productivity generates its own problems, such as the increased amount of effort necessary to maintain a larger establishment or the loss of freedom to do other than maintain an expected high quality of work. Especially for artists, our society offers few sinecures. In addition, there were the losses associated with age—loss of loved ones, loss of physical energy, loss of looks. For reasons such as these, there was little mood of having "made it" among the always productive in their 50s. Several of them felt exhausted from the pressure they were under, disappointed that they had not achieved all they would have liked, or sad that their greatest successes were probably behind them. On the other hand, they continued to be open not only to these depressive feelings but to new creative possibilities.

DISCUSSION

In the spring of 1958, 12 Mills College seniors emerged from a van and began arriving at the door of the Institute of Personality Assessment and Research (IPAR). They had come for a one-day assessment, rather than the whole weekend that our previous studies had included. They were the same age and same sex, dressed almost alike in skirts, sweaters and bobby socks. When it was all over and time for the IPAR staff to do their Q sorts, the staff complained loudly that they were barely able to match some names with faces. Remembering those assessments, I am intrigued that the Q sorts predicted the area and trajectory of productivity of the creative nominees over 30 years.

What was it that the IPAR staff registered? They must have observed how firmly and positively rooted the young women were in their own psyches (as opposed to "floating" or being apologetic or rigid) and whether they were conventional or had something of the outlook of an explorer, seeker, or rebel. Whatever else the psychologists noted, these characteristics were enough, in hindsight, to define their ego identity.

I like to think of the creative young person as having an identity achieved and yet unfinished, in process. Although these characteristics can be conceptualized as a pattern of personality traits, the use of identity concepts directs attention to the young women's thinking about the adults they wanted to become, to the different paths they took as traced by demographic markers, and to the values and commitments that they entertained and sustained or did not sustain.

The ego identity patterns make useful contact with life course concepts, such as the Beard-Simonton hypotheses about creative productivity. The Beard-Simonton hypothesis alludes to the importance of integration of ideas and emotionally involved search for both area of creativity and trajectory of productivity (Simonton, 1984).

Studying area of creativity, we found that among ever-productive women who scored high on both dimensions of ego identity, those women who would go into the arts scored higher on emotionally-involved search and that those who would go into other fields scored higher on integration. A comparable finding was obtained at age 43.

The groups with different productivity trajectories (always, early, late, and never) showed distinctive patterns over time on the achieved and moratorium dimensions. In college and again at age 43, high scores on both dimensions distinguished women who were productive at age 52, whether they had always been productive or had begun their careers late. Thus the combination of integration and openness to conflicts and to new ideas and possibilities seems to be a stable feature of personality of women who can sustain creative productivity or shift from another realized identity to a creative career in middle age. The hypothesis that early and late career trajectories would be associated with differences in integration (achieved identity) was supported at both ages 21 and 43. The hypothesis that never-productive nominees would have low scores on emotionally involved search (moratorium dimension) was also supported. There was modest evidence for the predicted shift on the moratorium dimension, late careerists increasing and early careerists decreasing relative to other groups between late adolescence and middle age. These findings will be elaborated presently.

The productivity trajectories of the women were strikingly associated with life path. Adolescent ego identity appears to have affected decisions about marriage, work, and children, thus defining a context for future achievement efforts. The problem of succeeding in both work and relationships was conspicuous in these women's lives. Characteristics often associated with creative work, such as risk taking and commitment to creative endeavor, were shown in this study to be manifested in life management skills that enabled the always-productive women to improve their niches and to persist after disruption and discouragement.

Although the constraints and structure of opportunity under which the sample operated were associated with their particular cohort, the groups we have identified fit conceptualizations of personality syndromes previously related to the actualization of creative potential. For example, the nominees who were low on the achieved dimension at age 21 tended in this sample to be conflicted individuals with ambitions but with limited ability to sustain relationships or work goals. They launched careers but could not maintain them at a high level. Their most difficult times in adulthood tended to involve loneliness or problems in intimate relationships. What Rank (1945) called the *neurotic type* and what Wink (1991, 1992) labeled the willful or *hypersensitive narcissist* have characteristics overlapping with these. Kahn, Zimmerman, Csikszentmihalyi, and Getzels (1985) also found relationships between a measure of ego identity in women with creative potential (art students) and the attainment of intimacy as evidenced in subsequent marital patterns. However, where the present study found that women low on achieved identity tended not to marry, Kahn et al. found that women low on ego identity tended to marry and divorce. Thus, the particular demographic expressions of problems in identity may vary from one context to another.

The creative nominee who was high on the achieved dimension but low on the moratorium dimension was never productive in a career. Her difficult times in adulthood often involved feelings of isolation soon after graduation, or, somewhat later, a sense of distortion in her life related to the needs or demands of her partner. What Rank (1945) called the *adapted type* or Wink (1991) the *giving type* has overlapping characteristics. There are a variety of reasons to adapt to conventional patterns. Conformity and resistance to risk taking or emotional arousal have been described as obstacles to creativity in shy people by Cheek and Stahl (1986), and their discussion seems applicable to a number of the creative nominees in the Mills sample who never actualized their potential in careers. However, there is life outside of careers. Some of these women were aesthetically sensitive and creative within a private or circumscribed sphere.

In college, creative nominees who would be productive late tended to have conventional goals formulated with individuality. Typically, they worked or went to graduate school for a few years after college, then became full-time homemakers. They only began serious careers in their 30s or 40s, often describing as most difficult and formative times in adulthood their midlife experiences in achieving an independent identity. Most of them saw themselves as helpers of others, and they had to discover the reasons for their reluctance to exert agency in their own careers when it seemed appropriate to do so.

The phenomenon of the person who first shows creative productivity in middle age is relatively unstudied, but seems to be common in women (Heilbrun, 1988). Whereas George Elliot became productive in middle age after entering a marriage-like relationship, the women who became productive late in the Mills sample usually did so in opposition to the marriage partner. One supposes that the characteristics of late-achieving women may vary from cohort to cohort, depending upon gender role prescriptions and work opportunities.

Finally, the nominees who would be productive always were the most consistent in emotionally involved search. Their most difficult and formative times in adulthood sometimes led to the abandonment by partners as they pursued these projects, so that they had to rebuild their lives. Their persistence attests to the power of creative motivation.

Although the group findings are coherent and useful, I would like to mention once again that exceptions and individual differences abound. For example, on the basis of her low scores on the achieved and moratorium dimensions at age 21, one nominee would be expected to have been productive only in young adulthood, if at all. But she integrated her life around her art and around a stable second marriage to a congenial fellow artist. Enduring as the creative personality tends to be, it is maintained by identity work that can falter or find unexpected sources of support.

ACKNOWLEDGMENT

This research was supported by NIH grant MH 43948.

REFERENCES

Albert, R. S. (1975). Toward a behavioral definition of genius. *American Psychologist, 30,* 140–151.

Albert, R. S. (1990). Identity, experiences, and career choice among the exceptionally gifted and eminent. In M. A. Runco & R. S. Albert (Eds.), *Theories of creativity* (pp. 13–34). Newbury Park, CA: Sage.

Arnold, K. D. (1993). Academically talented women in the 1980s: The Illinois valedictorian project. In K. D. Hulbert & D. T. Schuster (Eds.), *Women's lives through time* (pp. 393–414). San Francisco: Jossey-Bass.

Barron, F. (1965). The psychology of creativity. In *New directions in psychology* (Vol. 2, pp. 1–120.) New York: Holt.

Barron, F. (1972). Sex differences in self-definition and motivation. In *Artists in the making* (Ch. 4). New York: Seminary.

Beard, G. (1874). *Legal responsibility in old age.* New York: Russell.

Block, J. (1978). *The Q-sort method in personality assessment and psychiatric research.* Palo Alto, CA: Consulting Psychologists Press.

Bush, M. (1969). Psychoanalysis and scientific creativity with special reference to regression in the service of the ego. *Journal of the American Psychoanalytic Association, 17,* 136–90.

Cheek, J. M., & Stahl, S. S. (1986). Shyness and verbal creativity. *Journal of Research in Personality, 20,* 51–61.

Cox, C. M. (1926). *Genetic studies of genius: Vol. 2. The early mental traits of three hundred geniuses.* Stanford, CA: Stanford University Press.

Drevdahl, J. E., & Cattell, R. B. (1958). Personality and creativity in artists and writers. *Journal of Clinical Psychology, 14,* 107–111.

Dudek, S. Z., & Hall, W. B. (1991). Personality consistency: Eminent architects 25 years later. *Creativity Research Journal, 4,* 213–232.

Erikson, E. (1950). *Childhood and society.* New York: Norton.

Hart, B. (1990). Longitudinal study of women's identity status. *Dissertation Abstracts International, 50,* 4807-B.

Heilbrun, C. G. (1988). *Writing a woman's life.* New York: Ballantine.

Helson, R. (1967). Personality characteristics and developmental history of creative college women. *Genetic Psychology Monographs, 76,* 205–256.

Helson, R. (1985). Which of those young women with creative potential became productive? Personality in college and characteristics of parents. In R. Hogan & W. H. Jones (Eds.), *Perspectives in personality* (Vol. 1, pp. 49–80). Greenwich, CT: JAI.

Helson, R. (1987). Which of those young women with creative potential became productive? II. From college to midlife. In R. Hogan & W. H. Jones (Eds.), *Perspectives in personality* (Vol. 2, pp. 51–92). Greenwich, CT: JAI.

Helson, R. (1990). Creativity in women: Outer and inner views over time. In M.A. Runco & R. S. Albert (Eds.), *Theories of creativity* (pp. 46–58). Newbury Park, CA: Sage.

Helson, R. (1992). Women's difficult times and the rewriting of the life story. *Psychology of Women Quarterly, 16,* 331–347.

Helson, R., Elliott, T., & Leigh, J. (1989). Adolescent personality and women's work patterns. In D. Stern & D. Eichorn (Eds.), *Adolescence and work: Influences of social structure, labor markets, and culture* (pp. 259–289). Hillsdale, NJ: Erlbaum.

Helson, R., & McCabe, L. (1994). The social clock in middle age. In B. Turner & L. Troll (Eds.), *Growing older female* (pp. 68–93). Newbury Park, CA: Sage.

Helson, R., Mitchell, V., & Moane, G. (1984). Personality and patterns of adherence and non-adherence to the social clock. *Journal of Personality and Social Psychology, 46,* 1079-1096.

Helson, R., Roberts, B. W., & Agronick, G. (1995). Enduringness and change in creative personality and the prediction of occupational creativity. *Journal of Personality and Social Psychology, 69,* 1173–1183.

Hornstein, G. A. (1986). The structuring of identity among mid-life women as a function of their degree of involvement in employment. *Journal of Personality, 54,* 551–575.

Jaques, E. (1965). Death and the mid-life crisis. *International Journal of Psychoanalysis, 46,* 502–514.

Kahn, S. P., Zimmerman, G., Csikszentmihalyi, M., & Getzels, J. W. (1985). The relationship between identity and intimacy: A longitudinal study with artists. *Journal of Personality and Social Psychology, 49,* 1316–1322.

MacKinnon, D. W. (1962). The nature and nurture of creative talent. *American Psychologist, 17,* 484–495.

Mallory, M. E. (1984). Longitudinal analysis of ego-identity status. *Dissertation Abstracts International, 44,* 3955-B.

Mallory, M. E. (1989). Q-sort definition of ego identity status. *Journal of Youth and Adolescence, 18,* 399–412.

Marcia, J. E. (1966). Development and validation of ego-identity status. *Journal of Personality and Social Psychology, 3,* 551–558.

Marcia, J. E. (1980). Identity in adolescence. In J. Adelson (Ed.), *Handbook of adolescent psychology* (pp. 159–187). New York: Wiley.

Rank, O. (1945). *Will therapy and truth and reality.* New York: Knopf.

Raskin, E. (1936). A comparison of scientific and literary ability: A biographical study of eminent scientists and men of letters of the nineteenth century. *Journal of Abnormal and Social Psychology, 31,* 20–35.

Sheldon, K. M. (1994). Emotionality differences between artists and scientists. *Journal of Research in Personality, 28,* 481–491.

Simonton, D. K. (1984). *Genius, creativity, and leadership.* Cambridge, MA: Harvard University Press.

Suler, R. J. (1980). Primary process thinking and creativity. *Psychological Bulletin, 88,* 144–165.

Wink, P. (1991). Self and object-directedness in adult women. *Journal of Personality, 59,* 769–791.

Wink, P. (1992). Three types of narcissism in women from college to midlife. *Journal of Personality, 60,* 7–29.

Personal Force and Symbolic Reach in Older Women Artists

Lucinda Orwoll and M. Catherine Kelley

Previous research suggests that unusually creative men and women share the twin attributes of a strong, confident self and an unusual openness to affective, symbolic, and aesthetic experience (Barron, 1965; Dellas & Gaier, 1970; Harrington & Anderson, 1981; MacKinnon, 1962). Helson encapsulated this idea by defining the creative personality as "that of an individual in whom personal force combines with symbolic reach to overcome adversity and sustain productivity" (1985, p. 72). The themes of personal force and symbolic reach are particularly provocative because they bring together the "masculine" sensibility of self-assertion, self-confidence, and social dominance, and the "feminine" sensibility of receptivity, openness to inner experience, and aesthetic awareness. Is it the combination of these two orientations that accounts for the greater degree of androgyny of creative men and women when compared with their less creative counterparts (MacKinnon, 1962)? It may be that the most creative men *are* so because they have developed a feminine receptivity, which allows them access to symbolic, unconscious, and affective processes that they translate into outer expression. Creative women may have developed the necessary strength of self to face certain psychological and institutional obstacles that would discourage their less forceful sisters. To become productive, then, creative men and women face different challenges in being able to actualize their potentials.

Over the course of history, men have generally succeeded in realizing their creative talents more often and in grander ways than have women. For several decades, scholars have sought to understand the relative lack of eminent women in the arts. This disparity in achievement exists despite evidence of virtually no sex differences in creative potential (Kogan, 1976). In this chapter, we will focus on a group of older women who were able to actualize their creativity as accomplished visual artists. We wanted to explore whether the characteristics of personal force and symbolic reach would distinguish these women artists from a comparison group of less creative women. We were also interested in whether or not these groups would differ in antecedent early childhood experiences.

We believed that the characteristics of *personal force,* which we defined as having an extraverted sense of personal ascendancy, social confidence, and interpersonal dominance, could buffer many of the external and internal obstacles to achievement that creative women have traditionally faced. External obstacles include institutional barriers, lack of parental encouragement, pressures to conform to sex role expectations, childrearing and family demands, and biases in the evaluation of creative products (Greenacre, 1957; Helson, 1990; Nochlin, 1988; also see Rodeheaver, Emmons, & Powers, this volume). Without a strong sense of personal entitlement and assertiveness, such obstacles can effectively impede girls and women from actualizing their creative potentials.

Internal obstacles for females include what Labouvie-Vief (1992, in press) claims are pervasive cultural narratives, defining gendered prototypes for mind and self. The masculine narrative is one of heroic ascent, achievement, and creative expression; the feminine is one of descent, surrender, and idealization of others' accomplishments. As girls adopt a feminine identity, they internalize these narratives as templates for self-definition. The consequence is often a severe loss of self, conflict about agency and striving, and attenuation of the inner will and confidence for creative expression—in short, a lack of personal force.

The gender literature supports these ideas: Across many achievement situations, women often evidence lower levels of self-confidence, make less self-enhancing attributions, and experience more conflict about intellectual and creative pursuits than men (e.g., American Association of University Women, 1992; Beyer, 1990; Eccles, 1984; Gilligan, 1982; Lenney, 1977; Roberts, 1991).

Although these patterns are prevalent, not all women relinquish their claim to the so-called "masculine," heroic, agential, and creative path. Studies have found that manifestly creative women are generally less conventional and are more "independent," "adventurous," and "self-sufficient," compared with less creative women (Bachtold & Werner, 1973). A similar conclusion was the result of Helson's (1985, 1987) panel studies which followed creative women from college to midlife. She found that, among a group of women who were nominated as creative in college, those women who actualized their potentials in successful careers were higher in extraversion and social dominance, effective functioning, and complex cognitive style, and lower in adaptation to conventional patterns than the other groups. Helson speculated that these women were helped by their extraverted, dominant interpersonal style.

That it may require personal force to succeed as a woman artist is evident in the lives of many contemporary women artists, who confronted structural and psychological obstacles to achievement (Slatkin, 1993). For example, the American artist, Judy Chicago, in her 1973 autobiography, *Through the Flower,* documented the psychological and developmental processes that shaped her identity as a woman artist and chronicled her struggles for creative self-realization, within a context of a male-defined art world of the 1950s and 1960s. Chicago described her art school environment as discouraging to women students: "Continuing hostile comments from men and the absence of other serious women combine to make me conclude that *some* men didn't seem to like women who had aspiration as artists" (p. 28). She experienced difficulties finding her own artistic style, when her art teachers and colleagues rejected images that were "too overt in their femaleness" (p. 34):

> In order to be myself, I had to express those things that were most real to me, and those included the struggles I was having as a woman, both personally and professionally. At the same time, if I wanted to be taken seriously as an artist, I had to suppress anything in my work that would mark it as having been made by a women. I was trying to find a way to be myself, still function within the framework of the art community, and be recognized as an artist. This required focusing upon issues that were essentially derived from what men had designated as being important, while still trying to make my own way. (p. 40)

Despite these barriers, she possessed the strength of self necessary to actualize her talents. From an early age, Chicago was aware of her creative abilities and had a sense of her own worth, which carried over into her art school experience.

> Fortunately, I had a tendency to pursue my own objectives regardless of the message I received. This came partly from my irrepressible confidence that whatever I did was "terrific," partly from my drive and determination. . . . I had learned early that the world's perceptions of a person are

not necessarily true, so I tended to discount comments and attitudes that conflicted with my own sense of what was right. (p. 29)

Even when her work was ignored and criticized, she refused to relinquish her self-confident attitude, "My earlier naiveté about my situation as a woman artist was giving way to a clear understanding that my career was going to be a long, hard struggle. Fortunately, I knew that I was okay—that the problem was in the culture and not in me, but it still hurt." (p. 28)

> It suddenly dawned on me, . . . that I had simply refused to "read the signs" that told women to be "good girls" and to accept the second-class status of our sex. Since I never understood this message, I continued to behave in terms of my own self-expectations and according to the standards of equality I had absorbed from my family. Nonetheless, I couldn't entirely escape the realization that my ambition, aspiration, and dedication was somewhat unusual in women of my generation. But because I always demanded and got a place for myself in my classes, my relationships, and in my work, I was able to separate myself from that social conditioning that prompted other women to relinquish their goals. (p. 30)

As Chicago's experiences suggest, the ability of women to become productive, successful artists may depend, in part, on their having the personal force to withstand inner and outer pressures to doubt and withdraw.

What about the other factor that Helson defined as important to mature creativity? For us, *symbolic reach* connotes aesthetic interest, openness to the imaginative, access to nonlogical or unconscious sources, and a lack of conceptual rigidity. These have been identified as correlates of creativity (Arnheim, 1957; Barron, 1965; MacKinnon, 1962; Rose, 1964).

If personal force is more closely associated with a traditionally masculine approach, symbolic reach is more akin to the feminine (Milner, 1958). For example, some studies suggest women and men respond to primary process information differently (Fitzgerald, 1966; Pine & Holt, 1960), use different defenses (Cramer, 1990) and may have access to different kinds of self-information (Ashmore & Ogilvie, 1992). Certainly, psychodynamic theorists such as Chodorow (1978) and Benjamin (1988) and cognitive-developmental researchers such as Gilligan (1982) and Belenky, Clinchy, Goldberger, and Tarule (1986) have found similar trends. In philosophy and theology, the traditionally "feminine" realms have embraced the unconscious, irrational, and shadow elements, while the "masculine" has connoted consciousness, rationality, and control (Jung, 1971; Labouvie-Vief, in press; Reuther, 1983).

Milner (1958) argued that it is this so-called feminine mentality that Blake recognized in his *Illustrations to the Book of Job* as an essential component of the creative process which "undoes the over-fixed separation between self and other, self and the universe" (p. 88). Kohut described the creative individual as "less psychologically separated from his surroundings than the noncreative one; the 'I-you' barrier is not as clearly defined" (1987, p. 447). Similarly, Rose (1964) discussed the permeable ego boundaries that allow the creative person to:

> lose himself in order to find himself in a wider integration of time and space. He discovers the cosmos out of himself and expands the time interval of immediate consciousness. He grows through an expansion of ego boundaries. He can make use of art to help lead him out from concrete body imageries to a sense of the abstract, non-objective, timeless, and universal. (pp. 82–83)

The artist Ben Shahn (1964) evokes this awareness/transcendence of the self in creative experience: "Thus, in art, the symbol which has vast universality may be some figure drawn from the most remote and inward recesses of consciousness; for it is here that we are unique and sovereign and most wholly aware" (p. 29).

Earlier psychoanalytic writers (Kris, 1952; Schafer, 1958) have referred to a concept, "regression in the service of the ego," to explain this inner receptivity associated with the creative process (Wild, 1965). It involves the use of less rational modes of thinking, which incorporate preconscious and unconscious materials. Fitzgerald (1966) developed a measure of regression in the service of the ego, which was found to correlate with artistic pursuits and ego development (Costa & McCrae, 1985). Costa and McCrae (1985) used Fitzgerald's measure as a foundation for constructing their Openness to Experience scale of the NEO Personality Inventory. They found that women were higher than men on three dimensions of Openness to Experience—aesthetic sensitivity, openness to feelings, and preference for novel activities—but lower on intellectual curiosity.

The theme of symbolic reach resonated in Judy Chicago's use of art to symbolize and work through her emotional states:

> I repeated forms in an effort to establish a continuum of sensation. As I went along, the paintings became increasingly difficulty technically. But that difficulty seemed to be a parallel to the emotional risk they represented for me. The color systems I had been developing allowed me to establish a method of representing emotional states through color . . . (p. 56)

> . . . I was able to emerge from the many constraints of role condition-
> ing, for as I symbolized the various emotional states that comprised my
> personality, I gave myself permission to experience and express more
> aspects of myself. When I finished the paintings, I felt like icebergs were
> breaking up inside me." (p. 57)

In the study described in this chapter, we used data on personality and early life experiences to determine what would differentiate accomplished women artists from a control group of women. We focused our analyses on Helson's themes of personal force and symbolic reach. For personal force, we used variables that measured a sense of personal ascendancy, confidence, and dominance. For symbolic reach, we used variables that measured sensitive awareness and openness to a wide range of experiences, creative and psychological interests, and a tolerance for ambiguity.

A third set of variables assessed several aspects of psychological health and social functioning. We were interested in this dimension because studies on the psychological health and well-being of creative personalities have yielded mixed results (Golann, 1963). On one hand, many researchers link mature creativity with having a cohesive self, resolving inner conflicts, and transcending narcissistic limits (Helson, 1985; Kohut, 1987; MacKinnon, 1965; Wink, 1991). On the other hand, the complexity of the artistic personality may make conventional forms of adjustment less likely (Barron, 1965; Helson & Wink, 1987), and some work suggests that creativity is often associated with forms of psychopathology (Beeman, 1990; Jamison, 1993; Klingerman, 1980; Miller, 1990).

We were also interested in a fourth dimension: life history information that might differentiate the groups. Research suggests that the creative personality may develop in response to childhood conflicts and traumas (Helson, 1985; Miller, 1990). Creativity in adulthood has been associated with marked experiences in childhood of disruptive events and feelings of loneliness and isolation (Barron, 1975; MacKinnon, 1965; Roe, 1975). To assess childhood experience, we used subjects' narrative statements about their early lives and perceptions of their parents. We coded presence of information on childhood happiness, family environment, relations with parents, and artistic influences.

Finally, to measure intragroup differences in creativity among the women artists, we asked four art professors to independently rate the quality of samples of their work, which they submitted with their questionnaires.

SUBJECTS AND PROCEDURE

In this study, we used a peer nomination methodology to identify a national sample of women artists. The nominators were randomly selected from *Who's Who in American Art* (1990). The nominators identified visual artists, 50 years of age or older, whom they viewed as particularly creative.

Nominees were then contacted by mail and asked to participate in the study. We obtained data from 46 nominees, representing about a 58% response rate. They ranged in age from 60–89 years of age. A group of 39 well-educated, community volunteers recruited from a large, midwestern metropolitan area were included as a control sample. Nominees and controls were similar in age and background information; most were married, in good health and satisfied with their finances. Nominees and controls were similar in education: 72% (33) of the creative nominees attended college, 20% (9) attended art school; among controls, 79% (31) attended college, none attended art school.

VARIABLES AND THEIR MEASUREMENT

To assess personal force we used the 7 interpersonal orientation scales of the California Personality Inventory (CPI; Gough, 1987), which measure "the ways in which people deal with others and the ways in which they conduct themselves in the interpersonal context" (Gough, 1990, p. 39): Dominance, Capacity for Status, Sociability, Social Presence, Self-Acceptance, Independence, Empathy. We also used the California Self-Evaluation Scales (Phinney & Gough, 1985) to assess both general and creative aspects of self-esteem.

We measured symbolic reach with several variables related to a sense of openness, lack of rigidity, and permeable ego boundaries. Fitzgerald's (1966) Experience Inquiry was used to measure openness to experience or regression in the service of the ego. This scale assesses tolerance for and constructive use of regressive experiences, such as altered states and peak experiences, awareness of affective states, and irrational cognitions. Individuals who score highly on this measure show a looseness of repression, a lack of anxiety about the unusual or novel, sufficient ego strength to permit free discourse with experience, and a facility in shifting from more to less regulated thinking. A Tolerance of Ambiguity scale (Kirton, 1981) assessed the tendency to seek out, enjoy, or excel in situations where outcomes are not clear-cut and readily structured. We included questions about the use of the unconscious,

in which respondents rated the extent to which unconscious informa-
tion was relevant, knowable, and helpful in work or personal situations.
Finally, we used two CPI scales—Psychological Mindedness and Creative
Temperament—as further evidence of artistic and symbolic interests
(Helson, 1987).

To operationalize psychological health and well-being, we used the
CPI Well-being and Self-realization scales; Wink's CPI Narcissism scale
(Wink & Gough, 1990); a shortened version of the CES-D depression
scale (Radloff, 1977), four items from the Life Satisfaction Index A
(Neugarten, Havighurst, & Tobin, 1961), and the Satisfaction with
Relationships scale of the California Self-Evaluation Scales (Phinney &
Gough, 1985).

To assess childhood experiences, we used binary (presence vs.
absence) coding of two open-ended questionnaire responses, in which
subjects described their childhood and adolescent experiences and
their relationship with their parents, and responses to two items on
the Washington University Sentence Completion Test (Loevinger, 1976)
that dealt with mother and father. Each mention of a coding category
received a score of "1." After coding, categories were combined to create
the following childhood experience variables: Happy Childhood consisted of (a) having a happy or pleasant childhood and/or (b) feeling
loved by their parents; Unhappy Childhood consisted of (a) having an
unhappy childhood; and/or (b) feeling lonely and/or isolated or having
few friends; Family Problems consisted of a set of coding categories
involving mention of (a) childhood abuse or neglect; (b) parental discord, separation, and divorce; and/or (c) parental alcoholism or problem drinking; Childhood Stresses consisted of (a) death of a significant
person; (b) serious or prolonged illness; and/or (c) many or significant
moves; Creative Environment was comprised of having (a) a mother
who was herself creative or encouraged subject's creativity; (b) a
father who was himself creative or encouraged subject's creativity; (c)
other adults who encouraged subject's creativity; and/or (d) a culturally
rich environment (exposure to "the arts," music, theater, literature).

To obtain an independent assessment of the artists' creativity, we
asked art professionals to rate samples of the artists' works. Twenty-
seven women artists supplied representations of their art work; 4 did
not submit representations, and 15 representations were not included
in the study. Samples were excluded if they were photographs of poor
quality, photocopies, installations, conceptual art, and types of art for
which we had only one representation, such as coins, stained glass,
industrial design and fiber art. When artists sent more that one sample
of their work, we randomly chose one work to be evaluated.

All samples were mounted on 5"x7" or 8"x10" black poster board. Any identifying initials or signatures were concealed, and subject numbers were discretely recorded on the back of each work. No descriptive information about the size of the art work or media was provided for the judges, because some artists did not provide this information about their work. Art representations were viewed in a different random order by each judge (Amabile, 1982).

Three art professors from local universities and one professional artist evaluated the art representations. All had extensive experience judging art. The judges independently evaluated each art representation on the following dimensions: (a) technical skill; (b) originality; (c) expressiveness (i.e., the extent to which the structure expresses an underlying idea, feeling, or theme); (d) complexity (i.e., the extent to which the structure is composed of a number of interconnected and interwoven elements; and (e) aesthetic appeal (i.e., How would you rate this if you were to award prizes in a competitive art show?).

Judges examined the entire set of art work before beginning their evaluations. They then evaluated individual art samples in relation to the group, rather than against absolute standards for painting or sculpture (Amabile, 1982). Judges recorded their ratings on scales with 7 equally marked reference points, ranging from 1 (very low) to 7 (very high). Interrater reliability ranged from .65 to .78 using the Spearman-Brown formula for composite ratings (Shrout & Fleiss, 1979; Tinsley & Weiss, 1975).

RESULTS

DIFFERENCES BETWEEN CREATIVE AND CONTROL GROUPS

Using a multiple regression analysis (see Table 7.1) that controlled for education and health (based on a self-rating of health), we found that the creative women scored significantly higher on measures of personal force. That is, they were higher on all of the interpersonal orientation scales of the CPI and were higher on the general and the creative California Self-Evaluation Scales.

Women artists were significantly higher than the control group on all of the measures of symbolic reach: Experience Inquiry (openness to experience), Use of the Unconscious, Tolerance of Ambiguity, and the CPI scales of Psychological Mindedness and Creative Temperament. In addition, artists were significantly higher on the Baucom Masculinity Scale.

The groups did not differ, however, on measures of psychological health and well-being (Depression, Life Satisfaction, Narcissism, CPI

TABLE 7.1 Differences Between Artist and Control Women on Multiple Regressions Models Adjusted for Education and Self-Health

Variables	Difference Estimate	Standard Error
Error Personal Force		
CPI Scales		
Dominance	-3.21**	1.21
Capacity for Status	-2.65***	.72
Sociability	-3.10**	1.02
Social Presence	-3.31**	1.07
Self-Acceptance	-2.15**	.75
Independence	-2.70**	.85
Empathy	-2.81**	1.06
Self-Evaluation		
General	-3.43**	1.30
Creativity	-7.41***	1.15
Symbolic Reach		
Psychological Mindedness	-1.90**	.72
Creative Temperament	-3.17**	1.16
Experience Inquiry	-6.34***	1.79
Use of Unconscious	-1.10***	.17
Tolerance of Ambiguity	-4.21*	1.96†
Psychological Health, Well-Being, and Interpersonal Relations		
Well-Being	.51	.81
Self-Realization (V3)	-1.17	1.72
Narcissism	-2.68	2.48
Depression (CESD)	-.75	.74
Life Satisfaction	-.20	.14
Satisfaction with Relationships	-1.08	1.16
Other CPI Scales		
Normative Orientation and Values		
Responsibility	.63	.80
Socialization	1.42	1.17
Good Impression	1.47	1.41
Self-Control	1.65	1.43
Communality	.02	.49
Cognitive Style		
Tolerance	.82	.88
Achievement via Conformance	-.91	.79
Achievement via Independence	-1.41	.92
Intellectual Efficiency	-.58	.85
Flexibility	-.91	.96
Femininity/Masculinity	.18	.73
Baucom Masculinity	-6.00***	1.69
Baucom Femininity	1.30	.91

Note. Artists were coded 2; controls were coded 3.
*$p < .05$.   **$p < .01$.   ***$p < .001$.   †$p < .10$.

Well-Being scale, Satisfaction with Interpersonal Relationships). They were not different on other CPI measures of cognitive and intellectual functions (i.e., Achievement via Conformance, Achievement via Independence, Intellectual Efficiency, Flexibility).

We used *t*-tests to compare the groups on childhood experience variables. We found that creative women more frequently reported having an unhappy and/or lonely childhood than control women ($t = 2.15$, $p < .03$). Creative women also more often experienced a culturally rich environment in childhood ($t = 5.27$, $p < .001$). These categories included having creative parents, being exposed to art lessons, or other kinds of cultural and artistic experiences.

WITHIN-GROUP DIFFERENCES

Because the art ratings of technical skill, originality, complexity, expressiveness, and aesthetic appeal were highly intercorrelated ($r = .63$ to $r = .88$), we combined these ratings into a mean art rating. Using Pearson correlations, (see Table 7.2) we found that artists with higher art ratings scored higher on two symbolic reach variables: Use of the Unconscious and Creative Temperament. There was no relationship between the art ratings and measures of personal force, with the exception of Capacity for Status. This scale, which measures qualities related to striving for success, ambition, and independence, was negatively correlated with the art rating.

Regarding psychological health and social functioning, artists with higher art ratings scored lower on Life Satisfaction and Satisfaction with Relationships and, at a trend level, with the CPI Well-being and Self-Realization, (Vector 3) scales. Artists with higher scores were significantly higher on the depression measure.

Correlations showed that the artists whose work was rated higher were less norm following, as reflected on Socialization, which reflects a tendency "to be rebellious, dissatisfied, and nonconforming" (Gough, 1990). Other measures of norm following were also negatively correlated, but did not reach significance (Responsibility, Self-Control, and Good Impression). Art ratings were also significantly positively correlated with family problems and with childhood unhappiness and loneliness.

SEX DIFFERENCES

To put the findings on creative women in a broader context, we include a brief report on comparable analyses of males in our sample and analyses of differences between the artistic women and artistic

TABLE 7.2   **Pearson Correlations Between Art Ratings and Dependent Variables for Women and Men Artists**

Variables	Women Artists	Men Artists
Personal Force		
CPI Scales		
Dominance	−.31	−.01
Capacity for Status	−.56**	.19
Sociability	−.25	−.02
Social Presence	−.39†	−.04
Self-Acceptance	−.07	−.15
Independence	−.36	.33
Empathy	−.23	−.06
Self-Evaluation		
General	−.12	.12
Creativity	.45*	.29
Symbolic Reach		
Psychological Mindedness	−.10	−.24
Creative Temperament	−.09	.29
Experience Inquiry	.03	.26
Use of Unconscious	.51**	.32
Tolerance of Ambiguity	−.04	.37
Psychological Health, Well-being and Interpersonal Relations		
Well-being	−.40†	−.46*
Self-Realization (V3)	−.39†	−.18
Depression (CESD)	.49**	.0
Life Satisfaction	−.54**	−.23
Satisfaction with Relationships	−.51**	.06
Other CPI Scales		
Normative Orientation and Values		
Responsibility	−.33	−.38†
Socialization	−.51*	−.17
Good Impression	−.38†	−.18
Self-Control	−.34	−.25
Norm-Following (V2)	−.04	.02
Communality	−.32	−.04
Cognitive Style		
Tolerance	−.45*	−.38†
Achievement via Conformance	−.12	−.22
Achievement via Independence	−.12	.11
Intellectual Efficiency	−.46*	−.23
Flexibility	.04	.25
Femininity/Masculinity	.07	.04
Baucom Masculinity	−.34	−.16
Baucom Femininity	−.12	−.30

Note. N for female artist = 20; N for male artists = 20
*$p < .05$.   **$p < .01$.   ***$p < .001$.   †$p < .10$.

men. Forty-two male artists and 39 controls participated. They ranged from 60 to 90 years of age and were recruited in the same manner as the females.

Compared to the women artists, who were higher than control women on all measures of personal force, the male artists did not differ from the control males on any of these measures. Male artists differed from controls on several symbolic reach variables, however. Artists scored significantly higher on Experience Inquiry (openness to experience), Tolerance of Ambiguity, Use of the Unconscious, and Creative Temperament and, at a trend level, on Psychological Mindedness ($p < .07$). They also scored significantly higher on the CPI Femininity scale than control men. Unlike the women artists, the men artists did not differ from their control group on measures of personal well-being and psychological health, except a trend level elevation on Narcissism ($p < .07$). Coding of the childhood experiences of the male artists was not available.

When we directly compared the male and female artists, we found few differences. Women artists scored higher on two personal force variables, Sociability and Self-Acceptance, and on one symbolic reach variable, Use of the Unconscious. Male artists were higher on the CPI scales for Well-Being and Tolerance.

DISCUSSION

Although providing only part of the story, these results indicate that the sample of older women artists who were nominated as particularly creative were quite distinct from the sample of less creative women. This is evident on the measures of personal force, which we defined as combining self-confidence with social ascendancy, and on measures of symbolic reach, which included openness to experience, tolerance of ambiguity, use of the unconscious, as well as psychological and creative interests.

Our data suggest that artistic women, of this cohort at least, seem to balance two tendencies traditionally associated with masculine and feminine qualities. The women combined an external self, which could be receptive, imaginative, and flexible. This balancing, interestingly, appeared as well in the finding that the artistic women were less sextyped than the controls.

That the artistic males were also more androgynous than their control group was evident in higher scores on symbolic reach variables and on the CPI Femininity scale. However, the overall pattern of results comparing creative and noncreative groups differed markedly between the male and female artists. Most striking was the importance of personal force for the artistic women, who differed from control women across the board on these variables. In contrast, artistic men did not differ from control men on any of the personal force measures. These findings highlight the possibility that women with creative potential must develop a confident, self-assertive attitude along with symbolic interests in order to actualize their talents in productive work. Results comparing the male groups suggest that males with artistic potential must nurture a receptive, feminine openness rather than greater personal force to be distinguished from less creative males.

When we used art ratings to look for intragroup differences within the women artists, we found that measures of symbolic reach and norm questioning, but not personal force, were correlated with higher ratings. Based on this outcome, we suspect that greater personal force may be a necessary but not sufficient component of creativity in women: The utilization of symbolic, unconscious, and unconventional ideas further distinguish the most creative of the group.

Another striking finding was that women (but not men) artists whose work was rated higher scored worse on measures of psychological functioning (i.e., Well-Being, Self-Realization, Satisfaction with Life, Satisfaction with Relationships, and Depression) than the controls. Are these negative outcomes the price that creative women often pay for their inner openness and outer assertiveness? Are women of this cohort more vulnerable than younger creative women, because of the multiple gender-based deterrents, described by Chicago (1973) and others (Ruddick & Daniels, 1977), that the older women faced historically? Although we can only speculate at this point, these are questions that we hope to address in future research with a wider cross-section of ages. More information is needed also to clarify the relationship between early life experiences and adult psychological adjustment in the lives of creative persons. Our data, albeit limited, supports previous findings that creative adults report their childhoods to be less happy, more lonely, and involving more family difficulties than comparison samples.

If creative productivity requires a personality that blends masculine self-confidence and feminine awareness of symbolic realms, males and females should face different challenges to attaining such a balance. This study showed that, for older women artists, the inner creative aesthetic, while essential for artistic quality, must be matched by an inner strength of self, which is willing to claim and assert her talents, desires, and products. To be creative women in their times, these artists undoubtedly wrestled with the "inner demons of self-doubt and guilt and the outer monsters of ridicule or patronizing encouragement"

(Nochlin, 1988, p. 175). Unfortunately, many of the same pressures against female creativity still exist (Brown & Gilligan, 1992; Labouvie-Vief, 1994; Kerr, 1987). Young women of today can look to these creative, older women as models of strength and depth, finding encouragement to develop within themselves both facets of their creative personalities.

ACKNOWLEDGMENTS

This research was conducted under grant No. AG00114, Multidisplinary Research Training in Aging from the National Institute on Aging to Lucinda Orwoll, PhD.

We wish to thank Prof. Barbara Cervenka, Prof. Michael Kapitan, Dr. Billie Wickre, and Edee Joppich for their assistance with art ratings. We would like to thank Scott Davidson and Max Walker for their help with coding and Andrzej Galecki for his assistance with data analysis.

REFERENCES

American Association of University Women (1992). *The AAUW report: How schools short change girls.* Washington, DC: AAUW Educational Foundation.

Amabile, T. M. (1982). Social psychology of creativity: A consensual assessment technique. *Journal of Personality and Social Psychology, 43*(5), 997–1013.

Arnheim, R. (1957). The artist conscious and subconscious. *Art News, 56,* 31–33.

Ashmore, R. D., & Ogilvie, R. R. (1992). He's such a nice boy . . . when he's with grandma: Gender and evaluation in self-with-other representations. In T. M. Brinthaupt & R. P. Lipka (Eds.), *The self: Definitional and methodological issues.* Albany: State University of New York Press.

Bachtold, L. M., & Werner, E. E. (1973). Personality characteristics of creative women. *Perceptual and Motor Skills, 36,* 311–319.

Barron, F. (1965). *The psychology of creativity.* New York: Holt, Rinehart, & Winston.

Barron, F. (1975). The solitariness of self and its mitigation through creative imagination. In I. A. Taylor & J. W. Getzels (Eds.), *Perspectives in creativity* (pp. 146–156). Chicago: Aldine.

Beeman, C. A. (1990). *Just this side of madness: Creativity and the drive to create.* Berkeley, CA: University of California Press.

Belenky, M. F., Clinchy, B. M., Goldberger, N. R., & Tarule, J. M. (1986). *Women's ways of knowing.* New York: Basic.

Benjamin, J. (1988). *Bonds of love: Psychoanalysis, feminism, and the problem of domination.* New York: Pantheon.

Beyer, S. (1990). Gender differences in the accuracy of self-evaluations of performance. *Journal of Personality and Social Psychology, 59,* 960–970.

Brown, L. M., & Gilligan, C. (1992). *Meeting at the crossroads: Women's psychology and girls' development.* Cambridge, MA: Harvard University Press.

Chicago, J. (1973). *Through the flower: My struggle as a woman artist.* Garden City, NY: Penguin.

Chodorow, N. (1978). *The reproduction of mothering.* Los Angeles: University of California Press.

Costa, P. T., Jr., & McCrae, R. R. (1985). *The NEO personality inventory.* Odessa, FL: Psychological Assessment Resources.

Cramer, P. (1990). *The development of defense mechanism: Theory, research, and assessment.* New York: Springer-Verlag.

Dellas, M., & Gaier, E. L. (1970). Identification of creativity: The individual. *Psychological Bulletin, 73,* 55–73.

Eccles, J. (1984). Sex differences in achievement patterns. *Nebraska Symposium on Motivation, 39,* 97–132.

Fitzgerald, E. T. (1966). Measurement of openness to experience: A study of regression in the service of the ego. *Journal of Personality and Social Personality, 4,* 655–663.

Gilligan, C. (1982). *In a different voice.* Cambridge, MA: Harvard University Press.

Golann, S. E. (1963). Psychological study of creativity. *Psychological Bulletin, 60* (6), 548–565.

Gough, H. G. (1987). *California Psychological Inventory administrator's guide.* Palo Alto, CA: Consulting Psychologists.

Gough, H. G. (1990). The California Psychological Inventory. In C. E. Watkins, Jr., & V. L. Campbell (Eds.), *Testing in counseling practice* (pp. 37–62). Hillsdale, NJ: Erlbaum.

Greenacre, C. (1957). The childhood of the artist: Libidinal phase development and giftedness. *The psychological study of the child* (Vol. 12). New York: International University Press.

Harrington, D. M., & Anderson, S. M. (1981). Creativity, masculinity, femininity, and three models of psychological androgyny. *Journal of Social and Personality Psychology, 41,* 744–757.

Helson, R. (1985). Which of those women with creative potential became productive? Personality in college and characteristics of parents. In R. Hogan & W. H. Jones (Eds.), *Perspectives in personality* (Vol. 1, pp 49–80). Greenwich, CT: JAI.

Helson, R. (1987). Which of those women with creative potential became productive? II: From college to midlife. In R. Hogan & W. H. Jones (Eds.), *Perspectives in personality* (Vol. 2, pp. 51–92). Greenwich, CT: JAI.

Helson, R. (1990). Creativity in women: Outer and inner views over time. In M. Runco & R. S. Alpert (Eds.), *Theories of creativity.* Newbury Park, CA: Sage.

Helson, R. & Wink, P. (1987). Two conceptions of maturity examined in the findings of a longitudinal study. *Journal of Personality and Social Psychology, 53,* 531–541.

Jamison, K. R. (1993). *Touched by fire: Manic-depressive illness in the artistic temperament.* New York: Free Press.

Jung, C. G. (1971). Answer to Job. In J. Campbell (Ed.), *The portable Jung* (pp. 519–650). New York: Penguin.

Kerr, B. A. (1987). *Smart girls, gifted women.* Columbus, OH: Ohio.

Kirton, M. J. (1981). A reanalysis of two scales of tolerance of ambiguity. *Journal of Personality Assessment, 45,* 407–414.

Klingerman, C. (1980). Art and the self of the artist. In A. Goldberg (Ed.), *Advances in self psychology.* New York: International University Press.

Kogan, N. (1976). Sex differences in creativity and cognitive styles. In S. Messick (Ed.), *Individuality in learning.* San Francisco: Jossey-Bass.

Kohut, H. (1987). Forms and transformations of narcissism. In P. Ornstein (Ed.), *The search for the self.* New York: International University Press.

Kris, E. (1952). *Psychoanalytic explorations in art.* New York: International University Press.

Labouvie-Vief, G. (1992). Women's creativity and images of gender. In B. F. Turner & L. Troll (Eds.), *Growing older female.* Newbury Park, CA: Sage.

Labouvie-Vief, G. (1994). *Psyche and eros: Mind and gender in the life course.* New York: Cambridge University Press.

Lenney, E. (1977). Women's self-confidence in achievement situations. *Psychological Bulletin, 84,* 1–13.

Loevinger, J. (1976). *Ego development.* San Francisco: Jossey-Bass.

MacKinnon, D. W. (1962). The nature and nurture of creative talent. *American Psychologist, 19,* 484–495.

MacKinnon, D. W. (1965). Personality and the realization of creative potential. *American Psychologist, 20,* 273–281.

Milner, M. (1958). Psycho-analysis and art. In D. W. Winnicott, J.

Bowlby, I. Hellman, M. Milner, R. Money-Dyrle, E. Jaques, & J. Riviere (Eds.), *Psycho-analysis and contemporary thought.* London: Hogarth.

Miller, A. (1990). *The untouched key: Tracing childhood trauma in creativity and destructiveness.* New York: Anchor.

Neugarten, B. L., Havighurst, R. J., & Tobin, S. (1961). The measurement of life satisfaction. *Journal of Gerontology, 16,* 134–143.

Nochlin, L. (1988). *Women, art, and power and other essays.* New York: Harper & Row.

Phinney, C., & Gough, H. (1985). *California Self-Evaluation Scales.* Unpublished manuscript, Institute of Personality Assessment and Research, University of California, Berkeley.

Pine, F., & Holt, R.R. (1960). Creativity and primary process: A study of adaptive regression. *Journal of Abnormal and Social Psychology, 61* (3), 370–379.

Radloff, L. S. (1977). The CES-D scale: A self-report depression scale for research in adulthood and aging. *Applied Psychological Measurement, 1,* 385–401.

Reuther, R. R. (1983). *Sexism and God-talk.* Boston: Beacon.

Roberts, T. (1991). Gender and the influence of evaluations on self-assessments in achievement settings. *Psychological Bulletin, 109*(2), 297–308.

Roe, A. (1975). Painters and painting. In I. A. Taylor & J. W. Getzels (Eds.), *Perspectives in creativity* (pp. 157–172). Chicago: Aldine.

Rose, G. J. (1964). Creative imagination in terms of ego "core" and boundaries. *The International Journal of Psychoanalysis, 45,* 75–84.

Ruddick, S., & Daniels, P. (Eds.). (1977). *Working it out: 23 women writers, artists, scientists, and scholars talk about their lives and work.* New York: Pantheon.

Schafer, R. (1958). Regression in the service of the ego: The relevance of a psychoanalytic concept for personality assessment. In G. Lindzey (Ed.), *Assessment of human motives.* New York: Holt, Rinehart, & Winston.

Shahn, B. (1964). The biography of a painting. In V. Tomas (Ed.), *Creativity in the arts.* Englewood Cliffs, NJ: Prentice-Hall.

Slatkin, W. (1993). *The voices of women artists.* Englewood Cliffs, NJ: Prentice-Hall.

Shrout, P. E., & Fleiss, J. L. (1979). Intraclass correlations: Uses in assessing rater reliability. *Psychological Bulletin, 24,* 207–218.

Tinsley, H. E., & Weiss, D. J. (1975). Interrater reliability and agreement of subjective judgments. *Journal of Aging and Human Development, 22* (4), 358–376.

Who's who in American art. (1990). New York: Bowker.

Wild, C. (1965). Creativity and adaptive regression. *Journal of Personality and Social Psychology, 2,* 161–169.

Wink, P., & Gough, H. (1990). New narcissism scales for the California Psychological Inventory and MMPI. *Journal of Personality Assessment, 54* (3&4), 446–462.

Wink, P. (1991). Self- and object-directedness in adult women. *Journal of Personality, 59,* 769–791.

Context and Identity in Women's Late Life Creativity

Dean Rodeheaver, Carol Emmons, and Karen Powers

THE ADVANTAGES OF BEING A WOMAN ARTIST:

Working without the pressure of success.
Not having to be in shows with men.
Having an escape from the art world in your 4 free-lance jobs.
Knowing your career might pick up after you're eighty.
Being reassured that whatever kind of art you make it will be labelled feminine.
Not being stuck in a tenured teaching position.
Seeing your ideas live on in the work of others.
Having the opportunity to choose between career and motherhood.
Not having to choke on those big cigars or paint in Italian suits.
Having more time to work after your mate dumps you for someone younger.
Being included in revised versions of art history.
Not having to undergo the embarrassment of being called a genius.
Getting your picture in art magazines wearing a gorilla suit.

—The Guerilla Girls[1]

The Guerilla Girls were formed in response to an abysmal ratio of males to females (151 to 14) in the 1984 "International Survey of Recent Painting and Sculpture" at the Museum of Modern Art. In their struggle for the recognition of women artists, the Guerilla Girls don gorilla masks and use guerilla tactics. This includes creating posters with revealing statistics, such as the number of art publications, reviews, and feature stories about women artists.

Why the gorilla masks? 'They work anonymously to avoid retribution from galleries and museums and to allow the message to stand alone, unclouded by personalities' (Geitner, 1990, p. G-6). One Guerilla Girl notes: "It's amusing to see how important it is for people to know who we are so they can decide if they should take us seriously" (see Heartney, 1987). Comments, contributions, or requests for information about the Guerilla Girls may be addressed to The Guerilla Girls, Box 1056, Cooper Station, New York, New York, 10276.

INTRODUCTION

The interrelationship between social institutions, gender, and making a living at art provides the Guerilla Girls's raison d'etre; the connection of all of these to creativity is the focus of this chapter. In particular, we are concerned with the nature of creativity among women across the adult life course, with a special emphasis on later life contributions of women visual artists. This examination must be speculative however, as reviewing the literature on creativity, creativity among women, and creativity among older women is an exercise in diminishing returns. Psychological research currently does not permit any definitive conclusions concerning changes in creativity across women's adult lives; art historians have only recently begun to examine specific issues concerning aging women; and many women artists have been silenced by the institutions to which we devote much of our attention herein. Our goals, then, are rather modest: describing some of the developmental, social, and psychological factors related to creativity and artistic expression; examining the contextual factors affecting women's artistic achievements; and illustrating both using women artists over the age of 50.

PSYCHOLOGY DRAWS A BLANK: EMPIRICAL APPROACHES TO SEX AND AGE DIFFERENCES IN CREATIVITY

If you can recall the way you felt when describing your car's strange clacking noise to a mechanic, you can empathize with the first author— a psychologist—as he explained to the second author—an artist— how psychologists conceptualize creativity. There is definitely something going on, but the usefulness of psychologists' descriptions is yet to be decided.

Psychological studies of creativity vary in method and in hypotheses about age and sex differences (for example, see Bolen & Torrance, 1978; Crosson & Robertson-Tchabo, 1983; Ruth & Birren, 1985; Vaillant & Vaillant, 1990). More significant is the lack of consensus regarding just what creativity is.

Psychological definitions of what constitutes creativity are diverse and incorporate the process of creativity (Dowd, 1989), the source of creativity (e.g., the notion of basic talent, or *genius,* and the need for "appropriate experiences" for the nurturance of creativity; Abra & Valentine-French, 1991, p. 240) and the originality of creative products. Originality seems to be one of the most common characteristics of creativity as it is conceptualized in psychological theory (e.g., Abra, 1989; Dowd, 1989; Vaillant & Vaillant, 1990).

For practical and experimental purposes, however, psychologists have used a tautological definition of creativity; creativity is what is measured by tests of creativity, especially those measuring preference for complexity and divergent thinking. Creativity is quantified in a variety of ways, including number of test responses (fluency), their novelty (originality), and their diversity (flexibility); it is then correlated with gender, age, personality test results, or examined under experimentally induced problem-solving situations.

Such tests, while convenient and useful for generating numerical data, have been criticized because they do not clearly represent the construct *creativity* as it has been defined in theories of creativity across the life course—that is, they lack construct validity. A more immediate problem is the subjectivity inherent in the interpretation of creativity in many studies: Woodman and Schoonfeldt (1989) noted evidence of experimenter bias in interpreting males' responses as more creative than females'. In addition to the problems of construct validity and experimenter bias, there is a problem of predictive validity, which is most clearly represented by the samples used in creativity research. Most of the participants in creativity studies have not "by deed verified . . . their genuine creative productivity" (Abra, 1989, p. 107)—that is, these are typically studies of creativity among people who may not be especially creative (see also, Simonton, 1990).

Consequently, our ability to compare results and draw general conclusions from studies of creativity is mitigated by differences in operational definitions of creativity, differences in samples, and differences in the demands of the task as it represents creativity. Studies relying primarily on tests of creativity are suspect and we are uncomfortable trying to conclude that there are or are not sex differences in creativity in late life.

This state of affairs in the study of creativity has suggested an alternative, historiometric approach that simply examines life span creative achievements, assuming that "when we focus on those whose achievements history has eventually deemed 'great' beyond question . . . definition becomes superfluous" (Abra & Valentine-French, 1991, p. 236). Such an approach, primarily focusing on creative output at different ages, leads to the conclusion that there are age differences in creative output in different domains, and that there are sex differences, illustrated most notably by the relative absence of creative women. This is the issue to which we now turn, beginning with an examination of psychological theories related to women's creativity.

BACK TO THE DRAWING BOARD:
CREATIVITY, AGING, AND GENDER

Although empirical research on the subject is strained, psychologists have suggested various perspectives correlating creativity with aging and with gender. Some of these perspectives are cautious at best; others, unencumbered by data, are more wildly speculative. Those that seem most relevant will be addressed here.

CREATIVITY AND TOTAL OUTPUT

First, it is possible that the best predictor of creative output is the simplest: the more one does the more likely at least some of it is to be creative. Simonton (1990) has suggested that lifetime creative contributions depend on precocity (how early creativity began), longevity (how long one lives), and total lifetime output. These three factors are mitigated by a fourth, the area or domain of creativity: "Quantity and hence quality of output is apparently dependent solely on the particular form of creative expression" (Simonton, 1990, p. 324). Thus, the older one is, the more creative work one is likely to have produced, depending on how early one began and on the field in which one has chosen to work. (Abra [1989] has noted, however, that the relationship between quantity and quality may be the reverse of what Simonton suggests; that is, quality work may lead to greater quantity by virtue of the reinforcement one receives for it.) While Simonton does not explicitly address women's creativity, the applicability of his view is obvious: Women live longer than men, but their creative output would depend on equal access, especially early in life, to creative endeavors. That is, if creative men in the sciences peak early, as has been suggested, then women's creative scientific output would peak early only if they had the same access to those fields. Likewise, if artists generally peak late, men and women artists would be more likely to peak simultaneously if they had the same access to the art world early in their careers and continued to produce at equal rates. This apparently trivial point, we will show, is one of the most consistently addressed by art historians and artists themselves.

CREATIVITY AND POSTFORMAL THOUGHT

A contextualistic, cognitive approach has been suggested by Benack, Basseches, and Swan (1989), who see creativity as "a response to ill-defined problems, involving the breaking away from existing ways of thinking, creating relations among dissociated or even contradictory elements and resulting in novel and valuable products" (p. 204). In other words, creativity in adults demands the ability to tolerate ambiguity (ill-defined problems), consider opposing views, generate new ways of seeing a problem, and combine logic with intuition and emotion—a cognitive orientation that might be seen as postformal (beyond formal operations). In addition, this contextualistic approach engenders an expanded view of what constitutes creativity: ". . . people are 'authors' of their moral systems, their sense of personal identity, their views of politics, and their ways of understanding and relating to their children" (p. 207). That is, rather than focusing exclusively on cognitive processes related to creativity, the manner in which most people create their own lives should also be examined.

SOCIAL PSYCHOLOGICAL COMPONENTS OF CREATIVITY

While not specifically presenting a life course orientation on creativity, Amabile's (1983; 1989) social psychological approach is useful. In particular, Amabile's research suggests several conditions that might diminish creative ability: anticipating being evaluated for a creative product, being rewarded in a way that makes an intrinsically motivated task seem like work, eliminating the freedom that makes the task more fun, and facing competing and stressful demands. By contrast, early exposure to models (e.g., being the offspring of an artist), low authoritarianism and restrictiveness in the family, and encouragement toward independence can nurture creative ability. This view suggests that gender differences in creativity may arise from differences in how critically men and women expect their work to be evaluated (if they expect it to be evaluated at all), in reward structures, in role conflict and competing demands placed on the artist, and on socialization to roles as man, woman, or artist.

AGE-RELATED CHANGES IN CREATIVITY

Abra (1989) has addressed some issues that might predict changes in creativity due to the aging process. For example, cognitive factors may be related to age-specific changes in creativity: A decline in memory or in fluid intelligence may lead to a loss of creativity generally or of the flexibility required for originality. Similarly, changes in presumed motives for creativity may influence creative capacities. Specifically,

Abra suggests (1989) that creativity would decline concomitant with declines in the selfishness required to create; the fear of death (driving a desire for immortality), the self-confidence necessary for creative exhibitionism, and the tolerance for ambiguity that motivates a desire to find both novel problems and creative solutions. Finally, a decline in energy with age may exhaust the persistence that underlies any creative act. (It is quite possible, also, that creativity may facilitate successful aging and negate these declines, rather than vice versa.) These factors suggest some important considerations for gender issues in late life creativity; Abra's discussion of these issues (Abra, 1989; Abra & Valentine-French, 1991) is extensive enough to provide the point of departure for the rest of our consideration of gender and creativity.

HEREDITY AND PHYSIOLOGY

Perhaps the most controversial suggestion from the psychology of sex differences in creativity is that women's hormone, brain, and hormone-brain interactions reduce their creativity or channel it into areas different from men's. For example, this view posits that fluctuations in self-confidence, arousal, and mood related to hormonal changes would interfere with creativity since a potentially creative woman's sensitivity would be 'a sometime thing' (Abra & Valentine-French, 1991, p. 243; by extension, birth control pills and menopause might increase creative expression through freedom from the menstrual cycle).

Apparent brain lateralization differences have spawned the view that women are creative in different ways from men. (This view arises from men's seeming superiority at lateralizing and localizing functions in one hemisphere and women's seeming superiority at bilateral functioning.) For adherents of this view, women should be better at creative tasks using both hemispheres simultaneously (e.g., literature and dance) and poorer at activities involving, say, predominantly the right hemisphere (e.g., music and art). Finally, brain-hormone interactions suggest that women may be poorer at creative expression demanding spatial abilities (i.e., the visual arts). This view on hereditary differences as they apply to creative contributions is noted by Vernon (1989):

> It is entirely implausible that human society should approve of females becoming highly talented performers of music, dance, and drama, and even allowing them to become creative writers, while at the same time, disapproving of their becoming musical composers or painters. To me, this is the crux of the argument for attributing sex differences in creativity, at least in part, to genetic factors. (pp. 102–103)

EXPERIENCES SPECIFIC TO CREATIVITY

Differences in technical training and in education may produce significant differences in creative contributions. As we will see, the ability to innovate depends in great measure on the confidence one has in one's basic skills (which are acquired through training and practice). Sang (1981), writing from the perspective of a therapist who works with creative women, has described the absence in women's lives of what she calls "process models, . . . a kind of apprenticeship in which the learner has an opportunity to see, step by step, how another person deals with the nitty gritty, everyday aspects of her profession" (p. 46). This illustrates another point we shall make: Creative women have historically lacked same-sex role models.

Experiences Related to Childbearing and Childrearing

Bearing and raising children may affect creative output by impacting motivation, time, and energy. Abra and Valentine-French (1991) note Isadora Duncan's suggestion that no creative activity could equal childbearing: "Oh, women, what is the good of us learning to become lawyers, painters, or sculptors when this miracle exists?" (p. 255). Generally, then, procreation might reduce the uncertainty of one's purpose in life and diminish fears of death, thereby reducing some of the major existential motives assumed by psychologists to be important for creativity. By contrast, some women claim that parenthood has contributed to their creativity by placing new demands on their intellectual and emotional flexibility and by generating personal experiences they can draw on in their work (see Abra & Valentine-French, 1991). In any event, creativity requires persistence; children require competing time and energy. The relationship between childrearing, homemaking, and creative careers was investigated by Stohs (1992), who examined sex differences in the careers of middle-aged former students at the School of the Art Institute of Chicago. Marital status was not related to career pattern, but number of children was: women with the fewest children were the most likely to have had continuous careers.

Ironically, then, even though women live longer than men, they may actually spend fewer years at creative endeavors than their shorter lived male counterparts. And childrearing concerns may mean that "any later rise [in creative output] may reflect not genuine growth in the creative drive but its artificial suppression earlier" (Abra, 1989, p. 121).

PERSONAL CHARACTERISTICS
RELATED TO GENDER ROLE

The list of personal characteristics attributed to femininity and presumed to inhibit creative expression is endless. For example, passivity, unselfishness, and conformity are attitudes encouraged in women and are also "destructive to creative work" (Abra, 1989, p. 120). Women are also presumably socialized to lack confidence, autonomy, persistence, independence, competitiveness, and a willingness to take risks; to set their sights lower than men; and to need the approval of others too much to sustain creative activity (Abra & Valentine-French, 1991). Similarly, for Sang's (1981) construction of creativity as exhibitionism, socialization differences mean that women are less likely to be creative: The need to seek approval from others discourages exhibitionism among women.

Finally, Abra and Valentine-French (1991) note that midlife may be a time of potential change in gender identity: men may realize emerging nurturant and dependent qualities in themselves, and women may face a similar emergence of assertiveness and independence. Given these theories of late life androgyny, understanding personal characteristics is particularly important if women's heightened awareness of their assertiveness and independence also increases their creativity.

CULTURAL DIFFERENCES IN CREATIVITY
AND DOMAINS OF EXPRESSION

It is quite possible that some of the presumed differences in male and female creative contributions reflect cultural definitions of what constitutes creativity. Perhaps, as has been suggested about the labor force, women's creative contributions are less valued (and, hence, considered less creative, since value is inherent in many definitions of creativity) because they are women's contributions. And if there is any hereditary basis to creativity, it may occur through "specific creativities" (à la Howard Gardner's multiple intelligences) whereby one is "at promise" for a particular field: "Achievement, then, would depend on finding one's niche. . . . [H]istory's purported achievement differences may reduce to the arbitrary veneration of some activities over others, and different opportunities to try out various niches, because it is on this that finding one's niche depends" (Abra & Valentine, 1991, pp. 274–275).

In sum, psychological conceptions of gender, age, and creativity suggest a focus on several components of women's life course experiences. While there may be a hereditary or physiological basis for some differences in creative expression, those differences are magnified by several other factors: training and education; the availability of models; childrearing and homemaking roles and their effect on motivation, energy, and years of creative potential; personal characteristics attributed to feminine socialization; and cultural standards defining what constitutes creativity and to whom those creative outlets are open.

MEN AND WOMEN MAKING ART

We draw specific examples of issues in women's creativity from the visual arts. However, it is not our intention to suggest that all creativity is art, that all art is creative, or that all art is made by professionals. In other words, creativity, making art, and making a living at art are not always the same thing, psychologists's assumptions about creative contributions notwithstanding. These issues require elaboration by the second author.

AN ARTIST'S ASIDE

This section is an attempt to reconcile the psychological investigations of creativity with an artist's experience. In surveying the psychological research, I was struck by the absence of a central definition of creativity. This is not to suggest that artists have a ready definition, but then neither is creativity an issue of much interest to artists. (This is due not to anti-intellectualism but to a lack of necessity. As the painter Barnett Newman once remarked about a parallel issue, "Aesthetics is for artists like ornithology is for the birds" [Johnson, 1982, p. 14].) It does seem, however, that this fuzziness of conception hampers meaningful attempts to measure, quantify, or analyze creativity.

PSYCHOLOGISTS' CONCEPTIONS OF ARTISTIC CREATIVITY

Lacking clear definitions, many studies limit creativity (some to the point of speciousness) to performance on tests and exercises. Sampling producing artists (e.g., Crosson & Robertson-Tschabo, 1983) seems a laudable approach in that it transcends these limits by surveying individuals of demonstrable creativity. But in fact this approach only underscores a central failing of much of the writing about artists' creativity: it consistently confuses art with creativity. There is simply no necessary relation between the two concepts.

The art/creativity confusion is especially problematic when professional artists are discussed—for example, applying Amabile's (1983) social psychological research. The very factors that Amabile identifies as undermining creativity are precisely those that constitute the professional art world: evaluation (art criticism), work-like rewards (financial self-support), eliminating freedom (market pressures), and stress (competition and demands of dealers, curators, and collectors). This is most clearly the case in the contemporary art world, where art has become a commodity sold in markets governed by all the economic realities of late capitalism. What this discrepancy means is either that Amabile is wrong, or that the art world is incapable of producing creative work. The fact remains that at least some professional artists, some of the time, overcome (or respond to) these barriers, making creative work within an environment that Amabile suggests precludes creativity.

Some of the confusion of art and creativity derives from romanticized notions about artists and art making. For example, in his eclectic survey, Abra (1989) perpetuates the idea that creativity is motivated partly by a desire for immortality, which in turn stems from a fear of death. This approach begs the fundamental question because it fails to define creativity, then links creativity (whatever it may be) to similarly undefined psychological states. Furthermore, in my experience with contemporary artists, the association is insupportable. (Louise Nevelson said, "I've never feared death. To hell with it. I've met it daily and I want to feel I was [as] aware of it as possible" [Johnson, 1982, p. 46].) Sang's formulation of creativity as entailing exhibitionism is similarly deficient and reductivistic: It discounts creativity in favor of behavior that is typically considered pathological, it attributes a motive to artists that is not generalizable, and it lacks empirical support.

The work of Benack, Basseches, and Swan (1989), postulating creativity as a process of problem solving seems much closer to the mark. However, in making art, creativity is not only a matter of defining and solving the problem, but usually of generating it as well. The authors' expanded notion of the constitution of creativity—individuals as authors of their own lives—is also much more in keeping with most artists' experiences than scenarios of existential angst and mad genius. Furthermore, it reestablishes the value of creative activities which have generally been undervalued, in particular, the traditional household contributions of women.

I am also distrustful of descriptions of the visual arts as a right brain activity. Not only does the split brain hypothesis seem to result in simplistic applications, but diverse studies (e.g., Gazzaniga & Ledoux, 1978) stress the nature of the brain as an integrated (and integrative) system.

In this light, the theory seems to have little application to creativity. Additionally, the process of making visual art involves much more than the manipulation of spatial forms (a right brain activity). A work of art is not simply constituted by composition (design), technique, and/or mimesis: artworks usually proceed from a much more complex interweaving of the artist's philosophical stance, concern for art theory and art history, interest in specific problems, and so on. Thus, even if manipulating spatial forms is entirely a right brain activity, a work of art is much more than the product of such manipulation.

MARGINAL IDENTITY AND ARTISTIC CREATIVITY

Implicit in many of the conceptions of art/creativity discussed above is the popular characterization of artists as crazed and/or childlike victims of their passions. The titles (and especially the film versions) of Irving Stone's novels about Vincent van Gogh and Michelangelo (*Lust for Life* and *The Agony and the Ecstasy*) are prime examples of this characterization. While the art world has its share of dramatic and tragic stories, the biographies receiving notice—as in other public fields—tend to be those which are most extreme. Habituation to this image is objectionable: It positions artists on the social margin and denies them the status of responsible adults. Even when the marginalization is intended to be flattering (e.g., ascriptions of genius), it still relegates the artist to the social fringe. Additionally, any psychological theory based on these popular assumptions will fail in application because, once again, these extreme cases are not generalizable.

The consequence of marginalization for women artists is a double denial of their role in society: They are twice damned, once as women and again as artists. In this context, the relative lack of women composers and visual artists noted by Vernon (1989) can be understood without resorting to his theory of biological sex differences in creativity. One common alternative to Vernon's interpretation attributes the slight recognition of women artists not to a biological lack of creativity, but to women's cultural lack of authority. This view proposes that there are numerous cultural constraints operating against all artists' opportunities for fame. Within these constraints, women have been permitted to be creative dancers, singers, and actresses because these women play female roles, offering no competition to men and because they are interpreters of other artists' (usually males') works. Most often, they perform under male authorities within male-dominated contexts. As women playwrights, directors, writers, and choreographers are no more numerous in the canon than women composers or visual "fine" artists, it is the issue of authority which is central. This suggests that it is more permissible for women to be creative interpreters than creative producers, and the practice of assuming male pen names proceeds from awareness of that fact. Finally, sociobiological ideologies like Vernon's are, in turn, part of the mechanism of power whereby women are excluded from the creative realm.

One antidote to the conventional view of the marginalized artist is offered by Lucy Lippard (1984). She has referred to artists as "cultural workers," partly to overcome romantic stereotyping. While this approach proceeds from her politics, it is also broadly significant in its formulation of the artist as socially enmeshed. Proceeding from her conception of artistic creativity, we can see creativity not merely as an interior psychological state somehow equivalent to exhibitionism or mortality phobia, but as a process of engagement that situates the artist (and artwork) amidst social discourse.

THE PROBLEM OF ORIGINALITY

Although an artwork is an intricate synthesis of (at least partly preexisting) intellectual, personal, and physical components, art production is haunted by the specter of originality—and conceptions of creativity universally involve notions of originality. This is certainly true in the conceptions of psychologists, and emerges in the implicit assumption that works displaying originality must be good art. Even art historians have traditionally tended to equate good art with originality. But there have also been specific parameters—if one strayed too far from the art world discourse, one's work was ignored and/or lost. Being positioned outside the discourse has been a perennial problem for those who were socially outside the places of discourse: artists who were women, ethnic or racial minorities, the wrong social class, or geographically distant.

The visual art that is represented in the standard art history surveys (i.e., the work constituting the canon) generally owes its position to a positive assessment of its originality. This originality is usually stylistic—most simply, aspects of how the work looks. Thus the standard chronology for Western art (and European modern art in particular) is essentially a charting of stylistic innovations. In this view, a group of artists (the avant garde) reacts against the status quo, ultimately becomes the new regime, and is then fodder for the next group of stylistic innovators. This modernist conception of the history and nature of art as a succession of original styles is falling out of favor, due partly to its implication of progress in art. Recent thought has also focused on a critique of the "cult of originality" implicit in the modernist view (e.g., novelty as a criterion for valuing a work of art), and this approach appears in the work of both scholars and artists.

Indeed, a genre of artwork called *appropriation* has arisen which, in part, questions the possibility and/or meaningfulness of originality. Appropriation follows the lead of the artist Marchel Duchamp (1887–1968), whose paradigmatic "readymades" were merely everyday objects selected by the artist for display. (A 1915 readymade was a snow shovel titled *In Advance of the Broken Arm.*) Jean-Christophe Bailly writes, "[Duchamp] summed up his intentions as 'relating notions of aesthetic worth to a decision of the intellect and not to a facility or cleverness of the hand,'" (Bailly, 1986, p. 54). Duchamp's point was that the artist's act of selection can constitute a work of art.

Appropriation art also draws on such thinkers as Walter Benjamin, Jean Baudrillard, and Jacques Derrida in asking questions about authorship, representation, and mechanical reproduction. A concern for these questions is evident in the work of Sherrie Levine, who created a series consisting of rephotographed and represented photographs of earlier masters.

As Anne Hoy notes, "it is ironic that Levine's originality should derive from the thoroughness of her denial of originality" (1987, p. 122). The appropriationist example is important in its explication of the complex nature of originality, and its conception of the artwork as a system of signs within a broader cultural context. Further, its lesson may be that any theory of artistic creativity must go beyond the psychology of the individual to encompass the creative person as an element in a network of cultural relations.

CONTEXT AND IDENTITY IN THE VISUAL ARTS

Munsterberg (1983) has provided specific examples of changes in creativity with age among visual artists. There are artists, for instance, who appear to have created their own special style in old age *(Altersstil),* including Michelangelo, Rembrandt, Monet, and Matisse. Others are actually acknowledged to have done their best work in later life: Lovis Corinth, Christian Rohlfs, and Gauguin. Grandma Moses, who took up art in her 70s and painted over 1,000 works—is among those artists who didn't actually begin their careers until late life. Still others begin early and manage to remain productive throughout their adult years. Some eminent artists seem to have lost both creative power and vision in their old age. Munsterberg includes Picasso here, quoting the critic John Berger: "'[Picasso's later works] are no more than exercises in painting such as one might expect a serious young man to carry out, but not an old man who has gained the freedom to be himself.'" (Munsterberg, 1983, pp. 182–183). Dali may be another example; he is considered by some to have yielded too much to commercialism. Some artists were forced to give up art or exhibitions long before death, including Mary Cassatt, who suffered from vision and health problems and lost her eyesight by age 69. Kathe Kollwitz completed one of her more remarkable self-portraits only a few years before her death in 1947 at age 78, although the Nazis kept her from exhibiting after 1936. Finally, Munsterberg describes the work of some artists who continued into their nineties—Georgia O'Keeffe and Sonia Delaunay, for example—and notes that most evidence of such longevity is recent and has been largely characteristic of women.

Munsterberg's general review, however, fails to take into consideration a number of factors that differentiate the late life artistic contributions of men and women. With the exception of biographies of artists who happen to have been older women, especially work on Georgia O'Keeffe, art historians have not specifically addressed older women as a category of artists shaped by the aging process, sex, or social constructions of gender. However, they have noted a number of demographic, institutional and cultural issues that affect women's abilities to be artists across the life course.

Becoming an artist depends first on survival. When women's life expectancy was shortened by female infanticide or by death in childbirth, the number of women who could be artists, especially late life artists, was obviously diminished. Likewise, being an artist was difficult when marriage occurred at an early age, and was also related to the average number of children, size of household, and nature of family responsibilities (Slatkin, 1985). It may even be the case that the often-noted increase in women artists in the 19th century was related to a decline in the birth rate and to an increase in the number of unmarried women.

Demographic factors aside, artistic expression does not occur in a social, cultural, and political vacuum.

> The problem lies . . . with the naive idea that art is the direct, personal expression of individual emotional experience—a translation of personal life into visual terms. Yet art is almost never that; great art certainly never. The making of art involves a self-consistent language of form, more or less dependent upon . . . given temporally-defined conventions, schema, or systems of notation, which have to be learned or worked out, through study, apprenticeship, or a long period of individual experimentation. (Nochlin, 1973, p. 5)

There are three major problems faced by artists, then: preparing, earning a living (by selling their work or, by some other means), and gaining recognition (Baker, 1973).

As we noted earlier, innovation requires confidence in one's basic ability, and those abilities are acquired through training and practice (Slatkin, 1985). Historically, women have been denied access to the same education and training as men, and, even recently, art histories have denied women role models. For example, historical painting was the "highest" form of art from the Renaissance to the end of the 19th century (Nochlin, 1973). Since many historical paintings required nudes, training typically involved painting from live nude models. Yet, even into the 1890s, women were denied access to live nudes. Nor was art training in general available to women, although there were some exceptions. Until the 20th century, most women artists had fathers who were artists or, "later in the nineteenth and twentieth centuries, had a close personal connection with a strong or dominant male artist" (Nochlin, 1973, p. 30). Often women were expected to copy their fathers' methods and were given the most menial tasks to perform in the studio (Slatkin, 1985). Women were also excluded from much of the socializing among art students, from the arenas of male bonding: "bars, bistros, studios, artists' clubs, even whorehouses of the turn of the [20th] century. . . . Excluded from these forums, women did not become practiced in the craft of self-definition" (Munro, 1979, p. 27). The effect of these differences in training and education was certainly to reduce the output of women artists into this century. Nochlin goes so far as to declare, "We have suggested that it was indeed *institutionally* impossible for women to achieve excellence or success on the same footing as men, *no matter what* their talent, or genius" [italics added] (1973, p. 37).

Finally, cultural conditions for women's artistic expression include standards of what art is and who is to be an artist. The definition of what constitutes an important contribution to the world of art may include a new style or technique, a new format or composition, a new approach to an old subject, influence on other artists, or recognition by the general culture (Slatkin, 1985). If art history texts are any indication, until recently it could be concluded that women have produced few important contributions. Tufts (1981) describes one interview with a prominent author of art history texts, including this appraisal: "'I may very well in the next edition include a woman artist, but at least until the most recent edition [1978] I have not been able to find a woman artist who clearly belongs in a one-volume history of art'" (p. 151). Even women who were successful in their time have been diminished in or excluded from art histories. Additionally, the attitude toward women conveyed in some texts has been problematic, as illustrated by this quotation from a 1970s text: "'One of the greatest assets an artist can have is a wife who believes in him and his work. . . . A wife who is willing to endure hardships and disappointments on the long road to the fame that eludes most artists derives her pleasure and fulfillment from nurturing the creative spirits of her husband'" (Tufts, 1981, p. 153). While things have changed and art by women is incorporated in contemporary art histories, the point is still critical because the aging women artists with whom we are concerned would have had no same-sex role models if they relied on art history texts; nor could they have gotten the impression that art could be a woman's life.

Standards of what constitutes important art are still changing, not always in ways that increase the inclusion of women. Heartney has noted that the hope of the early 1980s for women's art was dimmed as it became clear that the time was really "about the reinstatement of painting as a dominant mode of expression and, with it, the tradition of the heroic male artist" (1987, p. 140). This focus on male artists was illustrated by the Museum of Modern Art (MoMA) survey exhibition that prompted the founding of the Guerilla Girls. As the art market boomed, a new emphasis on saleable art that was "decisively unfeminine" took shape. Public funding that had been instrumental in nurturing women's art was reduced, and, as the 1980 census showed, women were still less likely than men to be making a living at art. This last point suggests that cultural standards do not merely define what is art, but who is to be an artist. This issue has been with women since the time when they were forbidden by law to sign contracts, run businesses, or practice a trade. It has persisted in social class distinctions that kept upperclass women homebound and permitted them to practice crafts that were rarely considered fine art, and has emerged more recently in empirical research (e.g., Stohs, 1992) and in the 1980 census, which showed that only 38% of all artists were women and that women in art disciplines earned an average of $5,700 to the $13,000 earned by men.

In sum, whatever differences may exist between men and women at birth or even as a result of early childhood experiences, women's life-long contributions in the visual arts must be examined in the context of (a) vast differences in family, training, and education; (b) women's abilities to deal with competing expectations concerning childrearing and homemaking; and (c) their capacity to work within a context which only reluctantly values their contributions. Although the experiences of today's women artists are different, this is the history that embraces the experiences of older women artists. Age, if nothing else, is an accumulation of experiences in that environment.

We would suggest that these contextual issues are necessary for understanding women's artistic endeavors—but they are not sufficient. While these issues certainly will be addressed in the rest of this chapter, an additional concern lies with women artists' dynamic relation to what we consider to be a critical point of convergence between artist and developmental psychologist—and one that is rarely addressed by either: artistic identity as it encompasses women's motives for making art, their desire to find an artistic signature, and their ability to overcome substantial barriers to do so.

CONCEPTUALIZING ADULT IDENTITY

Although there are a variety of perspectives on adult identity (most based at least partly on Erik Erikson's view), they agree on one important issue: Adult identity must be seen as an act of integration. In essence, "physical characteristics, abilities, motives, goals, attitudes, values, and social roles [must be attributed] over time as belonging to the self" (Whitbourne, 1986, p. 179). This integrated sense of self, in turn, provides the basis for adults' perceptions of who they are and how they relate to society—that is, the means by which they "know themselves and . . . explain who they are to others" (Kaufman, 1986, p. 25). The development of such a social identity further requires the individual to consider how to prioritize multiple group memberships (e.g., class, race, gender, or age), their emotional significance and meaning, and the facets of identity they represent (Andrews, 1991). The outcome is an integrated framework which underlies the meaning assigned to the past, the ability to cope with the present, and the continuity necessary to anticipate the future. Paradoxically, though, continuity is always accompanied by discontinuity as new experiences can be expected to challenge the sense of self.

Identity is, then, not a product of adult development, but a process. As such, it is related to studies of creativity in two ways. First, identity formation itself may be seen as a creative act. Self-attributes are formulated and reformulated in a manner that is "ongoing, continuous, creative" (Kaufman, 1986, p. 14) as individuals integrate "areas of meaning with [personal and cultural] symbolic force—which explain, unify, and give substance to their perceptions of who they are and how they see themselves participating in social life" (p. 25). The creation of a life story is a fundamental part of adult identity formation. Second, the individual must integrate several facets of identity, one of which may be the definition of self as creative. For our purposes, this may entail efforts to maintain and prioritize a personally and culturally powerful artistic identity in relation to other powerful identities such as wife, mother, and aging woman. The writings of Anne Truitt—her life story— reflect these issues.

DEFINING THE SELF AS ARTIST: ANNE TRUITT

In 1974, the artist Anne Truitt decided to "record my life for one year and see what happened" (1982, p. 4); she continued writing until 1980, grappling with her definition of herself as an artist.[2] Her *Daybook* (the first of three such introspections) illustrates the evolution of an artistic identity—gaining awareness of how her work comes to be, dealing with the reactions of others, examining the competing sides of her own identity, and, most important, revealing the artist as she recognizes a sense of alienation and specialness.

Truitt seeks to understand the motives behind her own work, realizing that the process is unpredictable and does not always result in a product: "It sometimes happens unexpectedly. . . . a series of three sculptures may present themselves somewhere that seems high over my head in my consciousness. This can happen anywhere, . . . characteristically without any preparation on my part. . . . Less than a quarter of them ever reach actuality" (p. 93).

The artist's identity is public and is a condition of his or her work. Truitt reflects on one encounter with three visitors to her studio: "[They] took for granted that their own artistic context was the only one possible . . . They delivered their opinions as if from the reverberating halls of Zeus. . . . At the end of twenty minutes or so of solemn gazing and pronouncements, one of them said how nice the work would look in marble" (p. 139).

The artist's identity has many aspects, and they may occasionally compete with one another. Truitt is particularly evocative as she describes the relationship between the artist and the mother in her own self:

> It is becoming apparent to me that the mother and the artist do not
> speak much to each other, and when they do the speech is initiated by

---

[2] Some of Truitt's reflections on art and artistic identity are conveyed in a set of interviews with male and female artists over the age of 60 (Berman, 1983). They were absorbed in their work and committed enormous energy to it, and they were able to combine absorption and strength with tenacity and growing mastery of materials. They continued searching for something in their art and were convinced that it could come at any time and any age. They recalled that "they became artists not on a whim but because the idea of it consciously completed them as individuals" (p. 78); they rejected the notion of a new and different style—an *Altersstil*—but described a sense of their own evolution and enrichment as artists.

the artist who wishes to be off about her business. She chivies the mother to get herself time. Otherwise she views her as a source of knowledge, but of knowledge already assimilated—and here it occurs to me that the artist is giving the mother short shrift in a way that strikes me at this moment as rude. . . . The artist could not have come into herself without the mother's experience. . . . For the artist has grown out of that rich ground as surely as she has grown out of the student, the wife, the nurse, the friend. The fact that the mother is bothersome, takes up the artist's time with her demands, in no way reduces this fundamental reliance on her wisdom. The artist is also more dependent on the mother than she likes to acknowledge. (pp. 183–184)

Truitt's artistic identity is grounded in her childhood, and it is to that ground that she returns often in her writing: "I believe that I return so persistently to the insights of my childhood because what I think of as my nerve in art had its origin at that time in my first recognition that I was alien in the universe" (p. 225). Yet her recognition of that almost hidden sense of specialness comes late, in her fifth decade, as does her consciousness of its effects on her and her willingness to call herself an artist: "It slowly dawned on me that the more visible my work became, the less visible I grew to myself . . . It was as if the artist in me had ravished the rest of me and got away scot-free (p. 4). . . . I am an artist. Even to write it makes me feel deeply uneasy. . . . to think of myself as an artist was self-idolatry" (p. 44). Her efforts to define what it is that makes artists special and to accept that in herself constitute most of her writing; one metaphor evokes the essence of that struggle, a struggle we believe to be the key missing factor in both psychologists' and art historians' considerations of women's lifelong artistic careers:

Their [artists'] essential effort is to catapult themselves wholly, without holding back one bit, into a course of action without having any idea where they will end up. They are like riders who gallop into the night, eagerly leaning on their horse's neck, peering into a blinding rain. And they have to do it over and over again. When they find out they have ridden and ridden—maybe for years, full tilt–in what is for them a mistaken direction, they must unearth within themselves some readiness to turn direction and to gallop off again. (p. 26)

CONTEXT AND IDENTITY IN FEMALE
VISUAL ARTISTS: A COLLAGE

Our review of research and speculation regarding women's life span creativity suggests a scheme for examining women's late life artistic expression. We propose the following: Artistic contributions and innovations can and do continue into late life and, in some cases, emerge in late life. However, there are a number of contextual obstacles women must overcome to be able to make art and to make a living at it. In addition to this context, understanding women's artistic expression across the life course depends on our recognizing that they make art for a variety of reasons. Some make art because it's fun or because they have a vision that demands some form of expression—these women do not necessarily define themselves as artists. Others make art because they have to, because their artistic identity demands it. Those who most strongly identify themselves as artists may be better able to overcome contextual obstacles. In the rest of this chapter, we examine the interplay between context and identity in mid- to late life women visual artists through pieces of their life stories.

LATECOMERS TO ARTISTIC EXPRESSION

Artistic expression, one might suggest, does not diminish with age if even untrained individuals can discover their own talents late in life. Examples of productive artists who began their careers late in life and have been recognized commercially and/or aesthetically reinforce this claim. Such examples are informative, not because they necessarily demonstrate the potential for creativity in late life, as historiometric views might suggest, but because they illustrate the relationship between motive and identity and the context in which artistic contributions are evaluated. Latecomers to art, even recognized ones, do not necessarily identify themselves as artists. One example would be Grandma (Tressa) Prisbey (b. 1896), whose artistic expression began with a pencil collection. (See Figures 8.1 and 8.2). She claims that she needed a place to keep her approximately 17,000 pencils, so she used items collected from a landfill and created *Bottle Village*—9 buildings, a wishing well, a leaning tower of Pisa, a bottle tree, a fountain, and a wall of burned-out television tubes—which became a tourist stop in Santa Susanna, California. Grandma Prisbey also wrote her own brochures and gave tours of the "village." A number of explanations have been offered for her *Bottle Village* and other works of art: She was attempting to recapture the attention she got as a child, the trash she recycled brought back memories of better times, or the work represented the grief she felt over the deaths of siblings and six of her seven children. Grandma Prisbey says simply that she kept doing it because she was having a good time (Greenfield, 1986).

Similar stories of latecomers who do not self-consciously identify themselves as artists can be found in "folk art" programs, including the

FIGURE 8.1   Grandma Prisbey, *The Little Chapel.* Photo by Amanda Devine, 1977. Courtesy of Preserve Bottle Village.

Grass Roots Art and Community Efforts (GRACE) program in north-eastern Vermont.[3] The program was started by painter and sculptor Don Sunseri in the belief that "everyone has the innate ability to make art" (Straw, 1987, p. 3A). It provides art supplies, classes, motivation, and, increasingly, recognition for dozens of artists, most of whom are residents of nursing homes. Two of the artists, Dot Kibbee and Gayleen

---

[3] The information about GRACE was obtained from Don Sunseri. Information about the program and about traveling shows by GRACE artists may be requested at the following address: GRACE, RFD Box 49, West Glover, Vermont, 05875.

FIGURE 8.2   Grandma Prisbey, *Rumpus Room* (foreground) and *Round House* (background). Photo by Amy Skillman, 1982. Courtesy of Preserve Bottle Village.

Aiken, have been exhibited widely. (See Figure 8.3). Kibbee, a retired nurse, has never had formal training and does not want it, claiming that she wouldn't know what to do with it and that they wouldn't know what to do with her. She works in brightly colored acrylics (so the paintings can be washed), creating landscapes, animals, and patterns, most of which tell a story. Gayleen Aiken paints landscapes and her "Raimbilli cousins," a family she created when she was in grade school to pretend she had lots of cousins. (See Figure 8.4.) The paintings reflect Aiken's own love of making music with instruments from her past, ranging from nickelodeons to tiny harmonicas (Page, 1986).

Other latecomers are motivated by religious visions rather than artistic identity: "these 'self-taught artists' more aptly describe themselves as missionaries, mystics, mediums, spiritualists, clairvoyants,

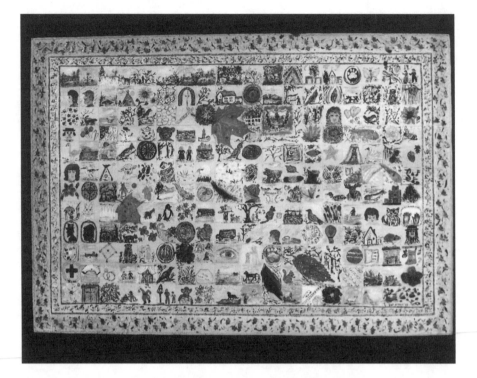

FIGURE 8.3 Dot Kibbee, *All That Glitters Is Not Gold,* 1989, acrylic with stones, feathers, seeds, leaves, thread, diamond dust, glitter, and a moth, 16½ x 24″. Photo by Michael Gray. Courtesy of the Grass Roots Art and Community Effort.

evangelists, and preachers" (Cubbs, 1991, p. 2).[4] For example, Mary LeRavin (who was born at the turn of the century and died in 1992), was instructed by God to create bone art adorned with jewelry, shells, glitter, and other materials and held together by a special "God-given glue" (Cubbs, 1991). (See Figure 8.5.) Bessie Harvey (b. 1928) dug up a piece of metal in 1972. (See Figure 8.6.) The face she saw in the metal

---

[4] Social activism—art with a social, political, or historical emphasis—is another motive underlying the work of untrained artists. Examples include the patchwork pictures (*arpilleras*) created by groups of Chilean women depicting experiences of the Chilean working class and the "disappeared," or the drawings by Hiroshima survivors solicited by a television broadcaster almost 30 years after the bomb was dropped (Brett, 1987). These works are not solely produced by women or by older women but they illustrate the range of motives behind artistic expression and they also demonstrate the need to consider the relation of artistic expression to social class and race.

FIGURE 8.4 Gayleen Aiken, *My Rainbilli Cousins March*, 1984, crayon on paper, 14″ x 17″. Photo by Michael Gray. Courtesy of the Grass Roots Art and Community Effort.

became an inspiration to translate her visions into art form. Now she sees faces everywhere and creates clay figurines and dolls made of branches, roots, and stumps and adorned with hair, jewelry, paint, and feathers (*Baking in the Sun,* 1987). But even religious visionaries can have multiple motives for making art: Mary T. Smith (b. 1904) has been recognized for the powerful religious messages she began painting in her 70s, but says she started "making pictures . . . to pretty up my yard" (*Baking in the Sun,* 1987, p. 72). (See Figure 8.7.)

The motives of folk artists and religious visionaries certainly differ, but these individuals are similar in one regard: they do not specifically identify themselves as artists, and may not be concerned with the question of artistic identity at all. After a lifetime of identity formation in which other facets of the self assume primacy, it may be difficult, unnecessary, or (because being an 'artist' connotes a specialness

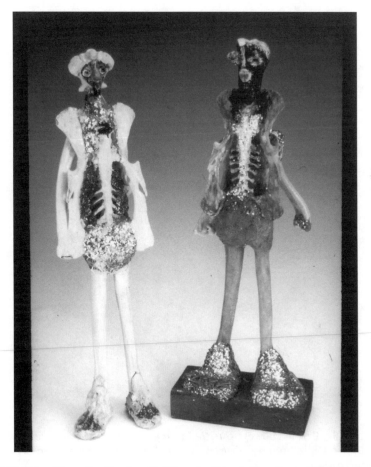

FIGURE 8.5   Mary Le Ravin, *California Black Panther,* 1990, bone and mixed media, 18 x 5½″ x 3½″ (left), *Goldilock's Fiance,* 1990, bone and mixed media, 17½ x 5 x 2½″ (right). Courtesy of the John Michael Kihler Arts Center, Sheboygan, Wisconsin.

about oneself) counter to their self-image for latecomers to develop an artistic identity.

In addition to illustrating how motive, artistic expression, and artistic identity can be distinct, these latecomers also reveal how valuation in art forms a backdrop for artistic identity. Why do others see them as artists if they do not see themselves that way? Cubbs (1991) has claimed that the art world's current appreciation of the art of religious visionaries is related to "its curious appearance—its novelty, idiosyncrasy, and

FIGURE 8.6   Bessie Harvey, *Untitled (Face)*, 1985, clay, paint, and plastics, 5½ x 5½″ x 4½″. Photo by Warren Zuelke. From the collection of Slyvia and Warren Lowe.

apparent strangeness" (Cubbs, 1991, p. 3). Another interpretation derives from the supposition that the expressive needs of folk artists and visionaries mirror those of other artists; hence the attraction of this art is that its lack of sophistication reflects the primacy of expressive needs over craftsmanship (Cubbs, 1991). Others suggest that the appreciation of untrained work serves as a rejection of the art world, with unsophisticated, innocent, or unskilled work as a purer form of art for the very reason that it is untrained. (For a related discussion of the *realpolitik* of fine art, see Sunseri's comments in Polston, 1991, p. 21.)

Whatever the interpretation, it is important to note that untrained latecomers have been recognized, and that the art world's valuation of art and of artists changes over time: "even 'bad art'. . . has become a

FIGURE 8.7 Mary T. Smith, *Jesus—I Come Back,* 1984, enamel paint on tin, 54″ x 28″. Photo by Warren Zuelke. From the collection of Sylvia and Warren Lowe.

new and lucrative category of sophisticated taste in the West" (Brett, 1987). However, those folk artists and visionaries without strong artistic identities are more likely to function independently, unconstrained by the art world's valuations.

RECOVERING ARTISTIC EXPRESSION IN MIDLIFE

A degree of withdrawal from society and concomitant involvement with the self may also make it easier for women to make art late in life—at least it may no longer be more difficult for them than for men. Latecomers to art may be freer from the constraints of family and of social roles than younger women. Frym (1979) interviewed women whose domestic roles placed their artistic careers and identities in moratorium until midlife. All of these artists described a struggle for artistic expression, a battle they began to win only after the age of 35.

For example, Helene Aylon, a painter, was married to an Orthodox rabbi. She described the difficulty of finding a time and a place to paint: "'In the afternoons I worked in the front room so I could look out the window at the children playing outside. But around five o'clock I quickly put all the paints away. The house smelled from turpentine so I cooked something with garlic and opened the windows'" (quoted in Frym, 1979, p. 21). Even after she was divorced and had her own studio, she still had to deal with her children's conflicting demands on her time and emotions: "'I'd see them off to school each morning, travel to the studio, meander around to get my bearings, do some work, and suddenly it was time to leave. I'd drive home around rush hour—start dinner at 8 o'clock at night sometimes'" (p. 24).

What is perhaps most striking about Frym's accounts of these interviews is not the context in which these women tried to make art, but their attitude toward the work itself. Frym concluded that women who begin their careers in earnest in midlife seem to exhibit enormous ambivalence about their intentions and the seriousness of their commitment to art. More than anything else, they speak of the conflicting demands of art and domesticity. Time may resolve these conflicting demands: Children grow up and husbands may be outgrown, allowing women to get back to their art. These women's ambivalence about an artistic career was paralleled by an ambivalence towards artistic identity is especially evident when contrasted with the lives of some prominent, lifelong artists.

LIFELONG CAREERS AS ARTISTS: FRANKENTHALER, NEVELSON, AND KRASNER

Because both the motive for making art and its context can change enormously over time, we have chosen to survey three women from the same period. They represent a narrow range within the art world but illustrate the importance to lifelong expression of finding an artistic identity, overcoming obstacles because that identity demands it, and continuing to evolve in that identity.

Helen Frankenthaler (b. 1928): One Signature

Helen Frankenthaler knew as a child that she was different; by the time she finished college, she was aware that art would make her a renegade: "'By then . . . I had the idea that I didn't want to repeat the patterns I had come from—certain parts of a domestic package that didn't attract me'"(quoted in Munro, 1979, p. 214). Artistically she is credited with facilitating the emergence of stain painting, a technique in which thinned paint is poured directly on a raw canvas (Johnson, 1982). Her work, *Mountains and Sea* (1952), is a seminal example of this approach. By the time she was in her twenties, she had already developed an economical and generalized style that was to become her oeuvre (Elderfield, 1982). Her expression of that oeuvre changed periodically. In her 30s, she moved toward minimal means of expression. In her 40s, she began to use acrylic paints and to create larger, brighter areas of solid color separated by areas of empty canvas. In her 50s her work began to demonstrate a new quality: "a fitful, expressive darkness, metaphor for a new level of feeling?—has begun to deepen the shadows in some of her recent works" (Munro, 1979, pp. 222–223). Later in that decade of her life, she started experimenting with stained work on paper rather than canvas, demonstrating its different qualities and intensity (Poirier, 1985).

By the late 1980s, questions were being raised about Frankenthaler's direction and the quality of her work. While one critic has dubbed her "the first major woman painter in recorded art" (Tatransky, 1985), others have chosen to damn her with faint praise: "An expedient but not entirely inapposite view situates Frankenthaler midway between the angst-fueled rituals of the abstract expressionists and the no-nonsense materialism of the color-field painters who succeeded her" (Bankowski, 1989, p. 147). Some are much less generous: "Frankenthaler is capable of gorgeous visual epiphanies, but hackneyed effects are almost as common. . . . it is nevertheless surprising that in her new work she takes no risks" ("Helen Frankenthaler," 1988, p. 189); or "Helen Frankenthaler has been on cruise control for nearly a decade. . . . Her recent works take no chances, make no attempt to explore other possibilities" (Yau, 1985, p. 86). The critics suggest that the Helen Frankenthaler who was approaching the end of her sixth decade had grown conservative. Their criticisms reflect an ongoing problem for any artist working over the life course: Regardless of one's early contributions (e.g., Frankenthaler's role in the development of color-field painting) the modernist art world demands novelty. Simultaneously, dealers want more of what sells. In Frankenthaler's case, it is also debatable whether the critics understood the importance of her work from the outset. They tended to consign her work to feminine stereotypes—remarking, for example, that she called on nature and intuition—when she was also an intellectual artist who understood modern art and innovated on the basis of that understanding (Parker & Pollock, 1981).

Perhaps Frankenthaler herself should have the last word on this question. She has asserted that, regardless of the work she does, there is always one signature. She has seen it in retrospectives featuring vastly different works. For example, "'In the late sixties I wanted to try my hand at more geometric shapes than those I had been painting previously. This meant I had to struggle to maintain my own identity'" (Galligan, 1989, p. 50). At 53, she saw herself as having evolved: "'Does life get better? Of course, one hopes one becomes more and more experienced, or profound, or stronger. Perhaps the work isn't better intrinsically, but I hope it reflects a combination of age, the worlds I have seen, my attitudes, fears, pleasures, and relationships'" (Shaw-Eagle, 1981, p. 182). Yet even at 61, she maintains an interest both in trying new things and in her signature: "'I'd like to get into sculpture again. I'm a little afraid of it and I'm not sure that sculpture is my domain—which could be a sign that it's very *much* my domain and I should fearlessly jump into it.'" (Galligan, 1989, pp. 48–49).

Louise Nevelson (1900–1988): What Is Right for the Self

Louise Nevelson was 60 when she finally started to receive broad acclaim for her sculpture. What kept her going for so many years was "her ability to throw herself energetically into her work and continue to evolve her own pictorial language" (Kronsky, 1985, p. 86)—that is, her belief in her own future and that the public simply wasn't ready for her work. (See Figure 8.8.)

Born in 1900, Nevelson first explored painting and printmaking before she turned to sculpture in the 1940s, possibly because of a great fascination with old and weathered wood. She claimed, "'From earliest, earliest childhood I knew I was going to be an artist. I felt like an artist'" (quoted in Berman, 1983, p. 78). She recalled being asked as a child what she wanted to be: "'I'm going to be an artist. No,' I added, 'I want to be a sculptor, I don't want color to help me. I got so frightened, I ran home crying. How did I know that when I never thought of it before in all my life?'" (Glimcher, 1976, p. 19). Her early conviction, which Kronsky called Nevelson's "intuitive sense of what is right for

FIGURE 8.8   Louise Nevelson, *Mrs. N's Palace,* 1964–1977, wood painted black with black mirror floor, 140″ x 239″ x 180″. Photo by Tom Crane. Photograph courtesy of the Pace Gallery, New York.

the self" (1985, p. 24), appears to have remained a part of her artistic identity; she noted later in life, "'If you know what you have, then you know that there's nobody on earth that can affect you'" (Kronsky, 1985, p. 86).

Perhaps Nevelson's conviction was related to two decisions she made early in her career, one of which seems to have earned her almost as much notoriety as her work. Feeling that marriage was compromising her responsibility to her art, she left her husband in 1931. Later she would note: "'I learned that marriage wasn't the romance that I sought but a partnership, and I didn't need a partner'" (Glimcher, 1976, p. 20). That same year, when her son, Mike, was eight years old, Nevelson left him with her mother in Maine so she could travel to Munich to study with Hans Hofmann. She remained in Munich for a time, then traveled to Vienna, Italy, and Paris before returning to New York in the summer of 1932 (Glimcher, 1976). She would later recall this event:

> The guilts and weights of separation, the weight of leaving Mike, was a great responsibility. I think people should think a million times before they give birth. The guilts of motherhood were the worst guilts in the world for me. They were really insurmountable. You see, you are depriving another human being of so many things, and the other party also knows it. That struggle blinds you. That's the price, the great price. (Quoted in Tully, 1990, p. 40; see also, Gardner, 1990).

Louise Nevelson's identity as an artist was lifelong, her creativity motivated by a conviction about what she was doing and a love of her art: "'Nothing—friendship, love, or anything—will come to such a harmony or unity as you come to in your work'" (quoted in Berman, 1983, p. 78).

Lee Krasner (1908–1984): Mrs. Pollock, the Widow, and Lee Krasner, the Artist

If one were to create a prototype of the woman artist as portrayed by psychologists and art historians, one would emerge with someone very much like Lee Krasner (See Figure 8.9). Krasner's identity as an artist emerged in relation to her family's religious background, her training, her relationship with the art community, and her identity vis-à-vis Jackson Pollock.

Krasner was the fifth of six children, and the first born in the United States, to a Russian Orthodox Jewish family from Odessa. Some have suggested that her work reflects her early experiences, surrounded by Hebrew books: calligraphic images in some of her work and the apparent manner in which she paints from the upper right part of the canvas. She recalls even as a child wanting to be an artist, although she didn't know what it meant: "'It seemed to satisfy some need in my personality'" (quoted in Berman, 1983, p. 78). As an art student, though, she lost her orthodoxy, replacing it with philosophy and with disdain for the role of women in Orthodox Judaism. Her final break with Judaism came when she married Jackson Pollock in a Reformed Church.

FIGURE 8.9 Lee Krasner, *Present Perfect,* 1976, collage on canvas, 50″ x 38½″. Photo by Art Mozell. © 1994 The Pollock-Krasner Foundation/Artists Rights Society (ARS), New York.

As an art student at the National Academy of Design she experienced a peculiar set of expectations: Women were supposed to paint in dark colors; her use of light and bright colors landed her in trouble: "'That was the first time I had experienced real separation as an artist, and it infuriated me . . . It reminded me of the synagogue and being told to go up not downstairs'" (quoted in Munro, 1979, p. 107).

Although she is now recognized as one of the important figures in Abstract Expressionism (in which gesture and feeling are conveyed through the physical act of painting, and which includes drip techniques and very large canvasses), this recognition came late and was very hard won. For example, in an attempt to claim some recognition from the art establishment, several abstract expressionist painters assembled a petition. The publicity attendant to the strategies of the "Irascible Eighteen," including a *Life* magazine pictorial, bypassed Krasner: She was neither asked to sign the petition nor to appear in the photograph. Indeed, though she had long been part of the New York art scene, the first comprehensive retrospective of her work opened in Houston in October of 1983, when she was 75 years old. Krasner was grateful to feminist efforts toward gaining exposure and opportunities for women artists, and found "it 'a little curious' that her male contemporaries in the New York School were given so many museum shows before she had even one. "'A retrospective,' she commented, 'shouldn't have to be so rare'" (Berman, 1983, p. 80). She attributed much of the lack of attention to her status as the wife of Jackson Pollock.

Krasner first became acquainted with Pollock in 1942 at a show including works by both artists. His work struck her as only a few others' (Picasso, Mondrian, and Matisse) had: she felt Pollock had achieved what she had been trying to accomplish. Indeed, she was among the first to recognize Pollock's importance. She introduced him to people who could appreciate his work, using her contacts, which were much broader than his (Landau, 1981, Nov.). She also introduced him to modern abstractionist work that facilitated his innovations; in turn, his drip technique helped her move away from her own formal training (Linker, 1982). Their relationship was mutually professional, as she recalls: "'We had a continuing dialogue about our work, although we kept separate studios and didn't visit each other unless invited . . . I honestly don't remember feeling competitive with him. He treated me like a professional painter'" (quoted in Glueck, 1981, p. 58).[5]

Others in the art world were not so ready to recognize her talent. Although some of Pollock's mates in the New York School admired her work, she didn't get any exhibitions (Nemser, 1975). The media treated her in an increasingly patronizing fashion, illustrated by one article from the *New Yorker* from August 5, 1950: "Pollock, a bald, rugged, somewhat puzzled-looking man of 38, received us in the kitchen, where he was breakfasting on a cigarette and a cup of coffee and drowsily watching his wife, the former Lee Krasner, a slim auburn-haired woman, who is also an artist, as she bent over a hot stove making currant jelly" (quoted in Landau, 1981, October, p. 110). Another story in *Time* magazine from 1958 entitled "Mrs. Jackson Pollock" reviewed Krasner's

---

[5] This working relationship has led to questions about whose innovation was whose.

work: "The pair made history: one with commotion—Jackson Pollock; the other with devotion—Lee Krasner who became his wife" (quoted in Landau, 1981, October, p. 110). As a result of these perceptions of her, Krasner's artistic struggle included the need to establish a separate identity from Pollock's.[6]

It was after Pollock's death in an automobile accident in 1956 that her work matured most. Indeed, in the 1960s, while other expressionists were languishing, her work started to grow. Her acceptance grew also, and the support of women artists in the 1970s exceeded anything her male contemporaries had given her (Brach, 1982). Her career was still handicapped in another way, though, because she had to handle Pollock's estate. As she described, "'There were a lot of vendettas against Mrs. Pollock, the widow, that had to be paid back to Lee Krasner, the artist'" (Rubinstein, 1982, p. 274).

Reviews of a show in 1981 (3 years before her death) suggest that age had not diminished the critics' view of Lee Krasner, the artist. Her work was described as fresh, full of youthful vigor, spontaneous, and intense, even violent (Baro, 1981; Cavaliere, 1981, Ratcliff, 1981). Recall that Abstract Expressionism required energetic gestures on canvasses that, in the case of this show, were 6 feet across. Krasner was 73 at the time of this exhibit, which included her most recent works. Her age apparently had not stifled her expression.

In sum, the ability of Helen Frankenthaler, Louise Nevelson, and Lee Krasner to create across the adult life course seems to have demanded the tenacity to overcome barriers, while permitting the expression of an identity that the artists recognized very early in life and considered essential to self-completion. The life stories of these women suggest, then, that context is important, but that artistic identity gives some women the capacity, as Munro has put it (1979), "to survive more than one death and rebirth."

CONCLUSION

Converging reports from psychological theorists, art historians, and artists themselves suggest a number of critical institutional factors related to women's creativity and artistic expression: differences in training and education as they relate to a chosen field; the demands of childrearing and homemaking; and the standards imposed by a culture

---

[6] This suggests a reciprocal issue not addressed here—the extent to which one's works shape self-definition. That is, how do artworks come to stand for an artist's identity?

that often denies women access to creative fields and then denies the creativity of their work, often simply because it is women who have done it.

Yet our examination of the careers of women artists suggests another issue rarely addressed in scientific studies of creativity. Despite institutional factors, artistic expression also seems to encompass an artistic identity. This identity was recognized very early by the lifelong artists we described, and its nurture depended on both specific experiences and on individual tenacity and perseverance. While it seems to compel some women to make art, not all women artists claim to have such an identity.

Is age a friend or a foe to creative women? While age presents some exhaustion of the energy necessary for a creative career, it also adds maturity to conception and execution. And, since most of the women discussed in this chapter spent decades expressing their artistic identities, age would seem to be a necessary component of artistic "signature."

This is an admittedly select sample of women. Most notably absent are those whose artistic expression survived neither institutional barriers nor age. A variety of other factors also affect motive, identity, and context: socioeconomic status, race/ethnicity, geographic location (i.e., provincialism), sexual orientation, and art trends. These factors would interact with age in ways not necessarily predicted by an understanding of gender. Perhaps of greatest concern, however, is the inherently reductionistic, decontextualized approach that has characterized the psychology of creativity. Creative people are sometimes 'operationalized' as those who use cognitive strategies assumed to predict creativity, including a preference for complexity and divergent thinking. The creative *process* is operationalized as that which results in a set of *products* that possess specific characteristics, most notably novelty and value. What is lacking is a concerted effort to study the manner in which people define themselves as creative and how that self-definition affects what they choose to do with their lives. If nothing else, we hope that the life stories we have presented here will lead to a consideration of the role of creative identity across the life course, keeping in mind the words of Rosemarie Castoro: "I didn't become an artist because there was a job vacancy."

ACKNOWLEDGMENTS

For readings of earlier versions of this chapter, we are grateful to Charles Matter, Gilbert Null, and Joyce Salisbury

REFERENCES

Abra, J. (1989). Changes in creativity with age: Data, explanations, and future predictions. *International Journal of Aging and Human Development, 28,* 105–126.

Abra, J., & Valentine-French, S. (1991). Gender differences in creative achievement: A survey of explanations. *Genetic, social, and general psychology monographs, 117,* 233–284.

Amabile, T. M. (1983). *The social psychology of creativity.* New York: Springer-Verlag.

Amabile, T. M. (1989). *Growing up creative: Nurturing a lifetime of creativity.* New York: Crown.

Andrews, M. (1991). *Lifetimes of commitment: Aging, politics, psychology.* Cambridge: Cambridge University Press.

Bailly, J.-C. (1986). Duchamp. New York: Universe.

Baker, E. C. (1973). Sexual art-politics. In T. B. Hess & E. C. Baker (Eds.), *Art and sexual politics* (pp. 108–119). New York: MacMillan.

Baking in the sun. (1987). Lafayette, LA: University of Southwestern Louisiana, University Art Museum.

Bankowski, J. (1989, May). Helen Frankenthaler. *Artforum,* pp. 147–148.

Baro, G. (1981, August/September). New York Letter. *Art International,* p. 104.

Benack, S., Basseches, M., & Swan, T. (1989). Dialectical thinking and adult creativity. In J. A. Glover, R. R. Ronning, & C. R. Reynolds (Eds.), *Handbook of creativity* (pp. 199–208). New York: Plenum.

Berman, A. (1983, December). When artists grow old. *ARTnews,* pp. 76–83.

Bolen, L. M., & Torrance, E. P. (1978). The influence on creative thinking of locus of control, cooperation, and sex. *Journal of Clinical Psychology, 34,* 903–907.

Brach, P. (1982, March). Tandem paint: Krasner/Pollock. *Art in America,* pp. 92–95.

Brett, G. (1987). *Through our own eyes: Popular art and modern history.* London: GMP Ltd.

Cavaliere, B. (1981, June). Lee Krasner. *Arts Magazine,* 34.

Crosson, C. W., & Robertson-Tchabo, E. A. (1983). Age and preference for complexity among manifestly creative women. *Human Development, 26,* 149–155.

Cubbs, J. (1991). Religious visionaries. In *Religious visionaries* (pp. 1–22). Sheboygan, WI: John Michael Kohler Arts Center of Sheboygan Arts Foundation, Inc.

Dowd, E. T. (1989). The self and creativity: Several constructs in search of a theory. In J. A. Glover, R. R. Ronning, & C. R. Reynolds (Eds.), *Handbook of creativity* (pp. 233–242). New York: Plenum.

Elderfield, J. (1982, February). Specific incidents. *Art in America,* pp. 100-106.

Frym, G. (1979). *Second stories: Conversations with women whose artistic careers began after thirty-five.* San Francisco: Chronicle Books.

Galligan, G. (1989, Summer). An interview with Helen Frankenthaler: "There are many more risks to take." *Art International,* pp. 45–52.

Gardner, P. (1990, December). Diana was always there. *ARTnews,* pp. 57–58.

Gazziniga, M. S., & Ledoux, J. E. (1978). *The integrated mind.* New York: Plenum.

Geitner, P. (1990, February 17). Masked women fight discrimination in art world. *Sunday Post-Crescent* (Appleton-Neenah-Menasha, WI), G-6.

Glimcher, A. B. (1976). *Louise Nevelson.* New York: Dutton.

Glueck, G. (1981, December). Scenes from a marriage: Pollock and Krasner. *ARTnews,* pp. 57–61.

Greenfield, V. (1986). *Making do or making art: A study of American recycling.* Ann Arbor, MI: UMI Research Press.

Heartney, E. (1987, Summer). How wide is the gender gap? *Artnews,* pp. 39–145.

Helen Frankenthaler. (1988, March). *Artnews,* pp. 189–190.

Hoy, A. H. (1987). *Fabrications: Staged, altered and appropriated photographs.* New York: Abbeville.

Johnson, E. H. (Ed.) (1982). *American artists on art: From 1940 to 1980.* New York: Icon/Harper & Row.

Kaufman, S. R. (1986). *The ageless self: Sources of meaning in late life.* Madison: University of Wisconsin Press.

Kronsky, B. (1985, May). The psychology of art. *American Artist,* pp. 24, 86, 88, 90.

Landau, E. G. (1981, October). Lee Krasner's early career. Part one: "Pushing in different directions." *Arts Magazine,* pp. 110–122.

Landau, E. G. (1981, November). Lee Krasner's early career. Part two: The 1940s. *Arts Magazine,* pp. 80–89.

Linker, K. (1982, February). Krasner/Pollock: A working relationship. *Artforum,* pp. 86–87.

Lippard, L. (1984). *Get the message? A decade of art for social change.* New York: Dutton.

Munro, E. (1979). *Originals: American women artists.* New York: Touchstone.

Munsterberg, H. (1983). *The crown of life: Artistic creativity in old age.* New York: Harcourt, Brace, Jovanovich.

Nemser, C. (1975). *Art talk: Conversations with 12 women artists.* New York: Scribner.

Nochlin, L. (1973). Why have there been no great women artists? In T. B. Hess & E. C. Baker (Eds.), *Art and sexual politics* (pp. 1–39). New York: Macmillan.

Page, C. (1986, Dec. 7). Gayleen Aiken paints with innocence. *Burlington (VT) Free Press,* 1D, 8D.

Parker, R., & Pollock, G. (1981). *Old mistresses: Women, art and ideology.* New York: Pantheon.

Poirier, M. (1985, Summer). Working papers. *ARTnews,* pp. 79–85.

Polston, P. (1991, May 16). Looking for art in all the wrong places. *Vermont Times,* 21.

Ratcliff, C. (1981, October). Lee Krasner at Pace. *Art in America,* p. 139.

Rubinstein, C. S. (1982). *American women artists.* New York: Avon.

Ruth, J., & Birren, J. E. (1985). Creativity in adulthood and old age: Relations to intelligence, sex, and mode of testing. *International Journal of Behavioral Development, 8,* 99–109.

Sang, B. E. (1981). Women and the creative process. *The Arts in Psychotherapy,* 43–48.

Shaw-Eagle, J. (1981, June). A conversation with Helen Frankenthaler. *Architectural Digest,* 172–182.

Simonton, D. K. (1990). Creativity and wisdom. In J. E. Birren & K. W Schaie (Eds.), *Handbook of the psychology of aging* (3rd ed.; pp. 320–329). San Diego: Academic Press.

Slatkin, W. (1985). *Women artists in history.* Englewood Cliffs, NJ: Prentice-Hall.

Stohs, J. H. (1992). Career patterns and family status of women and men artists. *The Career Development Quarterly, 40,* 223–233.

Straw, D. (1987, February 20). Amazing GRACE. *Country Courier,* pp. 3A–4A, 12A.

Tatransky, V. (1985, Summer). Helen Frankenthaler. *Arts Magazine,* p. 14.

Truitt, A. (1982). *Daybook: The journal of an artist.* New York: Pantheon.

Tufts, E. (1981, April). Beyond Gardner, Gombrich, and Janson: Towards a total history of art. *Arts Magazine,* 150–154.

Tully, J. (1990, February). Taking care of Diana. *ARTnews,* pp. 39–40.

Vaillant, G. E., & Vaillant, C. O. (1990). Determinants and consequences of creativity in a cohort of gifted women. *Psychology of Women Quarterly, 14,* 607–616.

Vernon, P. E. (1989). The nature-nurture problem in creativity. In J. A. Glover, R. R. Ronning, & C. R. Reynolds (Eds.), *Handbook of creativity* (pp. 93–110). New York: Plenum.

Whitbourne, S. (1986). *Adult development* (2nd ed.). New York: Praeger.

Woodman, R. W., & Schoonfeldt, L. F. (1989). Individual differences in creativity: An interactionist perspective. In J. A. Glover, R. R. Ronning, & C. R. Reynolds (Eds.), *Handbook of creativity* (pp. 93–110). New York: Plenum.

Yau, J. (1985, January). Helen Frankenthaler. *Artforum,* p. 86.

PART FOUR

Domains of Creativity

Artists, Art, and Arts Activities: What Do They Tell Us About Aging?

Martin S. Lindauer

Much of what we know about creativity and aging builds upon the seminal work of Lehman (1953). In a rather straightforward way, Lehman tallied the ages at which historical figures at different times and in various professions did what experts judged to be their best work. Thus, the number of times the authoritative texts in a particular field referred to a specific work was counted: the more often it was cited, the greater its originality, influence, and achievement. In this manner, Lehman found that the most creative efforts were systematically related to age: Creative works generally peaked relatively early in life, in the thirties. Only a few professions peaked somewhat earlier or later (e.g., mathematicians and novelists, respectively).

The youthful high point of creativity has been verified and extended among historical figures with only slight modifications (Simonton, 1984, 1990), although there are some who have argued for the older years (Bullough, Bullough, & Maddalena, 1978). Total productivity, which is correlated with creativity (Albert, 1975; Lehman, 1953, p. vii, 70–72), also declines fairly early, in the forties, for major historical figures in science, art, and scholarship (Dennis, 1955, 1966). The decline, furthermore, was more precipitous for artists than for scholars and scientists.

Among contemporary individuals, the same early peak-and-decline pattern characterizes their creativity test scores, their publications, and their citations by others (Allpaugh & Birren, 1977; Cole, 1979; Diamond, 1984; Horner, Rushton, & Vernon, 1986; Smith & Kragh, 1975). Thus, the span of time for the highest level of creativity is only about 10 years, ranging on average from the thirties to the forties.

The loss of creativity in the later years has rarely been questioned. Not only is it expected on the basis of most studies of creativity, but it is also affirmed by research on cognitive development; it too finds that mental decline characterizes aging (Salthouse, 1989).

The relatively restricted course of creativity is examined in this paper in the context of artists, art, and the response to art by non-artists. The reasons for focusing on art are discussed first. This is followed by a summary of recent work that challenges the early peak-and-decline model; and its basis in Lehman's and Dennis' data is critically reexamined. Extensions of the research to other old populations, including contemporary artists and others, are also reviewed. The chapter concludes with a discussion of the general implications of late life art, artists, and non-artists' response for art to the study of cognition and aging.

CREATIVITY, AGING, AND ART

A clarification of the course of creativity among old artists, a profession with several special characteristics related to both creativity and aging, could be useful. If early decline is not the rule in art, it may encourage a reexamination of creativity and aging in other professions, and support a more optimistic view of old age.

There are several reasons for associating art with creativity and age. The term *creativity* is often synonymous with the term *art*. Artistic works are also dramatic, visible, and clear depictions of creativity, when that term is defined as originality and influence. When creativity is thought of in terms of nonconformity and independence, artists' lives are also illustrative. The content of art also portrays universal themes about aging and old age, including societal values and attitudes (Achenbaum & Kusnerz, 1982). Further, unlike most other professions, artists continue to work until they die. It should, therefore, be no surprise to find that psychology has been interested in art, whether experimentally or therapeutically, since its earliest days (Arnheim, 1986).

Historical artists are particularly attractive, because their creative reputations have been well established by experts. Thus, the status of a Michelangelo or a Rembrandt is rarely if ever questioned, and it is hard to imagine that it might be in the future. The output of historically validated creative artists provides concrete indicators of sustained and original achievement of a high order over a lifetime. Further, since historical artists tend to be long lived, they provide a longitudinal record of lifelong achievement (Lindauer, 1991).

The accomplishments of historical artists stand in marked contrast to test scores, the index most often relied upon in studies of creativity among contemporary persons. Test scores, at best, are indirect measures of creative potential, and they are obtained under artificial test conditions that capture only brief periods of time. In addition, tests are usually administered to college-age or younger individuals whose creativity has either not been demonstrated, or if it has been, may not continue into adulthood.

There are, admittedly, problems with the historical record. It is incomplete, and the selection of artists and works is likely to be biased in unknown ways. Biographical information was not collected by scientists for the purpose of reaching generalizations about creativity and age. Further, historically creative people are unavailable for further study. There are also unavoidable ambiguities in determining the ages of artists, especially since not all paintings of the past were signed, and the ages of many artists who lived before the 1700s are unknown.

Authorities also disagree on who the creative artists were. A notable example are the studies by Kroeber and Sorokin on cultural differences in artistic creativity (summarized in Naroll et al., 1971, p. 183). Kroeber and Sorokin, in separate surveys, came up with very different tallies of great artists, 604 and 1,714, respectively. Consider the divergent numbers for 19th century artists: Italy had either 0 or 195, and Germany had either 20 or 200, according to Kroeber and Sorokin, respectively. More agreement was found for France (101 and 99 artists, respectively) and Spain (5 and 6, respectively). Disagreements are inevitable when the reputations of the total population of Western artists is in question. However, there is usually general agreement over the status of the greatest artists, a relatively small number who have made the most outstanding contributions, such as Michelangelo and Rembrandt. A survey of several introductory art history texts (e.g., Hartt, 1985) consistently found about 150 to 200 long-lived (60+) artists mentioned repeatedly (Lindauer, 1991). (Age 60 was used as the cutoff point because it takes into account the lower life expectancies in earlier time periods. Art historians also use age 60 to define old age art.) About 70 major artists lived past 80 (e.g., Chagall, Michelangelo, O'Keefe, Picasso, Rouault, and Titian).

Long-lived artists make up a relatively large proportion of artists, although the number can only be approximated. For example, 59% of the 294 artists discussed in at least one paragraph in a well-known art history text (Hartt, 1985) died when they were over 60; so did 76% (13) of the 17 artists in a list of the 1,000 most eminent men who ever lived

(Cattell, 1903). Other indications of artists as long lived are found in Lindauer (1993b). The works of many old artists are also distinguished by an "old-age style" (Arnheim, 1990; Lindauer, 1991; Munsterberg, 1983). After about age 60, some artists show marked and drastic changes in technique, affective tone, and subject matter. These are clearly seen, for example, in Michelangelo's two *Pietas,* one done early and the other late in his life; and in Rembrandt's life-long chronicle of himself in his self-portraits. The later works of other artists—for example, Goya, Titian, Renoir, Matisse, and Degas—are usually taken as illustrative of the old age style (Lindauer, 1991, 1993b). Old age for these artists was not a time of loss. Instead, it was a period when new modes of creative expression occurred. Shifts in late life efforts, at least among some artists, suggest that some aspects of creativity, like wisdom, may emerge only in old age. The presence of an old age style is also congruent with a positive model of life span cognitive development in which there is an emphasis on growth rather than loss. Thus, cognitive abilities of a high order, like problem solving and concept formation, can persist into old age (Perlmutter, 1988, 1990).

RECENT WORK ON LATE LIFE CREATIVITY

Recent research on the creative output of the West's greatest artists points to a later, more extended, and more variable period of creativity than previously believed (Lindauer, 1991, 1993a,b) . The world's masterpieces of art were produced in the artists' forties, rather than in their thirties. Similarly, the total productivity of the world's best known artists also declined relatively late in life, in the fifties and sixties, rather than the forties. Revealing these patterns, though, depended on distinguishing between long-lived artists and short-lived artists. Individual artists' patterns, however, were more variable. Thus, productivity was highest in the twenties and thirties for Duchamp, Chagall, Trumbull, Chardon, Bracque, and Ernst, when they produced 28% to 40% of their work. However, Degas did the bulk of his work (34%) in his forties, and Benton and Goya were most productive in their fifties. For Rouault and Corot, a peak occurred in their seventies when they produced 25% to 43% of their work. There are even more exceptional individuals. Picasso had three peaks: the forties, sixties, and eighties, when he accomplished 68% of his work. Matisse had four peak periods: in his twenties, forties, fifties, and sixties. He did 91% of his work in those decades.

Long-lived artists have the advantage of having more time to express their creativity—and most historical artists were long lived, even though they lived when life spans were short. The average age of death in several samples of Western artists was in their seventies (Lindauer, 1993b), and nearly all worked until they died. Thus, the romantic notion that artistic geniuses die young is not supported when the population of artists is considered, and not just a select few (like Van Gogh).

Lehman's (1953) analysis, however, included short-lived individuals, thereby underestimating the age of their maximum creativity, a bias pointed out by Dennis (1966). To illustrate, consider Lehman's analysis of the world's 28 greatest artists, defined as those whose works were most often referred to in art textbooks (see point #4, below). Their masterpieces were produced when they were between 32 and 36. But of the 23 artists for whom birth and death rates could be found, eight (35%) died when they were less than 60 years old (e.g., Raphael died at 38, Watteau at 47, G. Bellini at 47, and Hobbema at 48); their mean age of death was a relatively young 63.46. (Lehman did examine a set of long-lived artists, but these results are problematic for other reasons; see points #7 and #13, below.)

Dennis (1966) avoided an age bias in his sample of artists, scholars, and scientists by including only individuals who lived to 79 or older. Unfortunately, though, he did not include visual artists, a group which is especially long-lived, as noted above.

The noteworthy feature of long-lived artists—their old-age style (Arnheim, 1990; Lindauer, 1992c)—has hardly been recognized. Art produced after age 60 radically changed in subject and technique, compared to earlier efforts. This shift demonstrates that creativity continues into old age (although it may await the appreciation of succeeding generations), and that it can take new forms and directions.

In order to learn more about the old age style and its implications for late life creativity, it is important to identify artists who have it. Two studies addressed this question (Lindauer, 1992a, 1993b). In the first one, experts were asked about the old age style of over 200 artists. In the second study, untrained viewers, rather than experts, judged works of art (the former are less likely to base responses on their knowledge of artists). The difference between young-old pairs by 24 long-lived artists were judged on several dimensions, (e.g., "Rate the degree to which the pairs look as if they were done by the same artist").

Across both studies, at least 10 artists were distinguished by an old age style: Eakins, Goya, Kirchner, Klee, Mondrian, Monet, Picasso, Pissaro, Sargent, and Tobey. In contrast, at least six artists did not have an old age style: Copley, Hoffman, Manet, Marin, Stuart, and Tiepolo. Contrasts between their lives, works, and times will serve in future studies as useful starting points in extracting the factors which led to changes in their late life creativity.

Research on the distinctive characteristics of artists' old age works has been initiated with the development of a reliable set of descriptors (Lindauer, 1992b). Twelve art experts were given a list of descriptors culled from the literature and asked to choose those which best fit old age style. Fifty percent or more agreement was found on about 10 terms. They included, for example, expressions which described the work as a whole rather than specific references to technique, like "brushstroke," or the personal characteristics of the artist, or the reactions of observers. Also judged as appropriate were terms like "intense" and "economical" rather than "refined," "stylistic," or "skilled."

Evidence for late life artistic creativity conflicts with previous research, which points to a more restricted span, earlier peaks, and a uniform pattern of creativity (Dennis, 1966; Lehman, 1953). To resolve this discrepancy, the data by Lehman were reexamined. His work was chosen because it was the first major study that gave extensive support to a decline model of creativity, and has been a framework and empirical base for subsequent research. A review of his findings for artists will indicate that the presumed decline of creativity cannot be unequivocally demonstrated. Similarly, a reexamination of Dennis' (1966) work also raises questions about the apparent productivity of artists.

A REEXAMINATION OF LEHMAN'S FINDINGS

Lehman (1953) presented several sets of data for artists (pp. 70–85; 316–319). Eight of them indicated that creativity peaked at a relatively early age, falling within the age intervals 32–36, 30–34, or 35–39, depending on the sample investigated. Early peaks were found in the following samples:

1. 162 etchings by 27 non-British artists.
2. 53 paintings by 32 artists whose works are displayed in the Louvre.
3. 650 paintings by 168 artists whose work appeared in at least 2 of 60 sources (but see #10 below).
4. 40 paintings by 28 artists whose work appeared 10 or more times in 60 sources. These are labeled "the best artists." The 23 long-lived artists, discussed earlier, were taken from this set.
5. 67 paintings by 67 artists whose works appeared 5 or more times in 60 sources. These are considered the major artists.
6. 86 paintings by 86 artists whose works appeared less than 5 times in 60 sources. These are called the minor artists.

7. 61 paintings by 61 artists whose works appeared in 60 sources and who lived to 70 or older. These data for older artists were not noted by Dennis (1966) in his critique of the bias in Lehman's sample toward short-lived artists.
8. 61 paintings by 30 of the "most selective" (undefined) artists, taken from a larger set of 357 artists who produced 7,600 paintings (but see #11 below).

However, not all of Lehman's data showed an early peak for creativity; and some findings are either ambiguous or inconsistent with one another. The remaining five sets of data or analyses show either a decline later than the thirties, the age emphasized in the above analyses, or no decline. They are presented below:

9. 84 modern American paintings by 66 living artists peaked at age 40–44.
10. 1,684 paintings by 305 artists, whose works appeared at least once in 60 sources (see #3 above). This sample showed a marked rise in productivity, peaking at ages 90–99 (p. 75). Lehman calls this finding an "artifact," and speculated that it was due either to the inclusion of idiosyncratic artists, or the "bizarre judgments of some individual compilers" (p. 77). To control for these possibilities, Lehman used the more selective criteria noted in #3–7 above; that is, he used only those artists whose works were mentioned 2–10 times in the various sources.
11. 357 artists who produced 7,600 paintings showed a flat (no-change) pattern through at least ages 50–54 (but see #8 above).
12. 7,032 paintings by 135 artists, and 506 paintings by 152 artists, taken from #3 above, and labeled as "least" and "moderately selective." These groups reached their peaks at ages 32–45 and 42–47, respectively (the intervals are Lehman's). The basis for these labels are not indicated, but they presumably point to the number of times their works were referred to in the works cited in #3 above.
13. 302 artists who had produced 2,273 works whose mean age of "contribution" (not defined) was plotted against seven age intervals in which they had died. The intervals begin with "before 50" and end with "over 80." Several aspects of these data deserve additional comments.

First, the source of this information is not identified, but as far as can be determined, the data were not previously reported (Lehman,

1953, p. 318). Second, *contribution* was not defined, although it probably refers to the mean age of several works by each artist. Third, and most surprisingly, the range of age intervals excludes the forties and even the thirties—ages at which Lehman found peaks in productivity in other analyses. Fourth, and most importantly, there is little if any decline in this data, as described next.

The 308 contributions, arranged from the earliest to latest death dates, are distributed as follows: 36, 40, 42, 45, 46, 51, and 48, respectively. The 302 artists who produced the 308 works were distributed at each of the above age groups as follows: 47, 57, 43, 45, 35, 42, and 33, respectively. For example, at the last age interval ("over 80"), 33 artists (11% of the total number) had 48 contributions (this is 16% of the total output). A profile of this data reflects a slight increase in productivity with age and then it becomes either flat or slightly increases again during the later years.

The problematic aspects of these data are difficult to resolve, since Lehman's sources are not specified. "All of the available art histories in [a] University library were studied" (p. 75). But even if they were known and available for recalculation, most were old and hence suspect. Technical developments in dating art and in verifying authorship since Lehman's work was completed around 40 years ago have led to changes in attributions of artists' works. For example, the number of works attributed to Rembrandt has been markedly reduced since the turn of the century from about 1,000 to approximately 300. Thus, more recent scholarship would yield a more accurate list of the great works of art and the ages at which they were done.

Lehman's data on artistic productivity are therefore mixed, ambiguous, and even contradictory. Further, there are rather clear indications of sustained creative productivity in old age when long-lived artists were included (point #13 above). Additional doubts about the productivity of long-lived artists are raised when Dennis' (1966) data are reexamined.

Dennis combined the various subgroups under the larger categories of artists and their works, scholars, and scientists. However, the number of individuals studied and works included in different professions were very disparate. For example, seven groups were placed under the category "artists," including 25 dramatists, 176 composers of opera, and 109 chamber works and 803 plays (Dennis, 1966, p. 2). Thus, the productivity profile of artists in different fields is blurred by combined averages. Aggregate data, furthermore, mask a particular artist's output, an important consideration in a profession noted for its members' idiosyncrasies and uniqueness. Thus, the output-by-age for specific artists may not mirror the overall results. Unknown, therefore, is whether individual patterns for specific artistic groups conform to the general findings.

But the most serious problem with Dennis' sample is that it included only two artist groups, musicians, and writers. There were therefore no painters. Yet as emphasized earlier, many painters are long-lived (Lindauer, 1991). The exclusion of long-lived artists is not only puzzling and inexplicable, but has serious consequences for Dennis' findings (e.g., the productivity of artists declines more precipitously than that of scholars and scientists).

The reexamination of the seminal work on historical artists by Lehman (1953), as well as work by Dennis (1966), raises serious questions about the research methodology and findings that are the basis upon which many subsequent investigations (and expectations) about the development of creativity have been built. Thus, recent findings indicating that late peaks in creativity and productivity can occur, that stability rather than decline can be found, that the later years are characterized by individual differences between artists in productivity, and that new forms of creativity—the old age style (Lindauer, 1992a, 1992c, 1993a, 1993b)—are not unexpected. These encouraging findings have led in other directions, including the study of non-artists and their response to art, which will be reviewed in the next section.

ADDITIONAL EVIDENCE OF CREATIVITY WITH AGING

Contemporary artists also show an extended period of creativity (Lindauer, Orwoll, & Kelley, 1992). Questionnaires and self-ratings were completed by nominated artists who were 60 to 80 years old. Over most of their lives, declines were not reported in either quality (creativity) or quantity (productivity). In fact, the artists wrote that they became steadily better as they got older. However, they said a plateau was reached in their quantity of work around age 60. A leveling off, the artists indicated, was mainly the result of losses in physical strength and sensory abilities. But no ceiling was reported in the quality of work. With increasing age, artists said that they got better because they had learned and knew more, and building upon that, their skills became more polished. Indications of an old age style among contemporary artists appear to be more muted than they were for historical artists, for reasons that remain to be explored.

Other studies have shifted the focus from old artists to other old people and have examined their response to art and involvement in arts-related activities compared to younger groups (Lindauer, 1992b). The response to art requires a high level of cognitive ability in visualization, imagination, and aesthetic sensitivity. The results for non-artists, as for artists, also offer an encouraging picture of aging.

Representational and abstract art were rated by senior citizens and college students on 30 different dimensions—for example, meaningfulness, complexity, feelings aroused, ideas evoked, and interest. The two age groups differed only in two ways. First, the older subjects were slower to respond. Since they had more to say about the art than the younger sample (as indicated during and after the study), the longer latencies may reflect more time spent in thinking about the response. The second difference is that older viewers preferred representational art more than younger ones, perhaps because the art was more familiar or traditional. The two age groups also responded similarly in two sorting tasks. In one case, when younger and older subjects were presented with multiple works from the same and different artists, they grouped the same artists' works together equally well. In the other task, they similarly grouped a series of works by the same artists into younger and older works.

Age differences were also largely irrelevant in comparisons of the arts-related activities of 20-, 40-, 60-, and 80-year-olds (Lindauer & Perlmutter, 1992). Only the very old respondents, those in their eighties, did not participate as much as the other subjects did in most activities (writing, playing an instrument, and painting). However, the level of activity was the same in a few areas (e.g., music and sculpting). Attendance at different kinds of concerts, or at art museums, was also similar between ages. Hardly any age differences were found between the four age groups' rated interest in art or its importance, whether in general or for specific areas of art. High opinions of art not only held in the present, but also the past and the future.

CONCLUSIONS

Since artistic creativity does not peak or decline as early in life as previously shown, or as precipitously, if it declines at all, then by implication, similar losses are not inevitable in other professions. Studies of artists, art, responses to art, and arts activities, although limited to specialized occupations, materials, and behaviors, are nevertheless broadly applicable. Abilities found in artists, and processes which underlie the response to and behavior toward art, are also likely to be found in the general population, at least to some degree, assuming that some traits and abilities are normally distributed. Thus, creative achievement, sensitivity to aesthetic qualities, and engagement in art among the non-eminent and less creative are possible late in life. Imaginative and other higher order cognitive abilities need not decline or be lost with increasing age. They can continue into old age and may even flower. There are, therefore, some good reasons to be optimistic about late life potential and the presence of at least some positive outcomes with aging.

To support these possibilities, previous findings for areas other than visual art (e.g., music) need to be reexamined, and studies should be conducted of creative people outside of the arts (e.g., scientists and scholars). Any reexamination of previous data, or the initiation of new research along the lines followed in this chapter, needs to include both historical and contemporary figures, and the relatively young, the long lived (60+), and the very old (79+).

The equivalence between young and old age groups on complex tasks and activities that involve art encourages some optimism about the performance of the old on other tasks, too. The life course of complex cognitive processes that require aesthetic sensitivity, imagination, conceptualization, and problem solving can also be stable.

Age comparisons involving art have a methodological advantage, compared to relying on artificial materials and activities such as rote learning and memory for nonsense materials (Cornelius & Crespi, 1987). Young undergraduates will do better on simple tasks and material because they are "test wise." But some of this advantage is lost when faced with complicated stimuli like art which require a complex response. Under more demanding circumstances, older subjects can do as well as younger ones. Cognitive deficits, if any, are compensated by drawing upon a greater interest in and motivation toward meaningful tasks.

A new look at long-lived creative people in several professions, and a "first" look at higher order cognitive processes among the elderly when real-world skills in response to art are demanded would help revise the negative view of late life creativity and cognition generally (Perlmutter, 1988). As people approach and pass 50, 60, or even higher ages, they can therefore be more confident about the stability of certain cognitive abilities, and even the "late-blooming" of some. Different ages, even old age, present new demands, and these can evoke new capacities and sustain old ones. Old artists demonstrate how to successfully cope with, compensate for, and overcome the deficiencies of old age. Similar possibilities exist for an aging population faced with physical and sensory losses. Old age need not be a time of losses and handicaps only.

There are several provocative lessons that can be learned from artists. The substantial number who have remained creative into old age suggests that involvement in the arts may have a positive, healthy, and therapeutic effect on those who become involved with the arts late in life. In addition, people in many fields might want to consider working beyond the normal retirement age, as artists do. A long working life increases the possibility of a reconceptualization and redirection of one's efforts and talents, a shift similar to the old age style of artists. Change is only possible, though, if people are allowed and encouraged to work as long as they can. If retirement is required or chosen between 60 and 65, around the time the old age style emerges among artists, then any signs of a revitalization of one's work would be masked or lost.

The study of art in old age increases our awareness of the growth possibilities of aging. Our knowledge is not only more accurate, but also more optimistic. A realization that old age can be a time of gains, as indicated by the work of aging artists, or a time of cognitive stability, as shown by older non-artists' response to art and arts-related activities, gives a positive perspective on late life potential.

ACKNOWLEDGMENTS

The work reported in this paper was supported by a National Institute of Aging fellowship to the Institute of Gerontology, the University of Michigan. The author wishes to thank Marion Perlmutter for her encouragement and assistance.

REFERENCES

Achenbaum, W. A., & Kusnerz, P. A. (1982). *Images of old age in America: 1790 to the present.* Ann Arbor: Institute of Gerontology, University of Michigan-Wayne State University.

Albert, R. S. (1975). Toward a behavioral definition of genius. *American Psychologist, 30,* 140–151.

Allpaugh, P. K., & Birren, J. E. (1977). Variables affecting creative contributions across the adult life span. *Human Development, 20,* 240–248.

Arnheim, R. (1986). The other Gustav Theodor Fechner. In R. Arnheim (Ed.), *New essays on the psychology of art* (pp. 39–49). Berkeley, CA: University of California Press.

Arnheim, R. (1990). On the late style. In M. Perlmutter (Ed.), *Late life potential* (pp. 113–120). Washington, DC: Gerontological Society of America.

Bullough, V., Bullough, B., & Maddalena, M. (1978). Age and achievement: A dissenting view. *The Gerontologist, 18,* 584–559.

Cattell, J. (1903). A statistical study of eminent men. *Popular Science Monthly, 62,* 359–377.

Cole, S. (1979). Age and scientific performance. *American Journal of Sociology, 84,* 958–977.

Cornelius, S. W., & Crespi, A. (1987). Everyday problem-solving in adulthood and old age. *Psychology and Aging, 2,* 144–153.

Dennis, W. (1955). Variations in productivity among creative works. *Scientific Monthly, 80,* 277–278.

Dennis, W. (1966). Creative productivity between the years of 20 and 80. *Journal of Gerontology, 21,* 1–8.

Diamond, A. M. (1984). An economic model of the life-cycle research productivity of scientists. *Scientometrics, 6,* 189–196.

Hartt, F. (1985). *A history of art: Paintings, sculpture, architecture* (2nd ed.). Englewood Cliffs, NJ: Prentice-Hall.

Horner, K. L., Rushton, J. P., & Vernon, P. A. (1986). Relation between aging and research productivity of academic psychologists. *Psychology and Aging, 1,* 319–324.

Lehman, H. C. (1953). *Age and achievement.* Princeton, NJ: Princeton University Press/American Philosophical Society.

Lindauer, M. S. (1991, August). *Art in old age: What does it tell us about aging?* Paper presented at the American Psychological Association meeting, San Francisco, CA.

Lindauer. M. S. (1992a). *A survey of art experts on the characteristics of the old-age style.* Unpublished paper.

Lindauer, M. S. (1992b, August). *College students and senior citizens' responses to art.* Paper presented at the annual meeting of the American Psychological Association, Washington, DC.

Lindauer, M. S. (1992c). Creativity in aging artists: Contributions from the humanities to the psychology of old age. *Creativity Research Journal, 5,* 211–231.

Lindauer, M. S. (1993a). The old-age style and its artists. *Empirical Studies of Art, 11,* 135–146.

Lindauer, M. S. (1993b). The span of creativity among long-lived historical artists. *Creativity Research Journal, 6,* 221–239.

Lindauer, M. S., & Perlmutter, M. (1992). *Self-reported creativity, attitudes toward art, and arts-related behavior across the life-span.* Unpublished manuscript.

Lindauer, M. S., Orwoll, L., & Kelley, C. (in press). Aging artists on the creativity of their old age. *Creativity Research Journal.*

Munsterberg, H. (1983). *The crown of life: Artistic creativity in old age.* New York: Harcourt, Brace, Jovanovich.

Narroll, P., Raoul, B., Fohl, F., Fried, M., Holdreth, R., & Schaefer, J. M. (1971). Creativity: A cross-historical political survey. *Journal of Cross-Cultural Psychology, 2,* 181–188.

Perlmutter, M. (1988). Cognitive potential throughout life. In J. Birren & V. Bengston (Eds.), *Emergent theories of aging* (pp. 247–268). Hillsdale, NJ: Erlbaum.

Perlmutter, M. (Ed.). (1990). *Late life potential.* Washington, DC: Gerontological Society of America.

Salthouse, T. A. (1989). Age-related changes in basic cognitive processes. In M. Storandt & G. R. Vander Bos (Eds.), *The adult years: Continuity and change* (pp. 9–40). Washington, DC: American Psychological Association.

Simonton, D. K. (1984). Creative productivity: A mathematical model. *Developmental Review, 4,* 77–121.

Simonton, D. K. (1990). Creativity and wisdom in aging. In J. E. Birren and K. W. Schaie (Eds.), *Handbook of the psychology of aging* (3rd ed., pp. 320–329). New York: Academic Press.

Smith, G., & Kragh, U. (1975). Creativity in males and old age. *Psychological Research Bulletin, 15,* 1–17.

Artistic Vision in Old Age: Claude Monet and Edgar Degas

James G. Ravin and Christie A. Kenyon

The subject of creativity in old age is relatively unexplored in the field of the history of art. Art historians tend to focus on the late style of artists, instead, describing the evolution of artists' work. These investigations generally follow one of two paths. The first is an idealization of old age as a time of spiritual revelation, when the artist exposes an inner self that has previously been concealed by the vanities and ambitions of youth. Titian, Michelangelo and Rembrandt are artists whose late styles are often defined in these terms. In the second interpretation, late style is considered an inevitable product of the artist's loss of power and imagination. By this viewpoint, the artist is seen as having made a brave attempt to continue working beyond the peak of his creative power. Picasso and Munch have been described as artists whose careers did not end gracefully. There is a certain tone of regret to this form of criticism, similar to that directed at an athlete who does not know when to leave the game. Between these two poles there is room for a deeper understanding of how a creative person responds to the challenges of old age.

This study is limited to an investigation of the late work of Claude Monet and Edgar Degas. These two artists make an interesting comparison for their differences as well as their similarities. Both had long, productive working careers. Monet painted until the age of 85, the year before his death in 1926. Degas worked well into the middle of his seventh decade, with roughly 10 years of retirement prior to his death in 1917. Both artists were loosely bound by an early association with the group of painters called impressionists. They were never close friends. They differed in temperament and artistic approach. Monet was primarily a landscape painter who worked outdoors whenever possible. He had little interest in continuing the tradition of French painting through the conventional means of the academy. Instead, he chose subjects and developed a style that enabled him to capture the fleeting effects of nature as they passed before his acute and highly sensitive vision. Conversely, Degas was a student of the old masters of European painting. His subject matter included contemporary Parisian life as expressed in manners, occupations and appearance. Degas modernized the traditional subjects of the nude and the portrait and added new ones—ballet, the racetrack, the outdoor café. He was a consummate observer who, without moralizing, presented the modern figure in its natural habitat. Each artist sought to portray the world clearly. The fact that each suffered from progressive eye disease adds an importance to the work they created towards the end of their lives.

CLAUDE MONET

In 1890 Monet was 50 years old. He had begun an ambitious project of a series of paintings that presented the same subject under a variety of light and atmospheric conditions at different times of day. This was a more focused and systematic version of his earlier impressionist work. Monet moved from canvas to canvas as the light conditions changed. The works are those particularly associated with this artist—the grainstacks, the poplars, Rouen Cathedral. (See Figure 10.1.)

Except for the normal effects of aging, in 1890 Monet's eyes were not yet giving him the difficulties he was to develop in the first decade of the twentieth century. The problems he encountered in painting toward the turn of the century were not ocular in origin. Instead, he struggled with the problem of motivation. In July, 1890, he wrote "I am feeling very low and profoundly disgusted with painting. It is nothing but constant torture! Don't expect to see any new works; the little I have managed to do is destroyed, scraped off, or staved in" (Geffroy, as cited in Stucky, 1985, p. 156).

Just a few years later, as he approached 60 years of age, Monet looked to the past: "What I do know is, that life with me has been a hard struggle, not for myself alone, but for my friends as well. And the longer I live and the more I realize how difficult a thing painting is, and in one's defeat he must patiently strive on" (Fuller, as cited in Stucky, 1985, p. 203). Self-confidence was never Monet's long suit. Fortunately for

FIGURE 10.1   Monet. Antibes Seen from La Salis. Oil on canvas 28⅞ x 36¼ inches. 1888.
Courtesy of Toledo Museum of Art, gifts of Edward Drummond Libbey.

him, he was able to rely most of his life on family and friends for support. His wife Alice, his stepdaughter Blanche (who was also his daughter-in-law) and his friend, the French statesman Georges Clemenceau, were reliable props for this artist as he aged.

Monet's eyesight became a problem early in the new century. By 1908 he was aware of difficulty seeing. This became apparent during a painting expedition to Venice. He recognized a difficulty with colors, but felt that his ability to handle forms was not affected. He may have relied on others in choosing tints, for the problem with colors is not easily noted in looking at the canvases he produced at that time. His depiction of space and depth in some of the Venetian scenes is not particularly well done. He was not happy with many of the works he created and destroyed many of them. An article about Monet, published in 1908, described his difficulties in sad terms: "Partly because of overstrain, partly because of dissatisfaction, M. Monet became extremely irritable and morose, and at last actually cut a few of his canvases to shreds" (Anon., 1908, as cited in Stucky, 1985, p. 251).

Monet could be temperamental. An American painter wrote: "His opinion of his own work was not, however, always calmly judicial. On one occasion, particularly disgusted at his own inadequacy, he decided to give up painting altogether. He was painting from his boat at the time, so overboard flew the forevermore useless paint box, palette, brushes and so forth into the peaceful waters of the little Epte" (Perry, 1927, as cited in Stucky, 1985, p. 181).

By 1912 he was having a great deal of difficulty with his eyes. His physician in the countryside, Jean Rebiere, MD, diagnosed bilateral cataracts. Monet consulted several ophthalmologists in Paris. One, Dr. A. Polack, must have been very sympathetic to Monet's plight, since he was an artist in addition to being a physician. Polack came to Paris in 1892 to study painting at the École des Beaux-Arts. He shifted to the medical school, where he wrote his doctoral thesis on the role of the refractive status of the eye in the education and work of artists. He became a professor of physiologic optics at the Institut d'Optique, a scientist at the Centre National de la Recherche Scientifique, and was director of the section of optics at the Laboratoire Scientifique of the Louvre (1953). Polack confirmed the diagnosis of cataracts, but advised surgery be deferred (Wildenstein, 1985).

Monet consulted another eminent ophthalmologist, Dr. A. Valude. Valude was an expert on cataract surgery, who had given an important presentation on this topic at an International Congress of Ophthalmology just a few years earlier. He was the author of a textbook of ophthalmology and coeditor of the *Encyclopedie Francaise d'Ophtalmologie.* He was a founding member of the Ophthalmological Society of Paris and an owner of the journal *Annales d'Oculistique* (Blodi, 1986). Valude's advice to Monet was basically the same as Polack's (Wildenstein, 1985). Monet was deathly afraid of surgery. He had discussed his problem at length with his friend Clemenceau, who was a physician as well as a politician. Following the visit to Valude, Clemenceau wrote Monet to reassure him he was not going to become blind. Monet's right eye was useless to him, since the cataract was nearly mature—the lens of the eye was opaque and blocked out incoming light, but Clemenceau wrote that the cataract in Monet's poorer seeing right eye could be operated on soon, and that "continuation of vision is assured" (Wildenstein, 1985, p. 77). Monet, ever anxious, preferred to do nothing more than try some eyedrops given by Valude.

Monet soon consulted a third ophthalmologist, Victor Morax, MD, who was long considered the dean of French ophthalmology. A productive researcher with a laboratory at the Institut Pasteur, and the coeditor of the *Annales d'Oculistique,* Morax was also an excellent surgeon and an enthusiastic teacher (Blodi, 1986, p. 643). He was in favor of surgery for Monet, but the artist was terribly afraid of any operation.

He was elated when he met, in Paris, a German ophthalmologist named Count Weiser. Weiser promised Monet a nonsurgical cure for cataracts if he would come to Germany for treatment. But the information Monet received about this doctor was so discouraging that he never took up the offer (Wildenstein, 1985).

Monet consulted a fifth ophthalmologist, Richard Liebreich, MD. The year was 1913, and the eminent Liebreich, at age 83, was a bit too old to be a vigorous surgeon. He, too, was an accomplished artist who had illustrated his important *Atlas of Ophthalmoscopy* and had studied at the École des Beaux-Arts. His article on the effect of eye disease on the artists Turner and Mulready had been published simultaneously on both sides of the English Channel, and had an enormous impact for decades. Edgar Degas was well aware of it. In 1913 Liebreich was ending an amazing career which had brought him to the highest ranks of medicine in three different countries.[1] He was, at that time, chair of ophthalmology at St. Thomas Hospital and Medical School in London, and Ophthalmic Surgeon to the hospital (Ravin & Kenyon, 1992).

Monet had left France during the Franco-Prussian War to avoid military service and also went to London. St. Thomas Hospital links Monet and Liebreich. Many of the paintings Monet created of the Houses of Parliament in the early years of the twentieth century were done from a room in that hospital. We do not know if they met before 1913, but certainly they had a lot to talk about. Liebreich examined Monet and found the artist had essentially no vision in his right eye. He prescribed glasses which had no power for the right eye. For the left eye his prescription was –175 sphere for distance, a moderate nearsighted prescription. For near, he gave +150 sphere, a moderately powered reading glass (Wildenstein, 1985).

During the next few years Monet refused to have anything done about his cataracts. He did very little artistic work during the war years of 1914–1917. Finding a physician to care for civilians was not easy, since most were busy with the troops. Monet was very interested

---

[1] He had been a student with Helmholtz in Germany, when the latter made the earth-shattering invention of the ophthalmoscope, and had been the right-hand man of von Graefe in Berlin. Graefe is generally considered to have been the greatest ophthalmologist to have ever lived. Liebreich reached the pinnacle of French ophthalmology when he surgically cured the mother of Empress Eugenie of glaucoma, prior to the discovery of local anesthesia. When Napoleon III's empire crumbled in 1870, Liebreich traveled to England with the imperial family.

in the cataract problem of the American impressionist, Mary Cassatt. Her ophthalmologist was another American expatriate, Louis Borsch, MD. Borsch also cared for the ocular problems of the author James Joyce. Unfortunately, neither patient did well. Cassatt underwent cataract surgery to one eye in 1917 and to the other 2 years later. Both eyes did poorly and Cassatt gave up her artistic career. The poor outcome of her treatment may have been due to complications of her diabetes or it may have been related to the radiation therapy she underwent for the diabetes. At any rate, her unfortunate surgical result could not have encouraged Monet to undergo the same procedure. He described his curiosity about Cassatt to Clemenceau in 1919. Aware she had just been operated upon, he said he was going to find out her condition after her operation, then make up his mind. He made up his mind to wait longer.

A representative of the press interviewed Monet in 1918. Monet described what had been happening to him during the previous 5 years:

> I no longer perceived colors with the same intensity, I no longer painted light with the same accuracy. Reds appeared muddy to me, pinks insipid, and the intermediate or lower tones escaped me. As for forms, they always appeared clear and I rendered them with the same decision.
>
> At first I tried to be stubborn. How many times, near the little bridge where we are now, have I stayed for hours under the harshest sun sitting on my campstool, in the shade of my parasol, forcing myself to resume my interrupted task and recapture the freshness that had disappeared from my palette! Wasted efforts. What I painted was more and more dark, more and more like an "old picture," and when the attempt was over I compared it to former works, I would be seized by a frantic rage and slash all my canvases with my penknife. (Thiebault-Sisson, 1927, pp. 45–46)

For a brief period of time he felt his visual problems had ceased. He still had difficulties with subtle, delicate colors viewed up close, but felt he could see better when he stepped a few feet away. He began to paint once more. His attempts at sketching made him feel he could not paint in bright light. He had difficulty distinguishing between colors that barely differed. He could still recognize vivid colors, especially if they were seen against a dark background. Since bright sunlight was overwhelming, he stopped painting during the middle of the day. Realizing that his choices of colors were poor, he destroyed many canvases. To avoid confusing pigments, he examined the labels on his tubes carefully, and kept the paints on his palette in a regular, unvarying sequence in order to minimize errors.

His paintings of waterlilies and weeping willows done between 1918 and 1922 reveal a loss of forms. The yellow-brown cataracts through which he saw the world filtered out violet and blue tones, as well as some of the greens. The paintings he created at that time included less and less of these colors, and more yellows, reds and browns.

In 1914 Clemenceau and some other individuals had encouraged Monet to give a group of waterlily canvases to the state of France, as Monet's contribution to the war effort. A plan to donate 12 large canvases was announced officially in 1920. The following year, Monet tried to extricate himself from this obligation. He felt that he was incapable of completing the task. Clemenceau, unhappy, even angry with Monet, realized that failure to complete this project would be an embarrassment to himself and to the artist. He persuaded Monet to sign a notarized document in formally committing him to donate 19 panels to France. The state agreed to house them permanently in a small museum, the Orangerie des Tuilleries, in the center of Paris, just off the Place de la Concorde.

Monet continued to be plagued by visual difficulties. He described the problem he was having in complying with the terms of his agreement in a letter dated May 8, 1922:

> I wished to profit from what little [remained of] my vision in order to bring certain of my decorations to completion. And I was gravely mistaken. For in the end I had to admit that I was ruining them, that I was no longer capable of making something of beauty. And I destroyed several of my panels. Today I am almost blind and I have to renounce work completely. (Stucky, 1979, p. 116)

Having outlived two wives and one of his two sons, Monet relied heavily on his friend Clemenceau for support. Since Clemenceau was a physician, and knew many members of the medical community, he had a strong influence on Monet when questions of health arose. At Clemenceau's urging, Monet consulted yet another ophthalmologist in September, 1922. This was Charles Coutela, MD. Coutela was an accomplished surgeon, who was later honored by being named a Commander of the Legion of Honor and a member of the Academy of Medicine (Offret, 1969).

In September, 1922, Coutela found that Monet could only see light and the direction from which a light source was projected into his right eye. His left eye could see only 20/200. Monet was still psychologically unprepared for surgery. Coutela prescribed eyedrops to dilate the pupil of Monet's left eye, in the very optimistic hope that this might allow more rays of light to penetrate the cataractous lens of his left eye and reach the retina. The attempt was doomed to failure because the cataract was too dense.

Monet must have been extremely anxious that this experiment would succeed. Before a week was up, he wrote enthusiastically to Coutela:

> It is all simply marvelous. I have not seen so well for a long time, so much so that I regret not having seen you sooner. The drops have permitted me to paint good things rather than the bad paintings which I had persisted in making when seeing nothing but fog (Monet, 1922b).

The effect was short lived, for Monet wrote Coutela again, in October, 1922, to make plans for surgery on his right eye (Monet, 1922c). But he could not convince himself to undergo an operation. In November he wrote Clemenceau of his apprehension and his nightmares, and said he was too tormented to have the surgery yet (Monet, 1922a). Clemenceau summoned all of his psychologic powers to convince Monet to have the operation. He continued to remind Monet of his agreement to finish the paintings for France.

Finally, In January, 1923, Monet underwent a two-stage cataract operation on his right eye. A preliminary iridectomy (excision of the superior part of the iris) was the first procedure. This was done at a clinic in Neuilly, a suburb of Paris. Later that month Coutela did a second procedure, an extraction of the cloudy lens (Dittere, 1973). Still extremely nervous, Monet was nauseated and vomited during the operation, to the consternation of his surgeon. Postoperatively, the 83-year-old patient was difficult to manage. He adapted poorly to the regimen of lying flat on his back for several days, without a pillow. Sandbags were placed alongside his body to prevent any movement. All he was allowed to eat or drink was some bouillon and lime tea. Both eyes were bandaged shut. Saying he preferred to be blind, rather than have his eyes covered, Monet tried to rip off the bandages. He was forcibly restrained from doing so. After discharge from the clinic, he returned home to Giverny. He was given a temporary pair of glasses to wear 3 weeks after surgery.

During the next few months, he developed a complication that caused him to undergo a third operation on the right eye. The posterior capsule of the lens, purposely left behind to add some structural stability to the eye, became cloudy. This was a common occurrence at the time, and still occurs today. Monet became depressed and refused to leave his bed. He wrote Coutela on June 22, 1923, saying:

I am absolutely discouraged, and as much as I read, not without effort, fifteen to twenty pages per day, outdoors from a distance, I cannot see anything with or without glasses [with the right eye]. And for two days black spots [floaters] have bothered me. Remember that it has been six months since the first operation, five since I left the clinic, and four that I have been wearing glasses. It has taken me four or five weeks to get used to my new vision! Six months that I would have been able to work, if you had told me the truth. I would have been able to finish the *Decorations* that I was supposed to deliver in April and I am now uncertain if I will be able to finish them as I would have liked. It is to my great chagrin that I regret having had this fatal operation. Pardon me for speaking so frankly and let me tell you that it is criminal to have put me in this situation. (Monet, 1923a)

Coutela responded quickly, reassuring Monet that this vision could be restored, and convinced him to undergo the required procedure. Today this can be done simply, with a laser. But in 1923, an operation was required, less difficult than what he had already been through. Rehospitalization was not necessary. From Coutela's perspective, here is what occurred:

Afterwards as had been predicted, the inevitable thickening of the capsule occurred: This did not make me anxious, but caused a difficult time for Monet. He was desolated. The period which followed at Giverny was a time of profound discouragement and despair; he saw himself blind forever and, completely demoralized, refused to leave his bed. When the eye calmed down after the first operation I proceeded with the extraction of this contrary membrane. This operation, done at Giverny, in his home [on July 17, 1923], allowed him to obtain visual acuity of 7/10 [about 20/30] with the correction of +10.00 + 4.00 x 90; I was reassured by the final result. (Dittere, 1973, p. 30)

The next step was to adapt Monet to a new way of seeing the world, through thick cataract glasses. This was not an easy project. Glasses of this type are obsolete today following the advent of intraocular lenses. Thick cataract lenses can induce distortion, magnification effects, and abnormal color perception. Monet had only one eye operated. He refused to have the second eye done. He could not use the two eyes together with his new glasses. The magnification effect of the strong lens for his right eye prevented this. Since his left eye still retained a yellow-brown cataract, his color perception with the two eyes differed markedly. Violets and blues could now come through to stimulate the retina of his right eye, but had difficulty penetrating the cataract in his left eye (Ravin, 1985). As an artist, he was acutely aware of these problems.

Monet complained that objects curved abnormally with his new glasses and that colors were strange. Coutela was not so troubled. On August 21, 1923, he wrote Clemenceau:

> His vision at near may be considered nearly perfect after correction . . . For distant vision the result is less extraordinary: Mr. Monet has 3/10 to 4/10 vision [20/50 to 20/70], which is not bad, but he will require a little bit of training because the vision for distance is more or less restricted. In brief, I am very satisfied. (Coutela, 1923)

Monet wrote a sad letter to Coutela, August 27, 1923, describing the difficulties he was having with the glasses:

> I have just received them today but I am absolutely desolated for, in spite of all my good will, I feel that if I take a step, I will fall on the ground. For near and far everything is deformed, doubled, and it has become intolerable to see. To persist seems dangerous to me. (Monet, 1923b)

Monet returned to painting, to complete the waterlily series. (See Figure 10.2.) He continued to have difficulties, both psychological and visual, as is apparent in this letter to Coutela dated April 9, 1924:

> For months I have worked with obstinacy, without achieving anything good. I am destroying everything that is mediocre. Is it my age? Is it defective vision? Both certainly, but vision particularly. You have given me back the sight of black on white, to read and write, and I cannot be too grateful for that, but I am certain that the vision of [this] painter . . . is lost, and all is for nothing.
>
> I am telling you this confidentially. I hide it as much as possible, but I am terribly sad and discouraged. Life is a torture for me. (Monet, 1924)

In the summer of 1924, still one more ophthalmologist was called in to care for the aging artist. This was Jacques Mawas, MD, an esteemed researcher based at the Rothschild Eye Foundation (Dubois-Poulson, 1976). Mawas was psychologically astute. He fit Monet with new lenses. Monet was easily discouraged and depressed:

> At night I'm constantly haunted by what I'm trying to achieve. I get up exhausted every morning. The dawning day gives me back my courage. But my anxiety comes back too soon as I set foot in my studio . . . Painting is so difficult. And a torture. Last fall I burned six canvases along with the dead leaves from my garden. It's hopeless. Still I wouldn't want to die before saying all that I have to say, or at least having tried to say it. And my days are numbered (Delange, Gordon, & Forge, 1983, p. 247).

Mawas worked hard with Monet. Monet described some of his difficulties to Mawas in March 1925:

FIGURE 10.2   Monet. Waterlilies. Oil on canvas 78¾ x 83¾ inches. Circa 1922–25.

Courtesy of Toledo Museum of Art, gifts of Edward Drummond Libbey.

I am quite late in giving you news concerning the outcome of my new glasses, but they arrived at such a bad period. I was very discouraged and I no longer hoped for better, so that I discontinued using these glasses which I probably might have accustomed myself to had they not completely disturbed me—eyesight trouble, the slightest color tones broken and exaggerated.

As soon as I am in a better frame of mind I will try to get used to them, though I am more than ever certain that a painter's eyesight can never be recovered. When a singer loses his voice he retires; the painter who has undergone an operation of the cataract must renounce painting; and this is what I have been incapable of (Monet, 1925a).

His depressive mood had improved by July, 1925:

Since your last visit my vision is totally ameliorated. I am working harder than ever, am pleased with what I do, and if the new glasses are better still I would like to live to be one hundred. (Hoschede, 1960, pp. 150–151)

His improved attitude was still present ten days later, in this letter to Dr. Coutela:

> I am very happy to inform you that finally I have recovered my true vision and that nearly at a single stroke. In brief, I am happily seeing everything again and I am working with ardor (Monet, 1925b).

Monet painted almost to the day of his death in December 1926. The 86-year-old artist had been a chronic smoker, and died of chronic obstructive pulmonary disease and cancer of the lung. A group of his waterlily canvases was installed in the Orangerie in 1927. They may be seen today in the same location.

EDGAR DEGAS

Ocular problems surfaced for Degas at an earlier age than for Monet. Monet first recognized his problem late in his seventh decade of life. Degas described severe loss of vision in his right eye at age 36. He had joined the National Guard in 1870, during the Franco-Prussian War. While practicing shooting with a rifle, he suddenly noticed he could not see the target with his right eye. His vision with this eye never improved. Diminished sight in the left eye came later; it was present by 1883. Degas mentioned the names of three ophthalmologists in his notebooks and letters (Guerin, 1947; Reff, 1979). Unfortunately, no medical records of these doctors are known to have survived.

Degas' letters and the notes of others tell us much about his eyesight and his treatment. The medical publications of the physicians mentioned by Degas give us information on the methods by which he was treated. Degas' artistic work adds more data.

Although Degas suffered depressive episodes throughout his life, he became even more reclusive, opinionated and negativistic as he aged. He could be most churlish and spiteful. Unlike Monet, he never had a spouse for emotional support. Monet's late works are lighter thematically than those of Degas. The waterlilies are more lyrical topics than the somber ballet dancers and nudes of Degas' late works. Each artist simplified his style as he aged. Thicker, broader brushstrokes and less detail are apparent in each artist's works.

Degas described the effect of his visual loss in 1871, in a letter to Walter Sickert, a friend and fellow artist. He felt the strong light of the sun caused him great difficulty in painting outdoors: "I have just had and still have a spot of weakness and trouble in my eyes. It caught me at Chatou, by the edge of the water in full sunlight, while I was doing a watercolor, and it made me lose nearly three weeks, being unable to read or go out much, trembling all the while lest I should remain like that." (Guerin, 1947, p. 177)

In 1873 Degas traveled across the Atlantic to New Orleans, Louisiana, where several relatives on his mother's side lived. He found the intense sun of the South caused him problems that did not occur in northern France: "The light is so strong that I have not yet been able to do anything on the river. My eyes are so greatly in need of care that I scarcely take any risk with them at all. A few family portraits will be the sum total of my efforts" (Guerin, 1947, p. 125). In two letters written to Tissot later that year, Degas stated: "This infirmity of sight has hit me hard. My right eye is permanently damaged," and "I shall remain in the ranks of the infirm until I pass into the ranks of the blind. It really is bitter, is it not? Sometimes I feel a shiver of horror" (Guerin, 1947, p. 34).

Sickert described Degas' eyesight, and showed that both his eyes were severely damaged. "It was natural that during the years when I knew him (from '83 onwards), that he should sometimes have spoken of the torment that it was to draw, when he could only see around the spot at which he was looking, and never the spot itself" (Sickert, 1923, p. 308). Sickert's notes indicate that Degas' central vision was affected in both eyes. This loss of central vision means his visual acuity must have been 20/200 or less, which is legal blindness. Studies of Degas' works over time, evaluating the artist's use of line, are consistent with this low level of vision. (See Figure 10.3.)

Several pairs of glasses were tried. Four pairs are still available for examination in the Museé d'Orsay. They were of little benefit. Degas often wore tinted lenses, to protect himself from excess light. He obtained some help from a magnifying glass.

Degas struggled with psychological problems as well as ocular difficulties. Actually, the psychological ones came first. Statements are available from his twenties on that reveal recurrent episodes of sadness and self-doubt. At age 25 a friend described his mood as depressed, his actions as "indecisive and indolent" (Koenigswarter, as quoted in Boggs, Druick, Loyrette, Pantazzi, & Tinterow, 1988, p. 85).

Degas described himself at age 31 in unflattering terms:

> I was or I seemed to be hard with everyone through a sort of passion for brutality, which came from my uncertainty and my bad humour. I felt myself so badly made, so badly equipped, so weak, whereas it seemed to me, that my calculations on art were so right. I brooded against the whole world and against myself (Guerin, 1947, p. 171).

Degas never married. Without a wife to rely on, his sources of companionship were family and friends. He managed to alienate some of his closest friends through his despicable behavior at the time of the

FIGURE 10.3   Degas. Study in nude for dressed ballet dancer. Bronze 28½ inches high. 18979–80.
Courtesy of Toledo Museum of Art, gifts of Edward Drummond Libbey.

Dreyfus affair, in the 1890s and later. In 1877, at age 43, Degas told the wife of a fellow artist, "Living alone, without a family, is really too hard. I never would have suspected it would cause me so much suffering. Here I am now, getting old, in poor health, and almost penniless. I've really made a mess of my life on this earth" (Boggs, Druick, Loyrette, Pantazzi, & Tinterow, 1988, p. 216).

During the decade of the 1870s Degas knew the vision in his right eye was severely damaged. He lived in fear of loss of vision in the left eye. In 1878, a critic noted that Degas, "with whom I am in danger of becoming a friend, [is] a man of wit and an artist of merit, threatened by blindness . . . who consequently spends hours in a dark and desperate mood, matching the gravity of his condition" (Boggs et al., 1988, p. 312).

At age 50 his mood had not improved. He wrote:

> Is it the weight of my 50 years that makes me as heavy and as disgusted as I am? They think I am jolly because I smile stupidly, in a resigned way.

I am reading *Don Quixote*. Ah! happy man and what a beautiful death . . . Ah! where are the times when I thought myself strong. When I was full of logic, full of plans. I am sliding rapidly down the slope and rolling I know not where, wrapped in my bad pastels, as if they were packing paper. (Guerin, 1947, pp. 80–81)

In surveying his half century of life, his conclusions were not happy ones. In another letter that same year Degas wrote:

If you were single, 50 years of age (for the last month), you would know similar moments when a door shuts inside you and not only on your friends. You suppress everything around you, and once all alone you finally kill yourself, out of disgust. I have made too many plans; here I am blocked, impotent. And then I have lost the thread of things. I thought there would always be enough time. Whatever I was doing, whatever I was prevented from doing, in the midst of all my enemies and in spite of my infirmity of sight, I never despaired of getting down to it some day (Boggs et al., 1988, p. 28).

For the major retrospective exhibition of Degas' works in 1988–1989, Degas' late years were arbitrarily considered to have begun in 1890, the year he was 56 (See Figure 10.4). The section on his late years

FIGURE 10.4   Degas. The Dancers. Pastel on paper 24½ x 25½ inches. Circa 1899.

Courtesy of Toledo Museum of Art, gifts of Edward Drummond Libbey.

describes Degas as having become overly serious, without the wit and humor of his earlier years. Deterioration in mind and spirit accompanied his physical aging. On occasion, though, he conceded there could be a psychological basis for some of his physical complaints. In 1896 he wrote "everything is long for a blind man, who wants to pretend that he can see" (Guerin, 1947, p. 199). Degas' sadness comes through to the reader of these passages in a deeper way than in the case of Monet. Monet's landscapes, although literally blue, are uplifting. Degas' late human figures are colder, less animated, more featureless than his earlier work. But despite their physical and psychological problems, both artists created masterpieces in their late years.

REFERENCES

Anon. (1953). *Bulletins et Memories, Societe Francaise d'Opthalmologie. 66,* xci-xcii.

Blodi, F. C. (1986). *Hirschberg's history of ophthalmology.* Bonn: Wayenbourg.

Boggs, J. S., Druick, D. W., Loyrette, H., Pantazzi, M., & Tinterow, G. (1988). *Degas.* New York: Metropolitan Museum of Art.

Coutela, (1923). [Letter to Clemenceau dated August 21, 1923]. J. G. Ravin, (Trans). French Ophthalmologic Society, Paris.

Delange, R., Gordon, R., & Forge, A. (1983). *Monet.* New York: Abrams.

Dittere, M. (1973). Comment Monet recouvra al vue apres l'operation de la cataracte. [How Monet recovered his sight after a cataract operation]. *Sandrama, 32,* 30.

Duboise-Poulsen, A. (1986). Jacques Mawas 1885–1976. *An.d'Ocul, 209,* 325–331.

Guerin, M. (1947). *Degas letters.* Oxford: Cassirer.

Hoschede, D. J. (1960). *Claude Monet ce mal connu.* [Claude Monet, who is poorly understood]. Geneva: Cailler.

Koenigswarter, A., (1988). *Degas.* In J. S. Boggs, D. W. Druick, H. Loyrette, M. Partazzi, & G. Tinterow (Eds.), *Degas,* p. 85. New York: Metropolitan Museum of Art.

Monet, C. (1922a). [Letter to Clemenceau dated November 9, 1922.] J. G. Ravin, Trans. French Ophthalmologic Society, Paris.

Monet, C. (1922b). [Letter to Coutela dated Sept. 13, 1922.] J. G. Ravin, Trans. French Ophthalmologic Society, Paris.

Monet, C. (1922c). [Letter to Coutela dated Oct. 20, 1922.] J. G. Ravin, Trans. French Ophthalmologic Society, Paris.

Monet, C. (1923a). [Letter to Coutela dated June 22, 1923]. J. G. Ravin, Trans. French Ophthalmologic Society, Paris.

Monet, C. (1923b). [Letter to Coutela dated Aug. 27, 1923]. J. G. Ravin, Trans. French Ophthalmologic Society, Paris.

Monet, C. (1924). [Letter to Coutela dated April 9, 1924]. J. G. Ravin, Trans. French Ophthalmologic Society, Paris.

Monet, C. (1925a). [Letter to Coutela dated March 25, 1925]. J. G. Ravin, Trans. French Ophthalmologic Society, Paris.

Monet, C. (1925b). [Letter to Coutela dated July 27, 1925]. J. G. Ravin, Trans. French Ophthalmologic Society, Paris.

Offret, G., (1969). Charles Coutela 1876–1969. *Archives d' Opthalmologie, 29*, 589–592.

Ravin, J. G., Kenyon, C., (1992). The meteoric career of Richard Liebreich. *Survey of Ophthalmology, 37*, 221–228.

Ravin, J. G. (1985). Monet's Cataracts. *Journal of American Medical Association, 254*, 394–399.

Reff, T. (1979). *The notebooks of Edgar Degas.* Oxford: Clarendon.

Sickert, W. (1923). Degas. *Burlington Magazine, 43*, 308.

Stuckey, C. F. (1979). Blossoms and blunders: Monet and the state, II. *Art in America, 68*, 116.

Thiebault-Sisson, F. (1927). Les Nympheas de Claude Monet a l'Orangerie des Tuilleries. *La revue de l'art ancien et moderne, 52*, 45–46.

Wildenstein, D. (1985). Claude Monet biographie et catalogue: Raisonne Lausanne et Paris. *Bibliotheque des Arts, 4*, 77, 108.

Aging, Writing, and Creativity

Carolyn Adams-Price

Throughout this volume, and in the literature on creativity, there have been three main approaches to the study of aging and creativity. The first approach is a creative persons approach. In this approach, the personality or cognitive characteristics of long-lived creative persons are studied, as well as the social or cultural factors that foster creativity. Examples of the creative persons approach are the chapters in this volume by Helson, Rodeheaver, Orwoll, and others.

The second approach is a "creative process" approach, in which a process at the bottom of creativity is postulated, and related to factors such as intelligence, divergent thinking, and problem solving. The chapters by Sinnott, Lubart and Sternberg, and Marsiske and Willis are examples of the creative processes approach.

The third approach, which I will emphasize here, is a "product-oriented" approach. In this approach, age changes in creativity are studied by examining the creative products of older people. They are compared to the creative products of the same persons when they were younger, or to the creative products of younger people, for style, contents, meaning, and the like; all of which may shed light on the nature of creating in late life, and which may ultimately involve new definitions of creativity. Comparing early and late life creative products is often called a search for *late life style*.

The search for late life style in literary products and other writings is the focus of this chapter. I will also expand the possibilities of the product-oriented approach to examine age changes in literary writing. In particular, I will discuss how creative writings can be analyzed objectively to test theories about aging and personality or aging and cognition. I will also discuss how a late life style might be identified using theory from life span developmental psychology to guide the selection of variables for study. Examination of these variables could then be related to the act of creating at different ages and in different stages of cognitive development.

WHY STUDY WRITING?

Writing is interesting to cognition and creativity researchers for a few reasons. The first reason is that writing is a task that is highly likely to be continued across the life span. Writing is a knowledge- and language-based cognitive task, and as such, may be more resistant to age-related decline than more abstract tasks like memory or spatial tasks. The second reason is that writing is a process that is likely to improve with experience, which may be acquired with age. As individuals develop expertise in writing, their writing style and their ability to convey meaning can change. The third reason is that the study of age changes in writing may help psychologists improve their understanding of creativity, as I will demonstrate in the next section.

DEFINITIONS OF CREATIVITY

Traditionally, some process-oriented researchers have defined creativity as a single set of cognitive processes distinct from, but not unrelated to, intelligence. One of the most commonly mentioned features of this process is divergent thinking, the ability to generate novel ideas (e.g., Guilford, 1956). Performance on divergent-thinking tests declines with age (e.g., McCrae, Arenberg, & Costa, 1987), suggesting that some cognitive processes thought to be involved in creativity are characteristic of the young.

Indeed, there is reason to believe that divergent thinking is directly related to thinking processes characteristic of young adults. According to Piaget and Inhelder (1969), cognitive development culminates in formal operational thought in adolescence. Formal operational thought is characterized by the ability to use abstract logic and theory to analyze and describe the world. The new logical processes of adolescents permit them to construct grand theories about politics, work, love, and so forth. The result is a great increase in the quantity of ideas they have, much as one sees in divergent thinking.

Unfortunately, the ideas the young have may be untested, egocentric, and relatively impractical, compared to the ideas that are characteristic of more mature thinkers (e.g., Blanchard-Fields, 1986). Most researchers in creativity suggest that creative ideas are not only novel, but are also useful or practical to the situation (e.g., Amabile, 1983). Sinnott (this volume) suggests that older people may come up with more creative, practical solutions to everyday problems.

Although the association of creativity and novelty appears frequently in the literature, it may not be suitable for describing the processes involved in some of the most famous creative products of all time. Creative products are not always novel; sometimes what makes a product creative is its style or its meaning rather than its novelty per se (Abra, 1989; Mudd, 1996). For example, Shakespeare often borrowed the plots of his plays from older stories and legends. Mozart created music in forms that were not at all unique for his time. Alternative definitions of creativity that may better fit great creators like Shakespeare or da Vinci include the definition of creativity as problem finding (Csikszentmihalyi & Getzels, 1971), or the creation of meaning (Erikson, 1988). The creation-of-meaning definition may be particularly relevant to literature because it is consistent with the way in which many contemporary literary critics evaluate creative products (i.e., by examining their meaning and symbolism).

Creativity probably involves several sets of cognitive processes rather than a single set of processes; processes which vary from domain to domain. Evidence for this comes from Simonton's (1984; 1990a) finding of widely different age peaks of creativity in different fields (e.g., mathematics vs. philosophy), which suggests that these fields require different cognitive processes. Similarly, Boden (1991), by suggesting that computers can mimic creativity in some fields but not in others, implied that there are large domain differences in creative processes, with some domains much more dependent than others on the nuances of language. Sternberg (1986) addressed the question more directly by asking experts in four fields to describe the characteristics of creative people in their field. He found that implicit definitions of creativity vary from domain to domain. For example, artists stressed risk taking and metaphoric processing in their definitions of creativity, whereas physicists emphasized problem solving.

The assumption that creativity equals novelty may be particularly inappropriate for characterizing creativity in writing. The value or worth of a piece of writing is not described by saying that it is novel. In creative writing, skill, style, and meaning may be more important determinants of overall quality (i.e., creativity) than the originality of the plot. The exact characteristics that determine the creativity of a piece of writing should be determined empirically, either by measuring appropriate features of the text directly, or by having those features rated by readers or critics.

The definition of creativity employed here is multidimensional. Creative products can have a number of different forms and still be considered creative. Creativity will be defined as the *result* of acts of self-expression which employ multiple cognitive and affective processes in the generation and translation of ideas into products. I will assume that the cognitive and affective characteristics of individuals of different ages influence the nature of the creative product produced at those ages, and thus, the nature of creativity at those ages. The approach I will take will be a combination of product- and process-oriented approaches, with the primary emphasis on aspects of the product that may enlighten us to the processes involved.

BACKGROUND ON THE PRODUCT-ORIENTED APPROACH

Product-oriented creativity research emphasizes the qualities of works deemed creative by professional or lay judges. Voss and Means (1989) suggest that the qualities most frequently associated with products that are creative are novelty, usefulness, and harmony or elegance. However, few researchers have compared products in older and younger artists for these qualities.

Because psychologists are not experts in the arts, the most prevalent product-oriented approach to creativity has focused on the number and type of products, rather than the specific contents or style of late life creative products. As stated earlier, Simonton (1984; 1988; 1990a; 1990b) has studied the output of the most creative individuals in history, and found that creative productivity peaks vary widely from domain to domain. Mathematicians and physicists tend to be most productive when they are in their twenties and thirties; by contrast, philosophers and historians reach their creative peak in their sixties. Among writers, there are genre differences: lyric poetry tends to be produced early in life, but epic poetry and historical fiction are produced late. From these genre differences, Simonton (1990a) concludes that in some domains, individuals must acquire and integrate huge amounts of knowledge to make a contribution. The more dependent the domain on knowledge, the later the creative peak for that domain.

Simonton (1990a; 1990b) has also indicated that although creative production may peak earlier and later in some fields, in general, the most creative individuals tend to remain creative across the life span. The obvious question that follows from this observation is whether there are age changes in the style or contents of creative products that are similar to the age changes in the types of products. For example, Do late life creative products include large amounts of information organized meaningfully?

A few researchers in artistic domains have begun to look directly at creative products for evidence of age differences. Art historians have taken the lead in this area, looking for age differences in the style and content of late life art works. The classic work here is by Arnheim (1990), who suggests that late life art is characterized by loose brushstrokes and intimate emotional scenes. In this volume, Ravin and Kenyon discussed the case histories of Monet and Degas, including changes in their style of painting that may be compensations for changes in vision accompanying eye disease.

One reason that art historians have been interested in changes in the style and content of late life art is because many of the greatest artists have been remarkably prolific in very late life. Lindauer (in this volume) found that most historical artists were extremely long lived, and continued to work as artists until they died. Lindauer also explored some methods of determining late life style. He asked research participants to guess whether a work is early or late, to see if they performed better than chance. The same participants were also asked to rate the unidentified works on variables thought to differ in early and late works. This method allowed Lindauer to examine differences in the effect of early and late works on perceivers.

Regarding literature, there has not been a great deal of discussion of late life style. Literary critics have been reluctant to make generalizations about age changes in literature for two reasons. The first is that literary experts, like experts in some other fields, have found the topic of aging distasteful and depressing (Wyatt-Brown, 1991). The second reason is a general distaste for the reductionist nature of the scientific method. Many literary critics believe that systematic examination of the commonalities of writers is inconsistent with the enjoyment of literature, because its goal is to remove the uniqueness of the piece (e.g., Cohen-Shalev, 1990; Milic, 1991; Wyatt-Brown, 1990). According to Milic, many literary critics, particularly those who are followers of postmodernism, believe that a literary work exists as a unified, unchangeable creation that is more than simply the work of an author, and thus, information about the author or about authors in general is not relevant to understanding a work. Cohen-Shalev (1990) provided an example of this principle in his comparison of two literary critics' analyses of Wordsworth's midlife poems. The earlier critic, writing in 1950, analyzed Wordsworth's poems in the context of aging, while the later critic, writing from a postmodernist perspective, ignored issues related to aging or other issues directly related to the author.

The belief that a literary work exists as an unchangeable whole is inconsistent with evidence that successful writers tend to revise their works many times before they feel they are finished. Some authors continue to revise their works long after they are published. For example, Yeats' late life poems are largely intriguing reworks of earlier poems (Bornstein, 1989). Getzels and Csikszentimihalyi (1976) have remarked that one of the differences between creative individuals and noncreative individuals is that the former are more likely than the latter to view their works as changeable.

CREATIVITY AND THE CONTENTS
OF LATE LIFE WRITINGS

An obvious place to begin the search for age differences in writing is with a discussion of the contents of writing. By content, I mean the actual words, ideas, themes, characterizations, and philosophies that are consciously chosen and explicitly expressed in the writings. Content may refer to molar qualities of a literary work, such as theme, topic, or social status of the characters, or it may refer to more molecular information, such as the integrative complexity of arguments in the story, or the emotional maturity of the characters. The important questions to ask are (a) To what extent does the content of late life writings differ from earlier writings? and (b) To what extent does the content of late life writings reflect developmental changes in the author's creativity or perspective on life? These ideas may shed light on life span development, cognition, or the nature of creativity.

Before discussing content, it is important to mention that content has its limitations as an indicator of developmental changes in authors. The mere presence of a particular theme or type of character may or may not directly relate to the author's personal concerns or cognitive skills. For example, portraying a character as one-dimensional does not mean that the author is only capable of creating one-dimensional characters. Similarly, it would be a mistake to assume that the presence of violent or sexual images implies a preoccupation with those images. Nevertheless, changes in the themes or characters can reflect the concerns or skills of the author.

CONTENT AND PERSONALITY

A few scholars of English literature have suggested that older writers write about different themes than younger writers (e.g., George, 1986; Woodward, 1980; Wyatt-Brown, 1988). Abra (1986) has examined both humanistic and experimental approaches to age changes in creative writing. He suggests that older writers are more philosophical and cynical than younger writers. In some authors, this style change interferes with the quality of the writing.

A number of researchers in developmental and personality psychology have used written materials, such as diaries, personal papers, and literary products, to examine developmental changes in the lives of individuals (e.g., Wrightsman, 1981; McAdams, 1988; Stewart, Franz, & Layton, 1988). Most of these researchers have used writing samples to verify the importance of developmental themes at different stages of the life span or to examine the impact of life events on personal concerns. Wrightsman suggests that although many of these researchers have employed personal papers, such as letters and diaries, more standard literary products, such as essays, short stories, and novels may be used as well. Personal documents and literary products have been examined using both quantitative content analysis techniques and qualitative methods such as hermeneutics or phenomenology (McAdams, 1988). The goal pursued by personality psychologists who examine personal papers is not to define creativity per se, but to see if the concerns of writers, as evidenced by the themes in their works, coincide with the stages of development, as defined by traditional developmental theorists, such as Erik Erikson (1982). For example, do young adult writers emphasize identity themes more than writers in other age groups, and do elderly writers emphasize generativity or integrity themes? Personality psychologists are using personal papers and literary products as if they were projective personality tests. To the extent that these researchers are using systematic content analysis techniques to answer specific questions about age differences in the themes of literary products, these methods are appropriate.

One way in which writing can be analyzed is to tally the frequency of particular themes. Simonton (1983; 1986) examined age changes in themes included in Shakespeare's plays and in great Greek plays, as represented in the *Syntopicon* of *Great Books of the Western World.* He found that late Shakespearean works were less likely than early works to concern love or to include the themes of political or commercial rivalry (although Simonton suggests that Shakespeare may have avoided these themes in late life for political reasons). Comic or satirical themes increased and then decreased with age. Later works by both Shakespeare and the Athenians emphasized themes of the divinity of government, money, and religious and mystical experiences. Adams-Price and Perlmutter (1990) looked for words related to old age in early and late short stories by 20 of the most famous American authors, equally divided between male and female. There were no differences between early and late works in the frequency of age-related words, but female authors included more age-related words than male authors. In addition, we found that older authors included more old characters in their stories, but the older characters who appeared in early stories were more likely to be positive characters than the older characters in late stories.

Researchers like Stewart (Stewart & Healy, 1986; Stewart, Franz, & Layton, 1988) have used content analysis methods of scoring adapted from the Thematic Apperception Test or from Erikson's writings. Stewart, for example, has examined the diaries and letters of Vera Brittain at different ages, coding these writings for Eriksonian themes, such as identity, intimacy, and generativity (Stewart & Healy, 1986; Stewart et al., 1988). Stewart and colleagues have found that writings from Brittain's teens and 20s emphasized identity themes, while writings from her 30s and 40s emphasized generativity themes.

COGNITION

In order to examine the relationship between late life literary products and cognition, it is important first to review some trends in cognitive aging research. These trends might suggest directions for research in late life writing style. Conversely, an examination of late life writing style may illuminate cognitive aging.

A common theme in current research on cognitive aging is late life potential (Perlmutter, 1990). Researchers have found that older people are more variable in their cognitive performance than younger people, and while decline is characteristic of some, it is far from characteristic of all. Thus, researchers interested in successful aging have begun to study the cognitive processes of those who age successfully, to see how they are different from the cognitive processes of younger people and of less successful agers. These researchers assume that the cognitive processes of successful agers show growth in some areas of thinking that compensates for declines in other areas of thinking (e.g., Baltes, 1987). Areas in which older people are likely to show growth demand considerable knowledge, effective strategies, or expertise that individuals have acquired over time. Thus, to the extent that writing is a cognitive process that involves a great deal of planning, strategy, and organization, it may take a long time to acquire—and longer to develop—true expertise. Research by Flower (e.g., Carey & Flower, 1989; Flower, Schriver, Carey, Haas, & Hayes, 1987) suggests that writing is indeed a process involving considerable strategy and organization, and that as such, minimal writing competence develops later than competence in most other areas of cognition.

One age-related change in cognition with implications for writing is postformal reasoning. *Postformal reasoning* involves the ability to reason about complex situations with more than one right answer, and to understand and integrate contradictions. (See Sinnott, this volume.) Researchers have suggested that older people are more likely than younger ones to understand and express the complex and contradictory nature of emotions (Labouvie-Vief, DeVoe, & Bulka, 1989). If these hypotheses are true, then examples of postformal thinking and complex emotions should be present in the writings of older people. They would be reflected in content rather than style, because they would occur sporadically, rather than permeating the whole text.

One recent study looked directly at writings for examples of age changes in cognition. Haviland and Kramer (1991) examined the diary entries of one young writer, Anne Frank. They tracked Anne Frank's emotional experiences as described in her diary, and correlated peak experiences with changes in cognitive complexity and formal thinking. They found that later writings by Anne Frank included more examples of complex thinking, and that peak emotional experiences usually preceded increases in cognitive level. Adams-Price, Brennan, and Tubb (1993) found that women included more examples of high emotional complexity in early stories than in late stories, while males showed a reverse order. These findings are consistent with gender differences in emotions early and late in life, which suggest that women become more stoic with age, while men become more expressive (e.g., Gutmann, 1987).

It has also been suggested that increased use of metaphor is related to postformal thinking (Boswell, 1975). Adams-Price and Perlmutter (1990) reported that famous authors used more literal metaphors in late life short stories than in earlier short stories, but not more nonliteral metaphors. Literal metaphors are metaphors with one, fairly obvious meaning. Nonliteral metaphors have more than one possible interpretation.

Two studies have examined age changes in integrative complexity in writers. Porter and Suedfeld (1981) studied the correspondence of famous authors. They found that integrative complexity increased with age, but declined 5 years before the authors' deaths. My colleagues and I (Brooks, Heaps, & Adams-Price, 1993) examined political columns written at four 7-year intervals, and found that columns written the first year were lower in integrative complexity. Intriguingly, integrative complexity was negatively correlated with writing style as measured by the Gunning-Fog Index, an index of reading difficulty computed from sentence and word length.

AGE DIFFERENCES IN THE STYLE OF WRITINGS

Winter (1969) defined literary style as "a pattern of recurrent selections from the inventory of optional features of a language" (p. 3). Elements of style include vocabulary, tone, sentence length or structure, and dialect. Famous writers are often known by the distinctive style of their writing, much as painters are known by their style of painting. For example, Faulkner is known for extremely long, convoluted sentences and Hemingway is known for a much sparser style.

A common way to approach literary style is to examine the tone of literary works. For example, literary scholars have suggested that late poems are characterized by a calm, meditative tone, and an increasingly personal voice on the part of the narrator (Woodward, 1980). By contrast, others have suggested that late life writings tend to be angry or cynical (George, 1986). Still other scholars (Wyatt-Brown, 1988) have suggested that the style of late life writings is influenced by events in the life of the writer. Literary analyses of style along these lines are intriguing, but the methodology has not yet been developed to be useful to cognitive aging researchers.

Researchers in statistical stylistics have described a variety of features of literary language that can be examined empirically to determine authorship or compare one author to another. Milic (1991) suggests that "stylisticians" can use statistical methods to address the question of consistent quantifiable writing styles that distinguish writers from one another.

In the 1960s, several researchers attempted to use computational methods to analyze writing style in famous authors (Dolezel & Bailey, 1969; Milic, 1991; Mosteller & Wallace, 1963). Assuming that style remains relatively constant for a particular author, but varies greatly between authors, Mosteller and Wallace (1963) used computational features of texts (e.g., mean sentence length and adjective-verb ratios) to determine the likely authorship of disputed manuscripts.

In the 1980s, Simonton (1986) analyzed the features that distinguish dramatic works that are recognized as highly creative. He reported that great plays have more quotable lines and present a broader range of philosophical issues than minor plays. The examination of the attributes that distinguish between creative products of high quality and lower quality is a very promising approach.

However, with the exception of Simonton, researchers have failed to use this intriguing technique to look at changes in writing style over time. Potter (1991) suggests that statistical stylistics has rarely been used to answer empirical questions because researchers have no theory to guide them toward variables that are worth examining. Theories of linguistics or cognitive aging could guide researchers in statistical stylistics toward the most important variables for study.

Cognitive aging researchers have begun to look at age differences in some aspects of style, such as syntax or vocabulary. Recent research on aging and productive language processes indicates that writing style may change with age in nonprofessional writers. Kemper (1990) has found that elderly subjects use fewer complex sentence structures than younger subjects in speech and writing. In her studies of diary entries written over decades, she found that late life diary entries had a more complex episode structure, but used fewer complex sentences. In particular, she found that late life diary entries contained fewer left-branching subordinate clauses (i.e., fewer clauses that interrupt the main clause). She explained that older persons do not use left-branching clauses because they are harder to remember. However, it could also be argued that older writers avoid left-branching clauses because they are harder to understand. Older writers may have learned that simple prose is readable prose. In a recent survey of amateur and professional writers aged 20 to 88, young writers said that they lengthened their manuscripts upon revision, but older people claimed that they shortened and simplified theirs (Adams-Price, 1991).

Bromley (1991) also found evidence of a decline in the complexity of writing in late life, reporting a modest decline in sentence length and complexity in the writings of older individuals. However, he also reported a positive correlation between vocabulary and age. Thus it seems that there is some evidence that syntactical writing style simplifies with the age of the writer, but other variables, such as vocabulary, may get more complex.

Less is known about age changes in the syntactical writing style of distinguished writers. Professional writers, as experts, may have more conscious control over their writing styles, and as a result, may show more individual patterns of change. Some authors may choose a so-called artistic style that utilizes complex sentence structures, such as left-branching clauses. Other authors, however, may choose simpler sentence structures in late life, to make themselves better understood by the intended audience. Edel (1979) found that Henry James' writing style got more complex with age. He used longer, more complex sentences in his late life writings. Simonton (1986) found several age changes in the style of Shakespeare's plays. He found that the proportion of prose increases and then decreases in a backwards J. He also found age-related increases in weak endings (lines ending in auxiliary verbs, prepositions, or pronouns), and in lines containing run-on sentences.

The comparative structure of the writings of young and old persons is another topic that needs to be explored, but that presently remains uninvestigated. Do older people write stories with the same story or plot structures as younger people? As stated earlier, Kemper (1990) suggests that the episode structures of late life diary entries are more complex than the episode structures of earlier ones. A related topic that may provide insight into older people's story-writing style is their storytelling style. Cynthia Adams (Adams, 1991; Adams, Labouvie-Vief, Hobart, & Dorosz, 1990) has examined age differences in written story recall. She found that older people tend to use a more interpretive, metaphoric style than adolescents while telling existing stories. By contrast, adolescents literally repeated the story, sticking more closely to the original propositions. Although this research examines recall rather than writing per se, the implication is that late life storytelling may be more oriented toward meaning than earlier storytelling.

MEANING, LITERATURE, AND LATE LIFE STYLE

The final section of this chapter deals with the third component of late life creative writing: the creation of meaning. Meaning has many definitions, from the linguists' division of meaning into denotative and connotative meaning, to the existentialists' discussion of the meaning of life. A discussion of meaning has been particularly problematic for researchers interested in literature, because literature has many layers of meaning, a concept called the *polyvalence convention* (e.g., Halasz, 1989; Schmidt, 1982). The interpretation of these layers is the stuff of literary criticism.

A valued feature of literature is its *shared meaning;* those meanings which are apparent and significant to readers (Halasz, 1989; Howard, 1991). Although the response of readers depends on their knowledge and emotional tendencies, some texts are more evocative than others (Colvin & Bruning, 1989; Halasz, 1989; Simonton, 1983). Such shared meanings can be examined empirically, for example, through phenomenological techniques or rating scales. The emotional impact of literature on different individuals is analyzed in reader response research.

There may be age differences in the production of personally meaningful stories, with older persons producing the most meaningful stories. Theory in life span developmental psychology suggests that older people are strongly motivated to search for life's meaning in anticipation of their deaths (e.g., Butler, 1963; E. Erikson, 1982; J. Erikson, 1988). Butler suggests that the drive to find meaning in life motivates older people to share the stories that define their lives through communication with others, through autobiographical writings and other means. Pivotal stories that help people define their lives are called *life scripts* (e.g., Linde, 1993). Little is known about age differences in life scripts, but life scripts may figure more prominently in the writings of older people. The desire to preserve these life scripts may result in a new interest in autobiographical writing. Autobiographical writing can help older adults find closure on their lives. It also allows them to pass on wisdom that they have acquired.

Joan Erikson (1988) has suggested that the meanings in the writing of older people are akin to wisdom. Borrowing heavily from Jung, she suggests that the creative products of older people contain layers of meaning drawn from their lives, and that it is these layers that make the works creative, not novelty. Along these lines, Howard (1991) suggests that a primary feature of great literature is that it contains meanings toward which readers are drawn and with which they can empathize. Such meanings might be called *empathic resonance.* Empathic resonance is not dissimilar to Simonton's (1983) notion of "issue richness." Texts with empathic resonance contain realistic and genuine characters, and a sense of timelessness. They make sense of life's complexities and contradictions. Empathic resonance may also be related to wisdom, in that current theories of wisdom include empathy and the ability to understand life's complexities (e.g., Orwoll & Perlmutter, 1990). Further, if complex cognition and wisdom increase with age, older adults' writings should show higher levels of empathic resonance than the writings of younger people, although empathic resonance is certainly not limited to the writings of older people.

PRELIMINARY DATA ON THE EMPATHIC RESONANCE OF LATE LIFE STORIES

I have collected some preliminary findings relevant to the hypothesis that that older writers create stories high on empathic resonance. A methodology for late style methodology similar to that suggested by Lindauer (this volume) was employed. Short stories written by advanced amateur writers were read by young and old persons, and rated on dimensions relevant to empathic resonance. Readers did not know the age of the authors. Six short stories written by young people and published in six volumes of a yearly campus literary magazine were selected, and six similar short stories published in an anthology of writings by an elderly writers' group. The stories were matched for length and topic. The two samples were similar in that both included short stories written by skilled amateur writers. However, the short stories written by younger people were a slightly more select group of stories. Short stories published in the campus literary magazine were selected on a competitive basis from a pool of about 100 entries per volume. Each volume contained 15 pieces, of which only two or three were short stories. Short stories in the elderly writers' anthology were selected on a cooperative basis from a pool of some 400 short stories, poems, and other short pieces. The volume contained 135 pieces of which 40 were short stories. The mean age of the younger authors was 21, while the mean age of the elderly authors was 79. The young authors were bachelor's or master's students. The older authors included three with a bachelor's degree, two with no college, and one with a doctorate.

Thirty college students aged 19–35 and 30 adults between ages 55–81 read the stories, with no information on the authors' ages. Each reader was randomly assigned to read one of two packets of stories, containing 3 elderly and 3 young adult stories. Results indicated that both young and old readers preferred the stories of the elderly authors. The stories of the elderly authors were rated as better written, more meaningful, more timeless, more realistic in terms of events and characters, and easier to follow than the stories of the young authors. Contrary to expectations, however, no age differences were found for the authors' perceived understanding of people, the plainness of the language, or the importance of the story to the author. There was only one interaction between the author's and the reader's age. Older people, but not younger people, rated the stories written by older people as more meaningful, suggesting that meaningfulness may be partially cohort specific. However, no such interaction was found for timelessness, quality of writing, psychological realism, and the other variables. Thus, for this sample, the stories of older people seem to have had more empathic resonance.

CONCLUSION: WRITING AS AN EXPRESSION OF CREATIVITY

In this chapter, I have suggested that age changes in personality and cognition may affect late life writings. Late writings reflect the concerns of older writers, as well as the complexity of their thinking about life. Gerontological research and theory can be used to guide the selection of variables for study in late life literature.

One theme of this chapter has been that late life writing has a different form and purpose than earlier writing. Late life writing is often written in a simpler, more straightforward style than earlier writing, possibly reflecting a desire to communicate directly. However, the narrative structure of late life writing may be very complex. Since style can come under conscious control, this change may not appear in all older authors, or at least in all professional ones. Developmental theory suggests that late life writing may be more autobiographical than earlier writing. However, to date, this hypothesis has not been tested. Future research should determine if the writing of older people is more autobiographical than the writing of younger people.

I have also suggested that late life creative writing may be high on empathic resonance, the qualities of timelessness and believability that make readers enjoy the story and identify with the characters. Stories high on empathic resonance are not unusual stories, but they are likely to be popular with average readers. As such, their value may not always be recognized by critics. Empathic resonance should not replace traditional definitions of creativity, but it might be considered an additional form of creativity; a convergent rather than divergent creativity. Furthermore, future research needs to better incorporate the concepts of reader response theory into an analysis of early and late life stories. For example, future research might identify the qualities of late and early stories with which readers empathize (See Adams-Price, 1993).

In short, definitions of creativity that emphasize novelty do not describe the qualities that make all creative products valued or valuable, and are particularly inadequate in accounting for the value of literary products. Furthermore, novelty-based definitions of creativity emphasize characteristics associated with adolescent thinking. By contrast, late life writing may reflect the positive aspects of late life thinking: synthesis, reflection, and even wisdom.

REFERENCES

Abra, J. (1986). Artistic creativity across the adult life span: An alternative approach. *Interchange, 4,* 1–16.

Abra, J. (1989). Changes in creativity with age: Data, exploration, and future predictions. *International Journal of Aging and Human Development, 28,* 105–126.

Adams, C. (1991). Qualitative age differences in memory for text: A life-span developmental perspective. *Psychology and Aging, 6,* 323–336.

Adams, C., Labouvie-Vief, G., Hobart, C., & Dorosz, M. (1990). Adult age differences in story recall style. *Journals of Gerontology, 45,* P17–P27.

Adams-Price, C. (1991, November). *Age, experience, and writing strategies.* Paper presented to the annual meeting of the Gerontological Society of America, San Francisco, CA.

Adams-Price, C. (1993, August). *Aging, life span development, and creative writings.* Paper presented as part of a symposium presented at the annual meeting of American Psychological Association, Toronto, Canada.

Adams-Price, C., Brennan, D., & Tubb, A. (1993, March). *Complex emotions in the early and late writings of famous authors.* Poster presented to the Southeastern Psychological Association Meeting, Atlanta.

Adams-Price, C., & Perlmutter, M. (1990, November). Style and perceptions of age and emotion in early and late stories. In C. Adams-Price (Chair), *Late-life artists and writers: Maturing of the psychology of creativity.* Symposium conducted at meeting of the Gerontological Society of America, Boston, MA.

Amabile, T. (1983). *The social psychology of creativity.* New York: Springer-Verlag.

Arnheim, R. (1990). On the late style. In M. Perlmutter (Ed.), *Late life potential* (pp. 113–120). Washington, DC: Gerontological Society of America.

Baltes, P. B. (1987). Theoretical propositions of life-span developmental psychology: On the dynamics between growth and decline. *Developmental Psychology, 23,* 611–626.

Blanchard-Fields, F. (1986). Attributional processes in adult development. *Educational Gerontology, 12,* 291–300.

Boden, M. A. (1991). *The creative mind: Myths and mechanisms.* New York: Basic.

Bornstein, G. (1989). *Poetic remaking: The art of Browning, Yeats, and Pound.* State College: Pennsylvania State University Press.

Boswell, D. (1975). Metaphoric processing in the mature years. *Human Development, 22,* 373–384.

Bromley, D. (1991). Aspects of written language over adult life. *Psychology and Aging, 6,* 296–308.

Brooks, J., Heaps, C., & Adams-Price, C. (1993, March). *Age changes in integrative complexity in political commentary.* Poster presented to the Southeastern Psychological Association, Atlanta.

Butler, R. (1963). The life review: An interpretation of reminiscence in the aged. *Psychiatry: A Journal for the Study of Interpersonal Processes, 26,* 65–76.

Carey, L. J., & Flower, L. (1989). Foundations for creativity in the writing process: Rhetorical representations of ill-defined problems. In J. A. Glover, R. R. Ronning, & C. R. Reynolds (Eds.), *Handbook of creativity* (pp. 283–303). New York: Plenum.

Cohen-Shalev, A. (1990). Developmental assumptions in literary criticism and their implications for conceptions of continuity and change in literary creativity. *Psychology and Aging, 5,* 79–85.

Colvin, C. A., & Bruning, R. (1989). Creating the conditions for creativity in reader response to literature. In J. Glover, R. Ronning, & C. Reynolds (Eds.), *Handbook of creativity* (pp. 323–340). New York: Plenum.

Csikszentmihalyi, M., & Getzels, J. (1971). Discovery-oriented behavior and the originality of creative products: A study with artists. *Journal of Personality and Social Psychology, 19,* 47–52.

Dolezel, L., & Bailey, R. W. (1969). *Statistics and style.* New York: Elsevier.

Edel, L. (1979). Portrait of the artist as an old man. In D. Van Tassel (Ed.), *Aging, death, and the completion of being* (pp. 193–214). Philadelphia: University of Pennsylvania Press.

Erikson, E. (1982). *The life cycle completed: A review.* New York: Norton.

Erikson, J. (1988). *Wisdom and the senses.* New York: Norton.

Flower, L., Schriver, K., Carey, L. J., Haas, C., & Hayes, J. R. (1987). *Planning in writing: A theory of the cognitive process.* (Office of Naval Research Technical Report, No. 1). Pittsburgh, PA: Carnegie-Mellon University.

George, D. H. (1986). "Who is the double ghost whose head is smoke?" Women poets on aging. In K. Woodward & M. M. Schwartz, (Eds.), *Memory and desire: Aging—literature—psychoanalysis* (pp. 49–61). Atlantic Highlands, NJ: Humanities.

Getzels, J. W., & Csikszentmihalyi, M. (1976). *The creative vision: A longitudinal study of problem solving in art.* New York: Wiley.

Guilford, J. P. (1956). The structure of the intellect. *Psychological Bulletin, 53,* 267–293.

Gutmann, D. (1987). *Reclaimed powers: Toward a new psychology of men and women in later life.* New York: Basic.

Halasz, L. (1989). Social psychology, social cognition, and the empirical study of literature. *Poetics, 18,* 29–44.

Haviland, J., & Kramer, D. (1991). Affect-cognition relationships in adolescent diaries: The case of Anne Frank. *Human Development, 34,* 143–159.

Howard, G. S. (1991). Culture tales: A narrative approach to thinking, cross-cultural psychology, and psychotherapy. *American Psychologist, 46*, 187–197.

Kemper, S. (1990). Adults' diaries: Changes made to written narratives across the life-span. *Discourse Processes, 13*, 207–224.

Labouvie-Vief, G., DeVoe, M., & Bulka, D. (1989). Speaking about feelings: Conceptions of emotion across the life span. *Psychology and Aging, 4*, 425–437.

Linde, C. (1993). *Life stories: The creation of coherence.* New York: Oxford University Press.

McAdams, D. P. (1988). Biography, narrative, and lives: An introduction. *Journal of Personality, 56*, 1–18.

McCrae, R., Arenberg, D., & Costa, P. (1987). Declines in divergent thinking with age: Cross-sectional, longitudinal, and cross-sequential analysis. *Psychology and Aging, 2*, 130–137.

Milic, L. (1991). Progress in stylistics: Theory, statistics, and computers. *Computers and the Humanities, 25*, 393–400.

Mosteller, F., & Wallace, D. (1963). Inference in an authorship problem. *Journal of the American Statistical Association, 18*, 275–309.

Orwoll, L., & Perlmutter, M. (1990). The study of wise persons: Integrating a personality perspective. In R. J. Sternberg (Ed.), *Wisdom: Its nature, origins, and development* (pp. 160–177). New York: Cambridge University Press.

Perlmutter, M. (1990). *Late life potential.* Washington, DC: Gerontological Society of America.

Piaget, J., & Inhelder, B. (1969). *The psychology of the child.* New York: Basic.

Porter, C. A., & Suedfeld, P. (1981). Integrative complexity in the correspondence of literary figures: Effects of personal and societal stress. *Journal of Personality and Social Psychology, 40*, 321–330.

Potter, R. G. (1991). Statistical analysis of literature: A retrospective on Computers and the Humanities, 1966–1990. *Computers and the Humanities, 25*, 401–429.

Schmidt, S. J. (1982). *Foundations for the empirical study of literature.* Hamburg, Germany: Luske.

Simonton, D. K. (1983). Dramatic greatness and content: A quantitative study of eighty-one Athenian and Shakespearean plays. *Empirical Studies of the Arts, 1*, 109–123.

Simonton, D. K. (1984). *Genius, creativity, and leadership: Histrionic inquiries.* Cambridge: Harvard University Press.

Simonton, D. K. (1986). Popularity, content, and context in 37 Shakespearean plays. *Poetics, 15*, 493–510.

Simonton, D. K. (1988). Creativity, leadership, and chance. In R. J. Sternberg (Ed.), *The nature of creativity: Contemporary psychological perspectives* (pp. 386–428). Cambridge, UK: Cambridge University Press.

Simonton, D. K. (1989). The swan-song phenomenon: Last-works effects for 172 classical composers. *Psychology and Aging, 4,* 42–47.

Simonton, D. K. (1990a). Creativity and wisdom in aging. In J. E. Birren & K. W. Schaie, (Eds.), *Handbook of the psychology of aging* (3rd ed., pp. 320–329). San Diego: Academic.

Simonton, D. K. (1990b). Creativity in the later years: Optimistic prospects for achievement. *The Gerontologist, 30,* 626–631.

Simonton, D. K. (this volume). Career paths and creative lives: A theoretical perspective on late-life potential. In C. Adams-Price (Ed.), *Creativity and aging: Theoretical and empirical perspectives.* New York: Springer.

Sinnott, J. D. (1984). Postformal reasoning: The relativistic stage. In M. L. Commons, F. A. Richards, & C. Armon (Eds.), *Beyond formal operations.* New York: Prager.

Sternberg, R. J. (1986). Implicit theories of intelligence, creativity, and wisdom. *Journal of Personality and Social Psychology, 49,* 607–627.

Stewart, A. J., Franz, C., & Layton, L. (1988). The changing self: Using personal documents to study lives. *Journal of Personality, 56,* 41–74.

Stewart, A. J., & Healy, J. M. (1986). The role of personality development and experience in shaping political commitment: An illustrative case. *Journal of Social Issues, 42,* 11–31.

Voss, J. F., & Means, M. L. (1989). Toward a model of creativity based upon problem solving in the social sciences. In J. A. Glover, R. R. Ronning, & C. R. Reynolds (Eds.), *Handbook of creativity* (pp. 411–427). New York: Plenum.

Winter, W. (1969). Styles and dialects. In L. Dolezel & R. Bailey (Eds.), *Statistics and style* (pp. 3–10). New York: Elsevier.

Woodward, K. (1980). *At last, the real distinguished thing: The late poems of Ezra, Pound, Stevens, and Williams.* Columbus: Ohio State University.

Wrightsman, L. S. (1981). Personal documents as data in conceptualizing adult personality development. *Personality and Social Psychology Bulletin, 7,* 367–385.

Wyatt-Brown, A. (1988). Late life style in the novels of Barbara Pym and Penelope Mortimer. *The Gerontologist, 28,* 835–839.

Wyatt-Brown, A. (1990). The coming of age of literary gerontology. *Journal of Aging Studies, 4,* 299–315.

CHAPTER TWELVE

Linguistic Creativity in Older Adults

Susan Kemper and Cheryl Anagnopoulos

Psycholinguistics commonly equate *generativity* with creativity. Generativity is the power of formal linguistic rules to create new and novel utterances through mechanisms such as recursion. Hence, the production of multiclause sentences, involving the recursive application of rules, is the hallmark of "creative" linguistic abilities. An example of a recursively generated sentence is "This is the dog that chased the cat that ate the mouse that lived in the house that Jack built." Analogical operations, such as applying morphological rules to transform one part of speech into another, are also treated as creative linguistic abilities. Examples might include: abridging "The Senators secretly conferred in the Senate cloakroom about the pending bill" to "The Senators cloakroomed the bill" and extending this new verb form as a nominal in "Cloakrooming legislation avoids filibusters." Recursion and analogy are powerful linguistic mechanisms which serve to expand a stock inventory of sentence forms or lexical items, thereby creating (or generating) an infinite number of novel utterances.

This sense of creativity has been extended to other linguistic abilities. It is from this perspective that the development of metalinguistic awareness in children has served as an account of the development of humor, language play, and figurative speech. Many forms of humor seem to reflect metalinguistic rule violations (Clark, 1978; Garvey, 1977; Hakes, 1980; Shultz, 1976; Shultz & Horibe, 1974; Sutton-Smith, 1976). Other forms of linguistic expression, such as storytelling, can be treated as rule-governed abilities, and their rules, like lexical and syntactic rules, are subject to recursion and analogy (Mandler & Johnson, 1977; Propp, 1968). Just as sentences can be extended through the use of recursion, so too stories can be recursive, involving nested sequences of problems and solutions, concatenated events, or multiple episodes.

Little is known about how these aspects of linguistic creativity relate to other aspects of creativity. Some might hold that recursion and analogy are basic components of linguistic competence and, hence, available to all individual speakers of a language as powerful linguistic devices for creating new and novel utterances. Thus, little individual variation would be expected and the creative application of linguistic rules should be independent of other forms of creativity. Alternatively, these mechanisms may be limited by other cognitive abilities which regulate their domain or range of application. Not all individuals may be able to produce multiple embedded clauses, morphologically derived forms, or elaborate narrative structures; if that is the case, the incidence of these forms or complexity metrics based on these forms, may be important individual difference variables (Cheung & Kemper, 1992) related to other forms of creativity. From either perspective, linguistic creativity is seen as distinct from literary creativity (Porter & Suedfeld, 1981; Simonton, 1975).

The research of Kemper (1987) and others (Kemper, Kynette, Rash, Sprott, & O'Brien, 1989; Kemper, Rash, Kynette, & Norman, 1990) suggests that linguistic creativity decreases with advancing age, reflecting a truncation or curtailment of grammatical rules. These researchers found that older adults' written and oral stories are less complex, syntactically, than those of younger adults. Syntactic complexity, in these studies, was defined by the use of multiclause sentences involving subordinate or embedded forms. Examples of multiclause sentences are given in Table 12.1. Multiclause constructions result from the application of recursive rules; recursion permits one clause to be generated "inside" another. Thus, this research suggests that adults' ability to generate recursive structures is limited by working memory restrictions on mental computations (Kemper, 1992a). It suggests, therefore, that linguistic creativity decreases in adulthood.

This research stands in sharp contrast to other research that documents a variety of more positive changes to older adults' language. For example, Kemper et al. (1990), Pratt and Robins (1991), and Pratt, Boyes, Robins, and Manchester (1989) have analyzed the personal narratives told by elderly adults; Kemper (1990) analyzed a 7-decade longitudinal record of diary entries. All three studies found that elderly adults created elaborate narrative structures that included hierarchically elaborated episodes with beginnings describing initiating events and motivating states, developments detailing the protagonists' goals and actions, and endings summarizing the outcomes of the protagonists'

TABLE 12.1 Example of Expository Statement

Left-branching clauses are bracketed [], right-branching are in braces {}. Cohesive ties, including pronominal reference (*my, I*), comparative terms (*greater, more*), causal connectives (*since*), ellipsis (*so*), and repeated lexical terms are italicized. Structural constituents are indicated in parentheses.

There are certainly some changes {I would have made}. At least it seems *so* from here. *My* lack of confidence in certain areas [emphasized to *greater* degree by *my* older brothers and sisters] [than should have been the case], led *me* {to feel} {*I* never lived up to *their* expectations of me} (problem). I should not have let {*their* loud and noisy criticism quiet me so easily} (solution). *I* should have considered the content of *criticism* more and the *critic* less (solution). *I* should have concentrated *more* and procrastinated *less* (solution). *I* should have tried much more {to discipline *myself*} (solution) and {to organize *my* work and life *more* carefully} (solution). [Since *my* talents were not tremendous], *I* should have sought places in community or literary fields {where *I* could have made a *greater* impact} (solution).

efforts. The elderly adults provided background information regarding the setting and story protagonists through the use of sequential and embedded episodes. The elderly adults also attached evaluative codas to their narratives which assessed the contemporary significance of these episodes.

The research studies also consistently obtained positive correlations between the age of the storyteller and ratings of the quality of the narratives. Naive raters as well as English teachers apparently agree on what makes a "good" story: good stories involve complex plots with multiple episodes and evaluative codas. Whether older adults have learned through experience to tell such stories or whether they simply have more interesting experiences and points of view to relate, their stories conform more closely to this ideal than those of young adults. This pattern of results confirms widely held cultural stereotypes of older adults as good storytellers. And, unlike the research focusing on grammatical rules at the sentence level, this work suggests that linguistic creativity increases in adulthood.

Kemper et al. (1990) suggested that these two aspects of linguistic creativity are interrelated. In their view, producing well-structured narratives requires working memory in order to hierarchically and serially organize story constituents. Similarly, producing well-structured sentences also requires working memory in order to hierarchically and serially organize sentence constituents. Hence, it appears that older adults sacrifice syntactic creativity in order to preserve narrative creativity as working memory limitations increase with advancing age.

Some support for this account comes from the examination of genre differences in the syntactic complexity of adults' language (Kemper et al., 1989). Different measures of syntactic complexity were obtained for written statements, oral statements, and oral answers to questions (see Figure 12.1). Mean clauses per utterance (MCU) can be taken as a general measure of syntactic complexity and the incidence of left-branching clauses (LEFTs) as a more sensitive measure of the load on working memory of novel syntactic constructions (Cheung & Kemper, 1992). The syntactic forms of the young adults and adults in their sixties varied widely from one speech genre to another; in contrast, the syntactic form of the 70- and 80-year-olds did not vary from one genre to another. For example, complex, left-branching constructions were nearly twice as common in the 60-year-olds' written statements as in their oral statements but equally infrequent in both types of statements from the 80-year-olds. This pattern suggests that the 60-year-olds created different speech styles, varying in syntactic complexity in response to different communication needs, whereas the older adults were no longer responsive to such differential communicative pressures, but used a restricted speech code in all contexts.

Narrative creativity interacts with syntactic creativity. When the demands of narrative creativity are high, less working memory capacity is available to meet the demands of sentence creativity, and as adults age, a loss of working memory will lead to a restriction of working memory capacity to be allocated among story level and sentence level needs. Consequently, syntactic creativity will be increasingly limited by narrative creativity as working memory declines.

Kemper et al. (1990) found a trade-off between narrative creativity and syntactic creativity (see Figure 12.2). Left-branching sentences were common in simple stories, which lacked a hierarchical structure, regardless of the age of the storyteller. Further, 60-year-olds were able to simultaneously create complex sentences and complex stories so that complex sentence forms occurred in their complex stories. In contrast, left-branching constructions were rare in the hierarchically structured, multi-episode stories created by 70- and 80-year-olds although they are common in their simple event sequences and one-episode narratives.

An alternative view of these same linguistic changes to adults' speech is that older adults have learned to avoid communication problems which arise from the use of complex constructions by shifting to a simplified, uniform speech register. Even young children have been observed to shift from one speech register to another, for example when they adopt different voices, vocabularies, and directive forms for

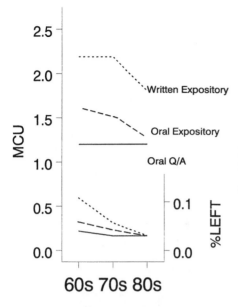

FIGURE 12.1   Genre differences in syntactic complexity.

Note: Adapted from Life-span changes to adults' language: Effects of memory and genre, by S. Kemper, D. Kynette, S. Rash, R. Sprott, and K. O'Brien, 1989, *Applied Psycholinguistics, 10,* p. 58. Copyright 1988; Cambridge University Press. Reprinted with permission.

different characters during imaginative play (Anderson, 1984; Hymes, 1972; Labov, 1970; Lakoff, 1977; Warren-Leubecker & Bohannon, 1989). One primary function of style shifting is adaptation to the communicative needs of listeners. It may be, therefore, that older adults have learned to enhance communication with their peers or others by being less creative, avoiding complex syntactic constructions. If so, the variability in young adults' speech can be taken as reflecting different social and communicative pressures for linguistic creativity, whereas older adults can be seen as having adopted a restricted, simplified speech code which does not vary from context to context or speech genre to genre.

In this chapter, these issues are investigated by contrasting two sets of narratives, collected 4 years apart, and two sets of expository statements, also collected 4 years apart. The analysis of these language samples will focus on syntactic differences between two speech genres, narratives and expository statements, and structural differences between simple and complex texts across the life span. Our hypothesis was that older adults are more creative than young adults with regards to the production of novel and complex text structures, but less creative in regard to syntactic forms that lead to communication problems and working memory problems.

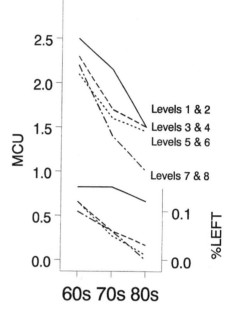

FIGURE 12.2   Structural differences between simple and complex narratives.

Note: Adapted from Telling stories: The structure of adults' narratives, by S. Kemper, S. R. Rash, D. Kynette, and S. Norman, 1990, *European Journal of Cognitive Psychology, 2,* pp. 217, 219. Copyright 1990; Lawrence Earlbaum Associates. Reprinted with permission.

LANGUAGE SAMPLE ANALYSIS

The language samples were obtained from a panel of older adults from the local community (see Table 12.2). All were participants in a series of studies of language production and comprehension. Language samples collected in Year 2 and Year 5 of the study were compared for this analysis; the statements collected in Years 2 and 5 and the narratives from Year 5 have not previously been analyzed. The initial report of the Year 1 language samples was reported in Kemper et al. (1989). A comparison of the language samples collected in Years 1 and 3 was given in Kemper, Kynette, and Norman (1992), which focused on syntactic changes related to working memory. Information regarding participant attrition from Years 1 to 3 can be found in Kemper et al. (1992); there was no further attrition after Year 3.

PARTICIPANTS

At the end of Year 5, there were 28 adults (19 women) from the original 60–69 group (mean age 69), 22 adults (12 women) from the original 70–79 group (mean age 78), and 12 adults (6 women) from the 80+ group (mean age 86).

TABLE 12.2 Description of the Participants

	Year 2	Year 5
60–69 years, *n* = 28		
Mean age	66.4	69.2
Education	15.1	—
WAIS vocabulary (Yr 1)	61.4	62.3
Digits forward	10.5	8.6
Digits backward	7.4	6.6
70–79 years, *n* = 22		
Mean age	74.8	78.5
Education	14.6	—
WAIS vocabulary (Yr 1)	62.6	63.2
Digits forward	9.9	7.5
Digits backward	7.1	5.7
80+ years, *n* = 12		
Mean age	85.4	86.9
Education	12.7	—
WAIS vocabulary (Yr 1)	61.5	63.4
Digits forward	8.0	6.4
Digits backward	5.1	4.3

Year 2

The participants were given two tests of working memory, the Digits Forward and Digits Backward tests from the Wechsler Adult Intelligence Scales-Revised (WAIS) (Wechsler, 1958); two tests of metalinguistic judgments, one written and one aural; and a test of prose memory. Researchers elicited a narrative from each adult, as well as an oral statement in response to the question "What changes have you observed over your life time?" The analysis of the metalinguistic judgments is reported in Pye, Cheung, and Kemper (1992), the prose comprehension study in Norman, Kemper, and Kynette (1992), and an initial analysis of the narratives in Kemper et al. (1990).

Year 5

The participants were retested using a battery of tests first administered in Year 1, including the WAIS Vocabulary, Digits Forward, and Digits Backward tests. In addition, a Sentence Span (Daneman & Carpenter, 1980) test first given in Year 3 was repeated. Four language samples were elicited: (a) oral answers to the questions about the participant's hobbies and occupations, (b) an oral response to the question "What piece of advice would you give a younger person?" (c) a written response to the question "Looking back, what would you do differently or change in your life?" and (d) an oral narrative. The oral narratives were prompted by reminding the participants of the oral narrative elicited in Year 2, and the participants were asked to repeat the same story. Only eight did so; the other participants told new stories. Approximately 50% indicated that they could not remember the earlier story and half that they wanted to tell a new story, one we had not heard before.

SELECTION OF MEASURES

On the basis of extensive analysis of many such complexity measures by Cheung and Kemper (1992), as well as complementary analyses of other linguistic aspects of these language samples by Kemper et al. (1989, 1990) and Kemper (1992b), six measures were selected for use in the present analysis: two measures of syntactic structure, two of semantic content, and two of text organization (see Table 12.3).

MCU

The mean number of clauses per utterance was calculated for each language sample. The number of syntactic clauses per sentence was determined by counting each main clause and each embedded or subordinate clause. Commonly embedded clauses include *wh* clauses such as "whoever did that" and *that* clauses such as "that I was right," which are used as nouns; relative clauses such as "who I admired," which modify nouns; and infinitive complements such as "to go to the store." Kemper et al. (1989) suggested that MCU was a more appropriate measure of adult language development than mean length of utterance (MLU), which is typically computed in the child language literature (Miller & Chapman, 1981).

LEFTs

The percentage of all clauses which were left-branching was calculated for each language sample. Use of LEFTs, therefore, provides a measure of the incidence of left embedding. Left-branching clauses occur as part of the sentence subject and include sentence initial subordinate clauses, such as "*After our two daughters were in school,* I went back to

TABLE 12.3   Language Sample Measures

MCU:	Mean clauses per utterance
LEFTs:	Incidence of left-branching clauses
PDensity:	Propositional density (per 100 words)
TTR:	Type-token ratio
CTies:	Cohesive ties (per sentence)

Level:
  Narratives
    Levels 1 & 2: isolated events and event sequences
    Levels 3 & 4: complex events and simple episodes
    Levels 5 & 6: expanded episodes and multiple episodes
    Levels 7 & 8: embedded episodes and episode sequences plus codas
  Expository Statements
    Description and attribute sequence
    Comparison
    Causation
    Problem-solution

college" and relative clauses modifying the sentence subject, such as "The thing *that I remember the most* is his honesty." LEFTs were included in the present analysis since they may be a more sensitive index of working memory processing problems than MCU (Kemper et al., 1989; Norman et al., 1992).

PDensity

The mean number of propositions of complete statements per 100 words was calculated for each language sample as an index of propositional density. Kintsch and Keenan (1973) have suggested that propositional density is a determinate of reading difficulty. It can also be interpreted as a measure of the semantic content of a language sample.

TTR

The ratio of lexical types (novel or different words) to lexical tokens (all of the words in a language sample) was calculated for each language sample. Type-token ratios are typically assumed to reflect lexical diversity such that a larger TTR characterizes those speakers who use many different words while smaller TTR characterizes those speaker who repeat many words or who use pronominal or elliptical forms (Templin, 1957).

CTies

Halliday and Hasan (1976) developed a system for classifying linguistic devices which tie one part of a text to another. These devices include: reference, ellipsis, lexical repetition, lexical substitution, and conjunction. The occurrence of each form of cohesion was identified and the mean number of cohesive ties per sentence was computed for each oral statement and narrative.

Level

The organization of the texts was also determined using two different systems of text analysis. The first was an interval rating scale which was applied to the narratives; it was based on a rating scheme devised by Botvin and Sutton-Smith (1977) and modified by Kemper (1990) and Kemper et al. (1990). This rating scale ordered the narratives in terms of eight levels of hierarchical organization. These eight levels of hierarchical organization were collapsed into four types of narratives: event strings and event sequences (Levels 1 and 2), complex events and simple episodes (Levels 3 and 4), expanded episodes and multiple episodes (Levels 5 and 6), embedded episodes and episodes sequences plus evaluative codas (Levels 7 and 8).

The second organizational model applied to the expository statements; it is based on the work of Meyer (1975) and Meyer, Young, and Bartlett (1989). Four types of expository texts were identified, roughly ordered in terms of increasing hierarchical organization as: descriptions or sequences, comparisons, causation statements, and problem-solution statements. This classification is ordinal but cannot be considered to be an interval rating scale.

LINGUISTIC CREATIVITY OVER THE LIFE SPAN

The goal of these analyses was to examine how the older adults' linguistic complexity or creativity changes over the life span. Linguistic creativity was assessed by examining complexity at two levels: the sentence level of embedded clauses and the text or structural level of narrative and statement forms. There is considerable variability in the syntactic complexity, semantic content, cohesion, and text structure of the language samples we studied. The overall pattern was one of a gradual gain of structural organization over time with advancing age, which was mirrored by a gradual loss of syntactic complexity, emerging first in complex text structures and gradually extending to simple ones.

Narratives Versus Expository Statements

In general, the 60-year-olds' narratives were considerably different than their expository statements, but 70- and 80-year-olds' narratives and expository statements did not differ in syntactic complexity or cohesion (see Figure 12.3). The 60-year-olds' narratives contained more clauses, more left-branching clauses, fewer propositions, and fewer cohesive ties than their expository statements. These syntactic

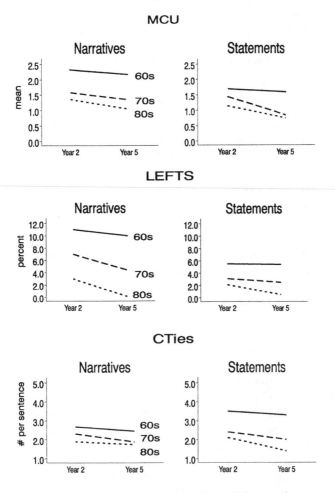

FIGURE 12.3 Syntactic complexity of narratives and expository statements: Mean clauses per utterance (MCU), percentage of left-branching clauses (LEFTs), and mean number of cohesive ties per sentence (CTies).

differences disappeared in the language samples obtained from the 70- and 80-year-olds; their narratives closely resembled their expository statements in terms of MCU, LEFTs, PDensity, and CTies.

Thus, it appears that the 60-year-olds' repertoire included at least two different speech styles, one characteristic of narratives and one characteristic of expository statements. The narrative style was somewhat more complex syntactically in terms of both clauses per sentence and incidence of left-branching clauses, than the expository style. When adjusted for word length, narratives also conveyed somewhat less content than expository statements, since more propositions and cohesive ties are packed into expository statements. Older adults, in their seventies and eighties, did not shift style when producing narratives and expository statements. Therefore, when it comes to syntax, we have concluded that younger adults are more creative than older adults.

SIMPLE VERSUS COMPLEX TEXTS

There is also considerable variability in the organization of the narratives and expository statements. The 80-year-olds told more complex narratives, particularly ones at Levels 7 and 8 with multiple, embedded episodes and evaluative codas than did the 60- and 70-year-olds. More complex narratives at Levels 7 and 8 were produced in Year 5 than in Year 2. Older adults also made more complex expository statements involving causation and problem-solution statements, although the clear preference was for comparison statements. Year 5 statements also were less likely to be descriptions and comparisons and more likely to involve causation and problem-solution plans than those produced in Year 2 (see Figure 12.4). Hence, when it comes to text structure, older adults become progressively more creative as they age.

A SIMPLIFIED SPEECH REGISTER?

Only three measures showed any effect of organizational structure: MCU, LEFTs, and CTies. Further, there was a complex interaction of age, year of study, and structure for these three measures that is similar for both the narratives and the expository statements. Figures 12.5 and 12.6 illustrate the interactions graphically.

Sixty-year-olds' production of multiclause sentences was relatively constant regardless of the structure of the narratives and shows little change over time. In contrast, 80-year-olds' production of multiclause sentences was initially much lower for complex Level 7 and Level 8

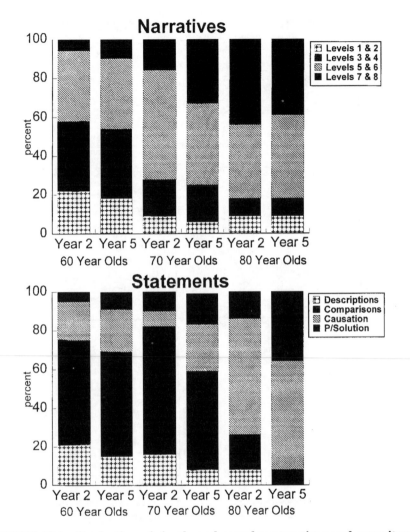

FIGURE 12.4 **Production of simple and complex narratives and expository statements.**

narratives but, over time, this effect of structural level extended to the Level 5 and 6 narratives as well.

A similar pattern held for the expository statements: 60-year-olds' production of multiclause sentences was stable for descriptions, comparisons, causation, and problem-solution statements, whereas 70- and 80-year-olds produced far fewer multiclause sentences in the more

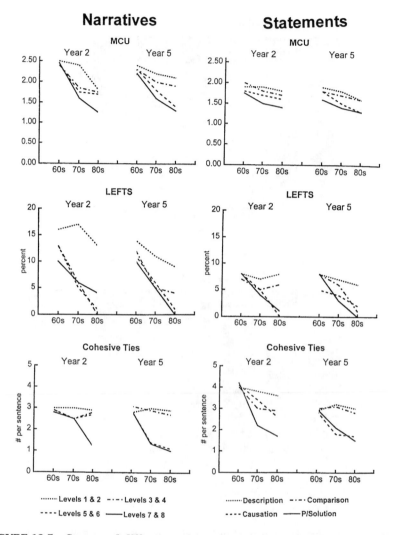

FIGURE 12.5   Structural differences between simple and complex narratives and simple and complex expository statements for MCU, LEFTs, and CTies.

complex problem-solution statements than in the other types. By Year 5, multiple clauses virtually disappeared from the older adults' causation statements as well as from their problem-solution statements, although multiclause sentences still occurred in their descriptions and comparisons.

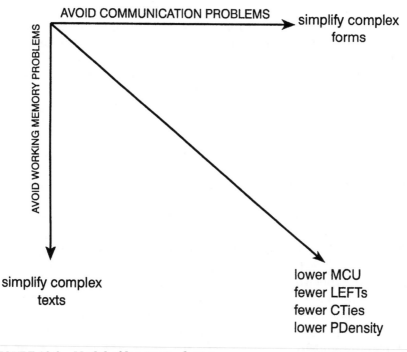

FIGURE 12.6   Model of language change.

Left-branching sentences showed a somewhat different pattern. Left-branching clauses were much less common for all speakers in the narratives at Levels 3 through 8 than in the simple, event sequences at Levels 1 and 2, but fewer left-branching clauses occurred in the Level 1 and Level 2 event sequences in Year 5 than in Year 2, for all speakers. Left-branching clauses occurred frequently in all types of expository statements made by the 60- and 70-year-olds, but only in the descriptions and comparison statements produced by the 80-year-olds.

Cohesive Ties were common in the narratives at all levels of complexity for the 60- and 70-year-olds but only the Level 1 through Level 6 narratives told by the 80-year-olds were cohesive. By Year 5, cohesive ties had disappeared from the Level 5 and Level 6 narratives by the 80-year-olds and the Level 5 through Level 8 narratives by the 70-year-olds. Cohesive ties were very common in all types of expository statements produced by the 60-year-olds, regardless of year. Cohesive ties were much less common in the problem-solution statements produced by the 70- and 80-year-olds and, by Year 5, in their causation statements as well.

Both narrative and expository statements gradually converged on the same simplified speech register with advancing age. This register is composed of simple single-clause sentences with few left-branching constructions and cohesive ties. Narratives and expository statements also diverged in terms of their organization or text structure—these structures began to increase in complexity, taking the form of multi-episode narratives and problem-solution statements.

CONCLUSION

Older adults may adopt a simplified speech register as a result of the convergence of forces. On one hand, in response to communication problems with peers or others, older adults may modulate their production of novel sentences including multiclause sentences. Left-branching clauses and clauses with many propositions and cohesive markers will be especially affected. As a result, syntactic differences between narratives and expository statements are gradually lost as older adults come to use fewer multiclause sentences in their narratives and multipropositional sentences in their expository statements. This force therefore represents a decline in linguistic creativity as syntactic differences disappear.

On the other hand, an accommodation to their own working memory limitations, arising from the structural demands of producing either complex narratives or expository texts, also occurs. This effect is a consequence of the gradual loss of working memory capacity with advancing age and the increasing creativity of older adults in the production of complex narratives with multiple episodes and evaluative codas or problem-solution types of expository statements. We have suggested that this accommodation contributes to the loss of syntactic complexity, because the working memory requirements of creating complex narratives or expository statements preempt those of creating complex sentences.

The result of these two forces—communication concerns and memory limitations—is the same: a restricted speech code characterized by single-clause sentences, low propositional density, and few cohesive ties. It does not vary from one speech context to another but does vary in response to the structural demands that different text organizational structures place on working memory.

This notion of a restricted code should not be confused with that of Bernstein (1971, 1973). Bernstein distinguished between elaborated and restricted speech on a number of dimensions; his restricted code was characterized as involving a restricted vocabulary, simplified syntactic forms, dependence on deitic forms, high contextualization, and personalization. Bernstein's restricted and elaborated speech codes were associated with social class differences and with educational success versus failure. While the older adult speech code we discovered resembles Bernstein's in that it is simplified syntactically, it differs from Bernstein's in a number of ways: its vocabulary is not restricted, as evidenced by the null effects on TTR, and there is no increase in the use of deitic forms, such as *this* or *that* or *here* or *there* (Kemper, 1990; Kemper et al., 1990). Finally, whereas Bernstein's restricted code was a result of cultural and social deprivation, this speech appears to be a functional accommodation to communication problems and processing limitations.

Older adults apparently know how to capture and maintain the attention of their audience by establishing the setting, describing the goals and motives of the characters, and structuring their stories as hierarchies of events and episodes. The use of these narrative forms, like the use of simplified syntax, is a reflection of the communicative goals of older speakers. Just as they may have learned to avoid syntactic complexities, older adults may have learned to use these narratives forms to enhance communication with their peers and others. Of course, these same narrative techniques may arise from the nature of the stories themselves. Older adults may use more complex narrative structures because they relate more complex sequences of events involving historically and contextually situated characters pursuing convoluted and intricate quests.

Similarly, older adults may have learned what it takes to convince or inform one another. Descriptive or comparative statements may be less convincing or less assertive than causation and problem-solution statements and, therefore, less persuasive or less informative. Hence, older adults may have learned to rely on more sophisticated forms of exposition involving the use of causation and problem-solution statements just as they have learned to avoid complex syntactic constructions because both complex expository forms and simplified syntax may enhance communication. Alternatively, older adults' knowledge and specialized expertise, as well as their historical knowledge and experience, may demand the use of more detailed arguments and more elaborated expository forms.

This gain in discourse-level creativity, as evidenced by the increased use of complex narrative and expository structures, may reflect two related phenomena. First, Simonton (1989) has suggested that the late life works of creative individuals, such as composers and authors, frequently peak in a "swan song," an exceptional effort which is "quali-tatively distinct" (p. 42) from other works; these last works of com-posers are brief, concise, and lacking in melodic originality, yet so expressive and aesthetically significant as to capture an enduring place in performance repertoires. Arnheim (1990) has also suggested that the late life style of artists, writers, and other creative individuals is qualitatively distinct. He suggests that late works reflect a contempla-tive detachment, an evenness of texture, and an assimilation and fusion of elements into an integrated world view. Although Simonton and Arnheim focus on the swan songs of exceptionally creative individu-als, a drive towards simplification combined with intersubjective life review and reassessment might also describe the narratives and exposi-tory statements of "ordinary" individuals.

Second, the gain in discourse-level structure may reflect the devel-opment of wisdom on the part of many older adults. Wisdom, while dif-ficult to define (see Baltes & Smith, 1990; Holliday & Chandler, 1986; Sternberg, 1990), is associated with old age. Wisdom is usually charac-terized as knowledge about human nature, social conduct, and life's uncertainties, as well as by the interpersonal skills of communication, conflict resolution, and problem solving. Although true wisdom may be relatively rare (Orwoll & Perlmutter, 1990), some elements of wis-dom may be evident in the narratives and expository statements of ordinary older adults. The use of elaborative discourse structures, com-bined with simplifications of syntactic structure, may be manifestations of the growth of wisdom as it pertains to effective communication, reflective judgment, and accumulated experiences.

ACKNOWLEDGMENTS

This research was supported by grants RO1AG06319 and KO4AG0043 from the National Institute on Aging. Portions of this work were pre-sented at the 1992 biannual Cognitive Aging Conference in Atlanta, GA. We would like to thank Hintat Cheung, James Jackson, Suzanne Norman, Kevin O'Brien, Shannon Rash, Richard Sprott, and, especially, Donna Kynette, for their assistance with this research.

REFERENCES

Anderson, E. S. (1984). The acquisition of sociolinguistic knowledge: Some evidence from children's verbal role play. *Western Journal of Speech Communication, 48,* 125–144.

Arnheim, R. (1990). On the late style. In M. Perlmutter (Ed.), *Late life potential* (pp. 113–120). Washington, DC: Gerontological Society of America.

Baltes, P. B., & Smith, J. (1990). Toward a psychology of wisdom and its ontogenesis. In R. J. Sternberg (Ed.), *Wisdom* (pp. 87–120). New York: Cambridge University Press.

Bernstein, B. (1971). *Class, codes, and control.* London: Routledge.

Bernstein, B. (1973). *Class, codes, and control II.* London: Routledge.

Botvin, G. J., & Sutton-Smith, B. (1977). The development of structural complexity in children's fantasy narratives. *Developmental Psychology, 13,* 377–388.

Cheung, H., & Kemper, S. (1992). Competing complexity metrics and adults' production of complex sentences. *Applied Psycholinguistics, 13,* 53–76.

Clark, E. V. (1978). Awareness of language: Some evidence from what children say and do. In A. Sinclair, R. J. Jarvella, & W. J. M. Levelt (Eds.), *The child's conception of language* (pp. 17–43). Berlin: Springer-Verlag.

Daneman, M., & Carpenter, P. A. (1980). Individual differences in working memory and reading. *Journal of Verbal Learning and Verbal Ability, 19,* 450–466.

Garvey, C. (1977). Play with language and speech. In S. Ervin-Tripp & C. Mitchell-Kernan (Eds.), *Child discourse* (pp. 27–48). New York: Academic.

Hakes, D. T. (1980). *The development of metalinguistic abilities in children.* Berlin: Springer-Verlag.

Halliday, M. A. K., & Hasan, R. (1976). *Cohesion in English.* London: Longman.

Holliday, S. G., & Chandler, M. (1986). *Wisdom: Explorations in adult competence.* Basel, Switzerland: Karger.

Hymes, D. (1972). On communicative competence. In J. Pride & J. Holmes (Eds.), *Sociolinguistics.* Hammondsworth, UK: Penguin.

Kemper, S. (1987). Life-span changes in syntactic complexity. *Journal of Gerontology, 42,* 323–328.

Kemper, S. (1990). Adults' diaries: Changes to written language across the life-span. *Discourse Processes, 13,* 207–224.

Kemper, S. (1992a). Language and aging. In F. I. M. Craik & T. A. Salthouse (Eds.), *Handbook of aging and cognition* (pp. 213–270). Hillsdale, NJ: Erlbaum.

Kemper, S. (1992b). Adults' sentence fragments: Who, what, when, where, and why. *Communication Research, 19,* 444–458.

Kemper, S., Kynette, D., Rash, S., Sprott, R., & O'Brien, K. (1989). Life-span changes to adults' language: Effects of memory and genre. *Applied Psycholinguistics, 10,* 49–66.

Kemper, S., Rash, S. R., Kynette, D., & Norman, S. (1990). Telling stories: The structure of adults' narratives. *European Journal of Cognitive Psychology, 2,* 205–228.

Kemper, S., Kynette, D., & Norman, S. (1992). Age differences in spoken language. In R. West & J. Sinnott (Eds.), *Everyday memory and aging* (pp. 138–152). New York: Springer-Verlag.

Kintsch, W., & Keenan, J. M. (1973). Reading rate and retention as a function of the number of the propositions in the base structure of sentences. *Cognitive Psychology, 5,* 257–274.

Labov, W. (1970). *The study of nonstandard English.* Urbana, IL: National Council of Teachers of English.

Lakoff, W. (1977). What can you do with words: Politeness, pragmatics, and performatives. In A. Rogers, B. Wall, & J. Murphy (Eds.), *Proceedings of the Texas conference on performatives, presuppositions, and implicatures.* Arlington, VA: Center for Applied Linguistics.

Mandler, J. M., & Johnson, N. S. (1977). Remembrance of things parsed: Story structure and recall. *Cognitive Psychology, 9,* 111–151.

Meyer, B. J. F. (1975). *The organization of prose and its effects on memory.* Amsterdam: North-Holland.

Meyer, B. J. F., Young, C. J., & Bartlett, B. J. (1989). *Memory improved: Reading and memory enhancement across the life span through strategic text structures.* Hillsdale, NJ: Erlbaum.

Miller, J. F., & Chapman, R. S. (1981). The relation between age and mean length of utterance in morphemes. *Journal of Speech and Hearing Research, 24,* 154–161.

Norman, S., Kemper, S., & Kynette, D. (1992). Adults' reading comprehension: Effects of syntactic complexity and working memory. *Journals of Gerontology: Psychological Sciences, 47,* P258–P265.

Orwoll, L., & Perlmutter, M. (1990). The study of wise persons: Integrating a personality perspective. In R. J. Sternberg (Ed.), *Wisdom* (pp. 160–177). New York: Cambridge University Press.

Porter, C. A., & Suedfeld, P. (1981). Integrative complexity in the correspondence of literary figures: Effects of personal and societal stress. *Journal of Personality and Social Psychology, 40,* 321–330.

Pratt, M. W., Boyes, C., Robins, S., & Manchester, J. (1989). Telling tales: Aging, working memory, and the narrative cohesion of storytellers. *Developmental Psychology, 25,* 628–635.

Pratt, M. W., & Robins, S. L. (1991). That's the way it was: Age differences in the structure and quality of adults' personal narratives. *Discourse Processes, 14,* 73–85.

Propp, W. (1968). *Morphology of the folktale.* Austin: University of Texas Press.

Pye, C., Cheung, H., & Kemper, S. (1992). Islands at eighty. In H. Goodluck (Ed.), *Psycholinguistic studies of island constraints.* New York: Reidel.

Shultz, T. R. (1976). A cognitive-development analysis of humor. In A. J. Chapman & H. C. Foote (Eds.), *Humour and laughter: Theory, research, and applications* (pp. 11–36). London: Wiley.

Shultz, T. R., & Horibe, F. (1974). Development of the appreciation of verbal jokes. *Developmental Psychology, 10,* 13–20.

Simonton, D. K. (1975). Age and literary creativity: A cross-cultural and transhistorical survey. *Journal of Cross-Cultural Psychology, 6,* 259–277.

Simonton, D. K. (1989). The swan-song phenomenon: Last-works effects for 172 classical composers. *Psychology and Aging, 4,* 42–47.

Sternberg, R. J. (1990). Wisdom and its relations to intelligence and creativity. In R. J. Sternberg (Ed.), *Wisdom* (pp. 142–159). New York: Cambridge University Press.

Sutton-Smith, B. (1976). A developmental structural account of riddles. In B. Kirschenblatt-Gimblett (Ed.), *Speech play.* Philadelphia: University of Pennsylvania Press.

Templin, M. (1957). *Certain language skills in children.* Minneapolis: University of Minnesota Press.

Warren-Leubecker, A., & Bohannon, J. N. (1989). Pragmatics: Language in social contexts. In J. Berko Gleason (Ed.), *The development of language* (2nd ed.). Columbus, OH: Merrill.

Creative Challenges and the Construction of Meaningful Life Narratives

Mark R. Luborsky

Q uestions about the quality of life experiences and their influence on the course and outcomes of old age have emerged in gerontology to complement the long-standing focus on health, biology, and policy. One component of the quality of life is an individual's sense of themes and meanings in their life. Emerging understandings about the nature and construction of personal meanings of life experiences extend our insights into effective functioning in later life. This chapter presents some new perspectives and findings about the construction and outcomes of personal meaning and examines the role of creativity in the processes of making meanings for one's lifetime.

Changes and losses to a person's social world and to physical functioning occur across the life span. These changes may become pervasive and more keenly felt in later life. A familiar gerontological refrain is that in old age increased demands for adaptation to changes occur at the same time as declines in exogenous resources (losses of family, friends, social networks, social roles and activities) and endogenous resources (physical functioning, health, cognitive function). Together the contexts and nature of these changes limit the capacity of elderly persons to alter the conditions they confront. Undiminished in old age is the need to exercise the human ability to make meanings for the self and the world. The popular and scholarly literature concur that the burden of recreating meanings becomes more acute in late life. There are many reasons. These include late life developmental tasks, such as generativity, related to existential issues and personal finitude (Alexander, Rubinstein, Goodman, & Luborsky, 1991; Kotre, 1984). In addition, attention to life meanings becomes more salient due to life course transitions in careers, family, intergenerational relationships, social identity, the sense of being a full adult person (Luborsky, 1994a), and bereavement (Luborsky & Rubinstein, 1989).

Gerontologists distinguish between primary coping (efforts aimed at changing the stimulus) and secondary coping (efforts focused on changing the perception and impact) and chart the progression from primary to secondary coping styles in later life (Pearlin, 1981). Yet the distinction is problematic because the active use of secondary coping strategies may itself be a form of primary coping. The continuous construction of personal life themes provides an example. I argue that personal life themes serve as both primary and secondary coping mechanisms. First, they provide core internal motivations. Thus, by redefining a life theme the primary internal stimuli are changed. Second, life themes also serve as resources for adaptation to external conditions; they provide a conceptual lens through which individuals reinterpret and alter the meaning and impact of events (Luborsky, 1995a).

We currently lack a full appreciation of the significant role of creativity in the autobiographic construction of a meaningful past, present, and future life. A subjective sense of vital meaning does not germinate automatically from the lifelong accrued body of facts, wisdoms, or static encyclopedic knowledge about the world (Labouvie-Vief, 1990; Sperber, 1974). Dynamic, fluid meaning making remains crucial for dealing with adversity in later life, as is shown by the emerging literature on the self-constructing and personal life narrative (Cohler, 1991; Luborsky, 1993a, 1993b, 1995a; cf. Labouvie-Vief, 1990). Current studies of the self-narrative tend to neglect important variations in styles and outcomes of the processes of meaning making. In particular, we lack a clear understanding of the nature of creativity in these processes.

My goal for this chapter is to explore creativity and its outcomes specifically in the domain of narrative meaning. The questions asked are, What kinds of creativity are involved in the creation of meanings in oral life stories, and How may these relate the speaker's intent or motives for the narrative? The term *creative challenge* is used to focus on the narrator's task of arranging the telling of past events in a style that expresses the current experience of meanings. For example, one challenge is to communicate salient personal meanings within the social expectations for the life narrative (e.g., story structure, coherence, intelligibility). Findings from the study to be discussed below demonstrate that while hallmarks of creativity are clearly observable in all stories, we need to develop concepts and methods especially attuned to the domain of narrative in order to identify variations in the types of creativity and those types that are related to well-being.

The chapter beings with a summary of emerging issues in research on creativity and the continuity of meaning at the level of the individual life biography. Second, I describe findings from a study of life narratives by elderly women and men, giving particular attention to the nature of creativity in narratives. Finally, key issues and dilemmas for future study are discussed.

EMERGING ISSUES ABOUT CREATIVITY

The expanding literature on creativity as reviewed by Adams-Price (this volume), Simonton (1989, 1990), Sternberg (1988), and Tardif and Sternberg (1988) testifies to the widening scope of concepts, issues, and problems for research. Two emerging issues concerning the contexts of creativity are of particular relevance: intentionality and domain specific characteristics of creativity.

Intentionality refers to the motive or purpose propelling the creative process (Barclay & Pettito, 1989; Csikszentmihalyi, 1988). That is, we need to ask what is the context of the intention and problem being addressed by the creator. This new question mirrors wider developments in the social and behavioral sciences. Factors related to individual agency, intentionality, and the motivating force of cultural models (D'Andrade, 1992; Luborsky, 1994a; Shweder, 1991; Stigler, Shweder, & Herdt, 1990) are now recognized as important aspects of narrative and creativity. These factors, in combination with cultural and practical knowledge or affect, may provide us with the richest explanations of societal and individual behavior.

Domain specificity refers to the need for concepts and measures of creativity that are tailored to specific arenas of activity. Simonton (1990) argues that creativity is not a singular uniform or global construct but differs greatly according to the challenges and medium of each specific domain of activity. For example, the creativity needed to solve logistics and supply problems for a military campaign is not identical with the creativity needed by a widow laboring to rebuild her life after the death of her husband. More sensitivity to different context-specific markers and styles of creativity will redress earlier overgeneralized approaches that spanned the vastly diverse realms of art, science and technology, and daily life. Studies of creativity have evolved from defining the characteristics of rare outstandingly creative persons to examinations of the results of common everyday creative endeavors. My interest in this chapter is to consider creativity as a component of daily functioning, with a particular emphasis on late life. Such studies help broaden creativity research by including societal processes (Simonton, 1990) to complement the traditional focus on exceptionally creative individuals. Adams-Price (this volume) exemplifies the product-oriented approach in which the nature of problem solving in response to specific challenges becomes an important facet of creativity. Similarly, Croply (1990), building on Nicholls (1972), examines the linkages between creativity in meeting everyday demands and positive mental health (see also Marslske and Willis, this volume). His work shifts the research focus from discovery of linkages between mental illness and exceptionally creative individuals to the characteristics of creativity that relate to growth and adaptation to routine daily life.

NARRATIVE CONSTRUCTION OF MEANING

Man is always a storyteller! He lives surrounded by his and others' myths. With them he sees everything in his life, no matter what befalls him.

Sartre, 1963

The personal narrative is a basic idiom and perhaps the primary way through which we construct knowledge (Bruner, 1990; Gee, 1985). Through narratives, individuals evaluate and interpret the personal salience and impact of events. The life narrative in particular plays a significant role in helping to foster personal resilience to adversity (Cohler, 1991). Narratives are a distinct mode of knowledge for meaning making. They tap longitudinally the personal experiences and processes of meaning making. Further, narratives and narrative insights are not readily reducible or translatable into other forms of knowledge. That is, their contents tend to elude assessment techniques employed by standardized measurement approaches in survey research or the structured health or mental health diagnostic categories.

The form of the self-narrative is not dictated by normative public statuses, the roles one holds, or even objective historical events; rather, it emerges from the interpretive interplay between the individual and society. The self-biography or narrative model focuses on the sense of one's own biography, which extends across the life to encompass family, community, and historical conditions and changes (Bury, 1982; Cohler, 1982, 1991; Gergen, 1984; Lieberman & Falk, 1971; Williams, 1984). Central to self-interpretation and well-being is the appraisal of life events as "on-time" or "off-time," judged by reference to the expectable life course (Seltzer & Troll, 1985). By *on-time,* we mean that the typical pattern of life stages occurs, and is seen at what people consider appropriate ages. The notion of a personal "life span construct" (Whitbourne, 1986) is similarly defined as the sense of one's own life course beyond age-sequenced social norms, roles and values. Whitbourne captures how these concepts concern core questions of meaning by framing the questions they pose: Who am I? What is happening to me? What does this mean about who I am? How do I feel about who I am?

Studies of everyday creativity direct us to examine creative production and innovation as a routine part of maintaining existing patterns of activity or processes in social life, not just in the innovation of a new form or process. For example, in the case of sustaining a sense of a continuity of personal meaning when faced with adversity from a crippling disease, the goal of creative efforts is not immediately knowable. It may be either to rededicate oneself to fulfilling lifelong values or to reorganize them into a new adaptive configuration.

CREATIVE CHALLENGES AND NARRATIVE MOTIVES

Three hallmarks of creativity are particularly relevant to the domain of narrative construction of personal meaning. These include: awareness of incompleteness, manipulation of implicit cultural categories that shape our thinking and actions (Sternberg, 1988; Simonton, 1990), and complexity of thought. In terms of creativity in life stories, we need to identify narrative devices that provide a sense of complete, continuing, and rich life meanings.

How do we recognize implicit cultural categories in daily life? Cultural categories are not always manifest. They are generally taken for granted rather than examined in daily life. Shopping for food—fish or eggs for example—illustrates this point. Federal agriculture rules do not require that each egg in a one-dozen carton of large eggs meet the grade and size on the label, only eight must do so. Yet when shopping we tend to study the contents for broken eggs but not for completeness of size. Similarly, more than a dozen species of fish are legally labeled as flounder for sale. During a routine day we seldom scrutinize the contents of such conventional categories in detail unless a problem arises.

Just as cultural categories are not readily apparent or examined in daily life, they are also not easily recognized as problematic by researchers (Luborsky & Sankar, 1993). The model of the normative social life course with stages and transitions is one such category. Awareness of the profoundly problematic nature of a normal life course and of differences in individuals' experiences and forms of expressing life stories is fairly limited (Luborsky, 1990, 1993a, 1993b). Later in this chapter, I describe how narrators whose lives were disrupted by calamity or disease find the cultural model of the normative life course ill-suited to express their story or a sense of the meanings in their lives.

Continuity of Personal Meaning

The concept of *continuity of personal meaning* (CPM), an intriguing construct entering gerontological discourse, directs us to question how individuals construct and interpret experiences of daily situations and lifelong conditions (Becker, 1993; Luborsky, 1993b). It focuses on the inner sense of an enduring individualistic identity, one that is separate from but related to the cultural category of personhood (Luborsky, 1994a). Continuity of personal meaning is defined as a generalization that a central personal value or belief in the past has continued thematically over the lifetime and fits within one's present-day self-image and hopes. These ideals, beliefs, and sentiments serve to organize experience, interactions, and hopes. The experience of continuity is a higher order perception about one's lifetime and identity that is separate from external events and social structures. The personal sense of continuity in life meaning is not predicted by the social meanings attached to normative social roles or activity patterns, and yet is crucial to effective functioning (Antonovsky, 1979; Cohler, 1982; Gutmann, 1988; Kaufman, 1987; Myerhoff, 1978; Whitbourne, 1986). Continuity theory posits that successful aging depends on the perception of continuing personal meaning (Antonovsky, 1979; Atchley, 1989; Lieberman & Tobin, 1983; cf. Huyck, 1989).

The sense of CPM may be a buffer or a resource that moderates the corrosive effects on health and well-being of physical and social losses in old age. As a resource it helps the elderly to preserve a sense of mastery and vitality, thereby buffering the impact of negative changes (Gutmann, 1988; Obeyesekere, 1982). Mortality effects are suggested for the frail elderly who sense disjunction in personal meanings as opposed to continuity (Lieberman & Tobin, 1983). Many questions remain about the nature of the CPM, how it is constructed, and its effects on health.

Three major streams of gerontological work on continuity are evident (Luborsky, 1993b; cf. Atchley, 1989; Becker, 1993). These can be described as structural, constructionist, and content perspectives. Each approach offers an incremental improvement over the previous one. The *structural view* posits that CPM is a fixed structure that endures over time. The rigid structure serves to mitigate the social and bodily changes experienced in late life. In this view a loss of continuity makes one vulnerable to decompensation and illness. Such a simplistic and static view ignores the contents and processes of creating the sense of continuity. Structural approaches have weak predictive power and do not account for variation in how people interpret objective events. Early gerontological research used this view to develop checklists of life events to predict well-being (Havighurst, 1963; Holmes & Rahe, 1967; Rosow, 1963). Creativity, to the structuralists, would be exercised to maintain the perception of permanence.

The *constructionist view* posits that basic personal life themes form during adult development (Whitbourne, 1986). From this vantage, CPM is achieved and constructed rather than fixed. The constructionist view is rooted in personal construct psychology (Landfield & Epting, 1987), symbolic interaction (Mead, 1934), and self-psychology (Kohut, 1977). The self-narrative (Gergen, 1984) posits an unfolding lifelong relationship between one's goals, plans, social obligations, and available resources and limitations. Bury (1982) and Williams (1984) argue that disrupted self-narrative processes caused by chronic disease lead to perceived illness states. Creativity is called for in the continual reinterpretation of experiences and cultural symbols, a process that provides the raw materials for identity continuity for community elderly (Kaufman, 1987) and nursing home elderly (Lieberman & Tobin, 1983). A limitation of the constructionist view is its failure to question the contents of meanings.

Content approaches include both a broad, simpler view and a narrow, more complex focus. The broad view posits that all human beings construct environments of meaning (Berger & Luckman, 1976; Frankl, 1978). The elderly need to be especially adept at managing meaning environments due to the diversity of losses they experience and diminished ability to change the conditions of their lives. Here, the research question is simply to determine if meanings are present or absent. For example, perceived losses of life meanings are one explanation of the long-term effects of bereavement. Grief arises due to separation from a loved one, but also from the loss of familiar meanings, habituated ways of life. Researchers report that acute mourning recedes after 2 years, but grief about the loss of cherished daily routines and sentiments persists for many years (Luborsky & Rubenstein, 1989; Zisook, DeVaul, & Click, 1982). Future work on narrative creativity needs to examine people's own sense of desired meanings and continuity.

The frail elderly actively manage continuity of personal meanings and cultural continuity as a means to preserve functioning. Feelings of belonging to a shared community of values help older people believe in the continuing significance (not obsolescence) of their values and ways of life (Myerhoff, 1984). Myerhoff (1978) concluded that the perception of continuity of personal meaning and habits is as important as finances and health for well-being in old age.

Narrow view approaches ask more critically which specific meanings and explanatory styles produce well-being; in contrast, the broad content views regard all meanings as adaptive. Uncritical approaches to CPM ignore different styles of interpreting experiences which produce healthy or unhealthy outcomes as demonstrated in psychological anthropology (Kleinman & Good, 1985; Cohler, 1982; Stigler et al., 1990) and in psychotherapy outcome research. Cognitive treatments for depression have demonstrated the pervasive influence of individual styles of explaining the meaning of events. Depression-prone people are disposed to make internal, stable, global attributions of causes for bad events. Such "depressenogenic" explanatory styles (Beck, Rush, Shaw, & Emery, 1979) are enduring, but they change with mood state, and can be changed and remain changed after successful psychotherapy (Seligman & Castellon, 1984). Of all three perspectives on CPM, this narrow view of specific meanings may call for the greatest expertise in meaning making by the individual. Here the individual has free reign in making subjectively salient meanings without the aid of fixed static structures or normative frameworks suggested by the other two perspectives on CPM.

To summarize, studies of the continuity of personal meaning describe the person's phenomenological experience of the world of normative categories and personally constructed personal meanings. Life narratives and life themes emerge from a subjective experience of CPM. Creativity is an integral feature because continuity and coherence in personal meaning are transcendent features; they are achieved at a metalevel by active reorganization and creation of meanings and identities. We need to discover how the widely shared collective categories and norms for the social life course mesh with or diverge from each individual's life experiences and meanings. In addition, each scientific theory about the continuity of personal meaning poses different research questions on creativity.

CULTURAL ASPECTS OF CREATIVITY, CONTINUITY AND INNOVATION

We need to ask to what extent our cultural predilection towards associating creativity with uniqueness and newness biases our work. It may be harder for us to recognize forms of problem solving and coping that make use of intensification and revitalization rather than innovation. An emphasis on innovation over continuity can apply to both individual and societal levels of analysis. The selective creation and reconstruction of core meanings are clear at the macrolevel of social systems.

One signature of explanatory power and generalizability is the discovery of a principle that is manifest at several levels of social life, from the macrolevel of social organization or social structure to the individual level. Just as at the microlevel there are personal meanings that serve to organize and give value to an individual's life, at the macrolevel there are core social meanings or *social charters* that serve to organize a whole society. The principles of a social charter are embodied in, for example, national constitutions, federal bills of rights, and religious tenets in literate societies (e.g., the Ten Commandments, the Bible, the Koran). The social charter specifies the ideals, goals, and rules for conduct between people, as well as obligations, rights, and duties to the community. The structure for life narratives is analogous to the frameworks guiding the charters of whole societies. These frameworks are made explicit by large-scale transformative or redemptive social movements. Familiar examples of such processes include fundamentalist religious movements, and millenarian (e.g., Native American Ghost Dance or Peyote Church; see Burridge, 1969) and charismatic movements. Alternatively, redemptive or fundamentalist movements may seek to rededicate members to revitalizing core traditional values (Wallace, 1970; Aberle, 1962). The mission of these movements is to reorganize the collective social narrative of a society, including the narrative myth of its origins, the proper behavior among its members, and its destiny in the world. These movements, focused on systemwide culture change, can shed light on the continual construction of conventional social life.

One important and little-studied question is, What challenges for creativity are posed by the ways people work to construct a personally meaningful life narrative within the context of the parameters defined by a normative life course pattern? The distinction between redemptive and transformative social movements has powerful heuristic properties to help explore how the normative life course serves as an implicit category that structures the life story meaning-making process. The form and content of one's life story emerges from factors beyond those dictated by the objective events and specific circumstances of the lifetime. Depending on the person's stance towards those events and intent in living and telling about the lifetime, we can observe that the socially given normative life course is either revitalized to reaffirm the person's sense of living a traditional life, or reorganized and transformed to express a sense of not having followed the normative sequences and statuses in life that are taken for granted by others.

CREATIVITY IN CONSTRUCTIONS OF LIFE NARRATIVES AMONG THE ELDERLY

Several types of creativity are discernible in oral life stories. The life story is a problem-solving task: The narrator faces the challenge of self-construction and self-expression using the oral genre of the life story. The individual's task is to find a way to effectively express his or her own sense of the life lived thus far by selecting and organizing myriad life experiences, personal beliefs, and opinions. In this section, I consider the question of how different types of creativity relate to individuals' sense of the continuity of personal meaning and to well-being.

METHODS

Oral life stories were collected from elderly women and men as part of a study of the construction and mental health outcomes of personal life themes among residents of a geriatric center. The study site includes twin apartment towers for the functionally independent elderly, a nursing home, Alzheimer's disease units, a full spectrum of in-house medical, psychological, and social services, and outpatient clinics.

Thirty-two subjects were identified by random selection from a computerized database of the entire population of approximately 1,100 residents. For this study, people with cognitive impairments were excluded. Sixteen subjects with a range of depressive symptoms including clinically defined Major Depression, and 16 nondepressed subjects (including 6 with a prior history of depression) were selected. The average age of participants was 84 (range, 71–92) and they had lived at the geriatric center for an average of 10 years.

Well-Being

Assessments of mental health were conducted independently by physicians, psychologists, and psychiatrists using established multidisciplinary clinical evaluation techniques. The purposeful comparison between depressed and nondepressed elderly was designed to maximize the contrast between moods related to self-constructed meanings for current and lifelong experiences and conditions. That is, it was hypothesized that the life meanings and sense of challenge in creating a narrative would differ between residents who are and those who are not experiencing profound sadness and depression.[1]

Life Stories

Oral tellings were elicited using a standardized method, the Sequence and Templates in Narratives (Luborsky, 1990), which consists of two sets of questions designed to elicit uninterrupted life stories. An initial story is typically 4–20 minutes long, and 15–35 minutes is usual for the whole section. The goal is to provide brief stories from the narrator's own perspective for systematic comparison rather than a standardized inventory of life events. It meets the formal criteria for sampling for meaning in cultural and qualitative research (Luborsky & Rubinstein, 1995).

First, a single query serves to elicit the story, "Now that we've met and talked for a few minutes I'd like to know more about you and your life. Would you describe your life for me; whatever comes to mind about it? Start where you like, take as much time as you need." By design, the prompt has few cultural propositions (D'Andrade, 1976; Metzger, 1974) or cues about a script to use for the reply. Phrases such as "important events in your life" are avoided since they evoke depersonalized simplistic accounts indexed to social norms (work, marriage, family) and seem to irk people: "Nothing special about me, I wasn't President or anything." Interviewers listen without interrupting until the informants state they have finished the story.

Second, informants are asked to depict their whole life using a pair of contrasting images or structures: a sequence of book chapters, and a mural with many scenes and themes. The goal is to probe a person's affinity for a particular image. The chapters frame provides a linear chronology of socially normative and bounded categories. The mural image provides for the simultaneous presentation of diverse experiences and events without attention to sequence, boundaries, and

---

[1] A consensus diagnosis was assigned by clinical staff by combining their independent findings during case conferences. The differentiations are: depression, to represent a range of depressive symptoms using the Geriatric Depression Scale (Yesavage et al., 1983) where scores of $S \geq 10$ and < 22) defined dysphoria, and including clinically defined major depression judged by DSM III-R checklist criteria for mood disorders, and non-depressed (GDS < 10). Residents with cognitive impairments are excluded (Blessed test scores > 7; Blessed et al., 1968).

coherence. The chapters and murals reveal chunks of salient life experience and meanings.

Creativity Assessment

Creativity was defined in terms of three aspects identified in the literature on creativity that are salient to the domain of narratives. First, the manipulation of implicit categories was operationalized in terms of the basic building blocks of the life story narrative. Specifically, we looked for how narrators use the underlying normative cultural life course script or categories of stages and transitions. Second, recognition of incompleteness was examined in terms of the closing sections of the story. We looked for direct statements that marked the narrators' attention to the completeness of the story. Third, complexity was defined in terms of the number of events or topics and perspectives presented.

Coding of verbatim transcripts of the audiotaped life stories was conducted using objective standardized coding procedures performed independently by two researchers. In addition to the narrative structure, complexity, and closings, content analyses were conducted to identify direct statements of life themes (Luborsky, 1994b) and of personal identity.

Readers should note that the format of the examples presented in this chapter follows a scientific convention designed to minimize several potential biases. A major challenge in presenting narrative materials in written form is to preserve and convey the natural intonation and rhythm with which the story is told. These features convey meaning. Failure to include these may "erase" important data from the research record even before they are analyzed. Conventions for laying out text on the printed page are deeply rooted in commonsense assumptions. These can contribute to a loss of data in narrative and discourse analyses. The transcripts in Figure 13.1 (p. 325) use punctuation to mark natural breaks or intonation units, referred to as "chunks" (Chafe, 1980) or meaning units. The comma or period is used to mark pauses and rising or falling tone rather than following conventions for proper grammar. Each chunk is started on a new line. The advantage is that natural units of meaning and talk by the narrator are presented, rather than artificially defined sentences.

FINDINGS

Several links are apparent between narratives and the sense of meanings and well-being in life. Differences in the sequential order of topics and the topics selected for narration illustrate several kinds of narrative creativity.

Manipulation of Basic Cultural Categories

One creative aspect of the life story is the structure of the story. The structure of the narrative is not preordained by the pool of life events and experiences. Creativity is also involved in the selection of particular events and topics to express the sense of the lifetime. The skeletal framework for the life story is observable in the way the speaker manipulates the normative categories of the stages in a cultural life course to tell the events of a lifetime. The cultural life course provides a shared social charter that gives meaning to the lifetime. People who judge that their life course follows the typical path gain a sense of belonging and of being on-time in relation to social norms for the life course. Returning to the broad scale social movements described earlier, the life narrative is analogous at the microlevel to the broad social charters at the macrolevel. That is, the narrative may be structured to present events, topics, and experiences in the individual's life that reaffirm and revitalize traditional collective societal values and ways of life. Alternatively, the events and experiences may be arranged to create a narrative that expresses a sense of loss, the failure or obsolescence of traditional values, or one that depicts new individualized meanings and values. The story structure itself is an object of subjective identification. Speakers may revitalize or instantiate the underlying traditional shared life course patterns when telling of their own life. On the other hand, when life takes a less well-trodden path, narrators may "transform" the traditional life cycle by rearranging both the order and the kinds of life stages and categories they present; they may also directly question the salience of these categories in their own life.

Results of coding the texts for the basic pattern to a lifetime were obtained by identifying each normative life stage, status, transition, and themes that express core cultural values. The coding categories established for use here were the basic script of American life. These include the approximate stages of: childhood, school, dating and marriage, work, and current life. Analyses indicated that each of the life stories included elements from the life course stages and transitions.

The life stories differed greatly in the organization of the narrative and the selective inclusion and exclusion of topics. Labov (1972) defined the essential quality of narrative speech as the presentation of a time-dependent sequence of clauses, where the order of the telling matches the order in which the events occur. That is, to alter the order in which events are told would change the event or its meaning. For example, "The dog behind me awoke and barked, I dropped the brick and shattered my foot," presents one sequence of cause and effect while "I dropped the brick and shattered my foot, the dog behind me awoke and barked" suggests a totally different situation. Thus, a fundamentally different meaning and meaning-making process is rooted in the sequence and the selection of elements in the story.

Five complete life story texts are presented in Figure 13.1. If we look at the stories by Celia, Steve, and Ben, we observe that the topics are presented in the order provided by the normative life course. They progress along the major life course stages and follow a chronologically linear form from early to late life. This manner of presentation serves to reinforce the speakers' overt assertion that their lives were usual and typical: "There was nothing unusual about my life," said Celia. In contrast, Maude and Rita present the events of their life in an entirely different order. They describe similar categories of youth, school, marriage, but do so in an order tailored to the personal sense or stance of a life filled with distress ("I had a bad life," said Maude) or of dire challenges ("I had nobody to depend upon," Rita told us). Maude and Rita were both diagnosed as clinically depressed; Celia, Steve, and Ben were not.

The contrast between narratives organized by the underlying shared normative life course and those organized according to the expression of a personal theme match findings from studies that examined life narratives from subjects in different ethnic groups and also elicited in other life stages and transitions, including bereavement. Lengthier discussions of these concepts and data are found in Luborsky, (1990, 1993a) and Luborsky and Rubinstein (1989).

At issue for studies of creativity is the display from a common set of social life categories (i.e., childhood, education, adulthood, marriage, retirement) and lifetime experiences (birth, growing up, school, friends, and family) of particular items according to whether the narrators' were or were not depressed. The narratives of depressed individuals, structured by a personal theme, have as their focus the dilemmas and conflicts related to core cultural values (independence, duty) in the grand design or social charter. In contrast, nondepressed narrators telling their life within the structure of the shared life course are challenged to inject a note of individuality. These narrators personalize the stages and transitions by interspersing remarks about personal tastes (art), interests (sports), and social standing (know lots of important people). The nondepressed speakers marshaled events, embodying implicit cultural categories as life course stages, to make a larger point about having led a satisfying and normal life.

Maude:

My life. What can I tell you. I didn't have a good day. I haven't had a good day.
Thank God I got my children to make me a little happy.
Outside of that I had a bad marriage. I had a bad life.

Rita:

I was. When I came here I was 14 years old. I had a sister to whom I came.
I went to work at 14. Took some schooling on my own. This is how I went on and worked.
I paid for my rent, I paid for my food. I was independent and I was 14 years old.
I had nobody to depend upon. My sister that I came to, she didn't know me, I didn't know her.
We were from one father, not one mother. And when she went to the US I was an infant.
But she knew just by corresponding there was a little sister here.
So the little sister was 14 years old when she came here.
And that, that's the whole story in a nutshell!

Celia:

There was nothing unusual about my life.
I grew up here, met my husband at a very, very young age.
But we didn't know that we were going to marry someday.
His sister, the one that sent me that note, was my Sunday school teacher.
And he was also in my class, I knew his brother very well. His brother was dating my girlfriend.
And, through him, I started going out with my future husband.
And we married at a very young age. And we had a wonderful, wonderful life together.
We had two sons. They married at young age too,
and I would say that they are now undergoing the same type of life that my husband and I had.
I have five grandchildren, I have eight great grandchildren.

Steve:

I was born and raised in Philadelphia. And I went to high school and college.
And er, some years back then I was in my twenties, I moved to Florida.
I lived in Florida 4-1/2 years. And I came back here.
And I was interested in art and had a gallery where I sold pictures, paintings, framing.
Framing was a prof, was the biggest item I had.
And I was on Chestnut Street, you know where that is?
17th and Chestnut. Which was the center of town. And I used to come to work by, I had my
automobile but I used to have a bus which brought me center of town.
And er, I met, scores of people that I have, friends, that I've known for years.
In, in the business that I was in I met judges, congressmen, priests, lawyers, doctors,
and then anyway, I became familiar with a lot of people.
Now sportswise, I was sports-minded. Played soccer as a, baseball as a boy.
What else could I tell you?

Ben:

Like I told you, I was born, I went to school, I got married,
I went into the Army, and I'm here.

FIGURE 13.1   Life stories of depressed and non-depressed elderly.

Permission was granted by the Gerontological Society of America to excerpt
several life stories from *The Gerontologist, 33*, 445–452.

An important conclusion concerns the fit between the speakers' current stances about their lives or the stories messages and the structure of the stories. In this study, no life stories were observed in which all the traditional life stages were stated in normative order and the narrator made the statements that life was unsatisfactory or depressing. The stories which were narrated with overt central themes and which did not adhere to the linear sequence of life course stages were told by elderly who were distressed and still actively engaged in making a sense of meaning for their lives.

To summarize, creativity in constructing a sense of continuity of personal meaning is vested either in the collective normative life course or the idiom of a personal life theme. It is important to note that the former expresses individuation, in that the narrator locates himself or herself as a member of the larger social system. In the latter case, where the life theme serves to express individuation, the narrator expresses a sense of separateness from others. The challenges in narrating a life are multiple. First, there is the basic problem of how to express the events and sentiments of the lifetime in an idiom that accurately reflects the individual's sense of personal continuity. Second, the challenge implicit to each narrative form is that each carries with it domain-specific demands to present a balanced account. For the life course formula, the challenge is to personalize the life script, whereas for the personal theme formula the challenge is to forge links with the collective social community. This brings us to consider the creativity evident in the narrative challenge as an attempt to come to terms with perceived "incompleteness."

RECOGNITION OF COMPLETENESS
AND INCOMPLETENESS

This factor is another hallmark of creativity. Narrators monitor the completeness of their accounts, as apparent in comments about the act of storytelling itself. A structural analysis identified story closings—the final topics presented by speakers. The story closing imparts information about the speaker's sense of completeness within the story structure. The closing also indexes the appropriateness of the narrative structure to the sense of how complete or successful the narrator was within the customary life path.

For example, speakers may apologize ("I can't tell you about childhood stuff . . .") or truncate their accounts ("I'll just limit it to my life here at the retirement home"). These explicit remarks convey the speaker's recognition of, and attempt to defuse, the sense of the incompleteness of their tale in terms of telling a whole lifetime. The focus of the stories differs between the two groups. The nondepressed speakers covered the entire life from early life to today, but gave less emphasis to more recent events. In contrast, the depressed narrators uniformly start the life story either in adulthood and midlife, or in current time. Interestingly, these later events contain episodes of later life losses and illness. The non-depressed narrate with less emphasis on these events, whereas the depressed narrators seem to delve into troubled times and do not link present day life with earlier life.

The closing sentences provide highly compelling information about the subjective recognition of incompleteness in life and in the life story. Several stories ended with overt narrative repairs. A *narrative repair* is an explicit statement recognizing that the story was not complete. Discourse studies have demonstrated that narrators and listeners alike are carefully attuned to judging whether a story is good and followable with a clear beginning, middle, and end (e.g., Cohler, 1991). Among these life stories the narrative repairs occurred in the stories structured by a personal theme rather than the normative life course. An example is the story by Rita. She reaches the end of her story and concludes by stating, "That's it in a nutshell." We can see that the story has not covered all the points covered by the complete stories. Thus, she had to signal very bluntly that she was done talking. The story is incomplete; it does not have all the features needed for a listener to spontaneously recognize the natural end to a complete story. Interestingly, the use of such metaphors occurs typically among the depressed narrators, several of whom used the "nutshell" ending.

The use of the metaphor of a nutshell can be diagnostic of a recognition of incompleteness. The formulaic "nutshell" closing invokes the very useful metaphor of a nutshell, suggesting a covering that encompasses a complete entity. Fernandez (1986) argues that the wish for a sense of wholeness best explains the power of an image to transform perceptions, and not any one particular trait(s) of the image itself. Here, the story elements themselves were not convincing. Metaphors serve as orienting constructs that sustain a sense of wholeness. They do so by dissolving prior images or disparate elements to give a fresh coherence to the multitude of events and periods of a lifetime. Guiding metaphors (e.g., nutshells) cross-reference separate domains of meaning to supply information from a familiar to a lesser known domain, thus merging them to form a new one. Reference to a central guiding metaphor serves to clarify who and where individuals are and what they are doing.

Depressed speakers are experiencing a sense of loss and incompleteness in life, and do not construct complete life stories from childhood to late life. They have very different story endings compared to nondepressed subjects. The type of endings exemplified by "that's it in a nutshell" were given only by depressed subjects. The story structure used by non-depressed speakers, the life course, comes ready-made with a complete story line from birth to death. These stories generally end with a description of current day life, and no overt claims to having told a complete story. There are no prefabricated solutions to the problem of ending a story based on the expression of a personal theme.

Degree of Complexity

Complexity is a key marker of creativity. In the life stories, complexity can be studied in terms of the diversity of topics used to represent the texture of the lifetime. The total number of words, number of topics, and words per topic were calculated. The mean number of words for all life stories was 330. The mean number of topics was eight. The mean number of words per topic was 78. The depressed speakers' mean number of topics (5) was half that of the nondepressed speakers' mean of 10 topics. Yet in terms of how much was said about each topic, the mean number of words per topic was equal between the two groups. Complexity in the description of the life varies across the narratives. Looking at the examples in Figure 13.1, the stories structured by personal themes contained fewer topics and a central topic or life theme. The stories structured by the normative life course presented more topics.

Fry's analysis of Americans' conceptions of the stages of the life course cautions us to interpret results in light of social structural position (personal communications). She found that systematic differences in the complexity and numbers of life stages identified by Americans were significantly predicted by the social class. People in higher social classes who have more opportunities for social and occupational mobility identified greater numbers of life course stages. People in the working and lower social classes who have less access to mobility and career opportunities identified far fewer life course stages. Thus, differences in the complexity of life narratives may reflect social class and gender differences as much as creativity in constructing meanings and life stories.

Pronouns

The *I* of the speaker is at the center of a life story. There are sharp differences in how narrators paint their lives. The speaker can be the constant center of attention or be intertwined with the unfolding of lifelong experiences and events. The cultural life course provides for a smooth, ready-made, integrated expression of the individual *I* and a host of successive social identities, roles, and activities. The narrative *I* in personal theme–organized accounts is mired in one trenchant conflict or self-perspective.

Earlier, I argued that we can not globally assign degrees of creativity without recognizing the types of challenges to self-expression posed within the domain of life stories. More precisely, the creative challenge for someone telling a story using the life course is to provide glimpses of the unique individual bearer and actor under the cloak of social roles. The challenge for the speaker providing a personal theme–structured life story is to establish links with collective community life, to show the common threads with shared social identities.

Analyses of the life stories identified that the first-person pronoun, *I,* occurs disproportionately among the depressed narrators. Among depressed narrators, the pronoun *I* accounted for 92% of all pronouns whereas it accounted for 66% of the pronouns used by nondepressed speakers. The difference is statistically significant, (p < .001) within a sample universe of over 10,000 pronouns in these 32 life stories. To tell their life stories, depressed speakers were overwhelmingly drawn to make a single "I" the center of the narrative. In contrast, the nondepressed speakers' life stories were not I-centered; rather, the narrators described themselves as engaged in a multiplicity of social and personal identities as part of the customary life cycle of social identities. The ability to take multiple perspectives is linked with positive mental health and social functioning; supportive therapy can help people regain a sense of well-being by developing such skills (Chandler, 1973; Selman, 1980). In the stories collected, the reflexive description of several different selves located in each life stage over the whole lifetime is linked with positive mental health.

To review, we have seen how life stories constructed with overt personal life themes are associated with depression. The illustrations have also suggested that the continuity of personal meaning is not a fixed, stable, internal construct. It is more accurately understood as the selective construction of meaning to provide a perception of permanence across health, personal, family, and historical changes. The explicit attention to constructing CPM in the narratives of depressed individuals may reflect a creative, meaning-making effort to cope with loss and discontinuity. The focus of meaning-making among non-depressed was to illustrate their integration within normative categories of social thought and life. The discussion highlighted how the actions of meaning making are influenced by health and mood states.

DISCUSSION AND FUTURE DIRECTIONS
FOR RESEARCH

Systematic comparisons within a set of life narratives provided several insights; the method for eliciting and analyzing sets of stories differs from single case study approaches. First, there are big contrasts between the life stories. These are categorical differences in the stories' organizing images, topic sequence, and focus, which are not matters of degree. Second, narrators express a clear sense of creative challenge in bringing closure or a sense of completion to a story. The observable ethnographic differences are also significant by reference to statistical and clinical diagnostic criteria.

One notable finding is that explicit personal themes are not a salient feature of all life history narratives. The differential distribution of themes across the set of stories is also relevant to the observation in the sociolinguistic and neuropsychological literature that older speakers tend to speak in more thematic and simple styles compared to younger adults. Similarly, Simonton (1989) has proposed what he terms the "late life swan song phenomena" to describe how artistic expression in late life evolves towards more simple and direct thematic representations. The life stories discussed here included both thematic and nonthematic accounts. The sample size is too small to lend itself to valid generalizations about mortality, but in the 3 years following the time these accounts were narrated, four of the speakers died; three of the deaths occurred among narrators using the thematic style, while only one was among those using the socially normative life course style.

Nondepressed, "normal," informants were more flexible in self-representations and preferred temporally linear stories built upon the shared image of the normative life course. Narrators who met the clinical criteria for depression presented stories rigidly structured around individual themes representing key personal concerns. Very different stories were told by nondepressed informants, who flexibly constituted multiple identities situated in each life cycle era and domain rather than asserting a single theme or identity across all stages of life.

One anthropological view is that the metaphor of the cultural life course per se (not the speaker) is a rich, flexible resource that facilitates the creative succession of meanings across time. The collective life course image serves as a palette with many potential colors, a resource of routinely changing life stages and identities. The normative life stage categories have multiple capacities. They deliver formulaic prefabricated meanings for experiencing and telling about life. The categories are also arenas for transition and personal growth

(Winnicott, 1971), pulling together and blending personal, situational, and cultural meanings to reconstruct a new sense of self across the lifetime. The single personal theme, in contrast, may be problematic and resistant to successive self-reinterpreting. It poses a singular, fixed, enduring global meaning less readily deconstructed and detached from the self; *unlike the life course there are no intrinsic transitions in a singular personal theme.* Such a personal identity or meaning is problematic for telling of situated selves. Apparently the personal thematic image and nonchronological style best articulates informants' sense of personal distress or conflict; they are as much "idioms of distress" (Nichter, 1981) as mental health ideals.

The image used to tell one's life story does appear as construct approximating experience for the total lifetime, one the narrators tell us is the most fitting and savory. We may conjecture that some lifetime images are not just unsavory, but regarded by some narrators as an ineffective way to make a point in speech (D'Andrade & Wish, 1985). For example, it may seem contradictory to assert your life was wrought with painful experiences, but to structure the story using the script of the conventional cultural life course.

The cultural life course, in contrast to the personal theme, emerges here as a more implicit, collective symbol. It helps to express the speaker's sense of individuation as a member within a whole society. In contrast, the idealized explicit personal theme indexes a negative individualistic or atomistic experience. Each image imparts a specific stance regarding the individual's overall sense of his or her present life. The structure of a narrative itself has very powerful affective and evaluative information about the speaker's feelings about the lifetime. More attention should be devoted to life stories' structures and to sequences as a whole. It may also be the case that personal style for achieving CPM may contribute to the nature of CPM making and the kinds of meanings the individual aims to assure. In this chapter, the focus has been on differences in the style of CPM and differences in the narrative expression of challenges and strategies posed for maintaining CPM.

The challenge for the explicit personal theme stories was to develop a coherent story and to link it to collective social life and experiences. Solutions provided by narrators in these accounts included a great deal of external conversational devices (e.g., overt storytelling openings, transitions, and closings). The challenge for stories told according to the linear social life course was to find ways within the story to convey interest or a compelling quality to keep the audiences attentive and to individualize the story to reflect the teller as a unique being.

Solutions provided by narrators adhering to the lifecourse formula include internal evaluative statements of affective intensity or importance and qualifiers to add personal qualities and experiences to the normative social roles and identities.

Acute methodological and empirical implications are posed by the diversity among the life stories. Notably, informants in this study used the formula of a single enduring self to express feelings of distress and marginality. The theme (Luborsky, 1994b) also conveys the speaker's appraisal of a lack of fit between personal, situational, and collective components of the self-representation in a smoothly unfolding biography. Themes may be an expression of distress, or reveal unresolved personal conflicts. This finding raises questions about the validity of applying theme techniques of analyses for many kinds of qualitative data where themes may not occur (Luborsky, 1993a, Luborsky & Sankar, 1993). It also directly challenges smaller scale qualitative research in gerontology that posits an enduring ageless self (Kaufman, 1987) as a marker of successful aging and well-being. I believe these findings can help to sensitize qualitative researchers to the need for reevaluating the validity of describing all lives in terms of a theme or themes. Gerontologists striving to empower elderly people by designing interventions which help them to reminisce and discover life themes may inadvertently reinforce oppressive culturally idealized concepts of a thematic self. The thematic life image is linked with personal distress and not well-being in the life stories discussed here. The implication for qualitative and quantitative gerontology is that we need a more appreciative attitude to the structural frames and content of entire life stories. Appreciation of these differences will broaden our understanding of individual lives.

The meanings in a life story may be those that are still being made, are yet unresolved, or were the resolutions to prior meaning dilemmas for the narrator and now are an important frame for the self. Specifically, stories organized by a personal theme are told by informants who find resolving personal meaning problematic and thus explicitly work to claim it. When the speaker does not see the social and personal life biography unfolding as expected, the collective life cycle images leave much of personal experience inchoate. Interestingly, the thematic stories provide the most vital and gripping accounts.

A personal identity or theme that is fixed and enduring throughout the life story occurred among informants who were experiencing a distressing sense of marginality or a disjunction in existential meaning. In contrast, narrators who presented multiple flexible, situated identities across the life story were culturally defined as healthy, normal people.

In some cases, the telling of a whole life was problematic and informants asked us to direct them: "You ask me the questions and I'll answer; it's too hard." These speakers tended to narrate the stories according to a personal theme, not the life course. This finding is counterintuitive to some models of identity process. We have come to anticipate a life history derived from the Western ideals of an explicit "life theme" that anchors an adult's sense of coherence and integrity and helps to organize experiences and events. But the personal themes, from an empirical view, may be a less valid construct for us to use to describe people whose life stories are modeled after a flexible, situated model of co-authored selves.

We found significant diversity in the challenge to be creative regarding the structure and the overt contents of the oral accounts. It takes creativity to maintain the flexibility needed to make many meanings. It also takes creativity to rigidly maintain a core theme across the changing contexts and demands of the whole lifetime. That is, the narrator's intent or purpose must be included along with affective and cognitive features to develop a comprehensive understanding of creativity.

To conclude, this study focused on one specific domain, the oral life narrative. The creative challenge for oral life narratives was found to differ widely according to the message and the style of talk pursued. Creativity researchers are increasingly acknowledging the value of developing domain-specific measures as a method to highlight interindividual differences in the creative challenges and solutions embedded in each persons' way of framing a story. The divergent creative challenges and solutions presented by different narrators remain ripe for further exploration. Discovery of the nature of creative challenges perceived by speakers engaged in other genres of narrative and discourse may help to refine and expand the findings discussed in this chapter.

ACKNOWLEDGMENTS

Support from the National Institute on Aging (#1RO1AG09065) and the National Institute of Mental Health (#P50MH40380) is gratefully acknowledged.

REFERENCES

Aberle, D. (1962). *The Peyote religion among the Navaho.* Chicago: Aldine.

Alexander, B., Rubinstein, R., Goodman, M., & Luborsky, M. (1991). Generativity in cultural context: The self, death and immortality as experienced by older American women. *Aging & Society, 11,* 417–442.

Antonovsky, A. (1979). *Health, stress, and coping.* San Francisco: Jossey-Bass.

Atchley, R. (1989). A continuity theory of normal aging. *The Gerontologist, 29,* 183–190.

Barclay, C., & Petitto, A. (1989). Creative activity in the context of real life. *New Ideas in Psychology, 7,* 41–48.

Beck, A., Rush, A., Shaw, B., & Emery, G. (1979). *Cognitive therapy of depression.* New York: Guilford.

Becker, G. (1993). Continuity after stroke: Implications of life course disruptions in old age. *The Gerontologist, 33,* 148–158.

Berger, P., & Luckman, T. (1976). *The social construction of reality.* London: Allen Lane.

Blessed, G., Tomlinson, I., & Roth, M. (1968). The association between quantitative measures of dementia and of senile change in cerebral gray matter of elderly subjects. *British Journal of Psychiatry, 114,* 797–811.

Bruner, J. (1990). *Acts of meaning.* Cambridge: Harvard University Press.

Burridge, K. (1969). *New heaven, new earth: A study of millenarian activities.* Oxford: Blackwell.

Bury, M. (1982). Chronic illness as biographical disruption. *Sociology of Health and Illness, 4,* 167–182.

Chafe, W. (1980). The deployment of consciousness in the production of a narrative. In W. Chafe (Ed.), *The pear stories: Cognitive, cultural, and linguistic aspects of story production.* Norwood, NJ: Ablex.

Cohler, B. (1982). Personal narrative and life course. In P. Baltes & O. Brim (Eds.), *Life span development and behavior,* (Vol. 4, pp. 205–241). New York: Academic.

Cohler, B. (1991). The life story and the study of resilience and response to adversity. *Journal of Narrative and Life History, 1,* 169–200.

Croply, A. (1990). Creativity and mental health in everyday life. *Creativity Research Journal, 3,* 167–178.

Csikszentmihalyi, M. (1988). Motivation and creativity: Towards a synthesis of structural and energistic approaches to cognition. *New Ideas in Psychology, 6,* 159–176.

D'Andrade, R. (1976). Propositional analysis of U.S. Americans' beliefs about illness. In K. Basso & J. Selby, (Eds.), *Meaning in anthropology.* Albuquerque: University of New Mexico Press.

D'Andrade, R. (1992). Schemas and motivation. In R. D'Andrade and C. Strauss (Eds.), *Human motives and cultural models* (pp. 23–44). Cambridge: Cambridge University Press.

D'Andrade, R., & Wish. (1985). Speech act theory in quantitative research on interpersonal behavior. *Discourse Processes, 8,* 229–259.

Fernandez U. (1986). The argument of images and the experience of returning to the whole. In V. Turner & E. Bruner (Eds.), *The anthropology of experience.* Chicago: University of Chicago Press.

Frankl, V. (1978). *The unheard cry for meaning.* New York: Simon and Schuster.

Fry, C. (1993). Personal communication.

Gee, J. (1985). The narrativization of experience in the oral style. *Journal of Education, 167,* 9–35.

Gergen, K. (1984). The self in temporal perspective. In R. Abeles (Ed.), *Lifespan perspectives and social psychology.* Hillsdale, NJ: LEA.

Gutmann, D. (1988). Late onset pathogenesis. *Topics in Geriatric Rehabilitation, 3,* 1–8.

Havighurst, R. (1963). Successful aging. In R. Williams, C. Tibbits, & W. Donahue (Eds.), *Processes of aging* (Vol 1). New York: Atherton.

Holmes, T., & Rahe, R. (1967). The Social Readjustment Rating Scale. *Journal of Psychosomatic Research, 11,* 213–218.

Huyck, M. (1989). Give me continuity or give me death. *The Gerontologist, 29,* 148–149.

Kaufman, S. (1987). *The ageless self, sources of meaning in late life.* Madison: University of Wisconsin Press.

Kleinman, A., & Good, B. (1985). *Culture and depression.* Berkeley: University of California Press.

Kohut, H. (1977). *The Restoration of the self.* New York: International University Press.

Kotre, J. (1984). *Outliving the self, generativity and the interpretation of lives.* Baltimore: The Johns Hopkins University Press.

Labouvie-Vief, G. (1990). Modes of knowledge and the organization of development. In J. Sinnott & C. Richards (Eds.), *Beyond formal operations: Comparisons and applications of adolescent and adult development models* (Vol. 2, pp. 48–62). New York: Praeger.

Labov, W. (1972). *Language in the inner city.* Philadelphia: University of Pennsylvania Press.

Landfield, A., & Epting, F. (1987). *Personal construct psychology, clinical and personality assessment.* New York: Human Sciences.

Lieberman, M., & Tobin, S. (1983). *The Experience of Old Age, Stress, Coping, and Survival.* New York: Basic Books.

Lieberman, M., & Falk, J. (1971). The remembered past as a source of data for research on the life cycle. *Human Development, 14,* 132–141.

Luborsky, M. (1990). Alchemists' visions, conceptual templates, and narrative sequences in life histories. *Journal of Aging Studies, 4,* 17–29.

Luborsky, M. (1993a). The romance with personal meaning in gerontology, cultural aspects of life themes. *The Gerontologist, 33,* 445–452.

Luborsky, M. (1993b). *Continuity of personal meaning and wellbeing in
later life: Concepts, critiques and findings.* Philadelphia: Philadelphia
Geriatric Center.

Luborsky, M. (1994a). The cultural adversity of physical disability, ero-
sion of full personhood. *Journal of Aging Studies, 8,* 239–253.

Luborsky, M. (1994b). The identification and analyses of themes and
patterns. In J. Gubrium & A. Sankar (Eds.), *Qualitative methods in
aging research,* pp. 189–210. Thousand Oaks, CA: Sage.

Luborsky, M. (1995a). The process of self-report of impairment in clinical research. *Social Science and Medicine, 40,* 1447–1459.

Luborsky, M., & Rubenstein, R. (1989). Ethnic differences in elderly
widowers' reactions to bereavement. In J. Sokolovsky (Ed.), *The
cultural context of aging* (pp. 229–240). Brooklyn, NY: Bergin &
Garvey.

Luborsky, M., & Sankar, A. (1993). Extending the critical gerontology
perspective: Cultural dimensions. *The Gerontologist, 33,* 440–444.

Mead, G. (1934). *Mind, self, and society.* Chicago: University of Chicago
Press.

Metzger, D. (1974). Semantic procedures for the study of belief systems.
In H. Siverts (Ed.), *Drinking patterns in highland chiapas.* Oslo,
Norway: Universitetforlaget.

Mishler, E. (1986). *Research interviewing.* Cambridge: Cambridge
University Press.

Myerhoff, B. (1978). *Number our days.* New York: Simon & Schuster.

Myerhoff, B. (1984). Rites and signs of ripening: The intertwining of ritu-
al, time, and growing older. In D. Kertzer & J. Keith (Eds.), *Age and
anthropological theory* (pp. 305–330). Ithaca, NY: Cornell University
Press.

Nicholls, J. (1972). Creativity in the person who will never produce anything original and useful: The concept of creativity as a normally
distributed trait. *American Psychologist, 27,* 717–727.

Nichter, M. (1981). Idioms of Distress. *Culture, Medicine, and Psychiatry,
121,* 962–970.

Obeyesekere, G. (1982). Sinhalese-Buddhist identity in Ceylon. In G.
DeVos and L. Romanucci-Ross (Eds.), *Ethnic identity, cultural conti-
nuities, and change.* Chicago: University of Chicago Press.

Pearlin, L. (1981). The stress process. *Journal of Health and Social
Behavior 22,* 337–356.

Rosaldo, R. (1989). *Culture and truth: The remaking of social analysis.*
Boston: Beacon.

Rosow, I. (1963). Adjustment of the normal aged. In R. Williams, C. Tibbits, & W. Donahue (Eds.), *Processes of aging* (Vol 1). New York: Atherton.

Sartre, J. P. (1963) *Psychology and imagination,* New York: Philosophical Library.

Seligman, M., & Castellon, C. (1984). Explanatory style change during cognitive therapy for unipolar depression. *Journal of Abnormal Psychology, 97,* 13–18.

Selman, R. L. (1980). *The growth of interpersonal understanding.* New York: Academic.

Seltzer, M., & Troll, L. (1985). Expected life history. *American Behavioral Scientist, 29,* 746–64.

Shweder, R. (1991). *Thinking through cultures.* Cambridge: Harvard University Press.

Simonton, D. (1989). The swan-song phenomena, last-work effects for 172 classical composers. *Psychology and Aging, 4,* 42–47.

Simonton, D. (1990). Creativity in the later years: Optimistic prospects for achievement. *The Gerontologist, 30,* 626–631.

Sperber, D. (1974). *Rethinking symbolism.* Cambridge, UK: Cambridge University Press.

Stigler, J., Shweder, R., & Herdt, G. (1990). *Cultural psychology: Essays on comparative human development.* Cambridge, UK: Cambridge University Press.

Sternberg, R. (1988). A three-facet model of creativity. In R. J. Sternberg (Ed.), *The nature of creativity* (pp. 125–147). New York: Cambridge University Press.

Tardif, T., & Sternberg, R. (1988). What do we know about creativity? In R. Sternberg (Ed.), *The nature of creativity* (pp. 429–440). New York: Cambridge University Press.

Wallace, A. 1970. *The death and rebirth of the Seneca.* New York: Knopf.

Whitbourne, S. (1986). *The me I know: A study of adult identify.* New York: Springer-Verlag.

Williams, G. (1984). The genesis of chronic illness: Narrative reconstruction. *Sociology of Health and Illness, 6,* 175–200.

Winnicott, D. (1971). *Playing and reality.* New York: Basic.

Yesavage, J., Brink, T., Rose, T., Lum, O., Huang, V., Adey, M., & Leirer, V. (1983). Development and validation of a Geriatric Depression Screening Scale. *Journal of Psychiatric Research, 17,* 37–49.

Zisook, S., DeVaul, R., & Click, M. (1982). Measuring symptoms of grief and bereavement. *American Journal of Psychiatry, 139,* 1590–1593.

Index